Guillaume de Machaut

THE COMPLETE POETRY & MUSIC

VOLUME 1

THE DEBATE POEMS

Le Jugement dou Roy de Behaingne
Le Jugement dou Roy de Navarre
Le Lay de Plour

MIDDLE ENGLISH TEXTS SERIES

The Middle English Texts Series is designed for classroom use. Its goal is to make available to teachers, scholars, and students texts that occupy an important place in the literary and cultural canon but have not been readily available in student editions. The series does not include those authors, such as Chaucer, Langland, or Malory, whose English works are normally in print in good student editions. The focus is, instead, upon Middle English literature adjacent to those authors that teachers need in compiling the syllabuses they wish to teach. The editions maintain the linguistic integrity of the original work but within the parameters of modern reading conventions. The texts are printed in the modern alphabet and follow the practices of modern capitalization, word formation, and punctuation. Manuscript abbreviations are silently expanded, and *u/v* and *j/i* spellings are regularized according to modern orthography. Yogh (ʒ) is transcribed as *g, gh, y,* or *s,* according to the sound in Modern English spelling to which it corresponds; thorn (þ) and eth (ð) are transcribed as *th.* Distinction between the second person pronoun and the definite article is made by spelling the one *thee* and the other *the,* and final *-e* that receives full syllabic value is accented (e.g., *charité*). Hard words, difficult phrases, and unusual idioms are glossed either in the right margin or at the foot of the page. Explanatory and textual notes appear at the end of the text, often along with a glossary. The editions include short introductions on the history of the work, its merits and points of topical interest, and brief working bibliographies.

This series is published in association with the University of Rochester.

Medieval Institute Publications is a program of
The Medieval Institute, College of Arts and Sciences

 WESTERN MICHIGAN UNIVERSITY

Guillaume de Machaut

THE COMPLETE POETRY & MUSIC

R. Barton Palmer and Yolanda Plumley

General Editors

VOLUME 1: THE DEBATE POEMS

Edited and translated by R. Barton Palmer

with Domenic Leo (art history) and Uri Smilansky (music)

TEAMS • Middle English Texts Series • University of Rochester

MEDIEVAL INSTITUTE PUBLICATIONS

Western Michigan University

Kalamazoo

**Library of Congress Cataloging-in-Publication Data
are available at the Library of Congress.**

ISBN 978-1-58044-252-7

Printed and bound in the United States of America

Guillaume de Machaut

THE COMPLETE POETRY & MUSIC

R. Barton Palmer and Yolanda Plumley
General Editors

ASSOCIATE EDITORS

Jacques Boogaart
Daniel Leech-Wilkinson
Domenic Leo
Tamsyn Rose-Steel
Uri Smilansky
Anne Stone

ADVISORY BOARD

Ardis Butterfield
Lawrence Earp
Donald Grieg
Deborah McGrady
Virginia Newes

GUILLAUME DE MACHAUT: THE COMPLETE POETRY & MUSIC

❧ CONTENTS

LIST OF ILLUSTRATIONS

Le Jugement dou Roy de Behaingne

Le Jugement dou Roy de Navarre

❧ ACKNOWLEDGMENTS

A project of this scope would have been impossible without institutional support and, even more important, substantial assistance from colleagues. Barton Palmer and Yolanda Plumley, the co-editors of *Guillaume de Machaut: the Complete Poetry and Music*, have been exceptionally fortunate in this regard. Key parts of the editing process have been supported by a generous grant from the Leverhulme Trust for which Plumley has been the principal investigator, while Palmer's participation, including released time from teaching and travel expenses, has been supported by the Calhoun Lemon endowment and the College of Art, Architecture, and the Humanities at Clemson University, whose dean, Rick Goodstein, deserves special thanks. The digitizing of previously published material, as well as the preparation of both front and back matter for each volume, has been handled with dispatch, energy, and expertise by TEAMS: The Consortium for the Teaching of the Middle Ages and the Middle English Text Series (METS), working in concert with Medieval Institute Publications (MIP). Their work is supported by a continuing grant from the NEH, and we are most appreciative of what their funding has made available to us. We are grateful as well for the wise counsel and enthusiastic support we have received from Russell A. Peck, general editor of METS, and Martha M. Johnson-Olin and Pamela Yee, assistant editors. Staff editors at METS have worked tirelessly and patiently on the several demanding tasks associated with the project; we owe a substantial debt to those editors, past and present: Leah Haught, Katie Van Wert, Alison Harper, Laura Whitebell, and Emily Lowman. Patricia Hollahan and Simon Forde, along with their staff at MIP, and the press's editorial board have been helpful, patient, and flexible, especially as in meeting the needs of an edition devoted to both verse and music, whose representation on the page is so very different. Palmer is mindful of another substantial debt, owed to the late J.J. Wilhelm, former editor of the Garland Library of Medieval Literature, in which series the editions and translations of three of the works in this volume originally appeared. J.J.'s vision was to make available to scholars and students usable editions and readable English translations of medieval works that for the most part had been previously accessible only to specialists. MIP and METS are devoted to the same worthy project, and J.J. would undoubtedly be pleased to see that the artistic legacy of Guillaume de Machaut is at last becoming available in its entirety to students of the Middle Ages.

I also wish to thank and mention the other people helping to create the entire project of *Guillaume de Machaut: The Complete Poetry and Music*. The Project is being edited by R. Barton Palmer (the poetry) and Yolanda M. Plumley (the music). The associate editors are Jacques Boogaart, Daniel Leech-Wilkinson, Domenic Leo, Uri Smilansky, Anne Stone, and Tamsyn Rose-Steel; Ardis Butterfield, Lawrence Earp, Donald Greig, Deborah McGrady, and Virginia Newes serve on the Advisory Board.

 # INTRODUCTION

After delivering a manuscript containing the works of Guillaume de Machaut to Count Louis de Male of Flanders, Eustache Deschamps dedicated a pair of ballades to his master in which he declares:

Dont vous estes honouriez haultement	And so you are highly honored
Car tous vos faiz moult honourablement	For all your works quite honorably
Chascuns reçoit en maint païs estrange	Are received by everyone in many a foreign land

Les grans seigneurs, Guillaume, vous ont chier,	Guillaume, the great lords hold you dear
En voz choses prannent esbatement.	And take pleasure in what you write.[2]

Deschamps observes further that Machaut "nourished" him and "paid him many kindnesses."[3] So perhaps we should consider his opinion of the older poet's reputation somewhat inflated by gratitude and personal admiration (we might add family obligation since Machaut was also Deschamps' uncle). And yet Deschamps is hardly the only contemporary writer to offer so favorable an opinion of Machaut's artistic accomplishments and their reception. Martin le Franc terms him a grand rhetorician, while Achille Caulier praises him as a renowned poet, according Machaut a place in his *Ospital d'amour* (*Love's Hospital*) alongside Alain Chartier, Boccaccio, and Petrarch in his pantheon of vernacular authors. We may safely conclude from such evidence that Guillaume de Machaut was one of the most famous and influential poets of fourteenth-century France.

---

[1] This biographical sketch details Machaut's relationship with the two patrons who figure in the interconnected works of the debate series, Charles of Navarre and Jean of Bohemia. The biographical sketches in other volumes of this edition, as appropriate, will emphasize Machaut's relationships with his other principle patrons, John of Berry and King Peter I of Cyprus. Furthermore, we here assess Machaut's artistic achievement primarily with reference to his literary works; more detailed discussion of his considerable contributions to the development of music in the fourteenth century can be found in the biographical sketches in the volumes of this edition devoted to his musical texts.

[2] Queux de St. Hilaire and Raynaud, eds., *Eustache Deschamps*, I.246, ballade 127. All translations in this volume are mine unless otherwise noted.

[3] Queux de St. Hilairie and Raynaud, eds., *Eustache Deschamps*, III.259. The text in question is ballade 447, which reads, referring to Machaut, "Qui m'a nourry et fait maintes douçours" (line 5).

Machaut's reputation rested on his production of an immense and varied corpus of works, many of which were composed for, and in honor of, the several grand nobles with whose courts he was at various times associated. As a musician, he wrote more than twenty motets and a polyphonic setting of the mass, the virtuosity and innovations of which have made him one of the most important figures of medieval music. As Elizabeth Eva Leach puts it, "what does differentiate Machaut from his contemporaries . . . is the central role of *music* within his literary output."[4] Of musical as well as literary interest is his extensive body of lyric poems in various fixed forms such as the *ballade* and the *virelay*. In fact, Machaut was largely responsible for the continuing fashion of this type of poetry.[5] A central aspect of Machaut's achievement is that he provided musical settings for many of these lyrics using recently developed forms of notation. Finally, following in the tradition of thirteenth-century love vision poetry, especially the *Romance of the Rose*, Machaut composed ten long narrative and didactic poems (*dits amoureux* or "love poems" as well as others with philosophical/religious or historical themes) and four shorter ones (which are all concerned with love). These poems, partly because of their love motifs and partly through what appears to be contemporary allusions, greatly pleased the noble audiences for whom they were originally intended. The considerable number of surviving manuscripts, some beautifully illuminated, testifies eloquently to this popularity. His *dits* exerted a substantial influence on other contemporary writers and some of the generation to follow, especially Deschamps, Oton de Granson, Jean Froissart, Christine de Pizan, and John Gower. And Geoffrey Chaucer's poetry evidences a close and reverent reading of narrative works by the French master. Machaut's *dits* include *Le Jugement dou roy de Behaingne* (*Judgment of the King of Bohemia*) and its sequel, *Le Jugement dou roy de Navarre* (*Judgment of the King of Navarre*), which constitute what is commonly referred to as his debate series. A third text, the *Lay de Plour* (*Lay of Weeping*), which is not narrative but lyric in form and set to music, is linked textually to the two debate poems and is thus included in this edition.

Because he was a low-born cleric (even though he was to become a servant of the noble and famous) little is known about Machaut's life beyond what is preserved in a few ecclesiastical documents and the poet's own works, which contain a fair number of biographical indications, though these are not always reliable. From documents which detail his appointment to different benefices, it can be inferred that Machaut was born at the beginning of the fourteenth century, probably in the village of Machault in Champagne. Since the same documents fail to accord him any of the titles which would indicate noble birth, we may assume he was not well born. This social status is consistent with the self-portrait that emerges from the poetry in which Machaut often makes his diegetic alter ego a humble or even cowardly clerk who moves uncertainly among his betters, the butt of mild class humor. The following passage from his *Fonteinne amoureuse* (*Fountain of Love*) is especially revealing:

Et comment que je soie clers	And though I might be a clerk
Rudes, nices, et malapers,	Who is ignorant, incapable, and inept,
S'ay je esté par mes .ii. fois	Yet I've been, by my two faiths,
En tele place aucune fois	In such a place several times

---

[4] Leach, *Secretary, Poet, Musician*, p. 2.

[5] For details see Poirion, *Le poète et le prince*.

Avec le bon Roy de Behaingne,	With the good King of Bohemia,
Dont Dieus ait l'ame en sa compaigne,	And may God keep his soul among His company,
Que maugré mien hantis estoie	And despite myself I was brave
Car il n'i avoit lieu ne voie,	Since there was no place, no path,
Ne destour ou fuïr sceüsse,	No byway where I knew to flee
Si couvenoit que hardis fusse.	And thus I had to be courageous.
	(lines 139–48)[6]

A similar passage occurs in the *Navarre*. Here a poet named Guillaume de Machaut encounters a beautiful and distinguished lady while hunting rabbits. Starting to dismount, Guillaume is dissuaded from such an unmannerly act of obeisance by the lady herself. Returning her greeting, the poet confides to his readers that he has learned well how to honor those of such higher station than himself (lines 739–59).

Various documents refer to Machaut as "master." This might mean that after an early education, quite probably in the cathedral school at Reims, Machaut pursued theological studies at a university, likely Paris, finishing with the grade of *magister*. But it also might mean nothing at all, for such a title is a common honorific. Machaut, however, did not go on to take holy orders, it can be assumed, since he is nowhere referred to as a priest and only served in offices like the canonicate which were open to those outside the priesthood. Most university students left after taking the master's degree to begin a career in secular or religious administration. Having secured a patron or a benefice, they might then return to the university to finish studies for the doctorate degree.

Through circumstances no longer known, Machaut became associated, while in his early twenties, with one of the most notable grand nobles of the era, Jean de Luxembourg, the king of Bohemia. It may have been that Machaut came to Jean's notice during one of the latter's sojourns in northern France; Jean had frequent dealings with the archbishop of Reims, a see with which Machaut may have been associated at an early age, and the archbishop perhaps effected an introduction. To the modern historian, Jean appears an extravagant and perhaps unstable figure. To his contemporaries, however, the king's fabled prodigality, the restlessness with which he sought to expand and consolidate the lands under his rule, and his reputed social finesse made him the very type of ideal ruler that would appeal to Machaut. In *Le Confort d'ami* (*Comfort for a Friend*) and other narrative works, Machaut speaks of Jean with the highest respect and reverence. Machaut also describes his experiences as Jean's secretary and chaplain. These include a sojourn at the castle of Burglitz (1323), a series of military expeditions through Poland, Russia, and Lithuania (1329), Jean's invasion of northern Italy (1330–31), and his involvement in Austrian affairs (1331). Ecclesiastical documents suggest that Machaut remained in Jean's service until the king's heroic death (he was led blind into the battle to fight) at Crécy in 1346.

Although he was so willing to provide information about his early association with Jean, Machaut offers few indications about any experiences with the king after 1331. This may mean two things. During the last fifteen years or so of his life, Jean's fortunes notably declined. Machaut does not mention the king's second marriage to the French princess Beatrice of Bourbon (1334); the loss of an eye (1337) and the king's desperate, often revengeful attempts to restore it; finally his complete loss of sight in 1339 and stubborn

---

[6] See Volume 3 of *Guillaume de Machaut: The Complete Poetry and Music*.

refusal to withdraw from a restless and active public life. Nor does Machaut recount military activities in the east, especially Jean's continuing difficulty in Bohemia (which culminated in the somewhat scandalous pillage of the synagogue in Prague) and renewed hostilities in Austria, where his victories were marred once again by questionable looting of a holy place. Machaut's silence may be a polite way of dealing with Jean's private sorrow and public troubles. After a long and effusive homage to Jean in the *Confort*, Machaut declares that he will not provide more details about his doings "on the other side of the Rhine," but that no one faults him.[7] Or his reticence may simply mean that he was no longer a member of Jean's entourage and so could not testify directly about what happened.

During his association with Jean, Machaut established a reputation as a writer with musical and, especially, poetical works. Evidence suggests that three of his longer *dits* were certainly composed and circulated prior to 1342: *Le dit dou vergier* (*The Poem About the Orchard*), the *Behaingne*, and *Remede de fortune* (*Fortune's Remedy*). It was their success that enabled Machaut to acquire other noble patrons after Jean's death.

Following Crécy, Guillaume must have found himself in a secure but unpromising position. Jean had secured him an appointment as a canon at Reims cathedral, but he apparently did not take up residence there until much later in life. In time, Machaut was provided with other ecclesiastical benefices, but these did not allow him to live in the rich state to which he had become accustomed while serving the King of Bohemia. But in the highest social circles of fourteenth-century France a noted poet was a highly desirable acquisition; Machaut did not spend much time without appropriate benefactors. As Claude Gauvard has said, "le véritable client est alors moins le poète que le prince" [the true client then was less the poet than the prince].[8] Perhaps surprisingly Machaut did not enter the service of Jean's heir and son, Charles, newly crowned emperor of Germany. Toward the end of his career, however, Machaut did dedicate the long crusading chronicle *La Prise d'Alexandrie* (*The Taking of Alexandria*) to him; this indicates that their relations must have been cordial at the least. And in this same work he mentions that he "performed much service for"[9] Charles' sister Bonne (Gutha), who had been married in 1332 to Jean, son of Philip VI, soon to become the next Valois king of France. It is likely that this means he was associated with the provincial court of Jean and Bonne in Normandy. Whether he served the duchess as he had her father (that is, as secretary and resident poet) is not known, but, significantly, he composed no *dits* (or at least none that survive) in her honor, that is, in which she would figure honorifically as a character, unless Lady Bonneürté in the *Navarre* is based on her. In any case, the association with Bonne was short-lived since she died on 11 September 1349, presumably of the plague which at that time was sweeping across northern France.

The opening of the *Navarre* tells us much of Machaut's activities at the time. Possibly resident in the kingdom of Navarre, Machaut recounts his melancholic reactions to the outbreak of the disease, foretold by astrological and political signs. Having made a good confession, the poet closes himself up inside his house and stops going to town (a move that may well have saved his life). He describes the various events that attended the attack

---

[7] See lines 3083–86 of the *Confort*, in Volume 2 of *Guillaume de Machaut: The Complete Poetry and Music*.

[8] Gauvard, "Portrait du prince," p. 26; see Poirion, *Le poète et le prince*, p. 196, for a similar view.

[9] *Prise d'Alexandrie*, line 769. See Volume 6 of *Guillaume de Machaut: The Complete Poetry and Music*.

of the disease: the persecution of the Jews, the appearance of wandering troops of flagellants, the mass burials of victims, the depopulation of the countryside, and desperate economic hardship. The disease at an end, Guillaume finds himself re-entering an unnamed but festive city, tired of burying its dead. The remainder of this work is fictive, a love debate that continues, in a complicated fashion, the one begun a number of years earlier in the *Behaingne*.

HISTORICAL CONTEXT AND PATRONAGE

Significantly, the patron who figures in the second judgment poem is Charles, the nineteen-year-old newly crowned king of Navarre (the official coronation took place in Pamplona on 27 June 1350). Charles was the eldest son of Jeanne, queen of Navarre (who had inherited the kingdom from her parents), and Philip, count of Évreux. Though chroniclers at the time and modern historians usually refer to Charles as the king of Navarre (the customary epithet "the Bad" was given him by a Spanish writer in the century following his death), this interesting and complex person, whose career became so connected to the important political developments of the age, was thoroughly French in culture and interests. He may more profitably be considered as count of Évreux and the investee of other properties, especially in the north of France, one of the great feudal vassals of the kingdom rather than a foreign potentate.[10]

How did Machaut meet Charles? Most likely in Normandy or in Paris, where Charles spent most of his early life. Jeanne was the daughter of Louis X of France and thus passed to Charles, through the female line, a direct connection to the royal house. Charles' younger brothers were Philip and Louis, also prominent French noblemen, while his sister Blanche was married to Philip VI of France. The family's relation to the Valois was made closer by the fact that young Charles himself was married to Jeanne, daughter of the soon-to-be Jean II, King of France; this was a marriage initiated and promoted by Jean, who apparently desired better ties with his cousin. Having a claim on the throne perhaps as good as that of the Valois, Charles inevitably attempted to press the merits of his case or, at least, increase his domains at the expense of his more fortunate rivals. He was aided in this by what, contemporary accounts suggest, were an engaging personality, a goodly amount of learning, and substantial cunning. In a history of his rival, Charles V, a contemporary chronicler characterizes the king of Navarre thus:

> C'estoit un petit homme, mais plein d'esprit et de feu . . . d'un oeil vif et d'une éloquence qui persuadoit tout ce qu'il vouloit, et avec cela si affable et si populaire, que, possédant en perfection l'addresse de se faire aymer tout autrement que les autres princes, il luy fut facile de gagner les esprits du peuple, et mesmes d'attirer à soy, et de débaucher plusieurs personnes considérables, de l'obéissance et de la fidelité qu'elles devoient au roi.

> [he was a little man, but full of spirit and fire . . . with a lively eye and an eloquence which persuaded everyone he wished to persuade, and in addition he was so affable and friendly that, possessing the ability to make himself more loved than any other prince, he found it easy to gain the hearts of the people, drawing them to his side, even corrupting several important nobles in the loyalty and devotion they owed to the king.][11]

---

[10] See Plaisse, *Charles, dit le mauvais*, for further details.

[11] Quoted in Plaisse, *Charles, dit le mauvais*, p. 17.

The difficulties between the Valois and their English cousins, also claimants to the throne of France, provided Charles with an opportunity to maneuver; his possessions in Normandy and Navarre, though eventually quite substantial, could not support a direct confrontation with his father-in-law, and yet these same possessions were, for obvious geographical reasons, of great strategic importance.

In order to understand Machaut's relationship to Charles of Navarre, which endured more than a decade and prompted the composition of the *Confort* we must at this point examine in some detail the events of the late 1350s in which patron and, to a lesser extent, poet both became embroiled.[12]

The first dispute between Jean and his Navarrese son-in-law arose in 1354 over the king's gift of the county of Angoulême to Charles, constable of France, a man, also of royal blood, who had been given the office held by Raoul of Brienne, recently executed by Jean as a traitor. Charles of Spain, cadet son of the royal house of Castille, was one of Jean's favorites, perhaps his lover as well (the rumor of a homosexual liaison was spread by Charles of Navarre, even to the Pope at Avignon, but Jean never answered the charge). As Charles of Navarre reckoned, the county of Angoulême belonged to him. By right his mother should have inherited the counties of Champagne and Brie (territories which her grandmother had brought to the crown in marrying Philip the Fair). When a minor, she had been tricked by her guardian and Philip VI of Valois into renouncing her claim to these counties in return for those of Angoulême and Mortain, as well as for fixed rents to be drawn on the royal treasury. The Valois had never permitted Jeanne possession of Angoulême or paid the compensation, and when Charles of Navarre became Jean II's son-in-law, he pressed this family claim strongly. Moreover, he was at the time promised a huge dowry in cash that was not paid.

Continually refused by Jean what he fairly considered his due, Charles was enraged to see the county of Angoulême pass to Charles of Spain as the result of what he could only understand as a deliberate affront to his personal honor. When Charles of Spain passed through Alençon on the night of 8 January 1354 (foolishly approaching the Navarrese stronghold of Évreux with no escort), he was waylaid at a local inn by Philip of Navarre and several of the king's cronies, including the count of Harcourt, the seigneur de Graville, a knight named Maubue, and the squire Colin Doublet. As he would later publicly acknowledge, Charles of Navarre gave the order for the assassination. In bed, stripped of his arms, and begging for mercy, Charles of Spain was cut down without pity. With his typical taste for the spectacular and gory, Froissart states:

> Lors le Bascon de Mareul et Radigo et quatre servans occistrent le dit Charles d'Espaingne connestable de France. Et l'occist de sa main et de son espée le dit Bascon de Mareul. Car il lui lança et bouta tout oultre parmi le corps ; et tant engoisseusement, villainnement et abhominablement l'apareillerent qu'ilz lui firent quatre vingt plaies.

> [then Bascon de Mareul and Radigo and four other squires killed the aforementioned Charles of Spain, the constable of France. Bascon de Mareul killed him with the sword in his hand. For he pierced and stuck him right through the body, and they did it so that he suffered great pain, was villainously and abominably treated, having eighty wounds.][13]

---

[12] This account is based on Plaisse, *Charles, dit le mauvais*; Bordonove, *Jean le Bon et son temps*; Cazelles, *Société Politique*; Deviosse, *Jean le Bon*; and Quillet, *Charles V*.

[13] Quoted in Plaisse, *Charles, dit le mauvais*, pp. 61–62.

Jean's reaction was a predictable rage and desire for vengeance. But Charles of Navarre had powerful allies at court, especially his aunt and sister, at that time the widows of Philip VI and Charles IV, who pleaded his case with Jean. There were even a good number of the king's council, ecclesiastics and nobles alike from the north of France, who sympathized with Charles of Navarre and what they viewed as his legitimate struggle against the crown. Many thought that the count of Évreux had acted only to restore his injured honor; Machaut apparently agreed, for, reviewing Charles' career in the *Confort*, he more than once affirms that his patron never did anything to merit the punishment he was then suffering (see especially lines 15–18 and 1832–35). Charles also arranged for the pope and other influential members of the Church to intervene, accomplishing this in what was then a novel way: by the writing of persuasive letters of explanation. Perhaps most effective, however, was the fact that Charles of Navarre sought aid, once again by elegantly written letters from his English cousin Edward III and the king's lieutenant, Henry of Lancaster.[14]

Fearing a coalition between England and Navarre (and a secure Norman base for operations against northern France), Jean allowed himself to be reconciled with Charles through the intercession of the Cardinal of Boulogne. As it turns out, the cardinal was an important member of what French historians term the Navarrese party at court and a vital source of information for Charles. Jean's political situation permitted no other course. Though submitting to his father-in-law, Charles was forced to give nothing, not even a public apology for his "crime." However he received the better part of the Cotentin, a territory then in dispute which made his Norman holdings even more strategically substantial and, as far as the Valois were concerned, more threatening. The Treaty of Mantes (signed in March 1354) established a temporary peace between the two rivals. Jean was at the time very much occupied with the English peace negotiations which, had he accepted the proposed final settlement, would have resulted in Edward III's taking possession of most of France. Reneging on the Treaty of Mantes (after some provocation), Jean was forced once more to deal with Charles of Navarre who, in 1355, was in the Cotentin and planning a voyage to England, where he was to resume his own negotiations. Jean appeased his son-in-law with the Treaty of Valognes (signed at an impressive ceremony of reconciliation on 10 September 1355). Once again Charles profited at the expense of his father-in-law and the latter's continuing fear of an Anglo-Norman alliance. He demanded and received the payment of his wife's dowry and even claimed financial compensation for the expenses incurred in raising an army (which was supposed to join an expeditionary force led by Edward III of England debarking at Cherbourg) to fight his sovereign.

The confrontation increased the popularity of Charles among the nobles of northern France, especially Normandy, a duchy which, for a number of reasons, was having its own difficulties with the king. It was during this sojourn in Normandy that Charles probably had the idea of plotting with the dauphin, Charles, recently put in charge, but not created duke, of Normandy (Charles, quite probably, convinced his impressionable younger cousin that his father was not going to give him his due). In October 1355, Jean was faced once again with the landing of an English army, but the campaign was short-lived and resulted in no significant gains for either side. He felt, perhaps, that with a lull in the war the time had come to deal decisively with Charles of Navarre. The details of a plot between his son

---

[14] For the original texts of the letters to Edward, see Plaisse, *Charles, dit le mauvais*, pp. 62–63.

and Charles of Navarre probably came to the attention of the king about this time; Jean had an excellent network of spies. As Friquet de Fricamps, one of Charles of Navarre's lieutenants, was to reveal much later under torture, the dauphin was encouraged by his cousin to ask in person for armed help from the emperor to save the kingdom from his father's misrule. Having raised a substantial force, Charles was then to return to join armies with the king of Navarre in order to capture and do away with his father.

Jean soon saw a perfect opportunity to defeat this conspiracy; the majority of Norman nobles had assembled in early April 1356 at Rouen to do homage to Charles and discuss issues of state, especially new taxes. With a substantial party of armed men, Jean surprised the convocation at the castle of Rouen on 5 April 1356, entering unnoticed through a back gate. Jean immediately had Charles of Navarre taken into custody. He dealt more severely with the noblemen in his retinue who had been involved in the killing of the constable of Spain. Harcourt, de Graville, Maubue, and Doublet were put into a cart to be transported to the gibbet, but, apparently fearing some trouble from the townspeople among whom Harcourt was especially popular, Jean ordered them unloaded halfway there and beheaded in the presence of his by then presumably quite terrified son Charles. Their bodies and heads were dragged in chains and installed on the city gibbet. Put in the personal custody of Arnoul d'Audrehem, the marshal of France, Charles of Navarre was taken to a number of prisons. First he was transported to the Château-Gaillard, then to the Louvre, then to the Châtelet (near Cambrai), and finally to Arleux-en-Palluel (near Douai). Contemporary accounts, based largely on what Charles was to reveal upon his release, confirm what Machaut hints at in *Confort*, namely that the king of Navarre was often harshly treated, in effect tortured during his captivity. Charles was not to gain his release until a year and slightly more than seven months had passed (8 November 1357).

For about six weeks Philip of Navarre tried to persuade Jean to let his brother go, but his efforts, and those of Charles' other friends and relations at court, were in vain. As a result, the Navarrese in Normandy made common cause with the English against Jean during the summer campaign of that year. But this fighting was soon to seem insignificant when at the beginning of autumn an English raiding party led by Henry of Lancaster made an attempt to link up with the forces of the Black Prince, who had invaded Poitou. Raising a huge army, Jean pursued the latter and in a remarkable and famous turnabout was defeated at Poitiers on 17 September. This was an event that Charles of Navarre, languishing in prison, might have regarded with some good humor, for the king who had put him in chains was himself made a prisoner (though in much less uncomfortable circumstances).

The absence of Jean and widespread dissatisfaction at the dauphin's initial lack of strong leadership probably contributed to the climate, long favorable to Charles of Navarre, which led to his eventual release. Somewhat inexplicably, Jean never publicized his reasons for arresting Charles, a fact to which Machaut himself refers in the *Confort* (see lines 1805–06); this contributed to the feeling, shared by the poet and many others, that the arrest was a miscarriage of justice that would be corrected by proper legal procedure (see the *Confort* lines 1815–24). Already at the meeting of the Estates General during October 1356, a call had been made for Charles' freedom, among other changes demanded by a party interested in the reform of the royal government (the session was eventually prorogued by the dauphin). It is interesting to note that Machaut demonstrates a good deal of sympathy for and agreement with the cause of reformation, although the *Confort*, to our knowledge, constitutes the poet's only public action in its support. One of the most prominent among the reformers was Jean de Picquigny, who was governor of

Artois. At about the very time Machaut was composing a poetic consolation for his imprisoned patron, Jean de Picquigny and other Picard nobles plotted and successfully executed Charles' deliverance from Arleux-en-Palluel; chroniclers disagree about the details of the escape, so we cannot be sure how it happened. There are hints in the *Confort* that he knew something of these plans; for after nearly eighteen months of captivity he decided to compose a political/moral work for Charles that was in many ways quite optimistic about his benefactor's eventual deliverance (see the *Confort* lines 1825–29, which even mention that the king has friends working hard for his release).

Rescued from his cell (perhaps by means of ladders and the connivance, forced or otherwise, of his jailers), Charles immediately began a political campaign to win support in what was, largely, a leaderless France. It is not clear, however, if he intended to take the throne or simply increase his own holdings during a period of crisis. Charles wrote sympathetic and thankful letters to authorities at Arras, letting them know that he did not hold the people of France responsible for his misfortune; he wrote the count of Savoy with similar intent. These documents, which have survived,[15] reveal a resourceful and resilient man eager to take advantage of the opportunities now available to him. Proceeding to Amiens, he received shelter from the respected canon Guy Quiéret; at Amiens he made a persuasive speech detailing his claims not only to Champagne and Brie, but also those to the throne of France, though he did not call for the deposition of Jean. Charles went on to Paris, where discontent with the dauphin was already in the air and he could count on enthusiastic support from an influential bourgeoisie. There he graciously accepted the hospitality of the monks at Saint-Germain-des-Prés; according to Jean de Venette, a contemporary chronicler:

> He watched for an opportunity, and when a large number of people had been summoned and had gathered in the Pré-aux-Clercs (the ditches round the monastery had not yet been dug), he stood upon the walls and began to preach to the people in a loud voice. Taking as his text these words in very good Latin, 'Because our Lord is just and hath loved justice, his countenance hath seen equity,' he expounded them to suit his purpose.[16]

We do not know what part Machaut may have played in Charles' campaign to win popular acceptance or support, but the fact that the king attempted in part to do so through scholarly/clerical methods is suggestive. Charles, however, was very well educated and loved learning, so he perhaps proceeded without support from the poet (who, it must be added, continued in his loyalty to the king as well; see the praiseworthy references to Jean's feats of battle at Poitiers in lines 2795–2818 of the *Confort*). Restored to a peace with the dauphin through the intercession of queen Jeanne and queen Blanche, his long-time allies, Charles staged an elaborate burial of the bodies of his executed friends, still hanging on the gibbet at Rouen; this took place on 10 January 1358. The dauphin had promised Charles the return of all his Norman holdings, but when he found it difficult to regain them, Charles broke the peace. Intriguing with Étienne Marcel, the leader of the merchants of Paris, who was himself organizing a formidable opposition to royal power, Charles made an attempt to secure a position in the capital, at that time unfriendly to the dauphin. This alliance likely lost him the support of many nobles and ecclesiastics. In any

---

[15] Quoted in part in Jean de Venette, *Chronicle*, pp. 226–27.

[16] Jean de Venette, *Chronicle*, p. 69.

case, an unusual chain of circumstances, too complex to be detailed here, led to both Marcel's death and the defeat of Charles' hopes.[17]

Hindsight suggests that Charles quite probably could have seized the throne had he either the nerve or desire in the summer of 1358. But was this indeed his intention? Among other modern historians Raymond Cazelles suggests not: though he certainly thought about becoming king of France, Charles possessed two clearer and not necessarily connected aims:

> profiter des embarras des Valois pour s'agrandir et s'enrichir . . . [et] il n'y aucun raison pour que le roi de France abandonne une partie de son royaume au roi d'Angleterre alors que lui-même estime avoir plus de droits qu'Edouard III" [to profit from Valois troubles and thus enrich and elevate himself . . . and there was no reason for the king of France to abandon half his kingdom to the king of England when he himself thought it by rights should be his own and not Edward III's].[18]

Allied with the English, Charles made war upon France, even in 1359 blockading the city of Paris by closing navigation off on the Seine in both directions. Stymied by the dauphin, Charles was once more forced to make peace. Throughout most of the next decade, Charles of Navarre remained an annoying but ultimately rather harmless enemy of his Valois cousins. He was able to continue and in some ways succeed in the position of leadership and responsibility that Machaut prepares him for with conventional wisdom and advice in the *Confort*. But he never became the royal leader around whom the somewhat inchoate cause of reform could organize itself. Defeated decisively by royal forces at the battle of Cocherel in 1364, Charles' fortunes began to decline precipitously in the late 1370s. In 1378, Charles suffered the confiscation of all his territories in France. Reduced to his Spanish possessions, he died in Pamplona on 1 January 1387, according to Froissart of a sudden illness brought on by a night of debauchery with a very young and beautiful girl. If this is true, it was a somewhat fitting end for a man whom Machaut characterizes in the *Navarre* as an enthusiast of the game of love.

After the *Confort*, Machaut never mentions Charles of Navarre again in any of his narrative poems, even though ecclesiastical documents and other evidence suggest that he remained associated with the king in some capacity for a number of years after his release. Machaut's career during this period demonstrates that the contractual relationship of patron and prince was flexible. Still attached to the king of Navarre, Machaut also became associated with a nobleman who, at least politically, would have been Charles' mortal enemy: Jean, the Duke of Berry, his brother-in-law and cousin. During the winter of 1359–60, Machaut lived through the siege laid to the city of Reims by the English and was even required, despite his age, to do some military service. In the spring of 1360 the French were required by the treaty of Brétigny to supply hostages in return for the release of the imprisoned king Jean (whose huge ransom his subjects were having difficulty raising). One of these was Berry, a man who, like Charles of Navarre, loved learning and the arts. Apparently in his service, Machaut wrote a consolation intended to comfort him, just as he had done for the king of Navarre. The *Fonteinne amoureuse*, however, offers a traditional love poem instead of advice and instructive exempla. *Le Livre dou Voir Dit* (*The*

---

[17] See Cazelles, *Etienne Marcel*, for details of Marcel's revolt.

[18] Quoted in Plaisse, *Charles, dit le mauvais*, pp. 78–79.

Book of the True Poem), written about the same time, hints that Machaut enjoyed patronage from yet another grand nobleman, Charles, duke of Normandy.[19]

In his later years Machaut, serving as canon, must have participated in a number of important public events, including the coronation of Charles V on 19 May 1364, in Reims. Among Charles' entourage was Pierre of Lusignan, the famous knight (he must have reminded Machaut of his beloved Jean of Bohemia), a man whose chivalric accomplishments the poet was later to chronicle in his *Prise*. During this time Machaut was probably more or less permanently resident at Reims, suffering from the afflictions (a cataract and the gout) he mentions in the *Voir Dit*. The records of the canonial chapter reveal that he died in April of 1377 and was interred alongside his brother Jean, who had died some time before.

ARTISTIC ACHIEVEMENT

Russian theorist Mikhail Bakhtin has famously suggested that in its relentless attraction to the written and not yet written, the modern novel is generically anti-generic, and is because it offers, in contrast with formal traditions such as the epic, a "new zone opened . . . for structuring literary images . . . the zone of maximal contact with the present . . . in all its openendedness."[20] With no fixed form or conventional matter, the novel is defined by its lack of a defining feature beyond the most unhelpfully vague: that it is prose fiction of a certain length. Had he been acquainted with the tradition of the late medieval *dit*, the form of verse narrative whose acknowledged master was Guillaume de Machaut, Bakhtin might have been inclined to view the novel's receptivity to languages, styles, and themes of all kinds as interestingly anticipated by the most popular form of a much earlier period. If the novel is, as he argues, a kind of *summa* or master form capable of re-orienting and re-presenting texts of all varieties, then this unlimited capacity to accommodate all imaginable sources is anticipated by the *dit* (roughly speaking, the tale), which is most importantly characterized by its attraction to the quotidian, the occasional, even the autobiographical and, in consequence, by its formal preoccupation with discontinuity and pastiche.

In its definite indefiniteness, the *dit* is by nature open to the textualizing or re-textualizing of whatever can be rendered in octosyllabic rhyming couplets. Such openness should, to a degree, dispose the form outward, toward the matter that might be incorporated. And yet, while he does not foreclose centrifugal possibilities of inclusion, Machaut simultaneously turns the *dit* inward, redirecting its openness toward its own ontology. However heterogeneous and syncretic, his *dits* are in a sense all of a piece since they are most notably characterized by a centripetality that leads them to focus on the social (dis)continuities of his authorship, as well as various aspects of his text-making practice. Across an impressively large oeuvre, this metafictional urge manifests itself in a continually re-inventive fashion, whose always surprising variety reflects the different materials (literary, personal, historical, etc.) on which each text draws. Such a balance between the outward and inward energies is proto-novelistic in the sense that, as Bakhtin suggests, the novel, though lacking a "unitary language" and disposed to reproduce all those it encounters,

---

[19] See Chailley, "Du cheval de Guillaume de Machaut," for further detailed discussion of this stage in Machaut's career.

[20] Bakhtin, *Dialogic Imagination*, p. 11.

locates the author at "the center of organization where all levels intersect."[21] The novelist is customarily an all-disposing ventriloquist who disappears into his various appearances. Like the other poets who imitate his example, however, Machaut does not only constitute the subjective source of the *dit*'s verbal flow. He is also either his own main character or an important subsidiary presence when characters of noble birth claim the narrative spotlight. In this insistence on the organizing energies as well as the representational possibilities of authorial singularity, the Machaldian *dit* proves generically ungeneric, as the subsequent developmental history of the form makes clear. His contemporaries Jean Froissart, Christine de Pizan, John Gower, and Geoffrey Chaucer, among others, produced so many similarly self-regarding texts — each of which is resolutely disposed toward uniqueness and disconnection, defying regularizing tendencies — that this particular inflection of the *dit* becomes the most recognizable literary form at the end of Middle Ages.

An embrace of disconnection and uniqueness constitutes the paradoxical formal ground of this impressive body of texts, which includes such diverse masterpieces as Froissart's *Prison amoureuse*, Chaucer's *House of Fame*, and Christine's *Livre du duc des vrais amans*. Unlike most medieval narrative, the *dit* eschews pre-existing cycles, the thematic corpora or *matières* that make possible a vast range of fictionalizing that is genetically related as for example in the various strands of the Arthurian tradition that so dominates literary production in the period. Like the novel, the *dit* resolutely resists any subordination of the individual text to ordinate traditions, which increase in cultural authority through continuing acts of invocation and re-use. Their cultural lives are characterized by the continual accretion of "range" to which each individual text contributes in terms of narrative mass, even as by its very existence each new text expands the possibilities for further imitation and linkage. Textual boundaries are never understood as closed, but rather as open to a continuation that can always inspire further continuation, producing complex, never-closed multiplicities (sometimes appropriately termed "cycles"). The *dit* is utterly different from matter-based narrative. The *dit* constitutes, in fact, the formal and thematic "other" to such impressively massive genres as the romance and the *chanson de geste*, with its invocation of speech (*dit* from *dire* "to say") perhaps pointing toward the unreproducibility of *parole*. The *roman*, by way of contrast, takes its name for the vernacular language in which it first appeared (*romanz* = French), and it fittingly shows affinities with the rule-governed nature of *langue*, in which the abstracting generalities of a constantly expanding repertoire customarily prevail over the idiosyncratic.

Another way of saying this is that almost without exception the *dit* exists in se and per se. Whatever transtextual connections it may establish are not mandated by a tradition that molds and prescribes even though Machaut's own oeuvre in some sense connects to the tradition of love poetry. His *dits* offer a perfect match between generic form and content. To repeat, the major structural motif of his narrative verse is the dramatization of his activity as a poet in the service of different great nobles. Such a focus is hardly surprising or unusual. In its insistence upon the unique, the unanticipated, and the ephemeral, the *dit* is strongly drawn toward the at least ostensibly autobiographical, most obvious source of emerging story (a truism about the connection between author and form that the modern novel, of course, clearly reflects).

---

[21] Bakhtin, *Dialogic Imagination*, p. 49.

And yet, the Machaldian *dit* continually escapes the confinement of the autobiographical. For this particular persona (if in complicated ways that connect to such modern notions as narrator and implied author) is identical with the poet who assumes the burden of continuing production. And this is a task that necessarily involves more that the narration of the self, generally including a substantial invocation of literary tradition in some form. The overall result, in any case, is an inward-regarding text constantly referencing itself as an aesthetic object in the making, whose confection (the various stages of which, to be sure, can also constitute the subject of further versifying) is the task the poet sets himself.

Long neglected as the productions of an inferior author who could do little more than imitate the truly grand monuments of an earlier age (especially the *Roman de la rose* and the *Ovide moralisé*), the narrative poems of Guillaume de Machaut have been revalued by the current generation of medievalists. Contemporary critics have especially appreciated the features of Machaut's *dits* dismissed by earlier scholars as "conventional:" the insistent literariness of the Machaldian text, its intricate (dis)connections to the poet's corpus and life, its playful celebration of the shifting, complicated relations among poet, public, and patron, its self-conscious re-making (and replacing) of literary models. The creation of a "post-modern" Machaut rightly has restored the poet's reputation by demonstrating that he should be read according to his age's conception of the literary (one intriguingly contemporary).[22] Current work, however, has slighted those aspects of the writer's oeuvre, particularly political and didactic elements, which do not fit such a model of textual self-containment. It is true, to paraphrase William Calin, that Machaut's narrative poetry is often about the writing of poetry by a poet;[23] but this interest is hardly global, and does not explain the generation or form of certain works. The lack of attention paid to that poetry reflects a judgment about literary categories that is thoroughly modern, not medieval: a division between the fictional, mimetic, and entertaining, on the one hand, and the occasional, rhetorical, and didactic, on the other. The modern critic and reader prefer texts of the first type, though this taste was not shared by their fourteenth-century counterparts.

Machaut was prompted to compose occasional poems because of events in his own and his patrons' lives. Both the *Voir Dit* and the *Navarre*, for example, offer themselves as responses to turning points or crises in the career of the poet (though it may well be that these "events" are themselves fictional, imagined in order to justify the works which respond to them). It is fairly certain that Machaut carried on a literary love affair with a much younger reader, and the first of his two *jugement* poems was perhaps found so objectionable by female readers that he was forced to compose a revision. But our only evidence for these "histories" is in the poems themselves. It is public knowledge, however, that Jean of Berry was forced by treaty obligations to leave France for England; the *Fonteinne amoureuse* refers, if vaguely, to this occasion, but also provides consolation for the sorrowful patron. This poem fulfills its occasional and didactic purposes through the construction of a traditional fiction. It is a love vision that assimilates Jean's grief (which presumably was a complex emotion) to the agony felt by a lover forced to part from his lady. The resulting text treats its occasion metonymically, offering an exposition of only those elements which can be expressed by poetic forms and conventions. The metonymy, in this case the figuration of

---

[22] For more on the "post-modern" Machaut, see Palmer, "Transtextuality and the Producing-I."

[23] See Calin, *Poet at the Fountain*.

Jean as a lover, means that occasionality becomes subordinated to the more general meanings of dream vision (e.g., that the nobleman's dream of Venus is not intended to represent Jean's particular, unique circumstances). Occasionality, in other words, is less a meaning in the text than a meaning which can be read into it. We do not need to know about the unfortunate turning of events in Jean's life to understand and appreciate the poem, though such knowledge helps us to locate a referential gesture that supplements our understanding and appreciation. The poem develops a series of general, conventionally acceptable meanings which can also be applied flatteringly to Jean's real life situation. Thus the patron's sorrow is less represented than alluded to. Occasionality in the two debate poems similarly incorporates autobiographical references into what is essentially a generic framework.

Because the later omnibus manuscripts of Machaut's complete poetry and music, including BnF, fr. 1584 (usually known by the siglum A) on which this present edition is based, to all appearances put the narrative *dits* in chronological order of composition, it is possible to establish that the *Behaingne* was the poet's second major work, likely following closely on his initial work, the *Dit dou Vergier*. Machaut's first *jugement* poem was followed more than a decade later by a sequel of sorts, the *Navarre*. The *Behaingne* revives a genre inaugurated some two hundred years earlier in which questions of love and gender are broached in debate form. Under Machaut's brilliant handling, the love debate genre went on to flourish for more than a century and a half, involving many, perhaps most, of the gifted authors of the later Middle Ages. The model he set stages a debate argued by two or more characters, each of whom speaks to a particular side of an issue concerning love. The discussion often takes place in the presence of a narrator figure in charge of recording the argument for a patron who will decide the matter. The whole case is written up as poetry, providing plenty of scope for lyrical expression of the joy and pain brought on by strong emotion. In the hands of the best poets, language and erudition are on display as much as sentiment. That is certainly the case with both the *Behaingne* and the *Navarre*.

POETIC LOVE DEBATES

Reaching back to the late twelfth and early thirteenth centuries, extended poetic debate in the topic of love existed already in what were called *débats du clerc et du chevalier* (debates of the cleric and the knight) or *jugements d'amour* (judgments about love). We have as examples of this genre half a dozen works, some in Latin and some in Old French, that stage a discussion in which ladies weigh the relative merits of clerics and knights and lovers. Consider, for example, the short Latin verse narrative *Idus Aprilus Habitum est Concilium Hoc in Monte Romarici (Council of Remiremont)*, written in the middle of the twelfth century and soon translated into French.[24] The *Concile* recounts the extraordinary events that supposedly took place at the monastery of Remiremont. The nuns have come together on the Ides of April, we are told, not to hear the reading of the Gospel but to discuss *amoris tractatus* (the "practice of love"). On one level, the poem satirizes those devoted to the religious life, who were famed, justly or unjustly, for a failure to observe the most difficult of vows. No men are permitted to attend this council except for "honest clerks," monks from nearby Toul, whose presence is welcomed and for whose "solace" the company of women has, in fact, been convoked. All the sisters know of love, but they have no physical

---

[24] For discussion and texts, see Oulmont, *Débats*.

experience of it. In a kind of mockery of religious service, the meeting begins not with a reading from the Bible but with a passage from the teachings of Ovid, which are declaimed by a certain Eve, who is said to be well skilled at following Love's commandments and offering sagacious advice to others. Eve is hardly attired in the modest garments of a nun. Instead, she is dressed like a courtly lady, wearing splendid clothes and adorned with precious jewels and flowers. She has come, so she says, to advise them never to hide the manner of life they have chosen for themselves — which, she says, is characterized by its exclusive devotion to, if not the physical presence of, carnal love and desire.

Elizabeth of Granges responds for the company, declaring that they have served Love to the best of their ability. Most important, the community has observed the rule of refusing to have sex with men (*viri copula*) and not accepting the companionship of anyone who does not belong to their "order." Elizabeth of Faucogney, however, offers a somewhat more expansive view of the sisters' behavior. They have never ceased enjoying, she declares, the grace, the worthiness, and the good memory of clerks — and they intend to continue loving them in this fashion.

Elizabeth of Faucogney then proceeds to catalogue the virtues of clerks as lovers. The clerk is gracious, kind, and attentive, full of courtesy and generosity. Experienced in love, he knows how to treat a woman well, bringing her appropriate presents and never failing to keep a promise. And he is faithful in his love, never abandoning a woman to whom he has joined himself. A knight, in contrast, is not worth the trouble or affection of a virtuous lady. His brand of loving is detestable, unfortunate, and short-lived. The sisters of the house at first sought out knights for lovers, but, realizing that they were deceivers, quickly abandoned them for clerks, who are famed for being blameless in affairs of the heart. And so any attachment to a knight has become forbidden to members of the company, she concludes. Such is the life they will continue to live, if it pleases Eve for them to do so.

One of the other nuns present has a different view, however. Clerks, she declares, are not as able in loving as Elizabeth has maintained. Those who share this opinion also belong to the "family of Love." Knights are worthy of respect because they love both war and pleasure. They fear no pain, whether it comes from love or wounds. In battle they are courageous, with a view toward gaining the ladies' affection and possessing the bodies of women.

Those who prefer clerks then state their case once again before Eve puts an end to debate. She affirms that clerks are able, sweet, and affable, while knights are fickle and given to foolish speech. Henceforth, these women should accept the proffered affection only of clerks. Women who shun this advice would not be admitted to their company until they repent and are granted absolution for the transgression.

The wisdom of clerks is to be preferred because, when women act foolishly, clerks will know where their best interest lies and direct them to pursue it. Eve orders that those who do not follow her injunction be excommunicated from the community and become objects of hatred. But pardon will quickly come to anyone who shows proper repentance.

Eve's judgment is that clerks make the best lovers, but, enforcing a double standard, affirms that nuns are to honor absolutely their vows of chastity. The *Concile* thematizes this new "doctrine" in a different fashion, making the question of how women should behave in love the subject of a debate that centers on the qualities to be expected in the men to whom they devote themselves. The *Concile* establishes the basic structure of the genre: a debate about an important aspect of the love experience — here the relative suitability of clerks and knights — which is eventually referred for adjudication to an appropriate authority figure.

Another text in the love debate tradition is worth a brief look. The thirteenth-century French *Jugement d'amours* (*Judgment of Love*) offers a distinctive variation on what was becoming a stock theme. One May morning two maidens, pretty and elegantly dressed, make their way to a pleasant garden where they intend to entertain themselves. After a walk through a valley filled with blossoms and the pleasant fragrances of the season, they find an olive tree, under which they sit and discuss a question of love. The first maiden, Blancheflor, sings the praises of the man, a clerk, with whom she has fallen in love, while Florence, her companion, argues for the superiority of her lover, who happens to be a knight. They can reach no consensus and decide to take their case to the God of Love, who with his knowledge and power, can resolve the dispute. On the appointed day, they make their way to Love's palace, a beautiful dwelling covered in flowers, but the door is barred and there is no porter to allow them inside. Suddenly two birds appear to conduct them to the divinity who is taking his rest on a bed of flowers. The god listens with interest and summons his council of "barons" who are all birds of different kinds. They debate the issue between champions representing the two positions. The champion who supports the knight is soon forced to admit that clerks are valiant and courteous and that all virtues are more evident in them than in any other men. Feeling her lover dishonored, Florence breaks into tears, moans bitterly, and dies. The poem ends with her burial as a martyr to Love.

The literature of love reaches its apotheosis in the thirteenth century with *Roman de la rose* (*Romance of the Rose*), a work of immense breadth and impact that is preserved in more than 250 manuscripts, a huge number for a medieval vernacular work. Its influence is correspondingly large. Virtually all love literature that follows over the next two centuries shows the impact of this work in some way, reproducing/rewriting, or taking exception to its contents, conceits, and characters.

The *Rose* consists of two parts, the first of approximately 4,000 lines and the second of an additional 18,000. It is conventionally assumed that the two parts were composed by different poets. Guillaume de Lorris is known as the author of the older portion, composed around 1230, which begins the story of a young lover who falls in love with a rosebud he sees in the Garden of Delight. The garden is the domain of the God of Love and his company, a group of allegorical personifications favorable to his powers. The second part of the romance, composed by Jean de Meun around 1270, describes the vicissitudes experienced by the lover but also incorporates long passages of exposition on all manner of topics, making it a compendium of knowledge as well as the resolution of the quest for the Rose.

The story is a dream vision that unfolds in the narrator's unconscious. Here, we find extensive meditations on love, debates about the central issues of the emotional life. Becoming the vassal of Love in the first part of the poem, the dreamer is aided in his pursuit of the Rose by Fair Welcome, who is driven off by Danger, Shame, and Fear before the lover can attain his goal. At this point, Reason rushes to the lover's rescue, urging him to give up on love, which, she maintains, is both unnatural, because not centered on procreation, and unreliably transient. An opposing view is offered by Friend, who emphasizes the positive aspects of the love experience, persuading the dreamer to disregard what Reason has advocated. In the poem's second part, the dispute over the value of love becomes even more elaborate, as a variety of other personifications appear to offer different perspectives. For example, a character known as the Old Woman, who has, perhaps foolishly, been given charge of the Rose's virtue, offers a disquisition on the rules of love, foolish counsel, promiscuity, and the blatant manipulation of unfortunate men. Her advocacy of an immoral surrender to impulse is opposed both by Nature, who recognizes that "laws" can be rejected by those who make use of their reason, and by Genius, whose view of love's essential connection to the procreative imperative reflects official Church doctrine. In the end, these points of view are, at best, uneasily reconciled. The lover does finally gain possession of the Rose, although his success is depicted in an extended military metaphor that shows his victory as a siege and assault on the tower protecting the Rose, a violent and overtly sexual ending to a tale that began in the most refined of registers. Most modern readers agree that the debate over the nature of love offered in the poem is never adequately resolved.

LE JUGEMENT DOU ROY DE BEHAINGNE

Though it was to reinvent a genre, Machaut's first judgment poem begins in a most conventional fashion, with the narrator's reminiscences of the adventures he passed through one late April morning, a time appointed by Nature and God for love. Love, he affirms, is an emotional experience that affects many men and women, bringing them both joy and pain. This narrator confesses to being an experienced and successful lover, so he can give himself over quite happily to the enjoyment of beautiful sunshine and reawakening nature. Following a nightingale, he enters a lonely glade, there to contemplate in solitude the indescribable beauty of the natural music he hears. This short opening (lines 1–40) draws explicitly on the *Roman de la rose* in which the archetypal Lover similarly falls prey to the enticements of springtime. In the *Rose*, after falling asleep, the lover experiences a vision of the Garden of Love, where the poem's complex, allegorical drama unfolds. In Machaut's reworking, however, the narrator does not fall asleep, but becomes witness to a different kind of drama that takes place nearby (lines 41–124).

The structure of the *Rose* has been invoked, but radically transformed. The elaborate interplay between allegorical personages that lends psychological and intellectual depth to the *Rose* has been altered in favor of a confrontation between two human characters, a man and a woman, unknown to one another, whose experiences in love — which are related in substantial detail — have been, up to a point, similar. Both have known not only the joy that love brings but the overwhelming and enduring sorrow that comes from its loss. Yet this loss, in their two cases, has intriguingly different sources, and the poem takes as one of its main themes the measuring of one loss against the other. Which of these distressed lovers suffers the greater pain? The issue is debated first (and inconclusively) by the protagonists, only later to be submitted as a question of love that is answerable by the king of Bohemia's courtiers, allegorical personages who each represent, in the tradition of the *Rose*, different and to some degree incompatible, aspects of the love experience.

Enjoying his springtime walk, the narrator spies an obviously troubled lady and a serving girl approaching down a lonely path. At the same moment, on the other side, he sees a knight walking down the same path. Thinking he may be intruding upon a lovers' meeting, the narrator hides in the bushes, becoming an involuntary witness to their encounter. The knight gives the lady a fair greeting, but she ignores him. Puzzled, he seizes her robe and questions her. She apologizes for her inadvertent rudeness; it seems she was lost in thought. Like a true gentleman, the knight offers his assistance, but it is declined since, as the lady declares, her difficulties are so severe that no one save God could alleviate them. Though sympathetic, the knight politely challenges her declaration, responding that his own suffering is more than any human being ever endured or indeed ever could. Their dispute leads almost to a joint undertaking as the lady and the knight will explain their troubles in full in order to determine who bears the greater burden of grief.

The lady begins her account of emotional distress by describing her dedication as "serf and vassal" to Love, who favored her with the affection of a knight who, in her view, was the best man who ever lived. His death, she maintains, has left her with an irremediable sorrow, the proof of which seems to be the dead faint into which she falls at the end of her speech (lines 125–205). After reviving her, however, the knight refuses to concede, remaining committed to his initial view, and in an even more elaborate response (lines 261–860) recounts his faithful service to the God of Love, which eventually earns him the reward of the young girl's heart. But Love's favor leads in the end only to misery, because his beloved throws him over for another man, betraying his trust. The bereaved lady, though sympathetic to his plight, is not persuaded that the jilted knight's suffering is worse, and she makes a telling point to support her contention (lines 881–928). She argues that since his beloved is still living, it is possible for him to regain her favor through loyal and patient service. In his rebuttal, the knight maintains the contrary: were she dead, he could forget the girl and be released from pain, but, being alive and forever unattainable, she will make him suffer endlessly (lines 929–1167).

Having reached an impasse, the two disputants obviously need a judge to decide the case, but, constrained by the rules of polite intercourse, neither wishes to nominate one. Nearly forgotten during the progress of the debate, the narrator once again assumes a prominent role, if quite a different one (lines 1185–1442). He is no longer free to lose himself in his own thoughts of love, awakened by the spring morning. Instead he must serve his betters in their time of emotional distress. Like the knight and the lady, he finds himself in a difficult position, for, though he wished to help them find a proper judge, he is embarrassed to reveal his presence. Chance soon intervenes. The lady's dog spots him hiding in the bushes and runs toward him, barking. This provides him with the opportunity to introduce himself. Confessing that he has heard all of their discussion, the narrator proposes the king of Bohemia as a judge to hear the case. The pair concur and the narrator quickly leads them to the nearby castle of Durbuy, where the king is in residence. Jean listens graciously to a summary of the disagreement provided by the knight (lines 1509–1608), and he then turns the issue over to his court for further discussion, charging his courtiers, sixteen allegorical personages with names such as Reason, Love, Youth, and Loyalty, to provide the proper explication of the issues involved.

Raison (Reason), who holds a position of prominence at court, speaks first, and in a long response (lines 1665–1784) confirms the correctness of the knight's argument, maintaining that, since love is a carnal affection, it cannot survive the death of the body. But the knight sees his unfaithful lady constantly and so cannot forget, even though Raison advises him to do so, because Jeunesse (Youth) and Amour (Love) urge him on in this mad error. Amour then intervenes (lines 1788–1811), agreeing with Raison's solution of the dispute, but challenging her view that the knight should abandon the love he feels because she has proved a traitor to him. In an emotional rejoinder (lines 1824–47), Loiauté (Loyalty) condemns the faithless behavior of the knight's beloved. She argues that Amour is wrong in demanding that the knight continue to love someone from whom he gets nothing but misery. Loiauté agrees with Raison that the knight suffers more because Amour holds him fast in a sorrow from which he cannot recover. Jeunesse finds herself in accord with Amour, asserting that the knight will never give up his love as long as her power can prevent it (lines 1857–1891). Like Amour, Jeunesse argues that the experience of love is reward enough, even if its object has proved unworthy, a position at whose foolishness and impracticality the king gently laughs, reproving Jeunesse for wanting to keep a faithful servant of Amour in such continual pain that he might die (lines 1900–14). So be it, says Jeunesse; he will then attain great honor as a martyr (lines 1915–20). Delivering his judgment, the king endorses the view that the knight suffers more than the lady. They have not assembled, he reminds them, to determine if that man should indeed continue to love the woman who has betrayed him (lines 1923–56).

And yet the debate does move from a weighing of the sorrows felt by the knight and the lady to a consideration of a much more difficult question, one that is, by royal command, never finally adjudicated: Should reason guide the behavior of those in love, who are under the powerful sway of both the affection itself and the impetuousness of their immature age? In this "digression," we see Machaut coming to grips with a dilemma developed more fully, if never answered decisively, in the *Rose*. The king, a mature man, sides with Raison, that when her grief passes, she will find another lover in accordance with natural imperatives. The assembled court assents unanimously to this judgment, though we can imagine that Jeunesse and Amour are not happy with the outcome, which endorses Raison's opinion that love does not survive the death of the body (lines 1716–23) and thus can exert but a limited power over those under its dominion. For eight days the courtiers attempt, with little apparent success, to assuage the suffering of the king's two guests, who are finally allowed to depart after receiving generous gifts.

Beyond the two questions of who suffers more and whether lovers should heed the dictates of the head rather than those of heart, the debate, if only indirectly raises a third question, which will become the focus of the poem's sequel: Who proves superior in love, men or women? The knight is judged the winner in the debate, an indication, perhaps, of the greater power of male reasoning and discernment — or it may be that the king has simply decided in favor of a fellow male. In any case, it is the knight's continuing devotion to his lady, however undeserving, that occasions the court's discussion of the relative claims of reason and emotion to direct human action. Moreover, the cause of the knight's sorrow is his lady's faithfulness, over which he has no control. Of the two women who figure in this poem, one is given to mistaken opinions (overestimating a misery that, it is predicted, will soon pass), while the other is a promiscuous betrayer of male trust, who inspires virtuous devotion only to inflict pointless pain on a man who merits, as all present agree, a quite different reward.

The poem's two men, in contrast, reflect the highest masculine ideals. Both are submissive to love and mindful of the proper service due the women to whom they have pledged themselves. These exemplary men suffer only because of what lies beyond their jurisdiction: for one, the vagaries of fortune leading to an early death; and for the other, the instability of a woman's heart that mocks the steadiness of the love bestowed upon it.

It could be argued, as a female figure of great authority does in the *Navarre*, that the author, who has created a fiction that so obviously favors men over women, has insulted the gentler sex. If this was unintentional, then she thinks that the author must be under the sway of that complex of incorrect notions about the "inferiority" of women that we term misogyny. Whether Machaut is guilty of this charge is the question that, with no little humor and irony, is debated in the *Navarre*, where the poet becomes his own main character. And so what was extratextual in the *Behaingne*, namely the author's intentions and his responsibility to advance only "true" opinion, becomes the center of the new work, as Machaut himself — or, more precisely, a humorously inept, fictional version of the poet — is called to account.

This transformation, however startling, is by no means unanticipated. An important feature of the *Behaingne* is its reflexivity, that is, its self-conscious presentation of the role the poet plays in court society. There is an unmistakable autobiographical strain in the poem, which gives voice to Machaut's likely uncertainties about his position — as clerk and commoner, but also as the designated spokesman of emotional idealism. At first, the narrator's solitude indexes both the importance of his subjectivity (which is a potential source of meditation on the love experience) and his openness to instruction or enlightenment, which should conventionally come, as in the *Rose*, in the dream that follows this figure's falling asleep in the springtime setting. The dramatic interchange between the knight and the lady, however, means that the narrator's solitude comes to indicate his sudden displacement from the debate to follow, as well as his conversion into an unseen and eavesdropping figure, the very image of Guillaume de Machaut the courtly poet, who attends to understanding the ideas advanced by the debating pair. Using his artistic powers, he will convert these ideas into poetry, as he confesses he has done in the work's coda (lines 2062–79). Giving way to the concerns of the class he serves, the narrator (and by extension Guillaume himself) is not content to be a simple witness, serving a narrating function that effaces itself behind the story. The role it fulfills is a larger one, for the poet, as Machaut sees it, is also a guide. His fictions are not just entertainments but are also intended to inform and comfort. If his experience in love must be denied the privilege of focus, the poet's duties as teacher and adviser cannot be so easily laid aside. That experience, however, offers no easy truths to be confidently endorsed. The conflict between Raison, on the one hand, and Jeunesse and Amour, on the other, does not finally admit a simple solution in favor of either clear-headed restraint or reckless self-abandon. The debate ends but does not conclude, much in manner of Machaut's most notable model, the *Roman de la rose*.

LE JUGEMENT DOU ROY DE NAVARRE

The *Behaingne* displays its indebtedness to the *Rose* in order to mediate its reception as one of both sameness and difference. In the *Navarre*, the concern with a love question leads not only to a debate between allegorical characters (most prominently Raison, one of the most important characters in the earlier allegory); it also leads to a representation of the central contradiction which defines the clerkly poet's role (a subject never raised by the two authors of the *Rose*). Similarly, the *Navarre*, though composed as much as a decade later and for a different patron, mediates its reception through a series of references to the *Rose*, though these are not, as was the case before, to the first part of that poem written by Guillaume de Lorris, but rather to Jean de Meun's continuation of Guillaume's narrative. Like the second part of the *Rose*, the *Navarre* offers a lively, occasionally raucous debate that raises the issue of anti-feminism. Furthermore, the debaters frequently use exempla of different kinds to make their points, though these exempla are not as fully developed as the similar ones in Jean's *Rose*. In addition, there is an important structural resemblance between the two works. The *Navarre* is the only work in the Machaut corpus which explicitly takes a previous poem as its subject matter or pre-text; in fact the work's full title in manuscript A, BnF, fr. 1584, is *Le Jugement dou Roy de Navarre contre le Jugement dou Roy de Behaingne* (*The Judgement of the King of Navarre against the Judgement of the King of Bohemia*). The transtextual link between the two works is thus established from the outset, and it is characterized by a desire for a correction or emendation, something similar to Jean's motives (or those of his narrator, at least) in continuing Guillaume de Lorris' unfinished poem.

[Handwritten note at top: deer Anthers are like a crown, bring it closer to the sky & make it sacred. They also fall off & regenerate (rebirth)]

[Handwritten notes in right margin: Deer 1) Christian Symbol of piety]

[Handwritten notes in right margin: Celtic: deer often turned into women in order to avoid being hunted, also the stag the king of the forest protector of all other creatures]

What prompted Machaut to write a sequel to one of his most popular works, a sequel that suggested the earlier poem was somehow deficient or faulty? Scholars have sometimes maintained that Guillaume had personal reasons for writing the *Navarre*. The *Behaingne*, it is inferred, must have been criticized for its unusual "doctrine" in noble circles; Guillaume's second judgment poem, then, would be an answer to those charges, an answer that could be seen as a retraction of the earlier judgment that cunningly does not refute it. The fact is, however, that we know nothing about the reception of the *Behaingne* beyond an evident popularity attested to by the large number of surviving manuscripts. We therefore have no good reason to think that the second judgment poem was motivated by anything other than what the *Prologue*, which the poet wrote toward the end of his career, tells us about Machaut's literary production; these "new" poems about love come into existence because Guillaume has undertaken to spend his intellectual career creating them. The *Fonteinne Amoureuse* and the *Confort*, it is true, are both motivated by extraliterary events: the departure of Jean of Berry for temporary exile as a hostage and Charles of Navarre's imprisonment by the king of France respectively. These events, however, are very clearly established as extraliterary motivations within the texts themselves (i.e., Charles is addressed by name and the anonymous nobleman in the *Fonteinne Amoureuse* is revealed to be Jean in a closing anagram). In contrast, the allegorical character Bonneürté, whose dissatisfaction triggers Guillaume's bungling defense of his earlier poem, can only perhaps be identified as a real figure in Guillaume's life. A prominent noblewoman attached to the French royal family, Bonne (daughter of the king of Bohemia), might be a model for this character. Machaut was well acquainted with her and undoubtedly shared the view of the court that she was especially virtuous, living up to her name. Although pure speculation, there are some intriguing reasons to suppose she might have been the model for Bonneürté. Bonne seems to have been an affectionate name; she was christened Jutta (Judith). Married to Jean of France, duke of Normandy, she might well have known Charles of Navarre personally; Charles was born in Normandy, where he inherited extensive lands and spent much of his early life. Bonne died of the plague in 1349, the same year Charles became king of Navarre. Charles later became a deadly enemy of Bonne's widower, Jean of Normandy, who became Jean II of France in 1350. But this is far from certain. The poem contains references to real events of that life; its opening section treats the narrator's melancholic reaction to the plague and other disasters of the years 1349–50. But these real events do not include any mention of attacks on Guillaume's reputation. It seems best, therefore, to conclude that the *Navarre* constructs the problems of Guillaume the protagonist for the purpose of generating a playful and entertaining text.

By making his previous poem the issue of a contentious debate, Guillaume is able to focus on a character other than the experiencing-I which he inherited from Guillaume de Lorris and which figures, as we have seen, in the opening of the *Behaingne*. In its place, the counter-judgment can offer a fictionalized version of the real Guillaume, a clerk protective of his literary reputation even as he is concerned about — must be concerned about — the reaction of the nobility to his representation of their experience. Thus Guillaume discovers in this poem a new way of understanding the "I" bequeathed him by tradition. The *Navarre* constructs the complexities and ironies of the producing-I, the self whose experiences with writing texts become the material of other texts written by the same self.[25] Machaut's focus on his own experiences (even when these are only "imagined" for the purpose of

---

[25] See Spearing, *Medieval Autographies*, for further discussion of this issue.

generating the text) is obvious from the beginning 540 lines of the poem, which treat, with accurate historical detail, the disturbing events of 1349–50 and the clerk's reaction to them. This section starts with an evocation of fall, the season of death and loss which suits historical calamity, and ends with the joyful coming of spring, when the passing of the epidemic allows the poet to resume solitary enjoyments — especially hare-hunting — and be open to the love experience, which here assumes a very untraditional shape. The movement from fall to spring and the attendant transformation of the historical subject into a character more suited to the love themes of courtly poetry have both encouraged numerous critics to view the opening part of the poem as a tedious irrelevance. Readers more sympathetic to Machaut's architectonic skill can stress thematic links of various kinds between the opening and the more conventional poetic fiction that follows. But the different parts of the poem become a difficulty only if we believe that Machaut was attempting to write a traditional love allegory and, for some dim reason, included an introduction which drew on tangential, historical material. The love allegory section itself, however, is hardly traditional, but in fact makes use of inherited structures in order to explore very different themes and issues.

Both parts of the *Navarre* in fact make it clear that the subject is the poet himself, first viewed, with great seriousness, as a historical person caught up in a tumult of events beyond his control, and then examined, rather humorously, as a bumbling versifier who slanders ladies even as he defends his attempts to exalt them. One important connection between the two parts of the poem is the poet's melancholy: the state of the world saddens him and then, with the disappearance of the disease, allows him pleasure again. Soon after, his hare-hunting is interrupted by the "call" from Bonneürté (Happiness) who sinks him back into a melancholy from which he is somewhat rescued by the lightheartedness of the debate's conclusion. Unlike the *Weltschmerz* that so affects him at the work's beginning, this melancholy can be (and is) overcome by Guillaume's gracious acceptance of the judgment against him and his cheerful agreement to do appropriate penance (which is the composition of three lyrical pieces in fixed forms with, this time, the "correct" doctrine).

If the true subject of the poem is the "real" Guillaume, then the historical references and analysis in the opening make good artistic sense: they ground the fiction which follows in the truth of the poet's experience. After referring to the cold north wind which has destroyed the greenery of summer (lines 34–36), the narrator describes how in the contemporary world there is no justice or truth, only a rapacious avarice that destroys social and familial trust; the result is a constant warfare that has brought down a heavenly vengeance in the form of destructive weather (lines 37–108). This description is a conventional, apocalyptic one (the topos is usually called *mundus senescit* or "the world grows old"), but it is followed by a return to the narrator's state of mind. The fall season had made him sad, and reflecting on the decay of the world sinks him into melancholy, which he tries to resist, following the wisdom of Ecclesiastes (lines 109–42). But, leaving behind the thoughts of social decay, the narrator considers those present ills which make him even more melancholic. These include ominous heavenly signs (lines 151–66), particularly the lunar eclipse of 17 January 1348, the various astrological configurations of that year widely interpreted as predicting the subsequent epidemic and the appearance of a fiery comet. Guillaume also makes reference to the great earthquake that devastated parts of Eastern Europe and Italy on 25 January 1348 (lines 167–80), a passage that mentions a heavenly rain of blood that boded ill. God revealed the meaning of these signs quickly by permitting a great outbreak of wars and killing, another apocalyptic reference with some basis in contemporary reality (e.g., the continuing hostilities of the Hundred Years' War, in which Machaut himself took some minor part). This long passage (lines 181–228) mentions as well the outbreak of anti-Semitism that accompanied the first appearances of the plague in northern Europe; like many at the time, Machaut believed that the Jews had poisoned wells and thus deserved the murderous fury of the persecutions which followed the spreading of these rumors (lines 229–40). Guillaume connects the phenomenon of wandering companies of flagellants to the disastrous events predicted by the heavens, even though this bizarre form of religious piety had come into existence during the previous century and continued to be active in Bohemia during the 1340s (lines 241–56). Because men were so intent on destroying themselves, Guillaume suggests, Nature decided to assist in this destruction by sending terrible storms to the earth, in expectation that the world would soon end; this weather, Guillaume suggests, was connected to the terrible mists that were said by many to have caused the epidemic, which immediately followed (lines 271–346).

Throughout this part of the poem, Guillaume gives the distinct impression that he is following one of the numerous Latin chronicles of the period, though no specific source has been identified. His selection of events (and their explanation as well) closely resembles what contemporary historians have to say about the outbreak of the epidemic. In any case, it is interesting that Guillaume here assumes the voice and manner of an historian's first-hand experience. The last part of his account is by far the most dramatic. God sees from his house that the world is everywhere corrupted, and so he sets Death loose on suffering humanity. Death is a beast so greedy and insatiable that he consumes heaps of corpses every day. The towns and villages are soon emptied of people; ditches must be dug in churchyards to bury the unnumbered dead. Guillaume says that no one will be able to count how many have died or will die (lines 393–99), an important indication that this part of the poem was indeed written during the epidemic. Pasture and field go untended because there are none to work or tend them (lines 408–430). At this point the narrator returns to his own reactions. Horrified by an imminent death, he confesses his sins thoroughly and resigns himself to the inevitable, closing up his doors and staying inside the whole winter (a precaution that probably saved his life). In this way he suffered less melancholy than he would have, for many of his friends died and were buried, a fact of which he remained ignorant. Finally, the end of the epidemic is signaled by merrymaking throughout the town, which Guillaume hears in his house. Asking one of his friends what is happening, Guillaume learns that the survivors are celebrating. He decides that he will do the same and goes to his horse and dogs, proceeding to some hare-hunting in the springtime fields. This is an activity that he defends with great seriousness, saying that its practice so absorbed him he would not have recognized anyone had they ridden up to him and spoken (lines 431–540).

At this point Machaut begins to reprise and adapt the structure of his earlier judgment poem. In the *Behaingne* the sorrowing lady, lost in gloomy thoughts, ignores the knight's greeting; this prompts their conversation and leads to the debate. Similarly, Guillaume's enthusiasm for hare-hunting here blinds him to the arrival in the fields of a "lady of great nobility," who, alerted to the poet's identity by her squire, sends him a message to appear before her. Indeed, she is the very lady whom Guillaume serves, although it is only later that he learns her name. This inconsistency conceals a hidden meaning, namely that Guillaume is unthinkingly aware he owes service to Bonneürté without knowing who she truly is or the power she wields over him. Like the traditional instructress figures of love allegory or the mysterious, supernatural ladies of Arthurian romance, Bonneürté appears to correct and enlighten her male subject. As it turns out, what she has to offer is advice about Guillaume's career; her judgment involves a renewal of the poet's contract to write about ladies and love in the appropriate fashion. As their debate develops, however, what is most significant is the fact that in this poem Guillaume takes the place of the knight as the male member of the debating pair. This change signals the most important difference of the *Navarre*. In the earlier poem, the narrator/clerk is displaced from the poem as the debate begins; here the narrator/clerk, no longer an anonymous and traditional figure but a fictional version of Guillaume himself, becomes the accused who must defend himself against the charges of Bonneürté. In the *Behaingne* the levels of traditional love allegory/debate and commentary on the poet's role in its making are kept distinct; the twist in the conventional structure of the poem calls attention to itself, focusing the reader on the narrator's role (and its reflection of the author's historical predicament as court poet/lyric voice). In the later judgment poem, on the contrary, the fiction itself becomes an examination of the poet's performance as poet.

 Instead of a response to a conventional *demande d'amors* (question of love), the debate here is more like a law suit in which the plaintiff makes a complaint whose rightness or wrongness is to be determined by an impartial judge. Unlike the interlocutors in the earlier poem, Guillaume is literally put on trial for an alleged crime: the promulgation of the "incorrect" view that the man whose beloved has betrayed him suffers more than the lady who has experienced the death of her lover. Bonneürté begins by faulting Guillaume for not noticing her arrival on the scene, a charge against which he defends himself successfully (lines 760–801). Then she accuses him of having sinned against ladies, but does not tell him how or when. Frustrated, Guillaume pleads for more specific information which, apparently impressed by the persuasiveness of his argument, she finally furnishes him, making reference to the conclusion reached in the *Behaingne* (lines 801–1038). Though she advises that Guillaume admit his fault immediately and correct his error by promulgating the opposite opinion (lines 1031–38), the poet refuses to do so because the original judgment is his published view. He resolves to win the debate if he can even though this means opposing himself to a grand and noble person whom he ought to, perhaps, unquestioningly obey. Guillaume's attitude here contrasts sharply with that of the character Guillaume in the *Prologue*; the latter is appropriately obedient, humble, self-effacing, and eager to please, agreeing wholeheartedly with everything Nature and Amour ask. In fact, in the light of the circumstances of literary production set out in the *Prologue*, the reaction of Guillaume to Bonneürté's charges is most surprising. Nature gives the poet Meaning, Rhetoric, and Music so that "in writing poetry you cannot fail at all" (I, line 17); the three natural children of artistic technique and content will make sure that his works will never "contain anything which will cause you to be blamed" (I, line 20).[26] This command hardly makes room for error, and that is because it does not grant Guillaume any control over what his works will contain. Certainly it does not authorize his willful disagreement with anything a figure of authority — especially a heavenly lady — might offer by way of correction.

Agreeing to debate the issue of his "error," Guillaume and the lady decide that the young King of Navarre, a man with amorous interests, shall be their judge. The pair ride on, accompanied by the lady's entourage, to a handsome manor house where she holds court. Described as a state of absolute repose and enjoyment, this manor house is a more

---

[26] See Volume 3 of *Guillaume de Machaut: The Complete Poetry and Music*.

realistic version of the traditional *locus amoenus* where love allegory is often set. There the poet is introduced to the twelve damsels who comprise the lady's court: these include psychological personifications.[27] The narrator relates that the lady is served well by her courtiers, who insures that she does only what is right and avoids all evil. It should be added at this point that the scheme adopted here is a fluid one; an important allegorical personage, Mesure (Moderation), appears later but is not introduced at this point. This long passage of description (lines 1155–328) is the poem's most impressive set piece. The appearance of the lady and her court dazzles the impressionable Guillaume, who for a moment is tempted to give up his defense; his strength, however, is restored by Raison (lines 1329–56). The lady then wishes to rehearse her complaint to the assembled court and, despite Guillaume's wish that they wait for the arrival of their judge, she does so impressively. As she finishes, the King of Navarre arrives by chance and immediately agrees to judge the dispute, picking appropriate members of Bonneürté's court to advise him (lines 1443–628). The debate finally begins with a long presentation of the case by the lady, who uses examples drawn from the bestiary tradition — the turtledove and the stork (lines 1629–702) — to argue that Guillaume is wrong.

Though he refuses Bonneürté's request to change his mind, Guillaume answers with extreme politeness, asking the judge's permission to speak, and simply restating his contention that the pain a man feels because of his beloved's infidelity is more severe than any other (lines 1703–68). Guillaume ends by asking for the judgment on his behalf, and this arrogance angers Attemprance (Temperance), who chastises him for wanting to circumvent proper legal procedure and for deliberately misinterpreting one of the lady's points. Attemprance suggests that the man, even though betrayed, can find relief in many ways, while the woman, seeing her lover dead, will suffer unending sorrow. And to illustrate her point, Attemprance introduces the debate's first exemplum, the story of a young girl who, upon learning her lover had been killed, soon dies despite the efforts of a host of doctors (lines 1769–2024). Guillaume agrees that the story is compelling, but finds in it a point for his side, namely that the lady died quickly and did not suffer long, while the cuckolded man finds no end to his misery (lines 2025–76). Reminding the court of something he had maintained in his earlier work (see the *Behaingne*, lines 1110–21; 1716–23), Guillaume states that the dead are soon forgotten, making the heart recover from grief. Once again, he asks for the decision on his behalf.

This time Pais (Peace) objects to his impertinence, declaring that he has not made enough argument to win the judgment. Intending to give Guillaume more to think about, she relates the death of Dido, who, betrayed by Aeneas, committed suicide. This exemplum diverts the course of the debate in a new way, because Dido did not suffer the death of her lover, but rather his faithlessness. Such a divergence is anticipated in the original judgment poem where the debate between Jean's courtiers about the issue of who suffers more soon turns to the question of whether Raison or Jeunesse should command the lover. Pais seems to be implying here that women have a greater capacity to suffer, whatever the cause. In any case, she also reproves Guillaume for stating that Nature overrides the commands of Amour, allowing the grief-stricken beloved to forget her loss. Amour, Pais suggests, always rules lovers and does not heed the wishes of Nature in any way (lines 2077–206). Guillaume, still polite, begs to disagree, relating the story of a clerk from Orléans whose

---

[27] For an intelligent discussion of the tradition behind Machaut's allegory here see Ehrhart, "Medieval Treatments of the Virtues."

distant lover proves unfaithful to him, marrying another man. Learning of her betrayal in a letter, the clerk goes mad and for the next twenty years lives in the wild like an animal, speaking to no one. Such a man, Guillaume avers, suffered a hundred times more pain than any woman who lost her lover (lines 2207–314). Foy (Faith) takes exception to Guillaume's exemplum, noting that he has not proved that the letter which caused the man to go mad actually was written by his beloved; her angry tone distresses Guillaume, and he asks her to stop threatening him (lines 2315–80). At this point Foy confers with Charité (Charity), and the latter is chosen to relate another exemplum, one which surely will prove Guillaume wrong. Charité tells the story of a rich man who, planting a sapling in his garden, goes to see it one day and finds it a full-grown tree. The story, as Charité explains it, signifies the behavior of the proper lover who, seeing his beloved grow into marriage with a powerful man, rejoices at her new-found station and happiness (lines 2381–532). Guillaume then challenges his opponents to prove only that no lady has ever suffered so much as to offer herself to death (has he forgotten the story of Dido, just related to him by Pais?). Honnesté (Honesty) doesn't address this point, but attacks his story about the clerk of Orléans, maintaining that, once mad, the man did not suffer at all. Guillaume's response is typically clerkly, a short disquisition on the distinction between primary and secondary causes which he thinks supports his view about the clerk's continued ordeal (though its relevance seems problematic at best).

At this point the debate turns completely toward the issue broached earlier by Pais, the supposed greater capacity of women to suffer. In a long speech (lines 2699–822), Franchise (Frankness) offers exempla from Classical literature, the stories of Ariadne and Medea, which, she believes, illustrate the point that women are made to suffer by men but emerge victorious in the end. Guillaume rudely attacks this argument, saying that he could easily find a host of examples to prove the opposite, namely that men have a greater capacity for suffering than women. He then relates one of the strangest exempla of the debate. A married woman has given her lover a ring on the condition that he never remove it unless she do it for him. One day her husband notices that the ring is missing and demands to see it. She sends a message to him asking for its return, and he sends it to her along with his finger in order not to break his word. Recognizing that extremes in loving are to be condemned, Guillaume suggests that the man surpassed all women in loyalty and suffering (lines 2823–924), Prudence (Prudence) does not agree, and she launches a long refutation of Guillaume's contention, which the poet ignores, preferring to return to the issue raised by Franchise. Though he recognizes that the debate has broadened to include an issue not mentioned in the beginning, Guillaume offers his opinion that men are far superior to women in love because there is nothing stable or firm about a woman's emotions or beliefs. These anti-feminist statements, he affirms, are endorsed by everyone, and that is why he advanced them in his poem (lines 3009–70).

These views give rise to an outburst which must eventually be settled by the judge, causing Guillaume to admit to some satisfaction and pleasure in seeing the assemblage of ladies so discomfited (lines 3157–62). Doubtance (Wariness) tells the story of Pyramus and Thisbé and Souffissance (Sufficiency) the tale of Hero and Leander as proof of women's capacity to endure. But Guillaume counters with the observation that in the latter case Leander suffered more since he suffered first (once again a somewhat dubious point). Thinking that the debate has continued long enough, the lady now asks the judge to go in private to deliberate. The judge and his advisers then leave, but Guillaume is informed of their proceedings by an attendant at court. Reviewing the aspects of proper judgment, the advisers condemn Guillaume unanimously. Mesure rebukes Guillaume for daring to debate such a noble and respected personage, for advancing a mistaken opinion, and for offering insufficient and dubious evidence in support of his position. Raison agrees, and when the court has reassembled with the accused, condemns him on these three counts (lines 3767–832). Seeing Guillaume saddened by the outcome, Raison reveals to him the identity of the lady and describes her immense powers; in the tradition of Boethius' Fortuna, Bonneürté distributes talents and wisdom to those she favors. Raison's long description of her providence particularly emphasizes the different gifts she accords to clergy and knights (lines 3839–4006). More reconciled to his fate, Guillaume asks to be sentenced, and the judge signifies to him that he owes three amends for his three different faults. Raison and the judge confer about the specifics of the sentence, a meeting which, Guillaume perceives, is somewhat lighthearted. Meanwhile Avis (Discretion) recounts the allegorical meanings of the different parts of Bonneürté's dress (lines 4075–170). The judge then returns to Guillaume and tells him he must compose three lyric poems, of different types, as penance. The poem closes with Guillaume's confession that he has made this poem in order to recognize his fault better and intends to present it to the lady along with his promise of continued service. Guillaume then expresses his desire to complete his penance quickly by composing a lay concerned with love.

In manuscripts B, E, and M the *Lay de Plour* follows the end of the judgment immediately; in F–G and A, the lay either is missing entirely or is found among the other lyric poems.[28] It seems that Machaut initially thought it should follow the narrative poem which is its pre-text but later changed his mind. I have included it as a continuation of the *Navarre*. The reader may judge whether Machaut's original plan is artistically successful or not (I happen to think it is, of which more below).

In assessing the artistic achievement of the *Navarre*, we must, I think, read the poem metafictionally, in the same way the original audience likely did. For we must, as did they, distinguish between the seriousness of Guillaume the character, who resents the accusations of Bonneürté and loses his composure as the trial begins to slip away from him, eventually mouthing, somewhat gleefully, the very anti-feminist statements he declared himself innocent of at the beginning; and the seriousness of Guillaume de Machaut the poet, who with remarkable *sprezzatura* puts his own poetry on trial in a work whose sophistication and finesse equally testify to his commanding, confident talent. The poem playfully treats the relationship of the poet to his *métier* and to his patrons, problematizing the very traditional poetics later enunciated in the *Prologue* by turning the poet's individual control over the content of his works (and the reputation they make or do not make for him) into an issue to be debated. Within the fiction, Guillaume's temerity is roundly condemned, as much, if not more than, the anti-feminism of which he proves himself guilty. But the poem itself testifies to the ways in which Guillaume, as creative source of his works, can forge something entirely new from the givens of tradition, including a different sense in which "poetic identity" can be represented. Focusing on the producing-I, the *Navarre* traces the ways in which authorial intertext, rather than traditional techniques and subject matter, "creates" poetry. The *Behaingne* generates the *Navarre*, which in turn generates the *Lay de Plour*. The audacity here is that Guillaume produces poetry which is intensely self-reflexive, thematizing the discontents of an author controlled by the reader, who consumes his work,

---

[28] The full list of manuscripts and shelf marks can be found in the Textual Notes on p. 369. N.b., Manuscripts F and G are part of a two-volume set of the complete works.

even as *Navarre* asserts the power of the poet to exceed or contravert the position assigned to him by tradition (i.e., here Guillaume the *writer* not the *lover*, is the main character). For this reason I believe the poet's original plan to have the *Lay de Plour* follow the end of the judgment poem was most effective artistically.

The *Navarre* is unlike all other medieval works in its complex exploration of the poetics of authorship, in its meditations on and comic reduction of the difficulties posed by a literary tradition and its underlying ideology to the creative author.

THE LAY DE PLOUR AND THE DEBATE SERIES

Though separate, the two debate poems and their lyric continuation clearly constitute a transtextual series. Machaut intended the two *jugements* to be read together, arranging that in his later collected works' manuscripts; the *Navarre* was presumably moved from after the *Remede* to follow the much earlier *Behaingne* directly. The series features the producing-I, a fictional reflex of the poet who is represented as struggling with the demands (including angry readers) of his chosen profession. The producing-I, however, is also the reflex of a transformed matter. In the transtextual course of the debate series, the *dit amoureux* genre becomes an exploration of authorial experience because the poet's activity is now available as content. This textual series, in large measure a meditation on its own making, is an artifact best accounted for, in a purely formal sense, by modernist theories of self-containment and "spatial form." And yet the impulse toward reflexivity and autotelism, however intriguingly contemporary its structural effects might seem, finds its distinctly late medieval source in the poet's complex connection to his patron and the court. The judgment series confirms Terry Eagleton's view of a literary work's material symptomaticness, the way in which it "bears the impress of its historical mode of production as surely as any product secretes in its form and materials the fashion of its making."[29]

As a structural feature, the figure of the poet who as poet can become his own subject is related to an aspect of the Machaldian oeuvre that has received some important and valuable study from Kevin Brownlee, William Calin, and others: what is usually termed intertextuality. For Brownlee, a key aspect of Machaut's career is the poet's well-documented concern for his collected works and, hence, his reputation:

> The arrangement of codices — in the thirteenth century largely the business of scribes . . . becomes with Machaut the business of the poet himself. Indeed the notion of organizing a codex is transferred by Machaut into the organizing of an oeuvre.[30]

And the *Prologue* that Machaut, late in his career, wrote for elaborate collections of his diverse works "involves the establishment of the poetic voice that will be speaking in all the works that follow."[31] A striking feature of some of Machaut's most renowned narrative

---

[29] Eagleton, *Criticism and Ideology*, p. 48.

[30] Brownlee, *Poetic Identity*, p. 15.

[31] Brownlee, *Poetic Identity*, p. 11.

poems is the manner in which they enfold other texts, particularly lyrical inserts, thus constructing themselves as self-generating or autotextual artistic objects.[32]

These aspects of intertextuality we might term global and textual respectively. They are concerned with the unity established for diverse works by a text that explains their compositional origin, and with the isolation of an individual text from the flow of literary tradition, the establishment of its self-sufficiency through the rhetorical figure of the *mise-en-abyme*. Though in divergent ways, both forms of intertextuality foster a sense of the uniqueness and separateness of Guillaume's artistic efforts. As such, they respond to the literary ideology of the court patronage system, which demanded adherence to traditional forms and materials, even as, by the end of the Middle Ages, that system had begun to encourage the building of an individual literary career by the artist called to make new his culture's literary inheritance.

The judgment series is an unusual if symptomatic response to late medieval literary ideology. In these works it is a question of the ties manufactured between texts in a series, a conception that depends on the ways in which subsequent texts can be understood as answers to previous ones. More than either global or textual intertextuality, such a method of connecting works emphasizes the role of the author, for he can now be imagined — and thus be represented — as a figure who must answer continually for (and hence in some way transform) what he has already written. The *Prologue* offers itself as an ur-text. In it Machaut delineates the hierarchies of creation which have brought about his selection as a creator of new poems (of which the *Prologue* itself, of course, is one). The individual works Machaut composes are imagined as generated by this call. The *Prologue* accounts for the oeuvre as a whole, not for the particularity and sequencing of separate works. The use of lyric inserts as *mises-en-abyme*, in contrast, creates autotexts whose rhetoric of self-generation belies any connection except to their poet-creator. The debate series offers yet another plan, for it imagines the poet in time, involved in a give and take with his patrons and with the literary tradition he serves. The difficult and multi-levelled connections among these three works index the vicissitudes (however fictionalized or idealized) of the poet's career, of creative acts that cannot be represented without reference to their reception (particularly judgments about their doctrinal conformity).

The judgment poems are thus dialogic or "open" in ways which the other works within the Machaut corpus are not. The debate which is the traditional (however modified) content of the *Behaingne* becomes the form which dictates the conception of the series (i.e., a debate about the debate), as the earlier poem becomes the question debated hypertextually (because the *Navarre* is a response to and modification of the earlier poem) as well as diegetically, because this response is generated self-consciously within the fiction, becomes the thematic matter of the new text.[33] The connection between the two poems cannot be described simply as an instance of intertextuality, as the co-presence of two texts.

The writing of the *Navarre* transforms the meaning of the *Behaingne*, identifying it as a problematic fulfillment of Guillaume's mission to write love poems with the proper doctrine; the *Navarre*, in fact, becomes a metatext, a commentary in the sense that it opens its hypotext to hermeneutic exploration, "speaking of it" as itself and thereby raising the question of what it says. We might go further and say that the diegetic transformation of

---

[32] See Calin, *Poet at the Fountain*.

[33] See essays in Plumley, Di Bacco, and Jossa, eds, *Citation, Intertextuality, and Memory*.

the *Behaingne* within the *Navarre*, the presence of the earlier poem as summarized content, constitutes the reduction of the *Behaingne* to a pretext. Bonneürté's desire is that the earlier poem be thought of as what we might call a disposable pretext, for she wishes its message replaced by a new judgment, by the new poem that her complaint provides the material for and is produced by (for, having poeticized his experiences with Bonneürté, Guillaume dedicates the freshly produced work to her). The *Navarre* itself, in turn, becomes a pretext, the explanatory preface for the *Lay de Plour*, which is the artistic penance called into being through the judgment passed against Guillaume by his patron, the lady, and her courtiers. Here is yet another text generated by a preceding one (in fact, by the two which precede it, since the *Behaingne* furnishes the content to be rewritten). Perhaps even more important, it is called into being by the encounter of the poet with the court, who uphold traditional love doctrine. This relationship is restaged within the debate itself. Ironically and appropriately, the lyric penance recalls the first poem in the series; the lady's complaints from the *Behaingne* are transformed from argument into a lyric complaint, which is a transvestite performance whose true speaker is the poet himself, taking seriously the judge's admonition to see the merits in the female point of view. Here the strident male (and clerical) tones of the narrator's voice from the *Navarre* ventriloquize the sorrows of female experience, but of course, and here is the humor, in an authentically poetic rather than authentically womanly fashion. The feelings evoked in the lyric outburst must be read within the context of the series as evidence of Guillaume's reformation, not as the personal product of emotional experience.

The debate series generates its own tradition. Such a refiguration of the traditional ground of allegorical love vision/debate poetry generates a radically different narrative persona. In the *Navarre*, the "I" that speaks is not the experiencing-I of the *Rose*, nor the clerkly narrator of an earlier literary tradition. Instead, it is the producing-I, the self whose experiences with writing texts become the material of yet other texts written by the same self (even, of course, as that self is written by its own texts). In the debate series, tradition becomes the earlier production of the poet; the rewriting that is the court poet's approach to newness becomes directed toward, and contained by, the oeuvre. The poet furnishes himself with a new voice, speaks through and beyond what he has already said, escaping thereby the power of what other writers have done before. At the same time, the *Navarre* constructs the dialogue of reception-production, fictionalizing the imagined negative response of listeners whose disagreement with the author furnishes the ground for a new, corrective series of texts, including the *Navarre* itself. In the debate series, the author's career is not represented as a command to produce which maps itself unproblematically over a series of texts that proceed like spokes from the hub of a wheel. Authorship, instead, is conceived as dialogic (like the texts it generates), as a series of bids and counterbids dependent for its continuation and shape on the answers furnished individual works by their aristocratic consumers.

The *Navarre* makes the reader understand the *Behaingne* as Guillaume's own, original contribution to textual production; and the *Navarre* identifies itself as, first, an exploration of that earlier text and as, finally, a rewriting of it. To put it somewhat differently, the new poem which inevitably transforms the old is required, but not because a tradition, in order to live, must be supported by the continuing production of new texts. The new work is required instead because a previous text has not been found to be the proper kind of rewriting (Guillaume allegedly has violated Love's command never to slander ladies). The *Behaingne* is allegedly nonconformist, unconventional. And so a new text is required to answer, atone for, and revise the one already composed. In this way, the issue of rewriting, of making a new text from the givens of the love poetry genre, becomes most directly connected to the author's consistency and integrity. It is the producing-I who is therefore both the voice and the theme of the debate series. The doctrine and form of love debate poetry become merely the source of this poem's engagement with the dilemmas and discontents of authorship.

Machaut's playful problematizing of his own role is ultimately humorous. Found guilty of heterodoxy, he is nevertheless not punished by the loss of his authority, his mandate to write; instead, he is simply required to compose more texts. In the repentant poet's hands, even the text of the *Navarre* becomes a gift he might bestow on his angry audience. It is interestingly transformed from a record of his recalcitrance into a monument of his rededication to proper love service, as it changes from a narrative representing experience to a made object, a codex that can be presented. The producing-I who composes the work is ultimately distinct from the beset and confused producing-I whose troubles and stupidity generate it. It is this distinction, figured in the text by the narrator's frequent silence as he witnesses the predicament of his former self, which allows the textual series to function both as an indictment (albeit fictionalized) of Machaut and as a testimony to his inventive skill.

It is thus strangely appropriate that Guillaume is assigned the penance of composing three lyric poems with the correct doctrine. The *Navarre* confirms his authorship in the very act of making amends for its evident and proven deficiencies. The debate series is resolutely open-ended, its second text called into existence by the reception of the first, and the second, in turn, to be replaced by three further texts, whose value is similarly to be determined by Guillaume's readers. The ultimate meaning of the series is the self-generating continuity of authorship, which can only be interrupted by the poet's inability or unwillingness to write more.

Fittingly, the scene at the end of the *Navarre* is echoed by the dramatic encounter of the *Prologue* but with a crucial difference. Here Guillaume accepts the command to write from Bonneürté, just as he agrees to become an author in the *Prologue* at the instance of Nature (Nature) and then Amour. Once again Guillaume humbly takes up the burden of what appears to be social and existential necessity. Like Nature, Bonneürté represents a number of forces. Both figures point toward the fact of patronage, that is, toward the existence of a class whose concerns occasion courtly poetry and who must be pleased by it. At the same time each figure suggests that the poet's calling is a unique, either natural or fortunate, gift which depends on him for its realization and furtherance. The difference is that the *Navarre* conceives authorship dialogically; Bonneürté does not furnish Guillaume with a command, but engages him in a debate. His oeuvre is thus imagined here as a never-ending struggle over the generation of meaning. Guillaume must realize the command he so readily and unproblematically accepts in the *Prologue*, but to do so he must submit to the ultimate authorship of those for whom he writes. Or at least he must apparently do so. The *Navarre*, we must remember, is most likely not an occasional piece, a response to some real attack on Guillaume's abilities and dedication, but rather an ingenious fabrication that allows him to colonize the love poem genre, to transform its content into a pretext and convert the "I" of tradition into its subject matter.

Machaut conflates authorial and emotional experience in the *Navarre*, just as he does in the *Remede*,[34] written during the same period of his career. But there are important differences of structure and rhetoric between the two works. The Boethian poem features a poet-lover whose production of a beautiful lay in honor of his beloved serves as the hypotext for both the love sorrow he suffers and the consolation which, with the aid of the heavenly Hope, he eventually experiences. Similarly, the *Navarre* offers a protagonist whose writing of a poem gets him into difficulty with the lady he is bound to serve faithfully and love. The publication of this text leads to a fractious, nearly damaging debate between him and his lady's twelve damsels, which culminates in his censure. Here the writing which causes difficulty but ultimately leads to happiness is not enfolded within the text; it is a public part of Guillaume's oeuvre. It exists in the *Navarre* only as a short summary. The *Navarre* does not treat the judgment of the earlier poem as a "reality" whose story world it would extend in the manner of a sequel. Instead the earlier judgment is represented as a text for which the author, named as the poet Guillaume de Machaut, is held responsible. The fiction of the *Navarre* is second degree. It has been constructed by the absorption into a later text of that which was extra-textual in an earlier one (i.e., the facts of authorship and reception). There is no question of any coincidence between amorous and authorial experiences because these belong to different layers of textual "reality." Or, to put it another way, we might say that the only experience that the *Navarre* (and by extension the debate series itself) can treat is authorial.

The *Navarre* functions more as metatext than simple transformation. Similarly, the *Lay de Plour*, reverting to a genre in which pure emotionality and its appropriate technical expression are at issue, furnishes a commentary on the *Navarre*. As a lyric, it provides a "correction" that implicitly goes beyond scholastic disputation to the roots of authorial feeling about love experience. An important aspect of the penitential rhetoric of this lyric is that it is a transvestite performance. On the surface at least, the poet's conversion stages, in so far as possible, the abandonment of the gender position Guillaume allegedly adopts in the *Behaingne* and so wrongfully defends in the *Navarre*. Finally, the contextualizing of the lyric implicitly asks the reader to judge it as an important element of the author's career (i.e., as textual evidence of his rededication to the proper service of ladies required of him in the *Prologue*).

At the same time, it is significant that Guillaume "corrects" the error contained in his first judgment by closely repeating central elements of what he had written. If the *Navarre* replaces the *Behaingne*, embodying as a text the wish of lady Bonneürté that the first judgment poem be effaced, the *Lay de Plour* in effect restores the *Behaingne* by containing and transforming it. As a metatext, the lyric reads the earlier judgment "against the grain," emphasizing the elements which had there been improperly marginalized. Furthermore, the reversion to a lyric form at this point in the series allows Guillaume to restage a move made in the *Navarre*. Guillaume's judgment in the *Behaingne* is not proven wrong so much as it never receives an adequate defense from the producing-I, who actually winds up mouthing unquestionably anti-feminist sentiments that clinch the case for the opposition. Similarly, a lyric penance makes it possible for Guillaume to avoid retracting his viewpoint. He accords the emotional turbulence of the sorrowing woman a special place (repressing male unhappiness with female fickleness and betrayal in the process), but the form does not constrain him to admit directly the error of his opinion. The *Lay de Plour* is an

---

[34] See Volume 2 of *Guillaume de Machaut: The Complete Poetry and Music*.

ironically subversive text, a testimony to Guillaume's obedience as a character to the wishes of his lady, but sly proof as well that Guillaume the author never surrenders final control of his versifying to the powers that he himself has decided to summon into diegetic existence.

The *Lay de Plour* accommodates two different voices, the voice of the producing-I and the voice of the character he recycles in order to further his role as author. The traditional lyric form remains technically intact; but the transtextuality of the debate series, the transformation which links one text to another, has in effect altered the reading strategy which Machaut's courtly audience must adopt to consume it. The poet shifts the rhetoric of the text, making his readers attend more to the work as a poem written by an author to achieve a particular effect than as a pleasing imitation of feeling and grief. Machaut speaks through the simulated emotions of his constructed persona to delineate once again the producing-I, the implied poet whose experience is authorial rather than emotional. The *Lay de Plour* exists to express authorial desire, or, to be precise, the author's desire for authorship; it exists dramatically in the manner of the traditional lyric only to the extent that the producing-I reveals himself as the ultimate voice that speaks it.

EDITORIAL POLICY FOR THIS EDITION AND TRANSLATION

Sources

Unlike most poets of the Middle Ages, Guillaume de Machaut was eager to present to the public his poetical and musical works as a unified oeuvre that would testify, in its breadth and variety, not to mention its demonstrated finesse, to his talent and accomplishment. This understanding of his compositional activities seems, from the evidence, to have occurred to the poet relatively early in his career, but it achieved its most impressive textual form late in his career. Though Machaut's works are sometimes found individually bound with those of other authors (this is especially true of the *Behaingne*, which seems to have enjoyed an unusual popularity), the more authoritative manuscripts offer more or less complete versions of the oeuvre and do not contain works by others. In attempting to establish the best witnesses for Machaut's various works, textual scholars evaluated the surviving manuscripts on the basis of what might be called a "growing contents" theory. Thus, the more complete manuscripts should be thought of as later and hence representative of the poet's final version of his works.[35] In the *Voir Dit*,[36] the character Guillaume de Machaut speaks of the book "where I have put all my compositions" (after line 6281; L33), establishing that there was at least one manuscript whose contents did grow the poet's compilation of fair copies.[37] In the past three decades or so, this theory has been challenged, both as a global explanation of the affiliation of the surviving manuscripts and as a protocol for establishing the "best text" to be used in editions of individual poems.[38] It may well be that one or more of the surviving manuscripts is "incomplete" because its contents were meant to suit the tastes of a particular patron. So

---

[35] See Hœpffner, I: pp. xliv–lii for an elaborate and persuasive demonstration of this view.

[36] See Volume 5 of *Guillaume de Machaut: The Complete Poetry and Music*.

[37] See Williams, "Author's Role," for a full discussion of this issue.

[38] See Keitel, "Musical Manuscripts" and Kibler and Wimsatt, eds, "Machaut's Text."

it follows that the dating and establishment of relative authority must rest on a careful examination of the evidence in each case. However, this does not mean that in deciding on the base text for an edition of an individual work the view that the more complete manuscripts carry no special authority can be laid aside lightly. How these issues affect the editing of the musical texts is discussed in full in the introductory materials of the several volumes of this edition devoted to Machaut's musical production.

The poems of Machaut are found either individually or in groups in seventy-three manuscripts that have either survived or can be postulated with some certainty.[39] Here follows a list of the five that include Machaut's last major work, the *Prise*, and thus seem to extend their completeness to the end of his active career:

A	Paris, Bibliothèque nationale, fonds français MS 1584
B	Paris, Bibliothèque nationale, fonds français MS 1585
E	Paris, Bibliothèque nationale, fonds français MS 9221
F–G	Paris, Bibliothèque nationale, fonds français MSS 22545–6
Vg	*olim* Marquis de Vogüé; now Ferrell 1, Parker Library, Cambridge

An earlier manuscript that lacks the final two major dits — the *Voir Dit* and the *Prise* — as well as the *Prologue*, but which, for a number of reasons carries considerable authority for the early works, is:

C	Paris, Bibliothèque nationale, fonds français MS 1586

Of the five later, complete works manuscripts, only A and F–G include a full version of the *Prologue* that Machaut wrote late in his career to serve as a literary explanation of why he devoted himself to the composition of verse and music. B includes a short, perhaps preliminary version of the *Prologue*. Vg lacks not only the *Prologue*, but some of the shorter works of Machaut's later career, and even though it does contain the *Prise*, it lacks the *Voir Dit*. While, like Vg, E lacks some of the short, later *dits*, it does include full versions of both the *Voir Dit* and the *Prise*. C lacks the *Navarre*.

A, E, and F–G undoubtedly relate closely to one another, but direct affiliations are difficult to establish. Of the three, A and F–G may well have been copied from the same source, but these two manuscripts do not regularly agree with Vg, B, and E, as one might expect in such a case. E sometimes furnishes readings superior to those of A and F–G. We can hardly doubt that A, E, and F–G are no more than one or two removes from Machaut's own fair copy, which, it is entirely possible, he may have edited during the preparation of these omnibus manuscripts. The fact that two substantial passages of the *Behaingne* have apparently been excised from A, and that these lacunae cannot be accounted for as scribal error or other material reasons (such as a missing folio), raises the strong possibility of authorial intervention in the preparation of this manuscript which, as shall become evident, we have other good reasons to believe was copied and assembled under the supervision of the poet himself. In any case, "authorized" versions of the different works may have circulated in different "final" forms. For this reason, the principle of common error cannot be invoked with any certainty in establishing a "correct reading."

---

[39] See Earp, *A Guide to Research*, for full details.

A has consistently, if not exclusively, been preferred by Machaut's literary (if not musical) editors because it offers reliable, if hardly error-free versions of his various texts. Ernest Hœpffner, Machaut's first modern, scientific editor, merits quoting on this point:

> In so far as the establishment of the text is concerned, priority must be given to the most complete manuscripts which contain in one form or another the last redaction of the works of Machaut, the definitive forms that the author wished to give them: A and F–G.[40]

A bears an additional cachet that distinguishes it absolutely from F–G. Its index is headed by a rubric, unique among all the Machaut manuscripts, that reads "Vesci lordenance que Guillaume de Machaut wet qil ait en son livre" (This is the arrangement that Guillaume de Machaut wishes his book to have). If we interpret "ordenance" more broadly to mean something like "form," this rubric might be understood as a testimony to the authenticity of the manuscript's witness to the author's intentions. Furthermore, the miniatures in *grisaille* throughout the body of the manuscript seem to be of provincial design, perhaps executed in Reims under the poet's supervision.[41] For these reasons, A has been selected as the base manuscript for the edition of the poetic works. Since there are compelling reasons to think it offers the best witness to Machaut's final intentions, the editorial policy adopted here accords priority to A in all matters. The two works in this volume are presented in fairly error-free form in A, and minor grammatical "errors" (if that is what they are) have been allowed to stand, while spelling variations have not been regularized. Obvious miswritings of various kinds (as opposed to misspellings, in so far as these two categories can be distinguished) have been noted and corrected. The several lacunae in the text of the *Behaingne* have been supplied from C; in the case of the two larger passages of this kind, the reader is invited to speculate on whether the cut-down or full version of the poem is the artistically superior. Accents, including the dieresis (or umlaut), are supplied to the original text; words written together that are normally separate are separated; abbreviations are expanded, but manuscript numerals are allowed to stand; u/v as well as i/j are treated in the modern fashion, with /v/ and /j/ reserved for consonantal use; capitalization follows modern practice, and the separation of initial letters from the first words in poetic lines has been abandoned. With these exceptions, the French text presented here is essentially the same as it appears in manuscript A, but of course with modern punctuation.

The facing English translations serve two quite different purposes which, in practice, have not always proved possible to reconcile. On the one hand, the English version is a guide for those reading the original, who might glance at it for assistance with a difficult construction or unfamiliar word. For such readers, the most useful translation is a version in which each French expression is rendered by an appropriate English equivalent. Basic syntactical and grammatical similarities between Middle French and Modern English make such translation possible, though often the result is awkward or unidiomatic. On the other hand, the translation also serves those with no knowledge of Middle French, for whom the best introduction to Machaut's poetry is a modern English version that reproduces not only the meaning of the original, but something of its style, though the version offered here

---

[40] Hœpffner, I:1.

[41] See Leo's "An Art Historical Overview" in the following section for further discussion of this important point.

does not pretend to equal the elegance of the original. Most lines of the translation do correspond to those in the original. To produce easily readable English, however, I have sometimes not been guided by Machaut's syntax. No attempt has been made to reproduce the rhyming octosyllabic couplets of the *Navarre* or the stanzaic form of the *Behaingne*.[42]

Music

The musical reading of the *Lay de Plour* presented here follows A alone; even where adjustments are required from that reading, they are made here without recourse to any other manuscript sources (for details of such instances, see the notes to the music, p. 377). By adhering closely to our base source and integrating illuminations from it, we offer a snapshot of a single tradition of transmission. Combining music and image into the text in their original positions enables the reader to appreciate the richness and subtlety of this tradition. As a consequence, the musical edition offered here is subtly different from its counterpart in Volume 10: *The Lays*, where the weight of evidence from the other manuscript sources sometimes calls for the adjustment of the reading from the base source, even where the version stated in our base source is also technically viable. A full list of the musical variants will be presented there, while the textual variants will appear in Volume 8: *The Lyrics I*.

In the score presented here, sharps and flats appearing above the stave are editorial. Brackets distinguish between more and less controversial suggestions. Detailed discussion of our editorial policy will appear in the music volumes of this complete edition. Further discussion about editorial approaches can be found on our project website, along with accompanying tailored scores and illustrative sound clips made by The Orlando Consort and Le Basile; http://machaut.exeter.ac.uk.

---

[42] Machaut's versification is discussed fully in the introduction to Volume 7: *The Lyrics I* of *Guillaume de Machaut: The Complete Poetry and Music*.

BnF, fr. 1584: An Art Historical Overview
By Domenic Leo[1]

With 154 miniatures in partially tinted and gilded *grisaille*, an appended bifolium with two large miniatures by the renowned Master of the Bible of Jean de Sy, and an "original" index, manuscript A, BnF, fr. 1584, ranks as one of the three most luxurious, complete-work manuscripts of Guillaume de Machaut's oeuvre, which were made in his lifetime.[2] Beyond MS A's importance to Machaut studies in general, however, it holds a special place in art historical scholarship. The first two images for the *Prologue* are deservingly recognized as masterpieces of late-fourteenth-century French manuscript illumination.[3] They are as remarkable for the artist's spectacular command of his medium as for his sophisticated and creative iconography.

The identification of the artists who painted in MS A is a critical issue. I believe there are five. Until now, it has been commonly accepted, based on the groundbreaking work of François Avril, that there are two artists: the well-known Jean de Sy Master who painted the two *Prologue* images; and the primary and otherwise unknown artist responsible for the main body of miniatures, the "Machaut Master." The latter's iconography is sometimes novel and nearly always inventive, making up for his maladroit style. Avril, foremost among the art historians to have analyzed MS A, wrote that, "[a]lthough this volume shows a strong stylistic kinship with other illuminated manuscripts executed for the court, it may

---

[1] A fully expanded version of this essay with color images can be found on the website for *The Works of Guillaume de Machaut: Music, Image, Text in the Middle Ages* (http://machaut.exeter.ac.uk/).

[2] Henceforth, the Jean de Sy Master. Two other manuscripts were painted during Machaut's lifetime. Manuscript C (BnF, ms. fr. 1586), of the mid to late 1340s, was in the collection of Charles, duke of Normandy, by 1363; Earp, *Ferrell-Vogüé Machaut Manuscript*, pp. 34–38, especially p. 31n20; Earp, *A Guide to Research*, 77–79; and Leo, "The Pucellian School," pp. 153–63. The Ferrell-Vogüé manuscript (MS Vg), of the 1370s, was in the duc de Berry's collection; on patronage see Earp, *Ferrell-Vogüé Machaut Manuscript*, especially pp. 38–44, and Leo, "Art-historical Commentary," p. 126. Two other complete-work, heavily illustrated manuscripts were painted posthumously. MS F-G (BnF. ms. fr. 22545–22546), was painted in the early 1390s. See Earp, *A Guide to Research*, pp. 90–92; Earp, *Ferrell-Vogüé Machaut Manuscript*, p. 38n72; and the forthcoming research on patronage by Plumley and Smilansky, "A Courtier's Quest." Manuscript E (BnF, ms. fr. 9921), of the 1390s, was also in the duc de Berry's collection; see Earp, *A Guide to Research*, pp. 92–94. The latest manuscript, Pm (New York, Pierpont Morgan Library M. 396), of c. 1425–30 is a partial complete-works manuscript; its iconographic program closely follows that of MS A. On MS Pm, see Earp, *A Guide to Research*, pp. 101–02; and Drobinsky, "Recyclage et création."

[3] On the *Prologue*, see Drobinsky, "*Peindre, poutraiture, escrire*," pp. 553–69; Perkinson, *The Likeness of the King*, pp. 218–31; and for an expansive analysis devoted to these two miniatures, see Leo, "The Beginning is the End." Leach, *Secretary, Poet, Musician*, pp. 87–103, has fused Leo and Perkinson's interpretations in her own important discussions of the *Prologue*.

37

have been illustrated in Reims . . . by a local illuminator who worked under the poet's direction."[4] In the 1981 exhibition catalogue for *Les fastes du gothique*, Avril added that the Machaut Master's style fits well within a group of manuscripts from the East of France, possibly Metz, that date to the third quarter of the fourteenth century.[5] But, apart from the Parisian sartorial finesse, there is no indication that this was made for the court. The comparison of the Machaut Master's style to that of Eastern France in general, or Reims in particular, remains highly problematic.[6]

Some scholars follow Avril's comparison of MS A to a French translation of Boethius' *Consolation of Philosophy* from Metz, though there is no substantial stylistic link between these manuscripts.[7] The artist of the Boethius manuscript uses a bold palette with a preponderance of brick red and orange whereas the artists of the Machaut manuscript use an elegant *grisaille*. Moreover, the *retardataire* style in the Boethius manuscript is most obvious, relatively speaking, in the cursory treatment of the drapery folds, the crude execution of the faces, and the ubiquitous use of figures with the so-called Gothic sway, an exaggerated *contrapposto*. In addition, although it is possible to recognize styles in general from Lorraine and Champagne c. 1300, is there a style specific to Reims in the 1360s and 1370s?[8]

The foundation of the Machaut Master's stylistic vocabulary is the adept use of *grisaille* for figures, buildings, plants, and animals. He uses contrasts between lighter and darker shades of gray for modeling but sharply defined grays and black to give the architectural components a three-dimensional appearance. The use of a heavy silhouette for the figures contrasts with the backgrounds, which are devoid of decoration (with the exception of the *Prise* frontispiece), and flattens the images. Certain elements of his style are fresh and spontaneous, as is his use of *portrait à l'encre* tinting. He sparingly applies translucent washes of colored ink for more delicate modeling. To focus attention on the more important images, especially frontispiece images, he uses densely saturated colors; for example, the *Prise* and the highly detailed artwork of the opening image for the *Dit de la Rose* (*The Tale of the Rose*). In his more finished work, he relies on a sharp, fine black line to pick out details, most apparent in the strands of hair and the outlines of the eyes.[9]

The Machaut Master was proficient in his trade, and quite inventive. The iconographer, no matter if it was the painter or another person, was well-read, and the *Roman de la rose*, the *Bible historiale*, and the *Ovide moralisé* figure prominently in the images. As the *Ovide moralisé* was the visual source for mythological tales in, for example,

---

[4] Avril, *Manuscript Painting*, p. 36.

[5] Avril, *Les Fastes du gothique*, p. 329, writes that this style "présente un caractère plus spontané et certains traits provinciaux qui cadrent bien avec la production de l'Est de la France telle qu'elle nous est connue par les manuscrits messins du milieu et troisième quart du siècle."

[6] This does not, however, preclude the possibility that MS A was illustrated in this city by an artist trained elsewhere.

[7] Montpellier, Bibliothèque de la Faculté de Médecine, MS H. 43. Notably Leach, *Secretary, Poet, Musician*, writes that "[the Montpellier manuscript] is a close match for the *style* of the *rest* of A" (original emphases, p. 96).

[8] See Avril, *L'Art au temps des rois maudits*, pp. 313–24.

[9] The Machaut Master uses this type of black line for Lady Fortune and the texts on the wheels she holds.

Fonteinne, so too did the *Bible historiale* provide the iconographic programs for the lengthy biblical stories used as exempla in the *Confort*.[10] Surprisingly, the artist demonstrates an intimate familiarity with Machaut's texts. He used pre-existing iconographic moduli from well-known sources when Machaut did the same with citations which derive from pre-existing sources in the text. For example, Machaut and the Machaut Master mined the *Roman de la rose*. This is most obvious in the highly finished opening image for the *Dit de la Rose*, where a cleric leans over a wattle-and-daub fence to pluck a large rose in the midst of a thorny bush (fol. 365v, A150). In a more subtle fashion, the artist visually cites *Rose* miniatures in the opening images of three of the dits, thereby highlighting Machaut's use of a dream vision construct. In the opening miniatures for the *Vergier*, *Behaingne*, and *Lyon*, the narrator discovers, enters, and enjoys a garden: the very heart of the *Rose*.[11] Meradith McMunn writes that "[t]he artist of MS A clearly uses the same imagery, figure placement, and postures that appear frequently in *Rose* manuscripts and it is very plausible that he is deliberately referring to *Rose* images."[12]

The Machaut Master created new imagery for Machaut's ever-growing body of poetry and music. The *Voir Dit*, for example, a late work, appears for the first time in MS A and the artist produced a rich body of innovative iconography. For example, he transformed an image of God creating land from a cloud-like mass in the frontispiece of an *Ovide moralisé* (Lyon, BM MS 742, fol. 1), into an erotic scene where Venus uses a perfumed cloud to envelop the narrator and his beloved who lie next to each other on a bed (fol. 255r, A130).[13]

Another artist, Hand 2, whose work only appears once, painted a man courting a woman in a large initial *L* on fol. 367r (A152), the first folio of a quire with the lays (L1, *Loyauté, que point ne delay*).[14] In keeping with the lyrics, a supplicating nobleman prepares to kneel, offering his folded hands in a sign of fealty and homage to his "liege."[15] He is dressed in a lovingly rendered depiction of period fashion. The woman coyly looks back at the nobleman, elegantly holding her right hand high in a gesture usually associated with conversation. At odds with the painting style used throughout MS A, this artist produced

---

[10] See, for example, the tale of Ceyx and Alcyone in the *Fonteinne* (fols. 157d–159v, A82–88) and the story of Susannah and the Elders in *Confort* (fols. 127v–129d, A54–60). For a discussion of Machaut's use of Ovid in the *Voir Dit*, see Blumenfeld-Kosinski, *Reading Myth*, pp. 130–70; and Mühlethaler, "Entre amour et politique." Drobinsky has worked extensively on the *Ovide moralisé* and its influence on illuminated Machaut manuscripts; see "Eros, Hypnos et Thanatos," and "Amants péris en mer,"(for the latter, plates VI–IX are *hors-texte*).

[11] Respectively: fol. 1r, A4; fol. 9c, A8; fol. 80v, A25.

[12] I am very grateful to Meradith McMunn who gave invaluable insight, via private communication, into the visual rapports between opening images.

[13] The convention for depicting a couple having intercourse shows them under the covers. Jacques Boogaart, private communication, points out that the artist is not following the text, in which Toute Belle is nude, wearing nothing "fors que les oeuvres de nature" [except what Nature had provided] (line 4022).

[14] On this lay, see Earp, *A Guide to Research*, pp. 338–39.

[15] This iconography is represented by a vassal or knight who kneels before a king or lord who, in turn, places his hands over the knight's. See Ladner, *Images and Ideas*, who discusses "commendation": "a sign of surrender connoting dependence, trust and fidelity" (pp. 220–21). For a detailed study of this iconography, see Carré, *Le baiser sur la bouche*, pp. 188–91.

an extremely fine miniature painted in the Parisian style. The artist uses a distinctive, thin, red-brown line to render their faces and hair. These portions are delicately modeled rather than heavily silhouetted.[16]

Hand 3, whose work only appears in the *Mass*, paints with a heavy line, which is reminiscent of a woodblock print. Despite the strokes of gray washes used for modeling, the images remain quite flat. This artist's most easily identifiable contribution comprises two historiated initials, both in the Agnus Dei of Machaut's *Mass* (fol. 449v).

The Artists of the Prise *Frontispiece*

The Machaut Master was fully capable of painting in a relatively finer style than that which predominates in the body of MS A. The best example is the dense composition on the opening page for the *Prise* (fol. 309, A 149). It is an ambitious, two column miniature, complete with bar extenders and marginalia.

Another artist painted a peacock in the right margin. His use of brilliantly colored green and blue washes and refined style demonstrates a command of the medium which appears nowhere else in MS A. The peacock may represent Juno, to whom the bird is sacred. The elderly man with shoulder-length white hair and a long beard in the historiated initial may be the work of another artist, as is evidenced by his treatment of the mouth as a single line making a "frown" with a red line transecting it in the middle. Furthermore, the colors of the background in the historiated initial and surrounding frame are not used elsewhere in MS A. The man in the initial cannot be Pierre de Lusignan, who wears a crown and wields a hatchet in the miniature. He is most likely Saturn, who plays an important role in the *Prise*, overseeing and directing the pantheon of Roman deities in the text (lines 169–180).[17] The lions on the lower bar extender and the butterfly above speckled with red, blue, and green, however, are the work of the Machaut Master. On the opening page of the *Prise*, the lion at left is a flip-side version of one on fol. 227, and the lion at right is a "finished" version of the sketch on the same folio. This treatment is a strong indicator that this quire was originally intended to stand on its own. Do the lions indicate a manuscript destined for royalty?

The Machaut Master took great care in painting this complex, crowded miniature. But who was responsible for the many roles necessary to create this manuscript? The sloppy application of the matte coral background may be a sign of hastiness. It is unique in MS A. Was it meant to be gilded? Perhaps, but a close observation reveals feathery, orange *rinceaux*. In sharp contrast to the amount of effort the Machaut Master expended to create the complex composition of the large miniature, the secondary decorative elements were finished hastily. The multi-colored sycamore leaves sprouting from the bar extenders do not relate in any manner to the sharply pointed leaves painted in *grisaille* on all other folios in the manuscript. This is a certain indication that the artist(s) responsible for this portion of the painting was pressed for time.

---

[16] See Earp, "Scribal Practice," p. 171n129, who discusses this initial in terms of *mise-en-page*, stating that it was drawn too large to allow for the entry of music, and therefore the original line of text had to be erased and moved lower to accommodate a small staff. This error demonstrates that the decoration was done *before* the entry of music in this manuscript.

[17] I thank Jacques Boogart, private communication, for his identification of the peacock and elderly man.

The Master of the Bible of Jean de Sy

The most refined work in MS A is by the well-known Jean de Sy Master, who painted on an appended bifolium at the head of the manuscript; perhaps his greatest and, surely, his most famous work of art (fols. E/A1 and D/A2).[18] He was active c. 1355–c.1380, although his most demanding works were in the late 1360s and throughout the 1370s.[19] He painted in at least fourteen major manuscripts during this period, and, based on the provenance of extant manuscripts, worked exclusively for the aristocracy.[20] The Jean de Sy Master's delicate creations and complex iconography are almost always fresh, unpredictable, and unique. His presence, in and of itself, and the superior quality of his work in MS A, are clearly signifiers of royal patronage.

The Prologue[21]

Near the end of a very long life and career, Machaut wrote a narrative poem entitled the *Prologue*.[22] It is now in two parts at the head of MS A; the first is a mistakenly inverted, appended bifolium on which there are two large miniatures painted by the Jean de Sy Master.[23] They accompany the first, lyric section of this poem. The second part is the work of the Machaut Master. The Jean de Sy Master's images create a visual counterpart to Machaut's new text., exposing the breadth and complexity of his musico-literary creations and operating as "portraits" of him.[24] For Charles V, these images would have preserved the face, accomplishments, and artistry of Machaut as a coveted possession of the *patrimoine* (and, no doubt, a cherished memory of his mother, Bonne de Luxembourg).

Dating MS A

Manuscript A was painted in the 1370s, ostensibly making it the last manuscript that Machaut himself may have supervised. Although Machaut's *Dit de la fleur de lis et de la marguerite* (*The Tale of the Lily and the Daisy*) and the *Prise* provide a *terminus post quem* of c. 1370, the assembly of separate fascicles may have been executed before, during, or after

---

[18] These images in the *Prologue* in MS A run "backward" because the folio was mistakenly inverted at one point in time, and it is still in that order. Hence, fols. E and D – A1 and A2 (in this order), are Earp's numbers. On the foliation, see Earp, *A Guide to Research*, pp. 145–46, 203–05.

[19] The Jean de Sy Master painted miniatures in another complete-works Machaut manuscript, MS Vg, where he headed a large and varied atelier. See Leo, "Art-historical Commentary," pp. 98–101.

[20] For a list of period manuscripts, including many painted by him, see Leo, "The Pucellian School," especially pp. 167–68.

[21] The *Prologue* will be discussed in detail in a subsequent volume.

[22] On the foliation and placement of the *Prologue*, see Earp, "Scribal Practice," p. 344; Earp, *A Guide to Research*, pp. 87–88; and Roccati, "Guillaume de Machaut."

[23] The title may not be his since its first and only appearance is in the later MS E; see Earp, *A Guide to Research*, p. 203.

[24] The use of the term "portrait" here will be discussed in following volumes with the *Prologue* and the *Voir Dit*.

this date (and Machaut's death in 1377).[25] Elements of fashion in the *Prologue* look forward to a new trend for men. Love's child, *Dous Penser* (Sweet Thought), is wearing a tightly fitted, very short doublet (*pourpoint*) padded as was the style over the chest. This figure's clothing has a subtle, surprising development. Normally the sleeve is fitted from shoulder to wrist with buttons to the elbow, as in the main body of MS A. But *Dous Penser*'s doublet is blousy from shoulder to elbow, at which point it is tight to the wrist. This looks forward to a new fashion trend — where sleeves are blousy up to the wrist (*bombards*) — for men that began in the second half of the 1380s.

Authorial Presence and Patronage

One of the most contested topics in Machaut studies is the possibility that the poet himself played a role in the creation of the manuscripts with his complete works, particularly manuscripts C and A. An inscription at the head of the index — *Vesci l'ordenance que G. De Machau wet qu'il ait en son livre* (This is the order that G. de Machaut wants to have in his book) — suggests authorial presence in the creation of MS A, whether or not it was finished according to Machaut's instructions while he was alive or after his death in 1377.[26] The complex image-text-music rapport in the earlier MS C (c. 1350–c. 1356), which has folios incorporating all three elements — as well as an exceptionally high quality of the illumination, flourishing, and script — all point toward Machaut's guidance. Did Machaut play any role in making MS A? I believe he was involved, but to what degree I remain uncertain. Was the footwork involved in creating an illuminated manuscript in Paris, so well documented by Richard Rouse and Mary Rouse, reduced to production within one atelier in Reims, and eventually fueled by a single person's mental negotiations, namely Machaut himself?[27] It would certainly not be a new practice. And what precludes assigning the "compilation" to a date after Machaut's death? There was surely an interaction with the Jean de Sy Master, ostensibly living and working in Paris, at a late date in MS A's production. So why make Machaut's death in 1377 a *terminus ante quem*?

Anne Walters Robertson[28] and Sylvia Huot are proponents of authorial presence in MS A, the latter writing that "[t]he codices of Machaut and Froissart were almost certainly organized by the authors themselves; Machaut may well also have designed, or at least influenced, programs of illumination for his works."[29] Using reception theory in part, Deborah McGrady, writes that "all lines of research point . . . to the vicinity of Reims where Machaut resided or . . . to an academic or cleric community."[30] For example, she writes that "the material quality of [MS A] points to the idea that [the codex] was produced for a

---

[25] *Lyon*, 1342; *Navarre*, 1349; *Alerion*, before c. 1350; *Confort*, 1357; *Fonteinne*, 1360–61; *Voir Dit*, 1363–65; *Marguerite*, 1364–69; *Lys*, 1369; *Prise*, after 1369.

[26] See Earp, *A Guide to Research*, p. 87, in his detailed description of MS A. On the "Index," most recently, see Leach, *Secretary, Poet, Musician*, pp. 86–87n3–4 and McGrady, *Controlling Readers*, pp. 88–105.

[27] Rouse and Rouse, *Manuscripts and Their Makers*, 1:261–84.

[28] Robertson, *Guillaume de Machaut and Reims*, p. 143.

[29] Huot, *From Song to Book*, p. 211 and especially p. 211n.

[30] McGrady, *Controlling Readers*, p. 83.

reader like Machaut."[31] But McGrady does not take into account the Jean de Sy Master's *Prologue* images, a certain stylistic signifier for royal ownership, thus precluding the possibility that MS A was ever intended for or kept in a cathedral library.

At present, I will have achieved my goal if this art-historical based study of MS A opens gateways for future scholars seeking out new interpretations of images, iconography, production, reception, patronage, and authorial presence. This in many ways defines the purpose and function of this project's massive undertaking whereby new translations and editions of texts and music will become available to all. For now, many of my insights and theories must remain hypothetical, speculative, sometimes provocative, and purposely open-ended. Above all, they are meant to foster interdisciplinary work which will incorporate new findings and broaden our horizons.

ILLUSTRATION COMMENTARIES

Le Jugement dou roy de Behaingne

The opening image for this poem includes the key elements describing the *locus amoenus* in the text: an enclosed garden, a stream, a tower, and a bird atop a tree [A8]. The narrator's identity, however, is blurred because he is dressed as a cleric and not a lover, as he describes himself in the text. The introduction to the crux of this poem begins on line 41. At this point the narrator first sees a knight approaching him on one side and a lady on the other, placing him in the area where they would converge. With his customary attention to detail, the artist has followed the text exactly in the second miniature [A9]. On the right, we see the knight, the lady, and her handmaid — even her small dog. At left, the artist has delicately painted three different types of trees. From an image-text perspective, the artist has captured the crucial moment when the narrator reveals himself (line 1215). The group, hands raised in astonishment, sees that the narrator is hiding amidst an area filled by leaves. The artist underscored the comedic element by showing only the narrator's head popping out from the vantage point. This also comments more deeply on the hierarchy of roles here, as the emphasis will be on the narrator's thoughts. His gendered body is obliterated by the forest, and his physical position is nearly as low as the dog's. In fact, he uses the dog as a means of meeting the group, returning it to the lady.

This is a clear commentary on the role that the narrator will play in the poem. He will be an arbitrator of love, but only as a pale reflection of the king's own role as magistrate. As the narrator defers judgment to the king, so too the king initially defers to the allegories Honor, Courtesy, Youth, Love, and Wealth. In the third miniature, the king is positioned frontally, a stiff figure seated on a throne [A10]. This symmetrical composition heightens the sense that the king is in perpetual stasis, a godlike figurehead, an eternally just persona, unlike the knight and the lady. This composition is unusual within this artist's repertoire in MS A, and to some degree in contemporary manuscript illumination. It is meaningful, however, in relation to the image of Love in the *Vergier* [A5] and God in the *Confort* [A53]. In the first, Love sits on a tree in a frontal pose, holding an arrow and a torch; ladies and men flank him. This forefronts his power. The second miniature depicts God in his majesty. He sits on an invisible throne surrounded by clouds. His direct gaze engages the viewer. He is invested with regal and spiritual iconographic elements. As God,

---

[31] McGrady, *Controlling Readers*, p. 82.

he has a cruciform nimbus and blesses (the viewer) with one hand. In the other, he holds an orb surmounted by a cross, a sign of his rule over heaven and earth. By creating compositional cross-references, the artist forefronts the king's authority.[32]

The final miniature shows the moment where the king makes his judgment [A11]. His gesture of tapping his left index finger on the palm of his right hand clarifies this reading. The lady and knight, both with their right hands on their hips, make two different gestures, perhaps the artist's way of portraying the outcome of the judgment in the knight's favor. The knight holds his hand up as if in conversation and the lady holds her hand over her breast, a touching means of conveying the wound in her heart.

Le Jugement dou roy de Navarre

There is only one image for the *Navarre*. It shows a meditative man looking out from his window with his hands crossed on the sill [A12]. Instead of taking an enjoyable walk in a lovely garden on a fine spring day, the narrator has sequestered himself indoors. This inventive manner of "creating a mood" to reflect the narrator's long-winded passages on the ills of the world attests to the artist's skill.

NOTES ON ILLUSTRATIONS

This system follows the format in Earp, *A Guide to Research*.

1. Earp #
2. (fol. #)
3. Insertion point / line number — the image is above the line in question.
4. Rubrics, unless otherwise noted, are above the image.

For example: A35 (fol. 2r) line 290: "The narrator writes a ballade."

To identify the placement of the miniature(s) on a single folio:
a: Column 1, recto
b: Column 2, recto
c: Column 3, verso
d: Column 4, verso

---

[32] Although the king is shown seated on a throne in the miniature, the text reads: "[The king] Was seated / In very great contentment on a silk rug" (lines 1472–73). It is on line 1493 that we read that the king was "enthroned."

ILLUSTRATIONS

N.B.: All miniatures are from manuscript A, BnF, fr. 1584, and reproduced with permission of the Bibliothèque nationale de France.

Le Jugement dou Roy de Behaingne [4]
1. A8 (fol. 9r) Line 1; *Ci aprés commence le Jugement dou Roy de Behaingne*. The Narrator, dressed as a cleric, stands in a lovely garden close to a castle with a stream; his hand to his heart as he watches a songbird atop a tree.
2. A9 (fol. 9d) Line 41; The narrator, hidden in bushes, is seen by the lady, with her handmaiden and dog, and the knight.
3. A10 (fol. 16v) Line 1185; The lady and fashionably-attired knight flank the King of Bohemia. The king is bearded and has long hair; he is wearing a crown and his garment is vaguely reminiscent of a toga. As with the depiction of God in Majesty (fol. 127b) in *Confort* and the enthroned Lady in *Le Dit de la Harpe* (*The Tale of the Harp*) (fol. 176v), he is depicted frontally, sitting on a throne with lion-head terminals.[33] The figures to each side gesture, denoting conversation, and the king raises his right hand as a priest would in blessing.
4. A11 (fol. 18v) Line 1509; The lady and knight stand at left with hands raised; the king, seated on a fabric-draped throne, taps his left finger in his right palm, as if meting out his decision.

Le Jugement dou Roy de Navarre [1]
5. A12 (fol. 22v) Line 1; *Ci aprés commence le Jugement dou Roy de Navarre contre le Jugement dou Roy de Behaingne*. Guillaume leans out the window of a castle.

---

[33] For a full description of *Le Dit de la Harpe* with extensive bibliography, see Earp, *A Guide to Research*, p. 223.

Figure 1. A8 (fol. 9r); *Ci aprés commence le Jugement dou Roy de Behaingne.* [Here begins the Judgment of the King of Bohemia.] The Narrator stands in a garden. (Photo: BnF)

🌿 LE JUGEMENT DOU ROY DE BEHAINGNE

fol. 9v	Au temps pascour que toute riens s'esgaie,
	Que la terre de mainte colour gaie
	Se cointoie, dont pointure sans plaie
	Sous la mamelle
5	Fait Bonne Amour a mainte dame bele,
	A maint amant et a mainte pucelle;
	Dont il ont puis mainte lie nouvelle
	Et maint esmay,
	A ce dous temps, contre le mois de may,
10	Par un matin cointement m'acesmay,
	Com cils qui tres parfaitement amay
	D'amour seüre.
	Et li jours fu attemprez par mesure,
	Biaus, clers, luisans, nés et purs, sans froidure.
15	La rousee par dessus la verdure
	Resplendissoit
	Si clerement que tout m'esbloïssoit
	Quant mes regars celle part guenchissoit,
	Pour le soleil qui dessus reluisoit.
20	Et cil oisel,
	Pour la douceur dou joli temps nouvel,
	Si liement et de si grant revel
	Chantoient tui que j'alay a l'appel
	De leur dous chant.
25	Si en choisi en l'air .i. voletant
	Qui dessus tous s'en aloit glatissant:
	"Ocy! Oci!" Et je le sievi tant
	Qu'en .i. destour,
	Sus .i. ruissel, pres d'une bele tour
30	Ou il avoit maint arbre et mainte flour

46

THE JUDGMENT OF THE KING OF BOHEMIA

At Eastertide, when every creature rejoices,
When the earth with many a gay color
Adorns herself, when Good Love leaves no wound but
       Pierces
5   The breasts of many pretty ladies,
Lovers, and young girls
(And this brings them many
       New joys and many cares),
At this sweet time, close to the month of May,
10   One morning I elegantly arrayed myself,
In the fashion of a man who loved most perfectly
       With a constant love.
And the day was just balmy enough,
Beautiful, clear, sunny, crisp and pure, without a chill.
15   The dew on the greenery
       Was shimmering
So brightly it completely blinded me
Whenever I looked upon it
Because of the sun shining down from above.
20   And the birds,
For the sake of the sweetness in that joyous new season,
Happily and with such grand celebration
Were all singing, so I moved to the call
       Of their sweet song.
25   Then I spied one among them in flight
Who soared above the others crying:
"Ocy! Ocy!" And I followed him until
       In a solitary byway
Above a stream, close by a beautiful tower,
30   Where there were many trees and flowers

Souëf flairant, de diverse coulour,
      S'ala seoir.
Lors me laissay tout belement cheoir
Et me coiti si bien, a mon povoir,
35   Sous les arbres, qu'il ne me pot veoir,
      Pour escouter
Le tres dous son de son joli chanter.
Si me plut tant en oïr deliter
Son dous chanter, que jamais raconter
40   Ne le porroie.

Figure 2. A9 (fol. 9d); The lady and the knight see the narrator. (Photo: BnF)

Mais tout einsi, com je me delitoie
En son tres dous chanter que j'escoutoie,
Je vi venir par une estroite voie,
      Pleinne d'erbette,
45   Une dame pensant, toute seulette
Fors d'un chiennet et d'une pucelette.
Mais bien sambloit sa maniere simplette
      Pleinne d'anoy.
Et d'autre part, un petit long de moy,
50   Uns chevaliers de moult tres noble arroy
Tout le chemin venoit encontre soy
      Sans compaingnie;
Si me pensay qu'amis yert et amie.
fol. 10r Lors me boutay par dedens la fueillie
55   Si embuschiez qu'il ne me virent mie.
      Mais quant amis,
En qui Nature assez de biens a mis,
Fu aprochiez de la dame de pris,
Com graçïeus, sages, et bien apris
60   La salua.
Et la dame que pensee argua,
Sans riens respondre a li, le trespassa.
Et cils tantost arriere rappassa,

Of different colors that smelled sweet,
    He perched.
Then I simply dropped to the ground
And hid myself as well as I could beneath the trees
35 So that he could not see me,
    In order to hear
The full sweet sound of his pleasant song.
It pleased me so to delight in hearing
His sweet singing that I could never
40   Describe it.

But as I was enjoying
His very sweet singing, on which I was intent,
I saw approach by a narrow path
    Covered with grass
45 A lady deep in thought and all alone,
Save for a little dog and a serving maid.
But her forthright demeanor showed clearly
    She was sorely distressed.
And on the other side, a short distance from me,
50 A knight of quite noble array
Came toward her right down the path
    With no companions;
So I thought they might be lover and beloved.
Then I pushed myself into the leaves
55 And was so hidden they didn't see me at all.
    Now when that lover,
To whom Nature had granted considerable gifts,
Approached that worthy lady,
He greeted her like a gentleman gracious,
60   Wise, and well mannered.
And so oppressed by thought was the lady
She passed him by with no response.
And at once the man retraced his steps,

         Et si la prist

65   Par le giron, et doucement li dist:
      "Tres douce dame, avez vous en despit
      Le mien salut?" Et quant elle le vit,
         Si respondi
      En souspirant que plus n'i atendi:

70   "Certes, sire, pas ne vous entendi
      Pour mon penser qui le me deffendi;
         Mais se j'ay fait
      Riens ou il ait villonnie ou meffait,
      Vuelliez le moy pardonner, s'il vous plait."

75   Li chevaliers, sans faire plus de plait,
         Dist doucement:
      "Dame, il n'affiert ci nul pardonnement,
      Car il n'i a meffait ne mautalent;
      Mais je vous pri que vostre pensement

80   Me vueilliez dire."
      Et la dame parfondement souspire
      Et dist: "Por Dieu, laissiez me en pais, biau sire,
      Car mestier n'ay que me faciés plus d'ire
         Ne de contraire

85   Que j'en reçoy." Et cils se prist a traire
      Plus pres de li, pour sa pensee attraire,
      Et ha dit: "Tres douce debonnaire,
         Triste vous voy.
      Mais je vos jur et promet par ma foy,

90   S'a moy volez descouvrir vostre anoy,
      Que je ferai tout le pooir de moy
         De l'adrecier."
      Et la dame l'en prist a mercier,
      Et dist: "Sire, nuls ne m'en puet aidier,

95   Ne nuls fors Diex ne porroit alegier
         La grief dolour
      Qui fait palir et teindre ma coulour,
      Qui tient mon cuer en tristesse et en plour,
      Et qui me met en si dure langour

100   Qu'a dire voir
      Nuls cuer qui soit n'en porroit plus avoir."
      "Dame, et quels mauls vos fait si fort doloir?
      Dites le moy; que je cuit recevoir
         Si tres grief peinne,

105   Si dolereuse, si dure, si greveinne,
      Si amere, que soiez bien certeinne,
      Il n'est dame, ne creature humeinne,
         Ne n'iert jamais,
      Qui tele peinne endurast onques mais."

110   "Certes, sire, je croy bien que tel fais

Took her
65   By the robe, and said softly:
"Sweet lady, do you scorn
My greeting?" And when she saw him,
        With a sigh
She answered so he waited no longer:
70   "To be sure, sir, I did not hear you at all
Because my thoughts prevented me;
        But if I've done
Something improper or wrong,
Please pardon me if you would."
75   The knight, making no further argument,
        Said softly:
"Lady, no pardon is needed,
For here there is no misdeed or ill will;
But I beg you please tell me
80   Your thoughts."
Then the lady sighed deeply
And said: "For God's sake, leave me in peace, fair sir,
Because I don't need you to increase the grief
        Or frustration
85   That they give me." With this, he began moving
Closer to her to draw out her thoughts,
And said: "Sweet and noble lady,
        I see you are sad.
But I swear to you and promise upon my faith
90   That if to me you reveal your trouble,
I'll do all in my power
        To put it right."
And the lady undertook to thank him for this,
Saying: "Sir, no one can help me,
95   And no one save God could alleviate
        The terrible grief
That mars and pales my complexion,
Binds my heart in sorrow and weeping,
Keeps me in such bitter misery
100   That, truth to tell,
There is no heart that could have more."
"Lady, what misfortune makes your pain so great?
Tell me, for I think I suffer
        A hurt so painful,
105   So miserable, so strong, so grievous,
So bitter that — of this you may be sure —
There's no woman, no human being,
        Nor was there ever one
Who endured such pain."
110   "Surely, sir, I firmly believe you

Ne portez pas a vo cuer que je fais.
                    Pour ce sarez
Ma pensee qu'a savoir desirez.
Mais tout avant, vos me prometterez
115   Que sans mentir la vostre me dirés."
                    "Tenez, ma dame.
Je vous promet par may foy et par m'ame
Que le penser qui m'esprent et enflame,
Et qui souvent mon cuer mort et entame
120   Vous jehirai
De chief en chief, ne ja n'en mentiray."
"Certes, sire, et je le vous diray."
"Or dites donc; je vous escouteray
                    Moult volentiers."

125   "Sire, il a bien .vij. ans ou .viij. entiers
Que mes cuers a esté sers et rentiers
A Bonne Amour, si qu'apris ses sentiers
                    Ay tres m'enfance.
Car des premiers que j'eus sa congnoissance,
130   Cuer, corps, povoir, vie, avoir, et puissance
Et quanqu'il fu de mi, mis par plaisance
                    En son servage.
Et elle me retint en son hommage
fol. 10v Et me donna de tres loial corage
135   A bel et bon, dous, graciëus, et sage,
                    Qui de valour,
De courtoisie et de parfaite honnour,
Et de plaisant maintient avoit la flour,
Et des tres bons estoit tout le millour:
140   Et s'ot en li
Gent corps faitis, cointe, apert, et joly,
Juene, gentil, de maniere garny,
Plein de tout ce qu'il faut a vray amy.
                    Et d'estre amez
145   Par dessus tous estoit dignes clamez,
Car il estoit vrais, loiaus, et secrez,
Et en trestous fais amoureus discrez;
                    Et je l'amoie
Si loiaument que tout mon cuer mettoie
150   En li amer, n'autre entente n'avoie;
Qu'en li estoit m'esperence, ma joie,
                    Et mon plaisir,
Mon cuer, m'amor, mon penser, mon desir.
De tous les biens pooit mes cuers joïr
155   Par li veoir seulement et oïr.
                    Tous mes confors

Bear not the same burden in your heart that I do.
     For this reason you shall learn,
These thoughts you wish to know.
Yet right away you'll promise

115   To tell me all your own without any lies."
     "Agreed, my lady.
Upon my faith and soul, I promise
That the thought that scorches and inflames me,
Often eating at my heart and rending it,

120   I'll reveal to you
Completely, and in nothing will I lie."
"Agreed, sir, and now I'll tell you."
"Speak, then, and I'll listen
     Most willingly."

125   "Sir, altogether now it's seven years or eight
That my heart's been serf and vassal
To Good Love, whose ways I've come to know
     Since childhood.
For when I encountered Love the first time,

130   I gladly put heart, body, strength, life,
My goods and power, what I had,
     At her disposal.
And as her vassal she retained me
And with a very loyal heart gave me

135   To a man handsome and good, gentle, wise, and gracious,
     Who was
The very flower of courtesy,
Perfect honor, and pleasant demeanor;
Of the very good indeed he was the best.

140   And the man had
A noble body, elegant too, gracious, well-formed and pleasing;
Young, genteel, graced with charm he was,
Full of all that a true lover requires.
     And he was acclaimed

145   Worthy of being loved above all others,
For he was true, loyal, and circumspect,
Discreet in what pertained to loving.
     And I loved him
So loyally I devoted all my heart

150   To loving him (no other thought was mine);
So in him was my hope, joy,
     And pleasure,
My heart, love, thoughts, and desire.
In every kind of goodness my heart could rejoice

155   Simply by seeing and hearing him.
     All my comfort

Estoit en li; c'estoit tous mes depors,
Tous mes solas, mes deduis, mes tresors.
C'estoit mes murs, mes chastiaus, mes ressors.
160   Et il m'amoit;
Par dessus tout me servoit et cremoit;
Son cuer, s'amour, sa dame me clamoit.
Tous estoit miens; mes cuers bien le savoit;
            Ne riens desplaire
165   Ne li peüst qui a moy dehust plaire.
De nos .ij. cuers estoit si juste paire
Qu'onques ne fu l'un a l'autre contraire;
            Einsois estoient
Tuit d'un acort; une pensee avoient.
170   De volenté, de desir se sambloient;
Un bien, un mal, une joie sentoient
            Conjointement,
N'onques ne fu entre eaus .ij. autrement;
Mais c'a esté toudis si loyaument
175   Qu'il n'ot onques un villain pensement
            En nos amours.
Lasse, dolente! Or est bien a rebours.
Car mes douceurs sont dolereus labours,
Et mes joies sont ameres dolours,
180   Et mi penser,
En qui mes cuers se soloit deliter
Et doucement de tous maus conforter,
Sont et seront dolent, triste, et amer.
            En obscurté
185   Seront mi jour, plein de maleürté,
Et mi espoir sans nulle seürté,
Et ma douceur sera dure durté
            Car sans faillir
Teindre, trambler, muer, et tressaillir,
190   Pleindre, plourer, souspirer, et gemir,
Et en paour de desespoir fremir
            Me couvendra;
N'a mon las cuer jamais bien ne vendra,
N'a nul confort n'a joie n'atendra,
195   Jusques atant que la mort me prendra,
            Qui a grant tort
Par devers moy, quant elle ne s'amort
A moy mordre de son dolereus mort,
Quant elle m'a dou tout tollu et mort
200   Mon dous amy
Que j'amoie de fin cuer et il my.
Mais aprés li, lasse! Dolente! Eimy!
Ne quier jamais vivre jour ne demi

Lay in him; he was all that pleased me,
All my solace, delight, and treasure.
He was my wall, my castle, and my refuge.
160   And he loved me;
Above all else he served and respected me.
He called me his heart, his love, his lady;
He was mine completely; my heart knew this well.
          Nor could anything
165 Displease him that should please me.
So true a pair were our two hearts
That one never opposed the other;
          Rather they were
Always in accord; one thought they shared.
170 They were the same in will and desire;
A single good, one ill, one joy they felt
          Together,
And it was never otherwise for these two;
Instead our love was so faithful
175 It never gave rise to an immoral thought
          Of any kind.
Alas! What sorrow! Now the opposite is true.
For my sweetness now is painful suffering.
My joys are bitter hurt,
180   And my thoughts,
In which my heart used to delight
And find sweet solace for every hurt,
Are, and will remain, painful, bitter, sad.
          My days
185 Will be dark and filled with misfortune,
My hope will lack all certainty,
And my pleasure will become enduring sorrow,
          For without fail
I will pale and tremble, startle with a change of mood,
190 Moan, cry out, sigh, and wail,
And in fear of despair
          Even shudder;
Nor will my sad heart experience any good;
No comfort, no joy will ever touch it
195 Until death seizes me,
          Death, who greatly
Wronged me by not bringing herself
To bite me with her painful bite
When of everything she stripped me and killed
200   My lover sweet,
Whom I loved with a pure heart, as he did me.
But alas — sorrow — what pain! I do not wish
To live on after him even a day or half of one

                        En si grief dueil;
205   Eins vueil morir dou mal dont je me dueil."
               Et je, qui fui boutez dedens le brueil,
               Vi qu'a ce mot la dame au dous acueil
                        Cheï com morte.
               Mais cils qui fu de noble et gentil sorte
210   Souventes fois li deprie et enorte
               Moult doucement qu'elle se reconforte,
                        Mais riens ne vaut;
               Car la dame que grief doleur assaut
fol. 11r   Pour son ami sent .i. si dur assaut
215   Qu'en li vigour et alainne deffaut.
                        Et quant il voit
               Que la dame pas ne l'entent në oït,
               Tant fu dolens qu'estre plus ne pooit.
               Mais nonpourquant tant fait que bien parçoit
220   Qu'elle est pasmee.
               Lors en sa main cueilli de la rousee
               Sus l'erbe vert; si l'en a arrousee
               En tous les liex de sa face esplouree
                        Si doucement
225   Que la dame qui avoit longuement
               Perdu vigour, scens, et entendement
               Ouvri les yeus et prist parfondement
                        A souspirer,
               En regretant celui qui desirer
230   Li fait la mort par loiaument amer.
               Mais cils qui ot le cuer franc sans amer
                        Dist: "Dame chiere,
               Pour Dieu merci, reprenez vo maniere;
               Vous vous tuez de faire tele chiere,
235   Car je voy bien que moult comparez chiere
                        L'amour de li.
               Si n'aies pas le cuer einsi failly,
               Car ce n'est pas preus, ne honneur aussi."
               "Vous dites voir, sire: mais trop mar vi
240   L'eure et le jour
               Qu'onques amay de si parfaite amour,
               Car je n'en puis eschaper par nul tour:
               Eins y congnois ma mort sans nul retour."
                        "Dame, or oiez
245   Ce que diray, et a mal ne l'aiez.
               N'est merveille se vous vous esmaiez,
               Car bien est drois que dolente soiés.
                        Mais vraiement
               On trouveroit plus tost aligement
250   En vostre mal qu'en mien." "Sire, et comment?

In such terrible grief;
205   I'd rather die from the pain that grieves me."
And I, who lay hidden within the brush,
Saw that at this word the lady with the gracious manner
Fell down as if dead.
Now he who was a type gentle and kind
210   Many times begged and exhorted her
Quite tenderly to take comfort,
But to no avail;
For assaulted by a grievous pain, the lady
Felt such a severe attack for her lover's sake,
215   Both breath and strength did fail her.
And when he saw
How the lady neither heard nor attended to him,
He was as pained as he could be.
Nonetheless the man realized
220   She had fainted.
In his hand he then gathered up some dew
From the green grass and sprinkled it over
Her tear-stained face
So gently
225   That the lady who for so long
Had lost strength, reason, and understanding
Opened her eyes and began to sigh
Deeply,
Bemoaning the man who made her desire
230   Death because of his faithful love for her.
But the man, whose noble heart lacked bitterness,
Said: "Dear lady,
For the mercy of God, get hold of yourself.
Carrying on like this will be your death
235   Since I see well that you pay most dearly
For loving him.
Yet let your heart not fail so.
It is neither worthy nor honorable."
"You tell the truth, sir, but it was quite bad luck I saw
240   The hour and day
I ever loved with such a perfect love
Because in no way can I escape it.
Instead, I see a death with no respite."
"Lady, now hear
245   What I will say, and please don't take it ill.
No wonder you are distraught
Since you are saddened.
Yet truly
A person could much sooner find relief
250   For your troubles than for mine." "Sir, how so?

Dites le moy, et de vo sairement
     Vous aquitez."
"Moult voulentiers, mais que vous m'escoutez,
Et que vo cuer de tristece gettés,
255   Par quoy toute vostre entente metez
     A moy oïr."
"Certes, sire, po me puis resjoïr.
Mais j'en feray mon pooir, sans mentir."
"Dont vous dirai quels maus j'ay a sentir,
260   Sans plus attendre.
Dame, tres dont que je me sos entendre
Et que mes cuers pot sentir et comprendre
Que c'est amer, je ne finay de tendre
     A estre amez;
265   Si que lonc temps, pour estre amis clamez
Eins que mes cuers fust assis ne donnez
N'a dame nulle ottroiez n'assenez,
     A Bonne Amour
Par maintes fois fis devote clamour
270   Qu'elle mon cuer asseïst a l'onnour
De celle en qui il feroit son sejour,
     Et que ce fust
Si que loange et gloire en receüst
Et que, se ja mes cuers faire peüst
275   Chose de quoy souvenir li deüst
     Ou desservir
Nul guerredon de dame par servir,
Qu'en aucun temps li deingnast souvenir
De moy qui vueil estre siens, sans partir,
280   Toute ma vie.
Tant qu'il avint qu'en une compaingnie
Ou il avoit meinte dame jolie,
Juene, gentil, joieuse, et envoisie,
     Vins par Fortune,
285   Qui de mentir a tous est trop commune,
Si en choisi entre les autres l'une
Qui, tout aussi com li solaus la lune
     Veint de clarté,
Avoit elle les autres seurmonté
290   De pris, d'onneur, de grace, et de biauté,
Et tant estoit humble et simple, a mon gré,
     Car, a voir dire,
On ne porroit en tout le monde eslire
fol. 11v Sa pareille, ne tous li mons souffire
295   Ne porroit pas por sa biauté descrire
     Parfaitement.

        Tell me, and you'll fulfill
                Your agreement."
        "Quite willingly, but listen to me
        And abandon the sadness in your heart
255   So you can give all your attention
                To hearing me."
        "Surely, sir, I can scarcely cheer up.
        Still, I'll do my best, and that's no lie."
        "Then I'll reveal to you what pains are mine
260   With no more delay.
        Lady, from that time I knew myself
        And my heart could feel and understand
        What loving is, I've never ceased striving
             To be loved;
265   So for a long time, to have the name of lover,
        Before my heart was securely placed or given,
        Or granted, or even inclined to one lady,
             I many times
        Devoutly requested that Good Love
270   Place my heart to the honor
        Of a woman in whom it would find a home,
             And that this would be
        So she would receive glory and praise thereby;
        And that if my heart could ever do
275   Anything to be worthy of attention
             Or earn
        Some reward from a lady through serving her,
        Love might sometime deign to remember
        Me, who would be her vassal, never to depart
280   For all my life.
        Finally it happened that among a company
        Including many pretty ladies
        Who were young, noble, happy, and amusing,
             I chanced by Fortune,
285   Whose custom is to lie to all,
        And from the others I picked out one
        Who, just as the sun surpasses the moon
             In brightness,
        Conquered all the others
290   In esteem, honor, grace, and beauty;
        And she was so modest and unpretentious, to my taste,
            That, truth to tell,
        No one could in the entire world find
        Her equal, nor could the whole world itself
295   Suffice to describe her beauty
             Perfectly.

Car je la vi dancier si cointement
Et puis chanter si tres joliement,
Rire et jouer si gracïeusement
300   Qu'onques encor
Ne fu veüs plus gracïeus tresor.
Car si cheveus ressambloient fil d'or
Et n'estoient ne trop blont ne trop sor.
          Son front estoit
305   Blanc et poly, ne fronce n'i avoit,
Sans vice nul compassé si a droit
Que trop large n'estoit, ne trop estroit;
         Et si sorcil,
Qui estoient de taille tres gentil,
310   Dessus le blanc sambloient .i. noir fil,
Dont il fussent prisié entre cent mil.
        Mais si .ij. oueil,
Qui de mon cuer vorrent passer le sueil
Par leur rigour et par leur bel acueil,
315   Pour moy donner le mal dont je me dueil,
         Furent riant,
Nom pas moult vair, por estre plus pongnant
Et plus agu, dous, humble, et attraiant,
Tous pleins de las pour loier .i. amant
320   En amour pure;
Et s'estoient clungnetant par mesure,
Fendus a point, sans trop grant ouverture,
Tout acquerant par leur douce pointure;
         N'a l'entrouvrir
325   Ne se peüst nuls homs qui soit couvrir
Qu'en mi le cuer ne l'alassent ferir
S'il leur pleüst, et pour euls retenir.
        Mais leurs regars,
Merci donnant par samblant, aus musars
330   N'estoit mie folettement espars;
Car quant lancier voloit .i. de ses dars,
         Si sagement
Le savoit faire et si soutivement
Que nuls savoir nel peüst bonnement,
335   Fors cils seur qui il cheoit proprement.
         Net, odorant,
Lonc et traitif, de taille bien seant
Avoit le nés au viaire afferant;
Car il n'estoit trop petit, ne trop grant.
340   Mais sa bouchette,
Petite a droit, vermillette, grossette,
Toudis riant, savoreuse, doucette,
Me fait languir, quant mes cuers la regrette.

For I saw her dance so debonairly
And then sing so very beautifully,
Laugh and play so graciously
300   That never yet
Was seen a treasure more elegant,
For her hair resembled golden threads,
And these neither too light nor dark.
    Her forehead was
305 White and smooth, no wrinkle there,
Without a flaw, of such correct proportion
It was neither too broad nor narrow.
    And her brows
Had a very noble shape
310 Beneath that whiteness and were like black thread,
And to be prized among a hundred thousand.
    But her two eyes,
Intent on passing the threshold of my heart
By their strength and fair welcome
315 To give me the pain that grieves me so,
    Were smiling,
Not really very gray, to be more piercing,
More striking, sweet, humble, and alluring,
All full of traps to snare a lover
320   In pure affection.
And they were modestly lowered,
Just big enough, not opened too wide,
Conquering all by their sweet piercing;
    Nor as they opened
325 Could any man prevent
Their going to strike his heart a blow,
If it pleased them, and claim him for their own.
    But their glance,
Seeming to grant mercy, to dawdlers
330 Was not at all unwisely parceled out,
For wishing to throw a dart,
    So craftily
Could it do so — and so subtly —
No one could ever truly know
335 Save him upon whom it properly fell.
    Flawless, dainty,
Long, and straight, of the proper shape
Was her nose, suited to her face,
For it was neither too big nor small.
340   But her little mouth,
Just small enough, rose in hue, somewhat rounded,
Always smiling, delicious, and sweet
Makes me languish whenever my heart sadly recalls her.

                    Quar qui l'oïst
345   Parler a point, et rire la veïst,
       Et les douceurs par saveur recueillist,
       Il la prisast seur toutes et deïst;
                    Que .ij. fossettes
       En sousriant faisoient ses joëttes,
350   Qui estoient blanches et vermillettes,
       Pour embelir, et un petit grassettes.
                    Et encor plus:
       Les dens avoit blans, sarrez, et menus,
       Et ses mentons estoit un po fendus,
355   Votis dessous et rondes par dessus.
                    Mais a merveille
       Fu sa coulour, des autres nompareille,
       Car elle fu vive, fresche, et vermeille,
       Plus que la rose en may, eins qu'on la cueille;
360   Et, a briés mos,
       Blanche com noif, polie, de biau gros
       Fu sa gorge, n'i ot fronce ne os;
       Et s'ot biau col dont je la pris et los.
                    Aussi est drois
365   Que je parle de ses bras lons et drois,
       Qui estoient bien fais en tous endrois;
       Car elle avoit blanches mains et lons dois.
                    A mon devis
       Avoit le sein blanc, dur, et haut assis,
370   Pongnant, rondet, et si estoit petis,
       Selonc le corps, gracïeus, et faitis.
                    Sans nul mestret
fol. 12r Avoit le corps par mesure pourtret,
       Gent, joint, joly, juene, gentil, grasset,
375   Lonc, droit, faitis, cointe, apert, et graillet.
                    Tres bien tailliez
       Hanches, cuisses, jambes ot, et les piez,
       Votis, grossez, bien et bel enjointiez,
       Par maistrise mignotement chauciez.
380   Dou remenant
       Que pas ne vi, dame, vous di je tant
       Que d' nature tout estoit respondant,
       Bien fassonné et de taille excellent.
                    Et ce seurplus,
385   Dont je ne vueil maintenant dire plus,
       Devoit estre sans comparer tenus
       A plus tres dous et a plus biaus que nuls.
                    Delié cuirien
       Blanc et souëf avoit, sus toute rien

> For whoever heard it
345 Speak so well and saw it laugh,
Received with pleasure its sweetness,
Would value it above all others and say as much;
> For her smile brought
Two dimples to her cheeks,
350 So white and colored like a rose,
Making them prettier and rounder.
> And there's even more:
Her teeth were white, small, and even,
Her chin a little cleft,
355 Arched below and rounded all above.
> Wondrously soft and clear,
Was her complexion, surpassing all others,
For it was vibrant, fresh, and pink,
More than any May rose before it's picked;
360 And, in a few words,
White as snow, smooth, pleasantly plump
Was her throat, not wrinkled or bony;
Her neck was beautiful, for which I prize and praise her.
> It's also fitting
365 I speak of her arms long and straight,
Which were in every way well fashioned;
For her hands were white, her fingers long.
> Just to my taste
Were her breasts — white, firm, and high-seated,
370 Pointed, round, and small enough,
Suiting her body, gracious and well shaped.
> Without a flaw
In proportion was her body,
Noble, well-shaped, lovely, youthful, genteel, amply fleshed,
375 Long, straight, pleasing, resilient, agreeable, and svelte.
> Very well shaped
Were the hips, thighs, and legs — the feet
Arched, plump, and well formed,
Cunningly shod with exquisite shoes.
380 Of the rest,
Which I did not see, lady, I'll tell you this:
All answered the requirements of Nature.
It was well fashioned and elegant in form.
> And this remainder,
385 Of which right now I'll say no more,
Must be considered beyond compare,
Sweeter and more beautiful than any other.
> Her delicate skin
Was white and soft; more than other women's

390   Resplendissant, si qu'on si mirast bien;
           Vice, tache n'i avoit fors que bien.
                  Douce et serree
           Avoit la char, tendrette de rousee,
           Mais de maniere humble et asseuree
395   Et de tres biau maintien estoit paree.
                  Et vraiement,
           Tant fu bele, que je croy fermement,
           Se Nature, qui tout fait soutilment,
           En voloit faire une aussi proprement,
400   Qu'elle y faurroit,
           Et que jamais assener n'i saroit,
           Se l'exemple de ceste ci n'avoit,
           Qui de biauté toutes autres passoit.
                  Et se vous di
405   Qu'onques encor en ma vie ne vi
           Corps de dame si tres bien assevi.
           Mais elle avoit .xiiij. ans et demi
                  Ou environ.
           Si que, dame, quant je vi sa fasson,
410   Qui tant estoit bele sans meffaçon,
           Dedens mon cuer la douce impression
                  De sa figure
           Fu telement empreinte qu'elle y dure,
           Ne onques puis n'en parti, dont j'endure
415   Mainte doleur et meinte durté dure.
                  Et sans doubtance,
           Eins que partis fusse de sa presence,
           Dedens mon cuer se ficha si Plaisence,
           En remirant sa douce contenance,
420   Que sachiez bien,
           Se j'eüsse l'avoir Othevien,
           Et sceüsse le scens de Galien,
           Et avec ce tuit li bien fussent mien,
                  Je tout heüsse
425   Guerpi par si, que veoir la peüsse
           A mon voloir, ou que faire sceüsse
           Chose a son vueil, dont plaire li deüsse.
                  Mais Fine Amour,
           Qui vit que pris estoie par le tour
430   De Plaisence, qui m'ot mis en sa tour,
           En remirant son gracieus atour,
                  Sans menacier
           .I. dous regart riant me fist lancier
           Parmi le cuer, et moy si enlacier,
435   Qu'il me sousmist en son tres dous dangier,
                  Sans repentir.

390 Resplendent — and one marveled;
There was no flaw or fault, only goodness.
              Sweet and firm
Was her flesh, tender with moisture,
But she was endowed with a manner humble

395 And assured — and she was beautifully groomed.
              And truly
She was so beautiful, I strongly believe,
That if Nature, who makes all things craftily,
Intended to make another woman just like her,

400   She would fail;
And that she'd never know how to do so
Had she not for a model the one
Who surpasses all others in loveliness.
              And so I tell you

405 I have never seen in all my life
A woman's body of such perfect shape.
And she was aged fourteen and a half,
              Or thereabouts.
So, lady, when I beheld her appearance,

410 Which was so beautiful, without any flaw,
Within my heart the sweet impression
              Of her face
Was so imprinted it still endures,
Nor ever since has it departed, so I suffer

415 Many pains and enduring miseries.
              And beyond all doubt,
Before I left her presence,
Pleasure so fixed itself within my heart
From marveling at her sweet face

420   You may be sure
If I possessed Octavian's riches
And knew all Galen's science,
If all goods were mine,
              I would have thrown over

425 Everything in order to see her
As I wished, or to accomplish something
She might have liked that would please her.
              But Noble Love,
Who saw me captured by the snare

430 Of Pleasure, who'd locked me in her tower
Because I'd marveled at the lady's gracious presence,
              Without threatening
Made a sweet and smiling look go
Straight through my heart to trap me

435 So I had to submit to her very sweet dominion
              Without repenting.

Si me plut tant cils dangiers a sentir,
Quant cils resgars se deingnoit assentir
A descendre sus moy que, sans mentir,
440   Je ne savoie
Qu'il m'avenoit, ne quele part j'estoie,
Car scens, vigour, et maniere perdoie;
Si durement par ses yex me sentoie
   Enamourez.
445 Adont desirs d'estre de li amez
En mon cuer fu si tres fort enflamez
Que puis m'en suis cent fois chetis clamez
   En souspirant;
Car tel doleur sentoie en desirant
450 Que ma vigour en aloit empirant
Et meint penser avoie, en remirant
   Son dous viaire;
fol. 12v Car volentiers li alasse retraire
Comment de cuer l'amoie, sans retraire.
455 Mais la paour d'escondire ce faire
   Me deffendoit;
Et d'autre part Bel Acueil m'apelloit;
Son Dous Regart riant m'asseüroit,
Et Dous Espoirs doucement ce disoit
460   En loiauté,
Et m'affermoit qu'onques si grant biauté
Ne pot estre, qu'il n'i heüst pité.
Si m'ont cil troi tant dit et enorté
   Que toutevoie
465 Je m'acorday que m'amour li diroie.
Helas! Einsi tous seuls me debatoie.
Mais quant mes maus retraire li cuidoie,
   Si paoureus,
Si veins, si mas, si las, si engoisseus,
470 Si desconfis, si tramblans, si honteus
Estoit mes cuers, et dou mal amoureus
   Si fort espris,
Qu'en li n'avoit scens, maniere, n'avis,
Einsois estoit com transis et ravis,
475 Quant bien veoir povoie vis a vis
   Sa biauté pure.
Lors estoit mors d'amoureuse morsure
Mes cuers et poins de joieuse pointure
Et repeüs de douce norreture
480   Par Dous Penser,
Qui ma dolour faisoit toute cesser
Et garison me faisoit esperer.
Einsi souvent avoie pour amer

So pleased was I to feel this domination
When her look deigned
To fall upon me that (I do not lie)
440   I didn't know
What was happening to me or where I was
Since senses, strength, and bearing I had lost,
So forcefully through her eyes was I
          Brought to love.
445   And thus the desire to be loved by her
Was so hotly inflamed within my heart,
I've since called myself 'poor captive' a hundred times
          While sighing;
For such misery did I feel in my desiring
450   My strength began to fail me,
And many thoughts I had while marveling at
          Her sweet countenance.
Now willingly I'd have gone to tell her
How with my heart I loved her with no hesitation.
455   Yet the fear of being refused prevented me
          From doing so;
Still Fair Welcome beckoned me;
His Sweet Look, smiling, reassured me,
And Sweet Hope sweetly told me this
460   In faith
And affirmed that so great a beauty
Could never exist without pity.
So these three spoke and encouraged me so much
          I agreed
465   After all to tell her of my affection.
Alas! In this fashion I declaimed all alone to myself.
But when I thought to rehearse my pains to her,
          So fearful,
Weak, beaten down, so weary and full of anguish,
470   So troubled, trembling, and shamed
Was my heart, and with lovesickness
          So grievously infected,
It lost all reason, composure, and wit.
In contrast, my heart was transformed and overwhelmed
475   When clearly, face to face, I could look upon
          Her pure beauty.
Then my heart was stung
By an amorous sting, pierced with a joyful point,
And nourished with sweet nourishment
480   By Sweet Thought,
Who relieved all my pain
And gave me hope for cure.
Thus often for Love's sake I experienced

     Joie et tourment.
485 Si demouray en ce point longuement,
   Une heure lie et l'autre heure dolent,
   Qu'onques n'osay requerre aligement
     De ma dolour.
   Mais nompourquant grant destresse d'amour,
490 Ardant desir, la crueuse langour,
   Ou j'avoie demouré par maint jour,
     Son Bel Acueil,
   Esperence de terminer mon dueil,
   Sa grant biauté, si dous riant vair oueil,
495 Et ce qu'en li n'avoit goute d'orgueil,
     Le hardement
   De requerre merci couardement
   Me donnerent; si li dis humblement,
   Moult tresmuez et paoureusement:
500   'Ma chiere dame,
   Vostre biauté mon cuer art et enflame,
   Si que seur tout vous aim, sans penser blame,
   De cuer, de corps, de vray desir, et d'ame.
     Si vous depri,
505 Douce dame, qu'aies de moy merci;
   Car vraiement je morrai d'amer ci
   Se de vo cuer, qui a le mien nercy,
     N'ay aligence.'

   Et quant einsi li os dit ma grevance,
510 Un pou muer vi sa douce samblance,
   Ce me fu vis, dont je fui en doubtance
     D'estre escondis.
   Mais ses regars m'asseüroit toudis,
   Et sa douceur et son gracïeus ris,
515 Si que par euls encor fu enhardis
     De dire: 'Helas!
   Gentil dame, pour Dieu, n'ociez pas
   Vostre loial amy, qui en vos las
   Est si laciez qu'il en pert tout solas
520   Et toute joie.'
   Lors se treï vers moy la simple et coie,
   Pour qui Amours me destreint et maistroie,
   Et dist: 'Amis, certes, riens ne vorroie
     Faire a nelui,
525 Dont il heüst grevence ne annuy;
   Ne l'en ne doit faire chose a autrui
   Qu'on ne vosist que l'en feïst a lui.
     Et, biaus amis,
   Il n'est nuls biens qui ne soit remeris,

          Joy and torture.
485   And I remained a long time in this state,
       One hour happy, sorrowful the next,
       For I never dared seek relief
          For my pain.
       Nonetheless this great distress from love,
490   This burning desire, this cruel languor
       In which I remained for many days,
          Her Fair Welcome,
       The hope of ending my pain,
       Her great beauty, her sweet, smiling gray eyes,
495   And that no whit of pride was in her —
          All this gave me
       The strength to beg for mercy
       Like a coward. And so I said humbly to her,
       Flushed and fearful:
500   'My lady dear,
       Your beauty so burns, inflames my heart,
       I love you above all else without impure thoughts,
       With my heart, my body, with true desire and soul.
          So I beg you,
505   Sweet lady, have mercy on me;
       For truly, I will die of love
       If from the heart that has turned mine black
          I find no relief.'

       And when in this fashion I dared tell her my grief,
510   I watched her sweet expression slightly change,
       As I thought, so I feared
          Being rejected.
       Yet all the time her look assured me,
       As well as her sweetness and gracious smile,
515   So by these I was emboldened enough
          To cry 'Alas!
       Gentle lady, for God's sake, don't kill
       Your faithful lover, who in your snares
       Is trapped so tight he forfeits all joy
520   And comfort.'
       Then she drew toward me, quiet and demure,
       The woman on whose account Love tortures and abuses me,
       And said: 'Friend, surely I would never want
          To do to anyone
525   What might pain or grieve him;
       And no one should do to others
       What he would not have done to him.
          And, sweet friend,
       No good deed goes unrewarded,

530   N'il n'est aussi maus qui ne soit punis.
         Si que, s'Amours vos a d'amer espris,
              Son guerredon
         Vous en rendra en temps et en saison,
         Se vous l'amez sans penser traïson.
fol. 13r   Et s'elle vous trouvoit autre que bon,
536   Ne doubtés mie
         Qu'elle ne fust vo mortel anemie,
         Ne que jamais garison ne aïe
         Vous fust par li donnee, n'ottroïe
540   De vos dolours.
         Si que, biau sire, alez devers Amours,
         Si li faites vos plains et vos clamours;
         Car en li gist vos mors et vos secours,
              Nom pas en moy.
545   Et pas ne sui cause de vostre anoy,
         Ce m'est avis, si que souffrir m'en doy.
         Plus ne vous say que dire, en bonne foy.
              Adieu vous di.'

         Adont de moy la bele se parti
550   Qui de si grant doleur me reparti
         Que par un po que mes cuers ne parti
              De son depart.
         Mais la douceur de son plaisant regart
         Par son dous art fist que j'en os regart
555   Que au departir de moy, se Diex me gart,
              Si doucement
         Me regarda qu'il m'iert vis proprement
         Que ses regars me disoit vraiement:
         'Amis, je t'aim tres amoureusement.'
560   Si que je fu
         Tous confortez par la noble vertu
         De ce regart qui puis m'a tant valu
         Qu'il m'a toudis norri et soustenu
              En bon espoir.
565   Et s'il ne fust, certeinnement j'espoir
         Que je fusse cheüs en desespoir,
         Mais riens qui soit ne me feïst doloir
              Quant ses regars
         Estoit seur moy en sousriant espars,
570   Si que, ma dame, einsi de toutes pars
         Me confortoit et aidoit ses regars
              De ma dolour.

         La demouray tous seuls en grant frëour,
         Si qu'en pensant commensai son atour,

530   No evil one unpunished.
        Thus if Love has urged you to love,
                She will reward you
        In her time and season
        If you love her with no thoughts of trickery.
535   And if she found you other than good,
                Don't doubt at all
        She would be your mortal enemy
        And that no help or cure
        Would ever be granted you by her, or given
540   For your pains.
        Therefore, fair sir, present yourself to Love
        And to her rehearse your moans and cries,
        For your rescue and your death lie in her,
            But not in me;
545   I am not the cause of your discomfort
        (Or so it seems to me) and should not suffer for it.
        In good faith I know not what else to tell you.
            I say goodbye.'

        At this that beauty took her leave from me,
550   She who had portioned out to me such pain
        My heart nearly broke in two
            At her leaving.
        But the sweetness of her pleasant look
        By its agreeable artfulness made me dare look upon her,
555   For as she left (may God protect me!)
            So sweetly
        Did she look my way it truly seemed
        Her expression actually said:
        'Lover, I love you with great affection.'
560   Therefore I was
        All comforted by the noble power
        Of the look that since has proved so precious
        It has always nourished and sustained me
            In good hope.
565   And had it not been so, I certainly expect
        I would have fallen into despair,
        But nothing on earth could pain me
            When her glance
        In a smile had so settled on me
570   That, my lady, in every way
        Her look consoled me, aided me
            In my distress.

        There in great turmoil I remained alone,
        And in my mind I began to marvel at

575 Sa grant douçour, sa coulour, sa valour
               A remirer,
     Son biau maintieng, son venir, son aler,
     Son gentil corps, son graċïeus parler,
     Son noble port, son plaisant regarder,
580   Et son viaire,
     Qui tant estoit dous, humble, et debonnaire
     Que de toute biauté fu l'exemplaire.
     Et quant j'eus tout remiré son affaire,
               Certes, j'avoie
585 Moult grant deduit et moult parfaite joie,
     Et pour tres boneüreus me tenoie,
     Pour ce, sans plus, que loiaument l'amoie,
               Si que depuis
     A li servir sui si tournez et duis,
590 Qu'en li servir s'est mis tous mes deduis,
     N'autre labour ailleurs faire ne puis.
               Si la servi,
     Amay, celay, doubtai, et oubeï
     Moult longuement, que riens ne me meri.
595 Mais en la fin tant l'amay et chieri
               Qu'elle vit bien
     Que je tendoie a s'onneur et son bien,
     Et que mes cuers l'amoit sus toute rien;
     Si que tant fis qu'elle me tint pour sien
600   En tel maniere
     Que de bon cuer riant, a lie chiere,
     Me dist: 'Amis, vesci t'amie chiere
     Qui plus ne vuet envers toy estre fiere,
               Qu'Amours le vuet,
605 Qui de bon cuer ad ce faire m'esmuet;
     Et vraiement, estre autrement ne puet,
     Car moult grant chose a en faire l'estuet;
               Pour ce m'amour
     Avec mon cuer vous doin, sans nul retour,
610 Si vous depri que vous gardez m'onnour,
     Car je vous aim dessus tous et honnour.'
               Et quant je vi
     Que ma dame m'apelloit son amy
     Si doucement, et que le dous ottri
fol. 13v M'avoit donné de s'amour, sans nul si,
616   Se je fui liez,
     Douce dame, ne vous en mervilliez;
     Car j'estoie devant desconsilliez,
     Povres, perdus, despris, et essiliez,
620   Sans nul ressort,
     Quant je failloie a son tres dous confort,

575 Her bearing, her great sweetness, her appearance,
   Her courage,
Her fair looks, the manner of her comings and goings,
Her noble body, her gracious speech,
Her genteel carriage, her pleasant look,
580   And her expression,
Which was so sweet, so humble and elegant
She was the paragon of all beauty.
And having marveled at all she did,
   I found, to be sure,
585 Much great delight and perfect joy
And considered myself quite fortunate
For no other reason than that I have since
   Felt such love,
Been so bent and dedicated to her service
590 That in serving her I find all my delight;
I have been able since to perform no other labor.
   And so I served her,
Loved, protected, respected, obeyed her
A very long time, and my reward was nothing.
595 At the last, however, I loved and cherished her so much
   She saw well
I intended only honor for her and good,
And also that my heart did love her above all else;
Thus I did enough so that she took me for her own
600   In such a way
That with a good and happy heart, a pleasant face
She told me: 'Lover, see here your own dear love
Who no longer will treat you haughtily,
   Since this is the wish of Love,
605 Who with a good heart has directed me to do this;
And, in truth, it cannot be otherwise,
Because something grand moves me to do so
   Since my love
And heart as well I present you, never to be returned,
610 And so I beg you guard my honor well,
For I love and honor you above all else.'
   And when I saw
My lady called me her lover
So sweetly and had bestowed upon me
615 Without reservation the delightful gift of her love,
   If I was happy then,
Do not marvel, sweet lady;
For until that moment I had been discouraged,
Forlorn, lost, exiled, and wretched,
620   With no recourse,
Lacking her quite sweet comfort,

Mais recouvrez, ressuscitez de mort,
Riche au dessus, pleins de grant reconfort,
   Et sans anoy
625 Fui, quant me dist: 'Amis, a ti m'ottroy
De tres bon cuer.' Et ce tres dous ottroy
Cent mille fois me fist plus grant qu'un roy,
   Si que la joie
Ne porroit nuls raconter que j'avoie.
630 Car tant fui liez que je ne l'en pooie
Remercïer ne parler ne savoie.
    Mais en la fin,
Com fins loiaus amoureus, de cuer fin,
Espris d'amer, sans penser mal engin,
635 Moult humblement li dis, le chief enclin,
   Et sans effroy:
'Dame que j'aim plus qu'autre, ne que moy,
En qui scens, temps, cuer, vie, amour employ,
Tant com je puis, nom pas tant que je doy,
640   Vous remercy
Dou noble don de vo douce mercy,
Quar tant m'avez puisamment enrichi,
Tant resjoï, si gari, tant mery,
   Que vraiement
645 Se quanqu'il ha dessous le firmament
Et quanqu'il fu et sera, quittement
Me fust donnez pour faire mon talent,
   Je ne l'amasse
Tant de cent pars que je fais vostre grace.
650 Si pri a Dieu que jamais ne mefface
Chose envers vous qui nostre amour efface,
   Et que vo vueil
Puisse acomplir, einsi com je le vueil
Faire, humblement, sans hautesse, n'orgueil,
655 Car, se je puis, assez miex que ne sueil,
   Vous serviray
Tres loiaument de cuer et ameray,
Et vostre honneur en tous cas garderay.
N'en dit, n'en fait, n'en penser ne feray
660   Chose envers vous,
N'envers autrui dont vous aies courrous.
Einsois serés ma dame et mes cuers dous,
Mes diex terriens, aourez dessus tous.
   Et sans doubtance,
665 Se je fais riens contre vostre plaisence,
Ne dont vos cuers ait courrous ne grevence,
Sachiez de voir que c'iert par negligence.'
   Ma dame, einsi

But now I was recovered, brought back from death,
Enriched beyond belief, filled with great consolation,
  And without tribulation
625 When she told me: 'Lover, I give myself to you
Most willingly.' And this quite sweet boon
Made me a hundred thousand times grander than a king,
  So that no one
Could describe the joy I felt.
630 For I was so happy I could not
Utter my thanks, was not able to speak.
  But in the end,
Like a lover loyal and pure, with a noble heart,
Inflamed to love, without a devious thought,
635 Very humbly, with lowered head, I told her
  Without difficulty:
'Lady, whom I love above all others, myself included,
To whom I devote reason, heart, time, life, and affection,
As much as I have power, but not as I should,
640 I thank you
For the noble gift of your sweet mercy
Since you have so greatly enriched,
So elated, so cured, so rewarded me
  That truly
645 If everything beneath the sky
Or all that was or will be
Had been given me entirely to do my will,
  I would not value it
A hundredth part as I do your mercy.
650 So pray God I never wrong you
In anything that might sully our love,
  And also that I might fulfill
Your will as much as I intend,
Humbly, not haughtily, not proudly,
655 For, if I can, much better than has been my wont
  I will serve you
Quite faithfully from my heart and love you;
And in all things I will guard your honor well.
Not in word, deed, or thought
660 Will I do anything
Against you or anyone that will make you angry.
Instead you will be my lady and my sweetheart,
My divinity on earth, adored above all others;
  And without a doubt,
665 If I do something against your pleasure,
Whatever might anger or torment your heart,
Know truly it would be through oversight alone.'
  My lady, in this manner

La merciay com vous avez oÿ,
670   Dou noble don de sa douce mercy.
       Et elle aussi me jura et plevi
              Moult durement
       Qu'a tous jours mais m'ameroit loiaument
       Sans moy guerpir et sans departement.
675   Einsi regnay en joie longuement
              Que je n'avoie
       Nulle chose qui fust contraire a joie,
       Mais envoisiez et reveleus estoie,
       Jolis et gais, trop plus que ne soloie.
680   Et c'estoit drois
       Qu'a mon pooir fusse gens et adrois,
       Car par cuidier estoie en tous endrois
       Li miex amez des amans et li rois.
              Mais quant Fortune,
685   La desloial, qui n'est pas a tous une,
       M'ot si haut mis, com mauvaise et enfrune,
       Moy ne mes biens ne prisa une prune;
              Einsi fist la moe,
       Moy renoia et me tourna la joe;
690   Quant elle m'ot assis dessus sa roe,
       Puis la tourna, si cheï en la boe.
              Mais ce fist elle,
       La traïtre, toudis preste et isnele
       De ceaus traïr qu'elle met dessous s'ele,
fol. 14r Pour ce que Diex et Nature la bele,
696   Quant il formerent
       Celle que j'aim, si fort se deliterent
       En la tres grant biauté qu'il li donnerent
       Que loyauté a mettre y oublierent.
700   Et bien y pert!
       Que je say bien et voy tout en apert
       Que ma dame, qui tant a corps apert,
       Que mes cuers crient, aime, obeïst, et sert,
              A fait amy
705   Nouvelement, sans cause, autre que my.
       Si que, dame, se je pleure et gemy
       Parfondement et di souvent: 'Aimy!'
              N'est pas merveille
       Quant sa fine biauté qui n'a pareille
710   Et sa colour vive, fresche, et vermeille,
       Et son tres dous regart qui me traveille,
              M'ont eslongié,
       Et qu'elle m'a dou tout donné congié
       Et de tous biens privé et estrangié.
715   Helas! Comment aroie je cuer lié?

I thanked her, just as you have heard,
670   For the noble gift of her sweet mercy.
And she in turn pledged to me and swore
      Quite adamantly
She would from this day forward love me loyally,
Never forsaking or deserting me.
675   And so for a long time I was crowned with joy.
      Nothing
Contrary to joy did I experience,
Instead was happy and full of celebration,
Much more jolly and gay than I had ever been.
680   And it was proper
I did my best to be kind and thoughtful,
Since it seemed in all ways I was
The best loved of lovers and their king.
      But when Fortune,
685   The betrayer, who does not treat everyone the same,
Had lifted me up so high, in an evil and miserly fashion
She valued my goods and me no more than a fig;
      Instead she frowned,
Denied me, turned her face away.
690   After she had seated me atop her wheel,
She turned it, and I tumbled into the mud.
      But she did this,
That traitress quick and ready on all occasions
To undo those she puts beneath her wing,
695   Because God and beautiful Nature,
      When they shaped
The woman I love, so greatly delighted
In the incredible beauty they bestowed upon her
They forgot to give her faithfulness.
700   And how evident it is!
For I know well and clearly see
That lady, whose body is so lovely,
Whom my heart respects, loves, obeys, and serves,
      Has taken a new
705   Lover without cause, someone other than me.
And so, lady, if I moan and cry
Quite bitterly and often utter 'Oh me!'
      It is no wonder
Since her pure beauty without peer,
710   Her vibrant complexion, fresh and rosy,
And that sweet look that tortures me still
      Have abandoned me,
And she has uttered her last goodbye
And, also, has deprived me of my every good.
715   Alas! How could my heart be happy?

                    Et a grant tort
          M'a retollu ma joie et mon confort,
          Et si m'a mis en si grant desconfort
          Que je say bien que j'en aray la mort,
720   Ne riens deffendre
          Ne m'en porroit, nés .i. seul confort rendre.
          Mais ce qui fait mon cuer partir et fendre,
          C'est ce que je ne me say a qui prendre
                    De mon anuy,
725   Car il m'est vis, se par Fortune sui
          Jus dou degré ou jadis montez fui,
          Par li en qui je ne me fi, n'apui,
                    A dire voir,
          Que nul mal gré ne li en doy savoir,
730   Car elle fist dou faire son devoir;
          N'elle ne doit autre mestier avoir
                    Fors de traïr
          Ceaus qu'elle voit monter et enrichir,
          Et de faire le bas en haut venir;
735   N'elle ne puet personne tant chierir
                    Que seürté
          Li face avoir de sa bonneürté,
          Soit de joie, soit de maleürté,
          Que sus ou jus ne l'ait moult tost hurté.
740   C'est sa nature:
          Si bien ne sont fors que droite aventure;
          Ce n'est qu'uns vens, une fausse estature.
          Une joie est qui po vaut et po dure.
                    C'est fols s'i fie!
745   Chascun deçoit et nelui ne deffie.
          Et se je di que la mort qui m'aigrie
          Puis demander a ma dame jolie,
                    Par quel raison
          Le ferai je, ne par quel occoison?
750   Elle s'est mise en la subjection
          D'Amours, a qui elle ha fait de li don
                    Entierement,
          Et vuet qu'elle ait tres souvereinnement,
          Com ses souvreins, seur li commandement
755   Si qu'el ne puet contrester nullement
                    A son plaisir;
          Eins li couvient en tous cas oubeïr,
          Dont, se ma dame ha plaisence et desir
          De moy laissier pour un autre enchierir,
760   Ce fait Amour,
          Nom pas ma dame, en qui tout a valour.
          Car elle fait son devoir et s'onnour

And quite wrongfully
She has taken back my joy and comfort,
Putting me in such great distress
I know well it will be my death,
720   Nor might anything
Save me from this or provide a single comfort.
But what tears and breaks my heart
Is that I don't know whom to blame
For my suffering
725 Since it seems that if I was shoved down
The ladder I once had climbed through Fortune,
Whom I do not trust or depend upon,
Then, to tell the truth,
I should feel no bitterness toward her,
730 Since in the deed she simply did her duty;
And she ought have no other task
But betraying
Those she watches mount up, grow rich,
As well as raising high those of low estate;
735 Nor can she love any person so dearly
She would issue
A guarantee for him to keep his luck,
Whether it is happiness or disaster,
And she would not suddenly move him up or down.
740   Such is her nature.
Her goods are but lucky happenstance,
Which is merely breeze, deceptive form.
They are a joy that hardly lasts and is worth little.
He's a fool who trusts it!
745 She deceives and defies all,
And if I say that the death destroying me
I can blame on my pretty lady,
By what logic
Would I do so and for what cause?
750 She has become subject to the rule
Of Love, to whom she gives herself
Completely,
And she is eager for Love to govern her
As her sovereign and to be under Love's command.
755 So she cannot go against
The wishes of Love;
Instead she finds it always necessary to obey,
And so it is my lady's pleasure and desire
To abandon me and cherish some other man,
760   Love does this,
Not my lady, who is completely worthy.
For she did her duty and the honorable thing

D'obeïr a son souverein signour.
                    Si qu'il m'est vis,
765   Quant par Amour d'amer estoie espris,
      Qu'en ce faisant Amours ha plus mespris
      Par devers moy que ma dame de pris,
                    C'est a entendre,
      S'Amours pooit par devers moy mesprendre.
770   Mais nullement je ne puis ce comprendre,
      Car longuement, com douce mere et tendre,
                    M'a repeü
      De ses dous biens au miex qu'elle ha peü,
      Ne je n'ay pas encor aperceü,
775   Pour nul meschief que j'aie receü,
fol. 14v   Que tout adés
      Elle ne m'ait com amie esté pres
      Et qu'el ne m'ait servi de tous mes més,
      De plours devant et de souspirs aprés.
780   C'est ma viande;
      Mon appetit plus ne vuet ne demande,
      Ne, par m'ame, riens n'est a quoy je tende
      Fors seulement a ce que mes cuers fende.
                    Einsi Amour
785   Croist en mon cuer au fuer de ma dolour,
      Ne ne s'en part, ne de nuit, ne de jour,
      Eins me compaingne en mon dolereus plour
                    Par sa bonté;
      Si que je di que c'est grant amité
790   Qui m'a esté mere en prosperité,
      Et encor est en mon adversité.
                    Si ne me puis
      Pleindre de li, se trop mauvais ne suis,
      Car sans partir de moy toudis la truis,
795   Ne je ne suis mie par li destruis,
                    Qu'elle ne puet
      Muer les cuers, puis que Diex ne le vuet.
      Car quant Diex fist ma dame qui me suet
      Clamer amy, dont li cuers trop me duet,
800   S'il et Nature,
      Quant il firent sa biauté fine et pure,
      Plaisant a tous seur toute creature,
      Heüssent lors en sa douce figure
                    Loyauté mis,
805   Je fusse encor appellez ses amis,
      Et ses cuers qui tant bien m'avoit promis
      N'eüst jamais esté mes anemis.
                    Pour ce di qu'en ce
      Nature et Diex feïrent ignorance,

In obeying her sovereign lord.
      And so, when Love
765   Inflamed me to love, I think
Love, so doing, wronged me more
Than my worthy lady did,
      That is to say
If Love indeed could wrong me.
770   But that I cannot understand at all,
Since for a long time like a sweet and tender mother
      She nourished me
As best she could with her sweet goods,
Nor have I yet perceived,
775   For any hurt I might have received,
      That she has been
Less than a friend by my side,
Serving me with all her meals,
Tears for starters and sighing for a sweet.
780   Such is my meat;
My appetite does not wish or ask for more;
And, by my soul, I am not drawn toward anything
Save what breaks my heart.
      And therefore Love
785   Grows in my heart in proportion to my pain,
Nor does she leave by night or day.
Instead she's my companion in my painful weeping
      Because of her goodness;
And so I maintain it is great friendship
790   To be my mother in prosperity
And in adversity the same.
      Then I should be
Quite wicked if I complained of her,
For I find her always at my side,
795   Nor does she destroy me in the least,
      For she cannot
Alter hearts since God does not wish it.
But when God made the lady who was wont to
Call me lover, for whom my heart feels such pain,
800   If He and Nature,
When they created her noble and pure beauty,
More pleasing to all men than that of any other,
Had they then in that sweet form
      Put loyalty,
805   I would yet be called her lover,
And her heart, which promised me so much,
Would never have been my foe.
      So in this matter I say
God and Nature did act in ignorance

810 Sauve l'onneur d'eaus et leur reverence,
     Quant il firent si tres bele samblance
             Sans loiauté.
     Car s'elle heüst cent fois meins de biauté,
     Et elle fust loyal, la grant bonté
815 De loiauté l'eüst plus honnouré
             Que s'elle fust
     Cent mille fois plus bele, et miex pleüst,
     Et en tous cas trop miex plaire deüst,
     Pour ce qu'en li riens a dire n'eüst.
820   Si que je croy
     Qu'a Bonne Amour, a Fortune, n'a soy
     Riens demander de mes dolours ne doy.
     Et en puis je riens demander a moy?
             Certes oïl!
825 Car je me mis de richesse en essil,
     De seürté en .i. mortel peril,
     De joie en dueil, par son regart soutil,
             Et de franchise
     En servitute ou on n'aimme, ne prise
830 Moy, ne mes biens, m'amour, ne mon servise,
     Ne ma vie vaillant une cerise.
             Et nompourquant,
     Il m'est avis que pas ne mespris, quant
     Je l'enamai, qu'en ce monde vivant
835 N'avoit dame qui fust si excellent,
             Ce disoit on.
     Si devins siens en bonne entention,
     Ne jamais n'i cuidasse, se bien non,
     Pour la grandeur de son tres bon renon,
840   Qui m'a destruit.
     Mais ce n'est pas tout d'or quanque reluit
     N'on ne doit pas tant amer son deduit
     Qu'on ne s'en puist retraire, quant il cuit.
             Et se je fusse
845 Tous li mieudres dou mont, je n'esleüsse
     Autre que li, ne miex je ne peüsse,
     Se loiauté en li trouve heüsse.
             Si ne m'en say
     Que demander et a qui m'en penray
850 Des griés dolours et des meschiés que j'ay.
     S'on m'en demande, a tous responderay
             Que ç'a fait Dieus
     Et Nature; dont c'est meschiés et diex,
     Quant il firent son corps en trestous lieus
855 Si bel, si gent, si dous, qu'on ne puet mieus,
fol. 15r   S'il fust loyaus.

810 (Saving their honor and the respect due them)
When they fashioned such a beautiful being
     Without loyalty.
For if she had been a hundred times less beautiful
And yet faithful, the great virtue
815 Of loyalty would have done her more honor
     Than if she had been
A hundred times more lovely — she'd then have pleased more;
And she should have been more kind-hearted
Because there would have been nothing to fault.
820   So I believe
That not Good Love, not Fortune, nor my lady
Should be blamed for my sorrows.
Then can I blame myself in any way?
     Yes, certainly!
825 For I betook myself from riches to wretchedness,
From safety to mortal peril,
From joy to pain through her subtle look,
     And from freedom
Into a servitude where no one loves or values
830 Me, my honor, affection, or service,
Or even my previous life as much as a cherry.
     Nonetheless
It seems I did no wrong
By falling in love with her, for in this world
835 There was no lady living as excellent,
     So they said.
Thus with good intention I became hers
And never hoped for anything but good
Because of the grandeur of her most impressive fame,
840   Which has destroyed me.
But all that glitters is not gold,
And no one should love his delight so much
He cannot abandon it when he thinks to.
     And had I been
845 The world's greatest man, I would not have chosen
Anyone save her, nor could I have done better
Had I found loyalty in her.
     So I do not know
Whom to blame or accuse
850 For the grievous pain and misfortune I suffer.
Were I asked, to all I would answer
     That God and Nature
Did this; so it is misadventure and sorrow
They made her body so beautiful
855 In every way, so noble, so sweet no one could do better
     Had it been faithful.

Si me penray a eaus .ij. de mes maus?
Je non feray, car il me sont trop haus;
Eins soufferray, c'est mes milleurs consaus
860   D'ore en avant.

Or vous ay dit la maniere comment
Amours me fist estre loyal amant,
L'estat, la guise, et tout le couvenant;
          Ce qui m'avint,
865   Comment pris fui, comment on me retint;
Comment de moy ma dame ne souvint;
Les biens, les maus qu'endurer me couvint
          Jusqu'au jour de hui;
Comment je n'ay aïe de nelui;
870   Comment vengier ne puis mon grief anui,
Dont a par mi me mourdri et destrui,
          Si que je di,
Se bien m'avez entendu et oÿ,
Que la doleur dont en morant langui,
875   Qui mon viaire a desteint et pali
          Par sa rigour,
Est de vos maus cent mille fois gringnour;
Car fine joie et parfaite douçour
Sont vostre mal encontre la dolour
880   Qui me martyre."
"Certes, sire, pas ne vous vueil desdire
Que vous n'aiez moult de dolour et d'ire,
S'einsi perdez ce que vos cuers desire.
          Mais toutevoie,
885   Il m'est avis, et dire l'oseroie,
Consideré vo dolour et la moie,
Qu'il a en vous meins dolour et plus joie
          Qu'il n'ait en moy.
Si vous en vueil dire raison pourquoy;
890   Vous m'avez dit que vous amez en foy
Ceste dame qui tant vous fait d'anoy
          Et amerez
De loyal cuer, tant comme vis serez.
Et puisqu'il est einsi que vous l'amez,
895   Certes, je croy que s'amour desirez,
          Car avenir
Voy po souvent qu'amours soit sans desir,
Ne que desirs d'amours se puist souffrir
D'esperence; et s'avez souvenir
900   Aucune fois
Dont, quant vos cuers est par desir destrois,
Il vous souvient de la bele aus crins blois,

Should I call these two to account for my woes?
I will not because they are too exalted for me;
Instead I shall endure; that's my best course
860   From this moment on.

Now I have told you how
Love made me a true lover,
The circumstances, the means, and all that was agreed;
  What happened to me;
865 How I was taken, how I was held;
How my lady does not think of me;
The joys, the sorrows I have had to endure
  Until this present day;
How I have help from no one;
870 How I cannot avenge my grievous hurt,
Which harms, destroys me so much
  That I say
(If you have heard me well and listened)
The pain in which I languish, dying,
875 Which has made pale and wan my face
  With its harshness,
Is a hundred thousand times greater than your pain;
For pure joy and perfect sweetness
Are your ills measured against the hurt
880   That tortures me."
"Certainly, sir, I would not deny
You feel much pain and anger
To have lost her whom your heart thus desires.
  But nonetheless
885 It seems to me, and I dare say it,
Considering your pain and mine,
You feel less hurt and more joy
  Than do I.
And I will tell you the reason why.
890 You have said to me you love faithfully
The lady who gives you so much distress
  And you'll love her
With a loyal heart as long as you live.
Since you love her this way,
895 I certainly believe you desire her love,
  For very seldom
Have I seen love exist without desire,
Or the desire for love to be able to last
Without hope; and memory comes to you
900   Sometimes,
So whenever desire devastates your heart,
You remember the beauty with the blond hair;

Dont vous avez des pensers plus de .iij.
          Si ne puet estre
905   Que vous n'aiez aucun penser qui nestre
       Aucune joie face en vous, qui remestre
       Fait la dolour qui si vous tient a mestre,
          Si qu'a la fie
       Par souvenir avez pensee lie
910   Qui vo dolour espart et entroublié.
       Mais la mienne jour et nuit monteplie
          Sans nul sejour,
       Et toudis croist li ruissaus de mon plour,
       N'avoir ne puis pensee par nul tour,
915   N'esperence de recouvrer m'amour.
          Mais par servir,
       Par honnourer, par celer, par cremir,
       Par endurer liement et souffrir,
       Par bien amer de cuer et oubeïr
920   Tres humblement
       Povez encore avoir aligement,
       Joie et l'amour de celle ou vos cuers tent.
       Si que je di que j'ay plus de tourment,
          Et moult visible
925   Est la raison, ce m'est vis, et sensible:
       Car de ravoir vo dame, c'est possible;
       Mais mon amy ravoir, c'est impossible
          Selonc nature."

       "Dame, d'onneur, de sens, et de mesure
930   A plus en vous qu'en autre creature.
       Car par vo sens mis a desconfiture
          Moult tost seroie,
       S'a vos raisons respondre ne pooie.
       Car vraiement faire ne le saroie
935   Si sagement, com mestier en aroie.
          Mais repeter
       Vueil vos raisons se j'y puis assener.
fol. 15v Vous argüez que j'aimme sans fausser
       Et amerai tant com porrai durer
940   Sans repentir;
       Et puis que j'aim, il faut qu'aie desir
       Qui ne se puet deporter ne souffrir
       D'esperence; et si ay souvenir,
          Qui esmouvoir
945   Me fait souvent a maint penser avoir.
       Certes, dame, ce vous ottroi pour voir,
       Fors seulement que je n'ay point d'espoir.
          Mais sachiez bien,

Of whom you have more thoughts than three.
　　　Then it cannot be
905 You never have a single thought to make
Joy grow within you and relieve
The pain so tightly binding you;
　　　So in the end
Through memory you have happy thoughts
910 That shove the sorrow out and make you forget it.
But mine multiplies day and night
　　　Without a rest,
And every day the stream of my tears increases,
And I cannot ever think about
915 Or have hope of recovering my love.
　　　But by serving,
By honoring, remaining discreet, respecting,
By happily enduring and suffering,
By loving well from the heart and obeying
920 　　　Quite humbly
You still might find relief, joy,
And the love of the woman your heart is drawn toward.
So I say I'm more tormented,
　　　And quite evident
925 Is the reason, it seems to me, and sound;
For it is possible to have your lady back,
But to have my lover back, that is impossible
　　　According to Nature's law."

"Lady, there's more honor, wisdom,
930 And moderation in you than in anyone else.
Now by your reasoning I should be undone
　　　Quite quickly
Could I not answer your arguments.
Yet truly I cannot accomplish this
935 With as much wisdom as required.
　　　But I intend
To go over your reasons if I can manage it.
You argue I love without deceit
And will as long as I live
940 　　　Without repenting;
And since I love, I must experience desire,
Which cannot do without or lack
Hope; and so I have memories
　　　That often
945 Move me to thinking many thoughts.
Lady, I certainly grant all you say
Save only that I have no hope at all.
　　　But mark well,

Dame, comment qu'il n'ait partout que bien,
950   Qu'en ce vostre entendement et le mien
Ne se joingnent, ne acordent en rien;
        Eins sont contraire,
Einsi com je le vous pense a retraire,
Quant poins sera. Mais ce ne vueil pas taire
955   Que vous dites qu'encor puis je tant faire
        Par honnourer,
Par bien servir, par souffrir, par doubter,
Par oubeïr, par loyaument amer,
Qu'en joie puis ma dame recouvrer;
960   Mais ce seroit
Moult grant maistrie au garder qui l'aroit.
Car en .i. lieu son cuer n'arresteroit
Nés que feroit .i. estuef seur .i. toit.
        Et vostre amour,
965   Qui tant avoit de pris et de valour,
Ne povez mais recouvrer par nul tour,
Dont vous avez veinne et pale coulour.
        Si qu'einsi dites
Que mes dolours sont assez plus petites
970   Que les vostres, dont je ne suis pas quites,
Ne que pas n'ay acquis par mes merites.
        Si respondrai
A ces raisons au mieus que je porrai,
Et sus chascune un po m'arresterai;
975   Si en dirai ce que j'en sens et say
        De sentement.

Dame, il est voirs que j'aim tres loiaument
Ce qui me het, c'est ma dame au corps gent,
Qui est ma mort et mon destruisement
980   Quant je li voy
Autrui amer, et n'a cure de moy,
Qu'elle deüst amer en bonne foy;
Si qu'a paine que tout ne me marvoy
        De ceste amour.
985   Car, s'elle amast ma vie, ne m'onnour,
En la doleur ou je vif et demour
Ne me laissast languir l'eure d'un jour
        Pour tout le monde.
Mais en vertu font monteplier l'onde
990   De la doleur qui en mon cuer habonde:
Amours premiers et ma dame seconde.
        Pour çe ay desir.
Mais quels est il? Il est de tost morir,
Car il n'est riens qui me peüst venir

Lady, though our intentions here are only good,
950 In this your understanding and my own
Do not accord at all, agree in nothing;
      Rather they are opposed,
As I think to make clear to you
When the time is right. But I will not pass over
955 In silence your statement that I can still do so much
      By honoring,
By serving well, suffering, respecting,
By obeying, by loving loyally
That I can in joy get my lady back.
960   For it would be
Quite a trick to keep her, whoever could
Since her heart would not remain in one place,
No more than a ball on a roof.
      And your lover,
965 Who was so strong and worthy,
You cannot recover in any fashion,
And so your color is wan and pale.
      So you say
My pains are much less
970 Than your own; and thus I have not triumphed,
Nor have I earned the judgment by my merits.
      For this reason I will answer
Your arguments as best I can,
And I will spend time on each one;
975 Also I will reveal what I think and know
      About my feelings.

Lady, it's true I love quite faithfully the woman
Who hates me, that is, my lady of noble form
Who is my death and destruction
980   When I witness her
Love another man and think no thoughts of me,
Whom she in good faith ought to love;
So I am almost driven mad
      By this love.
985 For if she loved my life or honor,
She would not for all the world
Let me languish one hour of a day
      In the state where I live and dwell.
But with great force they increase the tide
990 Of suffering that floods my heart:
Love first, and my lady second.
      For this reason I feel desire.
But what for? To die swiftly,
For nothing could possibly happen

995   Dont je peüsse esperer le garir.
             Et se j'avoie
    L'amour de li miex que je ne soloie,
    Ne sai je pas se je m'i fieroie.
    Certes, nennil! Pourquoy? Je n'oseroie.
1000   Car nourreture,
    Si com on dit, vaint et passe nature,
    Et toudis va, s'il ne se desnature,
    Li leux au bois — c'est la verité pure.
          Et par ce point
1005   En mon desir d'esperance n'a point,
    Mais a li joint desespoir si apoint
    Que je serai matez en l'angle point
           Dou souvenir,
    Que vous dites, qui fait en moy venir
1010   La pensee qui me fait resjoïr.
    Certes, de li ne puis jamais joïr,
           Ne n'en joï,
    Ne ne le vi, ne senti, ne oÿ,
    Puis que ma dame ot fait nouvel ami,
1015   Car adonques se parti il de mi.
          Si voeil prouver
    Que c'est la riens qui plus me puet grever
    Et qui plus fait mon cuer desesperer
    Que souvenir. Vous savez (et c'est cler;
1020   Chascuns le voit),
    Que, se jamez il ne me souvenoit
    De ma dame qui me tient moult destroit,
    Que ma doleur oubliee seroit.
          Et s'elle estoit
1025   Oubliee, l'oubliance feroit
    Qu'elle dou tout morroit ou cesseroit;
    Et ce garir de tous maus me pourroit.
          Mais qu'avient il?
    Cils souvenirs, par son engin soubtil,
1030   Me ramentoit le viaire gentil
    Et le gent corps pour qui mon cuer exil;
           Més engenrez,
    Nez et fenis est, et continuez
    Tous en dolour. Pour quoy? Pour ce qu'amez
1035   Cuiday estre quant amis fui clamez
          Tres doucement.
    Helas! Dolens! Or est bien autrement
    Quant ma dame aimme autre nouvellement.
    Et puet on pis, dame, s'on ne se pent?
1040   Certes, nennil!
    Car c'est pour mettre un amant a essil;

995   That would give me hope for cure,
        And had I
   A better love from her than I once had,
   I don't know if I would trust it.
   Surely I would not! Why? I would not dare.
1000   For nurture,
   As they say, conquers and overcomes nature,
   And always, if he doesn't go against his kind,
   The wolf makes his way to the woods — that's the simple truth.
       For this reason
1005   My desire has no hope at all,
   But despair is so confounded with it
   I will be checkmated
       By memory,
   Which, you said, gives rise in me
1010   To the thought that makes me rejoice.
   Surely I'll not be able ever to find joy in this thought,
       Nor have I yet enjoyed it
   And I have not seen, felt, or heard it
   Since my lady took a new lover,
1015   For that thought parted from me then.
       So I intend proving
   That this memory is what grieves me
   More and makes my heart
   Despair more. You know (it's clear,
1020   Everyone sees it)
   That if I never thought about
   My lady, who binds me so tightly to her,
   My pain would be forgotten.
       And were she
1025   Forgotten, the forgetting would make
   The pain die out completely or cease;
   And this could cure me of all my sickness.
       But what would happen?
   This memory, by its subtle trickery,
1030   Recalls to me the gentle face
   And the noble body for whom my heart breaks;
       Yet this memory is conceived,
   Born and perfected, endures
   All in suffering. Why? Because I considered myself
1035   Loved when I was called lover
       Quite sweetly.
   Alas! Sorrowful! Now it is quite otherwise
   When my lady has taken to loving another man.
   And could one do worse, lady, unless he hanged himself?
1040   Surely not!
   For such a thing sends a lover into ruination,

        N'eschaper hors de si mortel peril
        N'en devroit pas un d'entre cinq cent mil,
                Dont il avient
1045   Par maintes fois, quant de ce me souvient,
        Que mes las cuers dedens mon corps devient
        Si dolereux que pasmer me couvient.
                Et se pensee
        Par souvenir est en moy engendree,
1050   Quelle est elle? Elle est desconfortee,
        Triste, mourne, lasse, et desesperee.
                Et, par may foy,
        Je n'ai penser qui ne soit contre moy;
        Et se le pren au pis. Savez pour quoy?
1055   Pour ce qu'aler ma dame en change voy.
                Et se la joie
        Que j'avoie, quant en sa grace estoie,
        Ne fust plus grant que dire ne saroie,
        Ne ymaginer ne penser ne porroie,
1060   La grief dolour
        Qui me destreint en fust assez menour.
        Mais de tant plus que j'eus joie grignour,
        De tant est plus crueuse ma langour.
                Et que ravoir
1065   Puisse ma dame, ou je n'ay nul espoir
        — Ymaginer ne le puis, ne veoir.
        Se vous diray ce qui m'i fait doloir:
                Dame, y me samble
        Q'une chose qui se part et assamble
1070   En pluseurs lieus, et avec c'elle tramble
        Et n'arreste ne que fueille de tramble,
fol. 16r   Et n'est estable,
        Eins est toudis changant et variable,
        Puis ci, puis la, or au feu, a la table,
1075   Et puis ailleurs, c'est chose moult doutable.
                Car nullement
        On ne la puet avoir seürement.
        C'est droitement li gieus d'enchantement
        Que ce qu'on cuide avoir certeinnement,
1080   On ne l'a mie.
        Einsi est il, dame, quoy que nuls die,
        De ma dame, qui se change et varie,
        Donne et retolt, or het, or est amie,
                N'en une part
1085   N'est tous ses cuers, et s'aucuns y repart,
        Certes, je croy qu'il en ha povre part,
        Et que de li celle part tost se part.
                N'a droit jugier,

And not one man in five hundred thousand
Is apt to escape such deadly danger,
    And so it happens
1045   Often when I remember this
That the weary heart in my body becomes
So full of pain I have to faint.
    And if thought
Takes shape through memory in me,
1050   What is it? It's something with no comfort,
Sad, mournful, filled with sorrow, and despairing.
    And, by my faith,
I have no thought that is not my foe.
So this makes it worse. Do you know why?
1055   Because I witness my lady change her heart.
    And if the joy
I had when in her grace
Had not been greater than I could describe,
Or was able to imagine or even conceive,
1060   The grievous pain
Gripping me would be rather less.
But as much as I did once possess great joy
So is my suffering crueler.
    And that I could
1065   Get my lady back or have any hope of doing so
— This I cannot imagine or conceive.
And I'll tell you what makes me suffer:
    Lady, it seems
That something which separates and then unites
1070   In several places and likewise is in motion,
Keeps no more still than an aspen leaf,
    And lacks stability,
Instead is always variable and changing,
Now here, now there, at the hearth, at the table,
1075   And then elsewhere, is something to be very wary of.
    For in no way
Might any man possess it in security.
It must truly be the play of some spell,
For believing to have it for certain,
1080   One does not at all.
So it is, lady, whatever anyone might say,
With my beloved, who changes and varies,
Gives and takes back, now hates, now is a friend,
    And all her heart
1085   Is not in one place, and if anyone shares in it,
I certainly believe his portion is a poor one
And will soon be taken from him.
    Nor, to judge rightly,

Amans ne puet avoir homme si chier
1090 Qu'il le vosist avoir a parsonnier
En ses amours, sans plus nés par cuidier.
   Et pour ce a plain;
Ne puis avoir son cuer, dont je me plein;
Car cuers qui va einsi de main en main,
1095 S'on l'a ennuit, on ne l'a pas demain;
   Et toute voie
Et vrais amans li drois oisiaus de proie,
Car il ne vuet avoir pour toute joie
Fors tout le cuer de celle ou il s'otroie.
1100   Si que je di
Que vous rariés aussi tost vostre amy,
Comme on avroit mué le cuer de ly
Ad ce qu'il fust entierement en my
   Mis sans retraire.
1105 Car on ne puet le leu de sa piau traire
Sans l'escorchier, n'on ne puet d'un buef faire
.I. esprivier, ne aussi le contraire.
   Et, douce dame,
La coustume est partout d'omme et de fame
1110 Que, quant dou corps s'est departie l'ame
Et li corps est en terre sous la lame,
   Qu'en petit d'eure
Est oubliez, ja soit ce qu'on en pleure.
Car nuls n'en voy ne nulle qui demeure
1115 Tant en son pleur qu'a joie ne requeure
   Eins que li ans
Soit acomplis, tant soit loiaus amans,
Ne excepter n'en vueil petis ne grans.
Et vraiement, je croy que ce soit scens.
1120   Si en ferez
La coustume; pas ne la briserez
Car ja de nul reprise n'en serez,
Et de bon cuer pour l'ame prierez.
   Mais en oubli
1125 Ne puis mettre celle que pas n'oubli,
Car Souvenir la tient moult pres de mi
Sans departir jour, heure, ne demy;
   Et si la voy
Assez souvent, dont tous vis me desvoy,
1130 Quant longuement de mes yex la convoy,
Et je n'en ay joie, ne bien, n'avoy.
   Eins voy autrui
Qui joie en a. C'est ce dont me destrui;
Car s'elle amer no vosist moy ne lui,
1135 Les maus que j'ay ne pleingnisse a nelui,

Could a lover hold another man so dear
1090 He would want that one to share
His loving, plain and simple — that's not even in his thoughts.
          And because I clearly cannot
Possess all her heart, I lament;
For a heart that goes this way from hand to hand,
1095 Should some man own it at night, he won't come morning.
          And in any case,
The true lover is a proper bird of prey
Since he, as his joy, wishes nothing
But the whole heart of the woman to whom he is devoted.
1100   And so I say
You will get your lover back as quickly
As her heart will be so transformed
It will be granted me completely,
          Never to be withdrawn.
1105 For no man can remove the wolf's pelt
Without flaying him, nor can anyone turn
An ox into a sparrowhawk or vice versa.
          And, sweet lady,
The custom is universal among men and women
1110 That when the soul has departed the body,
And the body is in the ground beneath the tombstone,
          It is forgotten
In a brief while, though wept over.
For no man or woman I have seen has remained
1115 So long in mourning they fail to seek out joy again
          Before a year
Has passed, however faithful the lover,
And I will except neither those of high or low degree.
And truly I believe this is reasonable.
1120   So you will follow
This custom; you will not violate it at all,
For no one will reproach you;
And you will pray for the soul with a good heart.
          But I cannot
1125 Ignore the woman whom I do not forget
Because Memory keeps her very close to me
Without leaving for a day, an hour, not even half an hour,
          And I see her
Rather often, which at once undoes me
1130 Whenever I follow her with my eyes a long time
And I find no joy, no good, no guidance there,
          Instead witness another man
Taking joy in her. This is what destroys me;
For if she would not love either him or me
1135 I should have complained of my pains to no one;

           Eins les portasse
Dedens mon cuer humblement et celasse,
Et en espoir de joie demourasse,
Si que meschief ne dolour ne doubtasse.
1140   Ne departir
N'en vueil mon cuer, pour doubte dou partir,
Qui trop demeure en vie, et, sans mentir,
Je ne saroie amer a repentir.
          Et si seroie
1145   Faus amoureus se je me'en departoie,
Car sans nul 'si' li donnai l'amour moie.
Si l'ameray, que qu'avenir m'en doie;
          Et, par ma foy,
Si loiaument l'aim que j'ay plus d'anoy
1150   Cent fois pour li que je n'aie pour moy
Quant s'onneur voy amenrir; car au doy
          La mousterront
Ceuls et celles qui ceste ouevre saront,
fol. 16v Et meins assez en tous cas la croiront,
1155   Qu'a tous jours mais pour fausse la tenront.
          Car de meffait
C'est un vice si villain et si lait,
Car qui le fait, ja de pooir qu'il ait,
N'iert de tous poins effacié ne deffait.
1160   Pour ce conclus,
Dame, que j'ay de doleur assez plus,
Et que plus tost a garison venus
Seroit vos maus que cils dont sui tenus.
          Et jugement
1165   En oseroie atendre vraiement,
Se nous aviens juge qui loiaument
Vosist jugier, et veritablement."
          "Par m'ame, sire,
Et de ma part je vueil et ose dire
1170   Que de mon cuer le jugement desire.
Or regardons qui nous volons eslire
          Qui sans deport
Sache jugier li quels de nous a tort;
Car avis m'est que li maus que je port
1175   Est si crueus qu'on ne puet plus sans mort."
          "Dame, je vueil
Que li juges soit fais tout a vo vueil."
"Mais au vostre, biau sire, et si conseil
Qu'il ne soit fais fors par vostre conseil,
1180   Car vous l'avez
Premiers requis; pour ce dire devez."
"Certes, dame, or ne vous en lavez,

Instead, I would have borne them
Humbly within my heart and kept them secret,
Enduring in the hope of joy,
And thus I would fear neither misadventure nor pain.
1140   And because I fear desertion
I do not wish to take back my heart,
I who remain too long alive, and — it's no lie —
I do not know how to repent of loving.
              And I would be
1145   A faithless lover if I left her,
Because with no 'but' I gave her my love.
And I will love her whatever happens to me;
              And, by my faith,
So faithfully do I love her I feel a hundred times
1150   More pain for her than for myself
Because I see her honor ruined; for with their finger
              They will point her out,
The men and women who learn of this business,
And they will trust her much less in every way,
1155   For they will always consider her false.
              Now deception
Is a vice so base and ugly
That the person who indulges in it, however powerful,
Will never be completely cured or reformed.
1160   So I conclude,
Lady, that I feel much more pain
And that your ill will come sooner
To a cure than the one that grips me tight.
              And I would truly dare
1165   To expect the judgment,
Had we a judge who would decide
Faithfully and according to the truth."
              "By my soul, sir,
I intend and dare to say for my part
1170   That with all my heart I wish a judgment.
Let us look now to whom we would choose,
              Some man who without foolishness
Could determine which of us is wrong;
For the trouble I bear, it seems to me, is so cruel
1175   No one this side of death could endure more."
              "Lady, I want
The judge to be whom you wish."
"I yield to you, fair sir, and so I counsel
He be chosen by your advice alone,
1180   For you have
First sought him; so you must say."
"Surely, my lady, don't wash your hands of this now;

Mais vous, dites, pour ce que plus savez
Que je ne fais."

Figure 3. A10 (fol. 16v); The lady and knight flank the King of Bohemia. (Photo: BnF)

1185   Et quant je vi qu'il voloient que fais
        Fust jugemens de leurs dolereus fais,
        Mes cuers en fu de joie tous refais.
            Si ne savoie
        De .ij. choses la quele je feroie;
1190   D'aler vers eaus, ou se je m'en tenroie.
        Car volentiers mis les heüsse en voie
            De juge prendre
        Tel qu'a jugier leurs fais peüst entendre,
        Si souffissant qu'il n'i eüst qu'aprendre,
1195   Et qu'aprés lui n'i heüst que reprendre.
           Si m'avisay
        Moult longuement et pris mon avis ay
        Que j'iroie a eaus. Lors sans delay
        Je me levay et devers eaus alay
1200   Tout le couvert
        Parmi l'erbe qui estoit drue et vert;
        Et quant je vins si pres d'eaus qu'en apert
        Les pos veoir et tout a descouvert,
           Le petit chien
1205   Prist a glatir qui ne me congnut rien,
        Dont la dame qui moult savoit de bien
        En tressailli (je m'en aperçu bien),
           Si l'apella.
        Mais moult petit prisié son apel a,
1210   Qu'en abaiant li chiennes m'aprocha,
        Tant que ses dens a ma robe acrocha.
           Si le hapay,
        Dont il laissa de paour son abay.
        Mais en mon cuer forment m'en deportay,
1215   Pour ce qu'a sa dame le reportay,

Please, you say because you know much more
Than do I."

1185   And when I saw they desired
A judgment rendered in their painful cases,
Joy flooded my heart.
            And I did not know
Which of two things I would do:
1190   Move toward them or restrain myself.
For I would have willingly put them on the path
            Of finding a judge
Able to undertake ruling on their cases
So skillfully there would be nothing to do but learn from it,
1195   And afterward there should be no cause for dispute.
            So I deliberated
Quite a while and decided
I would go to them. Then I rose up
Without delay and made my way toward them,
1200   All unseen
Through the grass so green and thick;
When I had drawn near enough
To see them all in the open,
            The little dog,
1205   Who did not know me at all, began to bark;
And because of this the lady, who knew much of virtue,
Startled (this I clearly witnessed)
            And called him.
But he thought little of her summons
1210   Since, barking, the dog drew nearer
Until he tore with his teeth at my robe.
            So I picked him up,
And he stopped barking out of fear.
Now in my heart I secretly quite enjoyed this
1215   Because I returned him to his mistress

        Pour avoir voie
    Et occoison d'aler ou je voloie;
    Si que toudis son poil aplanioie,
    Mais quant je vins ou estre desiroie,
1220   Je ne fui mie
    Mus, n'esbahis; einsois a chiere lie
    Ay salué toute la compaingnie,
    Si com faire le sos de ma partie.
        Li chevaliers
1225   Qui sages fu, courtois, et biaus parliers,
fol. 17r Grans, lons, et drois, biaus, et gens, et legiers,
    Et d'onneur faire apris et coustumiers,
        Sans plus atendre
    Courtoisement me vint mon salut rendre.
1230   Et la dame ou Nature volt entendre
    Si qu'on ne puet sa grant biauté comprendre
        Vers moy se trait
    Moult humblement, doucement, et a trait.
    Car elle avoit moult gracïeus attrait
1235   Et le maintieng humble, dous, et parfait;
        Et cheveus blons,
    Les yex rians, plus vairs que nuls faucons,
    Et ses corps fu gens, joins, gentils, et lons,
    Et plus apers que nuls esmerillons;
1240   Et s'ot l'entrueil
    Grandet a point, maniere et dous acueil,
    Mais son attrait et son gent appareil
    Qui simples fu n'avoit point de pareil;
        Et si fu blanche
1245   Plus que la noif quant elle est sus la branche,
    Sage, loial, courtoise, et de cuer franche,
    Et si parfaite en toute contenance
        Qu'en loiauté
    Estoit assez plus bele que biauté;
1250   N'en li n'avoit orgueil, ne cruauté,
    Ne riens qui fust contraire a amité.
        Mais esplouree
    Fu moult forment sa face coulouree;
    Et nompourquant de coulour esmeree
1255   Et de fine douçour estoit paree.
        Si m'apella
    La dame, et puis m'enquist, et aparla
    Moult sagement dont je venoie la.
    Et je qui fu desirans d'oïr la,
1260   La verité
    De chief en chief li ay dit et compté
    Comment la vins et ou j'avoie esté,

And so to have the chance
And excuse to go where I wanted;
And all the time I stroked his fur,
But when I got where I wanted to be,
1220   I was not silent
Or embarrassed at all; instead with a cheerful face
I saluted all the company,
As I knew how to do for my part.
         The knight,
1225   Who was wise, courteous, and well-spoken,
Big, tall and straight, handsome, noble and graceful,
Well taught and accustomed to do the honorable thing,
         Without further delay
Graciously came forward to return my greeting.
1230   And the lady, in whom Nature wished to make clear
How no man could comprehend her great beauty,
         Drew toward me
Quite softly, quietly, and slowly,
For her appearance was very gracious
1235   And her carriage meek, pleasing, and beyond reproach;
         And her hair was blond,
Her eyes smiling, grayer than any falcon's,
And her body noble, well-shaped, pleasing, and long,
Formed better than a hunting bird's.
1240   And attractively spaced
Were her eyes, her manner and bearing pleasant,
Yet while her demeanor and noble dress
Were simple, they were beyond compare.
         Whiter she was
1245   Than snow on the bough,
Wise, faithful, genteel, generous at heart,
And in all aspects of her character so perfect
         Her loyalty
Was much more attractive than her beauty.
1250   In her was neither haughtiness nor cruelty,
Nothing contrary to friendship.
         Yet her face
Was stained by tears, much discolored by them;
Nonetheless she was endowed
1255   With a perfect complexion, a pure sweetness.
         And so the lady
Beckoned, then questioned me, asked
Very wisely how I had come to that place.
And I, eager to hear her,
1260   Related and told
Her the truth from beginning to end
Of how I had come there and where I had been

En tant qu'il ont leur meschief raconté.
            Lors dist en bas
1265   Li chevaliers par maniere de gas:
       "Je croy qu'il ait oÿ tous nos debas."
       Et je li dis: "Sire, n'en doubtez pas,
            Que voirement
       Les ay je oïs moult ententivement
1270   Et volentiers; mais n'aiez pensement
       Que je y pense fors bien; car vraiement
            Venus estoie
       Sus .i. ruissel, par une herbue voie,
       En ce vergier ou je me delitoie
1275   Es oisillons que chanter escoutoie.
            Et quant einsi
       Y fui venus, sire, je vous choisi,
       Et d'autre part ma dame venir vi.
       Si vous dirai, comment je me chevi:
1280   Je regardai
       Le plus fueillu dou brueil; si m'i boutai,
       Car de vous faire anui moult me doubtay;
       Et la vos biens et vos maus escoutai
            De chief en chief.
1285   Or m'est avis que de vostre meschief,
       Et ma dame qui tient enclin son chief
       Dou sien, sauriés volentiers le plus grief
            Par jugement.
       Si ne volez penre premierement
1290   Vostre juge, ne ma dame ensement.
       Pour ce venus sui aviseement,
            Pour vous nommer
       .I. chevalier qui moult fait a amer;
       Car de ça mer n'a pas, ne de la mer,
1295   Plus gentil cuer, plus franc, n'a meins d'amer;
            Car de largesse
       Passe Alixandre et Hector de prouesse.
       C'est li estos de toute gentillesse,
       N'il ne vit pas com sers a sa richesse;
1300   Eins ne vuet rien
       Fors que l'onneur de tout le bien terrien,
       Et s'est plus liés, quant il puet dire: 'Tien,'
       Qu'uns couvoiteus n'est de penre dou sien.
            Dieu et l'eglise
1305   Et loyauté aimme, et si bien justise
       Qu'on le claimme l'Espee de Justise.
       Humbles et dous est, et pleins de franchise
fol. 17v   A ses amis,
       Fiers et crueus contre ses anemis.

While they were recounting their misfortunes.
          Then the knight spoke
1265 Softly, in a joking way:
"I think he has heard all our debate."
And I said to him: "Sir, do not doubt it,
          For truly
I listened to it most attentively
1270 And willingly; but you must not think
My intentions are anything but good; for in truth
          I came here
From above the stream by a grassy path
Into these woods, where I found delight
1275 In the birds whose song I listened to.
          And after coming
To this spot, I noticed you,
And from over there, sir, I saw this lady arrive.
And I will tell you what I did.
1280   I searched out
The leafiest part of the greenery and hid,
For I greatly feared annoying you two;
And there I listened to your joys and sufferings
          From beginning to end.
1285 Now it seems to me you would
Eagerly learn through a judgment which one might be
The more grievous: your mischance or that of the lady
          Whose head is bowed.
You did not wish to be the first
1290 To select the judge, and neither did my lady.
So I have come forward here advisedly
          In order to name for you
A knight who does much to make himself loved,
For on this side of the channel or the other
1295 No heart is nobler, none more generous, none less cruel.
          Because in generosity
He surpasses Alexander and in prowess Hector,
He is the pillar of all nobility,
Nor does he live as a slave to his wealth.
1300   Instead he wishes nothing
Save the honor from every worldly good,
And he is happier when he can say 'It's yours!'
Than the greedy man is to take from his riches.
          He loves God,
1305 The Church, and loyalty, and governs so justly
He is called the Sword of Justice;
He is humble and pleasant, full of generosity
          For his friends,
Fierce and cruel toward his enemies;

1310 Et, a briés mos, de scens, d'onneur, de pris
En porte adés au dit des bons le pris
          Quel part qu'il veingne.
Et s'il avient que son anemy teingne
A son dessous, Nature li enseingne,
1315 Et ses bons cuers, que pité li en prengne.
          C'est noble sorte,
Car Prouesse partout s'espee porte,
Hardiesse le conduit et enorte,
Et Largesse si li ouevre la porte
1320   De tous les cuers.
A ceaus qui sont bon (je n'en met nuls fuers),
Avec euls est com sont freres et suers,
Grans et petis, moiens, et a tous fuers.
          Sire, et d'Amours
1325 Congnoist il tous les assaus, les estours,
Les biens, les maus, les plaintes, et les plours
Miex qu'Ovides, qui en sot tous les tours.
          Et se son nom,
Qui tant est bons et de noble renom,
1330 Volés savoir, dites le moy, ou non."
     "Certes, amis, dou savoir vous prion,
          Car onques mais,
Si come je croy, ne fu, ne n'iert jamais
Home qui fust en tous cas si parfais
1335 Comme cils est, et par dis et par fais."
          "Sire, s'enseingne
Crie Lembourc, et est roys de Behaingne,
Fils de Henry, le bon roy d'Alemaingne,
Qui par force d'armes, qui que s'en plaingne,
1340   Comme emperere
Fu coronnez a Romme avec sa mere;
Dont s'il est bons, c'est bien drois qu'il appere:
Car il le doit de mere et de pere.
          Si que, biau sire,
1345 Un tels juges seroit bons a eslire
Qui vous saroit bien moustrer et descrire
Li quels de vous sueffre plus de martyre.
          Et le prenez."
Li chevaliers respondi com senez:
1350 "Je croy que Diex nous ait ci amenez."
Et dist: "Dame, s'a juge le tenez,
          Je m'i ottroy."
Et la dame respondi sans desroy:
"Sire, tant oy dire de bien dou roy,
1355 Tant est sages, preus, et de bon arroy
          Que je l'acort."

1310   And to be brief, he always earns, so good men say,
       The highest esteem for his intelligence, honor, and worthiness
            Wherever he might go.
       And if it happens he gets the upper hand
       On his enemy, Nature teaches him,
1315   As does his own good heart, to pity the man.
           He sets a noble example,
       For Prowess everywhere carries his sword,
       Hardihood accompanies, encourages him,
       And for him Generosity opens the door
1320   Of every heart.
       To the virtuous (I make no exceptions),
       To those of all conditions, the great and small, those in between,
       He is like a brother and sister.
           Sir, of Love
1325   He knows all the assaults, the skirmishes,
       The joys, the pains, the sorrowing and moaning
       Better than did Ovid himself, who knew all its intricacies.
           And if his name,
       So excellent and of such gentle renown,
1330   You wish to know — or don't — then tell me."
       "Certainly, my friend, tell us, we beg you,
           For never yet,
       So I think, has any man been,
       Nor will ever be, as perfect in every way
1335   As is this one in both word and deed."
           "Sir, his battle flag
       Proclaims Luxembourg, and he is king of Bohemia,
       Son to Henry the good king of Germany,
       Who by force of arms, no matter who might bemoan it,
1340   Was crowned
       Emperor at Rome with his mother;
       So if this man is good, it is surely right he appears so,
       For this he owes to his mother and father.
           And so, fair sir,
1345   To choose such a judge would be wise,
       A man who could with skill demonstrate and explain
       To you both which one suffers greater pain.
           So choose him."
       Like a wise man, the knight answered:
1350   "I believe God has led us to this spot."
       And he said: "Madam, if you accept him as our judge,
           I will agree to it."
       With no foolishness, the lady responded:
       "Sir, I have heard so much good spoken of this king,
1355   Who is so wise, so brave, of such magnificence
           That I concur."

"Grant merci, dame; or sommes en acort.
Si pri a Dieu que le bon roy confort
Et qu'il nous maint temprement a bon port,
1360   Si que parler
Puissiens a lui, ou il nous faut aler."
Je respondi: "Bien vous say assener
La ou il est et, s'il vous plaist, mener.
          Certeins en sui,
1365   Car vraiement, je mengay yer et bui
Avec sens gens en chastiau de Durbui.
Et il y est, ne n'en partira hui;
          Ne ce n'est mie
Loing, qu'il n'i a ne lieue ne demie,
1370   Nom pas de ci le quart d'une huchie."
Li chevaliers d'aler la dame en prie
          Sans plus atendre.
La dame dist: "Je ne m'en quier deffendre,
Mais je ne say quel part la voie prendre."
1375   Je dis: "Dame, bien le vous vueil aprendre.
          Venés adés.
Je iray devant et vous venrez aprés."
Si q'en chemin me mis, d'aler engrés,
Et quant il ont veü Durbui de pres,
1380   Si s'arrestoient,
Et dou veoir forment se mervilloient,
Car onques mais en leur vie n'avoient
Veü si bel, ne si gent, ce disoient.
          Et, sans doubtance,
1385   Il est moult fors et de tres grant plaisence,
Biaus et jolis et de po de deffence.
Car se li rois d'Alemaingne et de France
          Devant estoient,
Cil de dedens ja pour ce ne lairoient
fol. 18r   Qu'il n'alassent hors et ens s'il voloient,
1391   Toutes les fois qu'a besongnier aroient
          En la contree.
C'est une roche en mi une valee
Qui tout entour est d'iaue environnee,
1395   Grande, bruiant, parfonde, roide, et lee;
          Et li vergier
Sont tout entour si bel qu'a droit jugier,
On ne porroit nuls plus biaus souhaidier.
Mais d'oisillons y a si grant frapier
1400   Que jour et nuit
La valee retentist de leur bruit;
Et l'iaue aussi seriement y bruit,
Si qu'on ne puet en nul milleur deduit.

"Many thanks, lady; now we are in agreement.
So I pray God may comfort the good king
And lead us safely to good harbor
1360   So we might
Speak to him wherever we must go."
I answered: "I know quite well how to tell you
Where he is, and, if you please, lead you there.
          Of that I am certain,
1365   For truly I ate and drank yesterday
With his entourage in Durbuy Castle.
There he yet remains and will not leave today;
          Nor is it
Very far from here, not even a league, or half,
1370   Not the quarter of a distance a voice will carry."
The knight then asked the lady to set out
          Without further delay.
The lady said: "I have no wish to refuse,
But I do not know which path to take."
1375   I said: "Lady, I am quite willing to show you.
          Come on.
I will go ahead, and you follow along."
And so I started out, eager to go,
And when they saw Durbuy Castle close at hand,
1380   They stopped
And greatly marveled at the sight
Since never before in their lives had they
Seen any place this beautiful, this noble, so they said.
          And, no doubt,
1385   The place is quite secure and extremely pleasant,
Beautiful and attractive, easy to defend,
For if the kings of both Germany and France
          Were before it,
Those inside need never give up
1390   Going in and out as they wished,
Anytime they had cause to move
          Into the countryside.
It is on a rocky mount in the middle of a valley
Thoroughly encompassed by a river
1395   That is huge, noisy, deep, rough, and wide;
          And the orchards
All around are so pretty that, to give them their due,
None prettier could ever be hoped for.
Within them, moreover, the birds make such a commotion
1400   That night and day
The valley echoes with their song.
And the river too gurgles pleasantly,
So one could find no greater delight.

              Et puis aprés

1405   A grans roches tout entour, nom pas pres,
        Eins sont si long dou chastel qu'il n'est fers,
        Engiens, ne ars qui y getast jamés.
              Mais la maison
        Sus la roche est si bien qu'onques mais hom

1410   Ne vit autre de plus belle façon,
        Car il n'i a nesune meffaçon.
              Et la fonteinne
        Est en la court, qui n'est mie villeinne;
        Eins est vive, de roche clere et seinne,

1415   Froide com glace et plus douce que Seinne.
              Mais le vaissel
        Ou elle chiet est tailliez a cisel
        D'un marbre fin, blanc, et bis, et si bel
        Que tels ne fu depuis le temps Abel.

1420   Sus la riviere
        Est la pree large, longue, et pleniere,
        Ou on trueve d'erbes mainte maniere.
        Mais revenir m'estuet a ma matiere.
             Quant la maison

1425   Orent veü, je les mis a raison,
        Et si leur dis: "De l'aler est saison.
        Alons nous en: car ci riens ne faison."
              Si en alames
        Tout le chemin et le pont trespassames,

1430   Ne ça ne la, nulle part n'arrestames
        Jusques a tant qu'a la porte hurtames.
              Mais li portiers
        La porte ouvri de cuer et volentiers.
        Je qui hurtai et qui fui li premiers

1435   Et de laiens estre assés coustumiers
            Parlai einsi:
        "Cils chevaliers et ceste dame aussi
        Viennent parler au roy s'il est yci."
        Et li portiers tantost li respondi

1440   Qu'il y estoit.
        Je dis: "Amis, pren garde s'on porroit
        Parler a li." Et li dist qu'il iroit.
        Mais tout einsi com de nous se partoit
             Pour aler sus,

1445   Uns chevaliers, biaus, et gens, et corsus,
        Jolis et gais, en est a nous venus;
        Honneur ot nom, et s'en sot plus que nuls.
             N'il ne vint mie
        Tous seuls a nous; eins li fist compaingnie

1450   Une dame bele, gaie, et jolie;

And then beyond
1405 There are cliffs all around, but not too close,
Instead at such distance from the castle that no weapon,
No siege machine, no arbalest could ever shoot at it.
But the keep
Above the rocks is so ably fashioned
1410 No man ever saw one of more beautiful form
Since it lacks faults of any kind.
And the spring
In the courtyard is by no means unpleasant;
Rather it flows free from clean and healthy rock,
1415 Cold as ice, sweeter than the Seine.
But the fountain
Into which it falls was chiseled
From fine marble, white and gray-brown, so beautiful
There has been none its equal since the time of Abel.
1420 Above the riverbank
The meadow is broad, long, and ample,
Where many kinds of grasses are found.
To my story, however, I must return.
After they had looked over
1425 The residence, I advised them,
Saying: "It's time to go.
Let us proceed; for we accomplish nothing here."
So we walked along
The length of the path and crossed the bridge,
1430 Halting neither here nor there
Until at last we knocked on the gate.
Now the porter
Opened the gate cordially and willingly.
I took the lead and knocked,
1435 Being rather familiar with the place,
And I said:
"This knight and this lady too
Have come to speak with the king if he is here."
And the porter answered me at once
1440 That he was within.
I said: "Friend, please find out if one might
Speak with him." And he said he would go.
Yet just as he was leaving us
To make his way above,
1445 A knight who was handsome, noble, broad-shouldered,
Friendly, and attractive approached;
His name was Honor, and he knew more about it than anyone.
And in no way did he come
All alone to us; instead a beautiful lady,
1450 Pleasant and friendly, was his companion,

Si ot a non la dame Courtoisie.
  Bien y parut,
Car aussi tost qu'elle nous aperçut
Nous salua, et puis biau nous reçut.
1455 Si fist Honneur, si com faire le dut.
  Adont endoy
Courtoisement, en riant, sans effroy,
Prirent chascun l'un d'eaus .ij. par le doy.
Mais Courtoisie, einsi com dire doy,
1460 Le chevalier
Acompaingna liement, sans dangier,
Et Honneur volt la dame acompaingnier.
Lors se prirent ensamble a desraisnier
  Si s'en alerent,
1465 Tout en parlant, la ou il les menerent,
Par les degrez de marbre qu'il monterent,
Tant qu'en la chambre au bon roy s'en entrerent.
  Et li bons rois,
Qui moult estoit sages en tous endrois,
1470 Loiaus, vaillans, liberaus, et adrois,
Et envers tous dous, humbles, et courtois,
  En moult grant joie
fol. 18v Estoit assis sur .i. tapis de soie,
Et ot .i. clerc que nommer ne saroie
1475 Qui li lisoit la bataille de Troie.
  Mais Hardiesse
L'acompaingnoit, et sa fille Prouesse,
Et doucement tint par la main Largesse,
Une dame de moult grant gentillesse.
1480 S'i fu Richesse,
Amour, Biauté, Loiauté, et Leesse,
Desir, Penser, Volenté et Noblesse,
Franchise, Honneur, Courtoisie, Jeunesse.
  Cil .xvj. estoient
1485 Avec le roy, n'onques ne s'en partoient.
Diex et Nature ottroie li avoient
Dés qu'il fu nez; pour ce tout le servoient.
  C'estoit grant grace.
Et s'il y a nul ne nulle qui face
1490 Chose dont nuls puist dire qu'il mefface
Raisons y est q'le meffait efface.
  Einsi se sist
Li gentils rois, et quant la dame vist,
Il se leva, et par la main la prist,
1495 Car Courtoisie a faire li aprist.
  Aprés pris ha
Le chevalier, et forment l'esprisa

And she was called Lady Courtesy.
>And, truly, this she seemed to be,
For as soon as she spied us,
She offered a greeting, then received us graciously.
1455 Honor did the same, just as he should do.
>And then the two of them,
Courteously, smiling, without ado,
Each took one of the couple by the hand.
But Courtesy, I should say,
1460 >Merrily
Accompanied the knight with no haughtiness,
And Honor intended to escort the lady.
Then they began to converse and in this manner
>They set out,
1465 Talking all the while, to where they were leading them,
Climbing some marble stairs
Until they at last entered the good king's hall.
>And the good king,
Who was wise in all circumstances,
1470 Loyal, valiant, generous, and well-mannered,
Kind, unassuming, and courteous to all,
>Was seated
In very great contentment on a silk rug,
And some clerk whom I cannot name
1475 Was reading to him the battle of Troy.
>But Hardihood
Was his companion, and Prowess too, that one's daughter,
And quite gently he was holding the hand of Generosity,
A lady of quite great nobility.
1480 >Wealth was present,
Love, Beauty, Loyalty, and Happiness,
Desire, Thought, Will, and Nobility,
Liberality, Honor, Courtesy, Youth.
>These sixteen were
1485 With the king and never left his side.
God and Nature had bestowed them upon him
At birth; and so all did him service.
>The favor was great.
And if a gentleman or lady ever did
1490 Something that could be called misdeed,
Reason was present to erase the fault.
>And in this way
Was the noble king enthroned, and seeing the lady,
He rose and took her by the hand,
1495 For this was what Courtesy had taught him.
>Afterward he received
The knight, and esteeming him greatly

Dedens son cuer, et puis leur demanda
Moult sagement dont il venoient la,
1500   Et leur enquist
De leur estre qui moult li abelist.
Li chevaliers a la dame requist
Qu'elle li vosist dire, et elle dist
      Que non feroit;
1505   Einsois deïst, que miex li afferoit.
Il respondi adont qu'il li diroit
De chief en chief tout einsi qu'il estoit,
      Jusqu'a la fin.

Figure 4. A11 (fol. 18v); The lady and knight stand before the King of Bohemia. (Photo: BnF)

"Sire," dist il, "Ci pres a .i. jardin
1510   Vert et flouri ou il a grant tintin
De rossignols; s'i vins hui a matin,
      Pour escouter
Leur biau service et leur joli chanter,
Comment que po s'i peüst deporter
1515   Mon cuer que riens ne porroit conforter.
      Mais toute voie
Einsi venus d'aventure y estoie,
Pleins et pensis de maus qu'Amours m'envoie,
Si vi venir par une estroite voie,
1520   Verde et herbue,
Ceste dame qu'avec moy est venue.
Si me sambla de maniere esperdue,
Si que tantost pris parmi l'erbe drue
      Mon adresse ay,
1525   Et mon chemin droit vers li adressai.
Et quant je fu pres, je la saluay,
Mais mot ne dist, dont je me mervillay,
      Ne onques chiere
Ne fist de moy, ne de oueil, ne de maniere.
1530   Et je qui fu mervilleus pour quoy c'iere,

In his heart, then asked these two
Quite wisely why they had come,
1500   Inquiring about
How they were, which greatly interested him.
The knight asked the lady
If she would speak to the king, and she said
             She would not do so;
1505 Instead, he should explain, it being more fitting for him.
Then he answered that he'd tell him
Everything step by step, just how the matter stood
             Right to the end.

"Sire," he said, "close by is a garden
1510 Green and flowery, where is a grand chorus
Of nightingales; I went there this morning
             To listen to
Their beautiful service and pleasant singing,
Though my heart could take
1515 Little pleasure because nothing can comfort it.
             However
When I had come to that spot by chance,
Full of the pains Love provides and thinking on them,
I saw arrive by a narrow path,
1520   Green and grassy,
This lady who has accompanied me here.
And I thought her manner distraught;
So at once I made my way
             Through the thick grass,
1525 Directing my steps toward her.
And, approaching, I greeted her,
But she said not a word, at which I wondered,
             And took no notice
Of me, not with her eye or manner.
1530 And, bewildered why this was so,

Dis belement: 'Tres douce dame chiere,

                    Pour quel raison

        Ne volez vous entendre a ma raison?'

        Et la tirai par le pan dou giron.

1535   S'en tressailli, dont sa belle façon

                    Coulour mua.

        Si respondi, que plus n'i arresta,

fol. 19r Et durement envers moy s'escusa

        De son penser a quoy elle musa.

1540   Et li enquis

        Pourquoy son cuer estoit einsi pensis.

        Finablement tant parlai et tant fis

        Qu'elle me dist tout ce que je li quis,

                    Voire par si

1545   Que par ma foy li juray et plevi,

        Quant elle aroit son parler assevi,

        Que le penser li diroie de mi.

                    Et dist einsi

        Qu'elle soloit avoir loial amy

1550   Qui loyaument l'amoit, et elle li.

        Mais la mort l'a de ce siecle parti,

                    Et la valour,

        Le scens, le pris, la prouesse, l'onnour,

        Qui fu en li, si comme elle dist, flour,

1555   Le fist estre des bons tout le millour.

                    Pour ce pensoit

        Parfondement, në onques ne cessoit,

        Et en pensant le plouroit et plaingnoit,

        Si que son vis en larmes se baingnoit.

1560   Pour ce maintient

        Que la dolour est plus griés qui li vient

        Pour son amy que celle qui me tient.

        Sire, et je di, faire le me couvient,

                    Tout le contraire.

1565   J'aim loyaument de cuer et sans retraire

        La plus tres bele et le plus dous viaire

        Qu'onques encor Nature peüst faire,

                    Qui me donna

        Jadis son cuer tout et abandonna.

1570   Son cuer, s'amour, son amy me clama,

        Et par son dit seur tous autres m'ama.

                    Or est ainsi,

        Sire, qu'elle n'a mais cure de my;

        Eins m'a guerpi, et fait nouvel amy.

1575   Et, par m'ame, pas ne l'ay desservi.

                    Et d'autre part,

I said pleasantly: 'So sweet dear lady,
            Why is it
You will not heed my words?'
And at the panel of her skirt I tugged.
1535   And she startled and her pretty face
            Changed color.
Without further pause she responded,
Fervently apologizing
For the thoughts preoccupying her.
1540   And I asked
Why she was so melancholy at heart.
At last I said and did enough
That she answered me
            So truthfully
1545   I swore upon my faith and pledged
That when she had finished speaking,
I would tell her my own thoughts.
            And so she said
She once had a faithful lover
1550   Who loved her loyally, as she did him.
But death took the man from the world,
            And the valor,
The intelligence, the worthiness, the prowess, the honor
That, she said, had in him their flower —
1555   These had made him the very best among good men.
            For this reason she was deep
In thought and never ceased being so,
And, while thinking, cried for and bemoaned him,
Bathing her face in tears.
1560   Therefore she maintains
The pain is more grievous that comes to her
On her lover's account than the grief that grips me.
Sire, I maintain (and must)
            Just the contrary.

1565   I love faithfully from the heart without desisting
The most beautiful woman, and with the sweetest face
Nature has ever been able to create,
            Who once gave
And abandoned her heart completely to me.
1570   She called me her heart, her love, her lover,
And said she loved me above all others.
            But now,
Sire, she no longer cares for me:
Instead she has thrown me over and taken a new lover.
1575   And, by my soul, I have in no way deserved this.
            Moreover

Mon guerredon ailleurs donne et depart,
Ne je n'en puis avoir ne part ne hart.
C'est ce, sire, pour quoy li cuers me part.
1580   Si m'est avis,
Consideré mes raisons, que j'ay pis
Que la dame, comment que ses amis
Soit trespassés, Diex l'ait en paradis!
          Sire, et cils clers
1585   Qui me samble gais, jolis, et apers,
Fu atapis ou jardin et couvers
En plus espés dou brueil qui est tous vers.
          Si sailli hors,
Quant li ot bien oÿ tous nos descors
1590   Si nous loa que li drois et li tors
Fust mis seur vous, et ce fu nos acors.
          Car longuement
Avoit duré de nous le parlement,
Et si aviens fait meint arguement,
1595   Si comme il est escript plus pleinnement
          Yci dessus.
Or sommes ci par devers vous venus
Par quoy li drois soit jugiés et sceüs,
Et que vos dis soit de nous .ij. tenus.
1600   Si que ce plait
Povez tantost terminer s'il vous plaist;
Car nous avons de vous no juge fait.
Sire, or avez oÿ tout nostre fait
          Entierement;
1605   Si en vueilliez faire le jugement,
Car nous l'avons desiré longuement,
Et ceste dame et moy devotement
          Vous en prions."

Quant cils li ot moustrees leurs raisons,
1610   Qui bien le sot faire com sages homs,
Li gentils rois qui moult estoit preudons
          Li respondi:
"Se Diex me gart, vous avez pris en my
Juge ignorant et de scens desgarni,
1615   Ne onques mais je n'oÿ, ne ne vi
          Tel jugement.
S'en saroie jugier petitement.
Mais nompourquant le conseil de ma gent
En vueil avoir; car je l'ay bel et gent."
fol. 19v   Lors appella
1621   En sousriant Loiauté qui fu la,
Amour, Juenesse, et Raison, qui parla

She bestows and shares out what was my reward,
Nor of this have I either share or portion.
For this reason, sire, my heart is breaking.
1580   And so I think,
Considering my reasons, to have it worse
Than the lady, since, although her lover
Has died, he may be with God in paradise!
        And, sire, this clerk,
1585   Who seems friendly and merry and knowledgeable,
Was hidden in the garden and covered up
In the thickest brush, which is all green.
        He emerged
After clearly hearing all our discussion
1590   And advised us to put the right and wrong of it
Before you, which was our agreement.
        For our talk
Had lasted a long time,
And we made many arguments,
1595   Just as it is written more fully
        Here above.
Now we have come before you
For the right to be judged and known
And your sentence kept by us both.
1600   Therefore you can end
This debate at once if it pleases you;
For we have made you our judge.
Sire, now you have heard all our dispute
        In full;
1605   So please render a judgment
Because we have desired one a long time,
And this lady and I earnestly
        Beg you for it."

After putting their cases to him,
1610   This man who knew well how to do so quite wisely,
The noble king, a very worthy man,
        Answered him:
"So God keep me, you have chosen in me
A judge who is ignorant and lacks discernment;
1615   And never before have I heard or seen
        Such a case.
And I know little about judging it.
Nonetheless I wish to hear the counsel
Of my court; for mine is both noble and good."
1620   Then, smiling,
He summoned Loyalty, who was present,
As well as Love, Youth, and Reason, who was the first

        Premierement, et puis leur demanda
               Li gentils roys:
1625   "Que diriés vous qui savez tous les drois?
        Cils chevaliers qui gens est et adrois
        Et ceste dame aussi a ces crins blois
              Sont venu ci
        Par devers moy, dont je les remercy,
1630   Et jugement vuelent oïr de my,
        Li quels a plus de mal et de sousci.
              La dame avoit
        Ami loial qui l'amoit et servoit,
        Et elle lui, tant comme elle pooit.
1635   Or est einsi que Mors, qui tout reçoit,
              Li a tollu.
        S'en a le cuer dolent et irascu,
        Car a son temps ot il si grant vertu
        Que nul milleur, ne nul plus bel ne fu.
1640   Le chevalier
        Sans repentir aimme de cuer entier
        La plus bele qui vive, a son cuidier,
        Et elle foy sans muer, ne changier
              Li a promis,
1645   Et retenus fu de li comme amis
        Et bien amez; il en estoit tous fis.
        Or a la dame en autre son cuer mis,
             Et li guerpi
        Dou tout en tout, et n'a cure de li.
1650   Et a ses yex voit la belle et celi
        Qui les dous biens a qu'il ha desservi.
             Or vous ay dit
        Pour quoy il sont venu oïr mon dit.
        Et sans doubte, cuers qui ainsi languit
1655   Se destruit moult, et a grant doleur vit.
            Si m'en devez
        Donner conseil au mieus que vous poez;
        Car chascuns est mes drus et mes privez,
        Et moult me fi en vous, bien le savez.
1660   Dites, Raison.
        Premiers oïr vueil vostre entention;
        Car vous m'avez maint conseil donné bon."
        Raisons, qui fu bele et de bon renom,
            Einsi respont:

1665   "Sire, je di que cil .ij. amant sont
        Moult engoisseus quant einsi perdu ont
        Ce qu'il aimment, et que li cuers leur font
            Si com la cire

To speak, and the noble king
                    Then asked them:
1625   "What say you who know all the laws?
         This knight who is noble and well-mannered
         And also this lady with the blond hair
                    Have come here
         Before me, for which I thank them,
1630   And they wish to hear a judgment from me
         As to which suffers greater pain and worry.
                    The lady had
         A faithful lover who loved and served her,
         And she him, as much as she was able.
1635   Now Death, who receives everyone,
                    Has taken him from her.
         So her heart is sorrowful and troubled,
         For in his time he had such great virtue
         There was none better, no man more handsome.
1640   The knight,
         Not repenting, loves with his whole heart
         The most beautiful woman alive in his opinion,
         And she pledged him her faith not to alter,
                    Not to change,
1645   And she accepted him as her lover,
         Loved him well — of this he was quite certain.
         Now the lady has given another man her heart
                    And thrown him over
         Completely in every regard, showing him no concern.
1650   And with his very eyes he sees this beauty and the man
         Who possesses the sweet goods he himself has deserved.
                    Now I have told you
         Why they have come to hear my sentence.
         And, doubtless, a heart languishing this way
1655   Quite destroys itself and lives in much pain.
                    So you are to offer
         Me advice in this matter, the best you can;
         For each of you is my intimate and friend,
         And I place much trust in you, as well you know.
1660   Speak, Reason.
         I want to hear your opinion first,
         For you have given me much good advice."
         Reason, who was beautiful and of good repute,
                    Answered thus:

1665   "Sire, I say that these two lovers are
         Greatly anguished because they have lost
         Those they love and so their hearts melt
                    Just as, before the flame,

Devant le feu se degaste et empire.
1670　Mais qu'il soient tuit pareil de martyre
Et de meschief, ce ne vueil je pas dire.
　　　　Ce qui me muet
Vous vueil dire puisque faire l'estuet.
Ceste dame jamais veoir ne puet
1675　Son ami vray einsi comme elle suet.
　　　　Si avenra
Einsi que puisque plus ne le verra,
Je ferai tant qu'elle l'oubliera,
Car le cuers ja tant chose n'amera
1680　　　Qu'il ne l'oublie
Par eslongier. Certes, je ne di mie
Qu'une piece n'en ait peinne et hachie,
Mais Juenesse, qui tant est gaie et lie,
　　　　Ne soufferroit
1685　Pour nulle riens qu'entroubliez ne soit.
Car Juenesse, sire, comment qu'il voit,
Met en oubli moult tost ce que ne voit.
　　　　Aprés je di
Qu'Amours n'a pas tant de pooir en li
1690　Que soustenir se peüst sans amy
L'eure du jour, ne sans amie aussy.
　　　　Et se l'un faut
Des .iij., li .ij. autres aront deffaut;
Qu'Amour, ami, et amie estre faut
1695　Tout ensamble, ou l'amour riens ne vaut.
　　　　Et puisqu'amie
Et Amours ont perdu la compaingnie
D'amy, certes, je ne donroie mie
De leur amour une pomme porrie.
1700　　　C'est assavoir,
Quant a l'amour qui est mondeinne, avoir.
fol. 20r　Car c'est tres bon de faire son devoir
Si que l'ame s'en puist apercevoir.
　　　　Mais il n'est ame,
1705　N'homme vivant, qui aimme si sans blame
S'il est tapez de l'amoureuse flame,
Qu'il n'aimme miex assez le corps que l'ame.
　　　　Pour quel raison?
Amour vient de charnel affection,
1710　Et si desir et sa condition
Sont tuit enclin a delectation.
　　　　Si ne se puet
Nuls, ne nulle garder qui amer vuet
Qu'il n'i ait vice ou pechié; il l'estuet,
1715　Et c'est contraire a l'ame, qui s'en duet.

The wax wastes away, grows smaller.
1670 But that they are just the same in suffering
And misfortune — this I do not intend to say.
What sways me
I will state since it is necessary.
This lady can never see
1675 Her lover true as she once did.
And so it will happen
Because she sees him no longer,
I will work to make her forget him,
For the heart will never love anything so much
1680 Not to forget it
As time goes by. Of course, I do not say at all
She will not feel pain and torment for a time,
But Youth, who is so very gay and happy,
Will not allow
1685 For any reason him not to be forgotten.
For Youth, sire, no matter what,
Makes one forget quickly what one does not see.
I state further
That Love does not have the power
1690 To sustain itself without the lover
Or the beloved for a single hour of a day.
And if one of these three
Is missing, the other two will fail;
For Love, lover, and beloved must remain
1695 Together or the affair is worth nothing.
And since the beloved and Love
Have lost the company of the lover,
I certainly would not give
A rotten apple for their love affair,
1700 And here is the reason:
This love is a worldly thing.
For love is quite good at doing its job
So the soul can feel it.
But there is no soul,
1705 No man alive, who loves this way without sin
When struck by the amorous flame,
Loving the body much more than the soul.
And why?
Love arises from fleshly attraction,
1710 And its desire and nature
Are inclined completely toward satisfaction.
So no man
Or woman who intends to love can prevent
Vice or sin from being part of it; it must be so,
1715 And this opposes the soul, which sorrows over it.

          Et d'autre part,
Tout aussi tost com l'ame se depart
Dou corps, l'amour s'en eslonge et espart.
Einsi le voy partout, se Diex me gart.
1720   Si que l'amour
De ceste dame, ou tant a de valour,
Apetise toudis de jour en jour,
Et aussi fait a ce fuer la dolour.
          Mais cils amis,
1725   Qui folement s'est d'amer entremis
Sans mon conseil et se s'i est si mis,
Li dolereus, qu'il en est tous remis,
          Les maus d'amer
Sont en son cuer qui li sont trop amer
1730   Qu'Amours le fait nuit et jour enflamer,
Ne il ne vorroit, ne porroit oublier
          Son annemie.
Savez pourquoy? Pour ce que Compaingnie,
Amour, Biauté, et Juenesse la lie,
1735   Et Loiauté, qu'oublier ne vueil mie,
          En grant folie,
En rage, en dueil, et en forsenerie
Le font languir, et en grant jalousie,
Et en peril de l'ame et de la vie.
1740   Car main et tart
Son dolent cuer de sa dame ne part,
Eins la compaingne en tous lieus sans depart;
Et cils qui est plus pres dou feu, plus s'art.
          Et Loiauté
1745   Si li deffent a faire fausseté.
Mais s'il heüst par mon conseil ouvré
Quant sa dame ot nuef ami recouvré,
          Il n'eüst pas
Continué l'amour; car, en tel cas,
1750   Se la dame chante en haut ou en bas,
On doit aler ou le trot ou le pas.
          Aprés li dist
Biauté qu'il fait miex assez, s'il languist,
Pour li amer, que se d'autre joïst.
1755   Si fait Amour. Juenesse le norrist
          Avec folour
En ce meschief, en celle fole errour,
Car il en pert le sens et la vigour.
Einsi languist li dolens en dolour;
1760   Car quant il voit
Que de s'amour, present li, autres joit,
Qui son amy appeller le soloit,

Furthermore,
As soon as the soul departs
The body, love leaves and distances itself.
I see exactly this everywhere, may God preserve me.
1720 And so this lady's
Love, which has so much strength,
Diminishes day by day,
As her suffering does proportionately,
But this lover,
1725 Who has rashly undertaken to love
Against my advice and embarked upon this course,
This unfortunate man, all weakened thereby,
Finds
The pains of love in his heart too bitter
1730 Because Love makes him burn night and day,
And he would not or could not forget
His enemy.
Do you know why? Because Companionship,
Love, Beauty, and joyous Youth,
1735 Loyalty too (whom I will not neglect)
Make him languish
In great madness, in rage,
In obliviousness, and in great jealousy,
And in the peril of his soul and life.
1740 For early and late
His sorrowing heart never leaves his lady,
But without departing is everywhere her companion;
And the man closer to the fire gets more burned.
And Loyalty
1745 Prevents him from proving false.
But had he acted on my advice
When his lady took a new lover,
He should not
Have continued the affair; for, in such a case,
1750 If the lady sings high or low,
The man must trot or walk.
Afterward Beauty
Told him he would do much better languishing
In love for her than in finding joy elsewhere.
1755 Love did the same. Youth fed him
On madness
In this misery, in this foolish error
So he lost strength and wit.
Thus the grieving man languished in pain;
1760 But seeing that other man,
With him present, rejoice in his beloved,
In this lady who used to call him her lover,

Il a le cuer si jalous, si destroit,
        Que c'est merveille
1765 Qu'il ne s'occist, ou qu'il ne s'apareille
D'occirre ce qui ainsi le traveille.
Et ce li met Jalousie en l'oreille.
        Et s'il avoit
L'amour de li, einsi comme il soloit,
1770 Qu'en feroit il? Certes, riens n'en feroit.
Car jamais jour il ne s'i fieroit.
        Et pour ce espoir
N'a de jamais autre solas avoir,
Puisque mettre ne puet en nonchaloir
1775 Ceste dame qui tant le fait doloir.
        Si que je di
Qu'il ha plus mal que ceste dame cy,
Et que son cuer est en plus grant sousci
Par les raisons que vous avez oÿ.
1780   Et, a mon gré,
Cils chevaliers en a moult bien parlé,
Car en escript l'ay ci dessus trouvé,
Et par raison s'entention prouvé.
fol. 20v   Ce m'est avis."

1785 Quant Raisons ot moustré tout son avis,
Amours parla, qui fu biaus a devis,
Et graciëus de maniere et de vis,
        Et dist: "Raison,
Moult bien avez moustree vo raison.
1790 Si m'i ottroy, fors tant que mesprison
Feroit d'oster son cuer de la prison
        A la tres bele
Pour qui il sent l'amoureuse estincelle.
Si vueil qu'il l'aint et serve comme celle
1795 Dont heü a mainte lie nouvelle,
        Car s'il pooit
Vivre mil ans, et toudis la servoit,
Ja par servir il ne desserviroit
Les grans douceurs que faire li soloit.
1800   Et se Plaisence,
Qui faire fait mainte estrange muance,
Li fait estre de sa dame en doubtance,
Doit il estre pour ce en desperence?
        Certes, nanil!
1805 Qu'en mon service en a encor cent mil
Qui aimment tuit pres aussi fort comme il,
Et si n'en ont la monte d'un fusil.
        Et s'ay povoir

His heart is so jealous, so distraught,
    It's a wonder
1765   The man does not kill himself or set out
To kill the one who torments him so.
And Jealousy puts this in his ear.
    And if he possessed
Her love as was his wont,
1770   What would he do with it? Surely, nothing.
For never a single day would he trust it.
    Therefore he has
No hope of ever having other comfort
Because he cannot cool in his affection
1775   For this lady who hurts him so.
    And thus I maintain
He feels more pain than this lady here,
And his heart experiences more anguish
For the reasons you have heard.
1780   And, to my satisfaction,
This knight has spoken quite well to them,
As I found all in writing here above,
And with reason he has proved his contention.
    Such is my view."

1785   After Reason had stated all her opinion,
Love spoke up, who was very good looking,
Gracious in manner and appearance,
    And said: "Reason,
You have quite ably made known your reasoning.
1790   And I agree, save it would be a grievous misdeed
To rescue the lover's heart from its prison
    Within the beautiful lady,
For whom he feels love's spark.
So it is my wish he love and serve her as one
1795   In whom he has found much happy news,
    For if he could
Live a thousand years and serve her every day,
Never by service would he merit
The great sweetness she was wont to show him.
1800   And if Pleasure,
Who has brought on many a strange alteration,
Makes him doubt his lady,
Must he then despair?
    Surely not at all!
1805   For in my service are a hundred thousand more
Who love almost as strongly as does he
And have for it not the price of a whetstone.
    And I have the power

De li garir et de li desdoloir,
1810 Mais il n'a mais fiance, ne espoir,
En moy; c'est ce qui plus le fait doloir."
        "Comment, Amours?"
Ce dist Raisons, "Est ce dont de vos tours
Qu'il amera sans avoir nul secours
1815 Celle qui ha donné son cuer aillours?
        Et qui vous sert,
Il n'a mie le luyer qu'il dessert?
Certes, fols est qui a servir s'ahert
Si fait maistre quant son guerredon pert."
1820   Aprés ce fait
Devers Amours, Loiauté se retrait,
Et dist einsi, que riens n'eüst meffait,
Se d'autel pain li eüst soupe fait.
        "N'il n'est raisons
1825 Pour ce, s'il est vrais, loiaus, et preudons,
Qu'il soit de ceuls qui batent les buissons
Dont li autre prennent les oisillons.
        Car se la dame,
Q'je repren moult durement et blame
1830 (Et c'est bien drois, car elle acuet grant blame
De muance faire en la haute game)
        Premierement
N'eüst osté son cuer de cest amant,
Qui tous estoit en son commandement,
1835 Amours, Amours, je parlasse autrement.
        Mais sans doubtance,
Quant il l'aimme de toute sa puissance,
Et sans cause le met en oubliance,
Il doit dancier einsi comme elle dance;
1840   Nom pas qu'il face
Chose de quoi il puist perdre ma grace;
Car s'il la laist, et ailleurs se pourchace,
Je ne tien pas qu'envers moy se mefface.
        Et si m'acort
1845 Dou tout en tout de Raison a l'acort
(Car elle fait bon et loial raport):
Que cils a droit, et ceste dame a tort."
        Et quant Juenesse,
Qui moult fu gaie et pleinne de leesse,
1850 Et qui n'aconte a don, ne a promesse,
Fors seulement que ses voloirs adresse,
        Ot escouté
Ce que Raisons ot dit et raconté
Et Loiauté, pou y a aconté,
1855 Car moult pleinne fu de sa volenté.

To cure him or worsen his pain,
1810　But he no longer has trust or hope
In me, and that is what makes him suffer most."
　　　　"How so, Love?"
Said Reason, "Is it then by your design
That the man will love without experiencing any relief
1815　The lady who has granted her heart elsewhere?
　　　　And he who serves you
Receives in no way the reward he deserves?
Surely, he's a fool to persist in serving
Such a master when he loses his wages."
1820　　　　After this,
Loyalty drew herself up in front of Love
And said no wrong would have been done
Had he made a sop from such bread.
　　　　"And it's not right
1825　If he is true, loyal, and worthy
That he should be one who beats the bushes
From which others take the birds.
　　　　For if the lady,
Whom I blame and condemn quite harshly
1830　(And quite rightly since she deserves
Much blame for proving fickle in this serious game),
　　　　Had not
First taken back her heart from this lover,
Who was completely under her control,
1835　Love, Love, I would have spoken differently.
　　　　But there is no doubt,
Since he loves her with all his might
And she for no cause ignores him,
He ought to dance the same dance she does;
1840　　　　This wouldn't be
Something that merits the loss of my favor,
But if he abandoned her and looked elsewhere,
I would not consider he had sinned against me.
　　　　So I concur
1845　Completely with all of Reason's conclusions
(For she has offered a good and true accounting):
The man is right, and this lady is wrong."
　　　　And when Youth,
Who is very gay and full of happiness
1850　And pays no mind to gifts or promises,
Only to what appeals to her,
　　　　Heard
What Reason had said and declared,
And Loyalty as well — she thought little of it
1855　Because she was quite full of her own willfulness.

             Et dist en haut:
"Certes, Raison, vostre science faut,
Et Loiauté, sachiés, riens ne vous vaut.
Car cils amis, pour mal, ne pour assaut

1860   Qu'Amours li face,
N'iert ja partis de la belle toupasse
Qui de beauté et de doulceur tout passe,
Et de fine colour; ja Dieu ne place
           Qu'il li avieigne

1865 Que ja d'amer la belle se refraigne!
Car s'a present ne veult, ne n'adaigne,
Au moins l'aimme il, et son cuer la compaingne.
           Dont n'est ce assez?
Doit il estre de li amer lassez?

1870 Certes, nennil! Car on n'est pas amez,
Ne conjoïnz toudis, n'amis clamez:
           Non est, sans doubte.
Raison, fols est amans qui vous escoute,
Ne qui ensuit vos dis, ne vostre route.

1875 Et qui le fait, je di qu'il ne voit goute.
           Et par ma foy,
Nous ferons tant, Amours, ma dame et moy,
Que son cuer yert si pris, et en tel ploy,
Que nuit, ne jour ne partira de soy.

1880   Ne vos effors,
Ne doubtez pas, ne sera ja si fors
Que li fin cuer de cest amant soit hors
De la tres belle ou po treuve confors.
           Qu'Amour, ma dame,

1885 Qui son cuer art, teint, bruit, et enflame,
Et moy qui sui encor a tout ma flame,
En ceste amour le tenrons; car, par m'ame,
           Il le couvient.
Et se des maus dolereus plus li vient

1890 Qu'a la dame qui dalés lui se tient,
Fors est assez; bien les porte et soustient."
           Lors s'avisa
Li gentils rois, et bonnement ris a
fol. 21r De Juenesse, qui einsi devisa;

1895 Mais onques meins pour ce ne l'en prisa,
           Qu'elle faisoit
Tout son devoir de ce qu'elle disoit,
Et de son vueil plus chier denree avoit
Que .x. livres de son profit n'amoit.

1900   Si dist: "Juenesse,
Bele dame, vous estes grant maistresse,
Qui cest amant tenés en grant destresse,

And she said loudly:
"Surely, Reason, your wisdom fails you,
And Loyalty, know that nothing is of any use,
For this lover, despite any pain, any assault
1860   Love may inflict upon him,
Will never be parted from that lovely topaz
Who in beauty and sweetness surpasses all others,
In pure color as well; may it never please God
        It comes to pass
1865 He holds back from loving such beauty!
For if at present she does not want, will not bend to him,
At least he loves her and his heart is her companion.
        And isn't that enough?
Must he tire of loving her?
1870 Surely not! For no one is loved,
Or treated kindly, or called lover every day;
        That's true beyond a doubt.
Reason, the lover is a fool who listens to you
Or follows your dictates or path.
1875 And whoever does, I say he can see nothing.
        And by my faith,
We will do much, Love, my lady, and I,
To so imprison his heart in such straits
That night or day it will not leave of its own accord;
1880   Nor will your efforts —
Don't doubt this — ever be strong enough
To make this lover's pure heart abandon
The quite beautiful lady in whom it finds so little comfort.
        Thus Love, my lady,
1885 Who burns, pales, scorches, and inflames his heart,
As well as I who am still in my prime
Will hold him fast in this love affair; for by my soul,
        So must it be.
And should more painful ills fall to his lot
1890 Than to the lady standing beside him,
His strength is sufficient; he bears and suffers them well."
        Then the noble king
Took stock and laughed heartily at
Youth, who had said these things;
1895 Even so he prized her none the less
        Since she only did
Her duty by saying what she had,
And he valued her wishes much more dearly
Than he loved ten pounds of his own profit.
1900   So he said: "Youth,
Beautiful lady, you are the great mistress,
Who holds this lover fast in such terrible distress,

En povreté, en misere, en tristesse,
Vous et Amours.
1905   Vez que li las a perdu tout secours,
Ne ses cuers n'a refuge, ne recours,
Fors a la mort, qui a li vient le cours.
Car travillier
Le volez trop, et dou tout essillier.
1910   Or a trouvé, s'il vous plaist, consillier
Bon et loial; laissiez le consillier;
Si ferez bien.
Car il est pris en si estroit lien
Qu'il n'i scet tour d'eschaper, në engien."
1915   "Certes, sire, de ce ne faire rien.
Eins amera
La tres bele pour qui tant d'amer a.
Et, s'il y muert, chascuns le clamera
Martir d'amours, et honneur li sera
1920   S'il muert pour li."

Quant Juenesse ot son parler assevi,
Li rois parla a euls et dist einsi:
"Nous ne sommes pas assemble yci
Pour desputer
1925   S'il doit amer sa dame ou non amer,
Mais pour savoir li quels a plus d'amer,
Et qui plus sent crueus les maus d'amer,
Si com moy samble.
Or estes vous en acort tout ensamble
1930   Que plus de mal en cest amant s'assamble
Qu'en la dame; ne pas ne me dessamble
De cest acort,
Einsois m'i tieng dou tout et m'i acort,
Que cils amans est plus long de confort
1935   Que la dame ne soit, que Diex confort.
Si en feray
Le jugement einsi com je saray,
Car tel chose pas acoustumé n'ay,

Et uns autres vraiement, bien le say,
1940   Miex le feroit.
Je di einsi: consideré a droit
L'entention de Raison ci endroit,
Et les raisons de vous qui volez droit.
Et Loiauté,
1945   Qui en a dit la pure verité,
Ne n'i chasse barat ne fausseté,
D'Amours aussi qui en a bien parlé,

In poverty, misery, sadness,
            You along with Love.
1905   You witness how the weary man has lost all help,
Nor does his heart find refuge or recourse,
Save in death, which quickly comes upon him.
            But you would
Torment him too much, estrange him from everything.
1910   Now he has found, if you please, a counselor
Good and true; let that person advise him.
            In this way you will do well,
For he is caught in so tight a place
He knows no trick or scheme to escape."
1915   "Surely, sire, I will do nothing of the kind.
            Instead he will love
The great beauty on whose account he feels such bitterness.
And should he die, everyone will call him
A martyr to Love, and it will do him honor
1920   If he does die for her."

When Youth brought her speech to an end,
The king spoke to them, saying:
"We have not assembled here
            To dispute
1925   Whether he should love his lady or not,
But rather to learn who feels greater unhappiness
And suffers more the cruel pangs of love —
            Or so it seems to me.
Now you all agree completely
1930   This lover feels much more pain
Than the lady; and in no way do I differ
            From this conclusion,
But support it firmly in every way and concur
That this lover is further from consolation
1935   Than this lady, may God console her.
            So I will judge
This case according to my understanding,
For in these matters I have no experience.

And truly another man, well I know it,
1940   Would do better.
I say this: in proper consideration
Of the opinion of Reason, here present,
And the arguments of you who are eager for justice,
            And of Loyalty,
1945   Who has spoken the pure truth in this matter
And does not resort to ruses or deception,
And also of Love, who has here argued skillfully,

         Et de Juenesse —
Que cils amans sueffre plus de tristesse,
1950   Et que li maus d'amours plus fort le blesse
Que la dame, ou moult a de noblesse,
         Et que plus long
Est de confort, dont il ont bon besoing.
Et pour ce di mon jugement et doing
1955   Qu'il a plus mal qu'elle n'a, plus de soing,
         Et de grevance."

Quant li bons rois ot rendu sa sentence,
Dont par Raison fu faite l'ordenance,
Li chevaliers iluec, en sa presence,
1960   L'en mercia,
Et, en pensant, la dame s'oublia
Si durement que nul mot dit n'i a.
Mais nompourquant en la fin ottria
         Qu'elle tenoit
1965   Le jugement que li rois fait avoit,
Car si sages et si loiaus estoit
Qu'envers nelui fors raison ne feroit.
         Adont li rois
En sousriant les a pris par les dois
1970   Et les assist seur le tapis norois,
Long des autres, si qu'il n'i ot qu'euls trois.
         Si leur enorte
Et deprie chascun qu'il se conforte,
Car se le cuer longuement tel mal porte,
1975   Il en porroit mors estre, et elle morte
         (Que ja n'aveingne!);
fol. 21v Mais chascuns d'eaus bon corage reprengne,
Car li cuers trop se destruit et mehaingne
Qui en tel plour et tel dolour se baingne;
1980   Et recorder
Voit on souvent qu'on doit tout oublier
Ce qu'on voit bien qu'on ne puet amender,
Ne recouvrer par pleindre ne plourer.
         S'einsi le font,
1985   Vers Loiauté, ce dit, pas ne meffont;
Mais s'en ce plour pour amer se meffont,
Homicides de leur ames se font
         Et de leur vie.
Aprés li rois appella sa maisnie;
1990   Si vint Franchise, Honneur, et Courtoisie,
Biauté, Desir, Leesse l'envoisie,
         Et Hardiesse,
Prouesse, Amour, Loiauté, et Largesse,

And of Youth —
That this lover suffers more sadness
1950 And love's pains wound him more grievously
Than they do the lady, in whom there is great nobility;
      And he is much further
From the consolation he truly needs.
And so I announce and render my judgment
1955 That he feels more hurt than she, more worry
      And distress."

After the good king offered his decision,
Whose logic had been proposed by Reason,
The knight thanked him there,
1960   In his presence,
And, lost in thought, the lady so forgot herself
She uttered nary a word.
Nonetheless in the end she granted
      She would accept
1965 The judgment the king rendered
Because he was so wise and loyal
He would do only right by everyone.
      Then the king,
Smiling, took them by the hand
1970 And seated them on the Norwegian rug
Far from the others, just the three of them.
      And he urged
And begged them both to take comfort,
For should the heart long bear such pain,
1975 He might die, and so could she,
      (May it never happen!);
Instead they should regain their senses,
For the heart destroys and harms itself greatly
Wallowing in such weeping and pain;
1980   And often repeated
Is the view that a man should forget
Whatever he cannot better
Or change by tears and lamentation.
      And, so doing,
1985 They should not sin against Loyalty, he said;
But crying so for love they did wrong,
Becoming the murderers of their own souls
      And lives.
Afterward the king summoned his court.
1990 So Liberality, Honor, and Courtesy,
Beauty, Desire, mirthful Happiness,
      And Hardihood,
Prowess, Love, Loyalty, and Generosity,

Voloir, Penser, Richesse, avec Juenesse,
1995   Et puis Raison, qui de tous fu maistresse.
         Si leur commande
Que chascuns d'eaus a honnourer entende
Ces .ij. amans, et qu'Amour leur deffende
Merencolie; aprés que la viande
2000   Soit aprestee,
Car il estoit ja pres de la vespree;
Et il ont fait son vueil sans demouree,
Com bonne gent et bien endoctrinee.
        Lors se sont trait
2005   Vers les amans, sans faire plus de plait,
Et chascuns d'eaus a son pooir a fait
Ce qu'il pense qui leur agree et plait,
        Qu'entalenté
En estoient de bonne volenté.
2010   Et li amant ont congié demandé,
Mais on leur a baudement refusé,
        Car Courtoisie,
Franchise, Honneur, et Largesse s'amie,
Li gentils rois, qui pas ne s'i oublie,
2015   Et chascuns d'eaus moult durement les prie
        De demourer.
Et il estoit pres heure de souper,
Et a ce mot on prist l'iaue a corner
Par le chastel, et forment a tromper;
2020   Si se leverent,
Et .ij. et .ij. en la sale en alerent;
Aprés leurs mains courtoisement laverent
Puis s'assirent, si burent et mengierent,
        Selonc raison,
2025   Car il y ot planté et a foison
De quanqu'on puet dire n'avoir de bon.
Aprés mengier, les prist par le giron
        Li gentils rois
Et si leur dist: "Vous n'en irez des mois,
2030   Car je vous vueil oster a ceste fois
Les pensees qui vous font moult d'anois."
        Le chevalier
Moult humblement l'en prist a mercïer,
Et aussi fist la dame qui targïer
2035   Ne pooit plus, ce dit, de repairier.
        Et finalment
Li rois les tint .viij. jours moult liement
Et au partir leur donna largement
Chevaus, harnois, joiaus, or, et argent.
2040   Si se partirent

Will, Thought, Wealth, along with Youth
1995 And then Reason, mistress over all, came forward.
   The king asked
That each strive to honor these two lovers
And Love should drive away melancholy
From them; and, afterward, a meal
2000   Be prepared,
For it was quite close to vespers.
And without delay they carried out his wishes
Like a retinue good and well instructed.
   They approached
2005 The lovers, offering no more debate,
And to the best of his ability each did
What he thought would please and suit them,
   For with good will
They were eager to do so.
2010 And the lovers asked for leave to go
But were adamantly refused,
   For Courtesy,
Liberality, Honor, and Generosity his friend,
The noble king, who did not forget himself at all,
2015 And everyone else quite fervently begged them
   To remain
Because it was nearly the dinner hour.
And as they talked, the call to wash sounded with horns
Throughout the castle accompanied by loud trumpeting;
2020   So the company
Rose and entered the hall two by two;
There they politely washed their hands
And sat down to eat and drink
   In moderation,
2025 For there was a great abundance
Of whatever one could request or have that is good.
After the meal, the noble king took them
   By the robe
And said to them: "You will not leave us for some time,
2030 Because my intention now is to free you
From those thoughts that so trouble you."
   The knight
Began to thank him quite humbly,
And likewise did the lady, who could delay
2035 No longer, she said, before returning.
   Yet in the end
The king lodged them eight days quite happily
And at their departure bestowed generously upon them
Horses, harness, jewels, gold, and silver.
2040   At the end of the eight days,

Au chief de .viij. jours et dou roy congié prirent,
Ou tant orent trouvé d'onneur qu'il dirent
Qu'eins si bon roy ne si gentil ne virent.
    Mais compaingnie
2045 Leur fist Honneur; aussi fist Courtoisie,
Juenesse, Amour, Richesse l'aaisie,
Et meint autre que nommer ne say mie.
    Car il monterent
Sus les chevaus et tant les convoierent
2050 Que chascun d'eaus en son hostel menerent,
Et puis au roy a Durbui retournerent.
    Ci fineray
Ma matiere, ne plus n'en rimeray,
Car autre part assez a rimer ay.
2055 Mais en la fin de ce livret feray
    Que qui savoir
Vorra mon nom et mon seurnom de voir,
Il le porra clerement percevoir
fol. 22r En darrein ver dou livret et veoir,
2060   Mais qu'il dessamble
Les premieres .vij. sillabes d'ensamble
Et les lettres d'autre guise rassamble,
Si que nulle n'en oublie ne emble.
    Einsi porra
2065 Mon nom savoir qui savoir le vorra,
Mais ja pour ce miex ne m'en prisera.
Et nompourquant ja pour ce ne sera
    Que je ne soie
Loiaus amis, jolis, et pleins de joie,
2070 Car se riens plus en ce monde n'avoie
Fors ce que j'aim ma dame simplet et quoie
    Contre son gré,
Si ay j'assez, qu'Amours m'a honnouré
Et richement mon mal guerredonné,
2075 Quant a ma dame einsi mon cuer donné
    Ay a tous jours.
Et ce mon cuer conforte en ses dolours
Que, quant premiers senti les maus d'amours,
A gentil mal cuide humble secours.

Explicit *le Jugement dou Roy de Behaingne.*

They parted, taking leave of the king,
In whom they found so much honor, so they said,
They had never seen a ruler this good or noble.
       And Honor
2045   Accompanied them, as did Courtesy,
Youth, Love, contented Wealth,
And many another I cannot name.
         For they mounted
Their horses and escorted them far enough
2050   To lead both back to their residences,
Afterward returning to the king at Durbuy.
        Here I intend to end
My account; I will rhyme no more,
For I have enough other matters to put in verse.
2055   But at the end of this book, I will see to it
        That anyone
Eager to learn my name and surname
Will be able to recognize them clearly
In the book's last verse, see them there.
2060   Let him simply remove
The first seven letters from the whole
And reassemble them in another fashion,
Neglecting or omitting none.
        In this way, whoever
2065   Wants to learn my name can do so,
Though he will not esteem me more.
Nevertheless, it will never happen
        I will not be
A lover loyal, pleasant, and full of mirth,
2070   For if in this world I possessed nothing
But loved my lady, humble and demure,
        Against her will,
Then I have enough, for Love has honored me
And richly rewarded my pain ever since
2075   I bestowed my heart upon my lady
        For all time.
What comforts my heart in its suffering
Is that when first I felt the pangs of love,
I expected a humble relief for a noble ill.

Here ends *The Judgment of the King of Bohemia.*

Figure 5. A12 (fol. 22v); *Ci aprés commence le Jugement dou Roy de Navarre contre le Jugement dou Roy de Behaigne* [Here begins the Judgment of the King of Navarre in response to the Judgment of the King of Bohemia]. Guillaume leans out the window of a castle. (Photo: BnF)

 ## LE JUGEMENT DOU ROY DE NAVARRE

fol. 22v   Au departir dou bel esté
             Qui a gais et jolis esté,
             De fleurs, de fueilles faillolez,
             Et d'arbrissiaus emmaillolez,
5   Arrousez de douce rousee,
             Sechiez par chaleur ordenee
             Que le soleil li amenistre,
             Et qu'oisillons ont leur chapitre
             Tenu de sons et de hoqués,
10   Par plains, par aunois, par bosqués,
             Pour li servir et honnourer
             Que tout ce couvient demourer
             Pour le temps qui, de sa nature,
             Mue sa chaleur en froidure
15   Un po aprés le temps d'autonne,
             Que chascuns vandange et antonne
             Qui a vingnes a vandangier,
             Et qu'on a a petit dangier
             Pesches, moust, poires, et roisins,
20   Dont on present a ses voisins,
             Que li blez en la terre germe
             Et que la fueille chiet dou cherme,
             Par nature, ou dou vent qui vente,
             L'an mil .ccc. nuef et quarente,
25   Le .ix^e. jour de novembre,
             M'en aloie par mi ma chambre.
             Et se li airs fust clers et purs,
             Je fusse ailleurs; mais si obscurs
             Estoit que montaingnes et pleins
30   Estoient de bruines pleins.

THE JUDGEMENT OF THE KING OF NAVARRE

At the passing of a beautiful summer
That had been pleasant and joyful,
Ornamented with flowers and leaves,
Adorned with shrubbery,
5   Drenched by sweet dew,
Dried by the seasonable heat
That the sun provided it,
A summer when the birds
Held their assemblies with song and hockets
10   Through meadows, arbors, and glades
In the season's service and honor
So all should linger
Despite the weather that, by its nature,
Changes summer's warmth into cold
15   A little after autumn comes,
When everyone who has vines to pick
Does his harvest and puts it into casks,
When, with little trouble, there is to be had
Drink made from peaches, must, pears, and grapes,
20   Which is shared with neighbors,
When the wheat sprouts in the ground
And the leaf falls from the oak
Because of nature or a gusting wind,
In the year thirteen hundred forty-nine,
25   On the ninth day of November,
I was walking about my room.
And had the air been clear and pure,
I'd have been elsewhere; but it was
So dark that the mountains and plains
30   Were full of haze.

Pour ce me tenoie a couvert
Quar ce qu'estre soloit tout vert
Estoit mué en autre teint,
Car bise l'avoit tout desteint,
35   Qui mainte fleur a decopee
Par la froidure de s'espee.

Si que la merencolioie
Tous seuls en ma chambre et pensoie
Comment par conseil de taverne
40   Li mondes par tout se gouverne;
Comment justice et verité
Sont mortes par l'iniquité
D'Advarice, qui en maint regne
Com dame souvereinne regne,
45   Com maistresse, comme roÿne
(Qu'Advarice engenre haïne,
Et largesse donne et rent gloire,
Vraiement, c'est parole voire,
Qu'on le scet et voit clerement
50   Par vray et juste experiment);
Comment nuls ne fait son devoir;
Comment chascuns quiert decevoir
Son proisme; car je ne voy pere,
Fil, ne fille, ne suer, ne frere,
55   Mere, marrastre, ne cousine,
Tante, oncle, voisin, ne voisine,
Mari, mouillier, amy, n'amie
Que li uns l'autre ne cunchie;
Et s'un en y a qui s'en garde,
60   Chascuns de travers le regarde
Et dist on qu'il est ypocrites,
Et fust sains Jehans li Ermites;
Come li signeur leur subgés pillent,
Roubent, raembent, et essilent,
65   Et mettent a destruction
Sans pitié ne compation,
Si que grans meschiés, ce me samble,
Est de vice et pooir ensamble.
Et on le voit assez de fait,
70   Ne riens tant cuer felon ne fait
Com grant pooir qui mal en use.
fol. 23r Or voy que chascuns en abuse,
Car je ne voy homme puissant
Qui n'ait puis .x., puis .xx., puis .c.
75   Tours, manieres, engiens, ou ars

And so I sheltered indoors.
For all that ordinarily was all green
Had been changed into another hue
Because the north wind had robbed everything of color,
35   Cutting down many a flower
With the coldness of its sword.

So there I suffered sadness
All alone in my room and thought
How the world in every way
40   Was ruled by barstool wisdom:
How justice and truth
Have been murdered by the iniquity
Of Greed, which in many realms
Rules as sovereign lady,
45   As mistress, as queen
(For Greed spawns hatred,
While Generosity gives, bestows glory;
Truly that's an irrefutable notion,
Which one can prove and clearly see
50   Through just and accurate experience);
How no one does his duty;
How everyone seeks to deceive
His neighbor, for I see no father
Or son, no daughter, sister, or brother,
55   No mother, stepmother, or cousin,
No aunt, uncle, or neighbor, man or woman,
No husband, wife, lover, or beloved
Such that one does not deceive the other,
And if anyone refrains from this,
60   Every man regards him suspiciously
And says he's a hypocrite,
Were he even St. John the Hermit;
How the lords pillage their subjects,
Rob, despoil, and mistreat them,
65   Put them all to death
Without pity or compassion
So that great misfortune, I think,
Comes from joining vice and power.
And one indeed often sees just this,
70   And nothing makes a heart so criminal
As great power when used for evil.
Now I witness everyone abusing it
Because I see no powerful man
Without ten, now twenty, now a hundred
75   Towers, troops, catapults, or arbalests

Pour pillier hardis et couars.
Car couvoitise les atrape,
Si que nuls de leurs mains n'eschape
S'il n'est dont tels qu'il n'ait que perdre.
80   A tels ne s'ont cure d'aerdre,
Car qui riens n'a, riens ne li chiet.
De tels gens riens ne leur eschiet,
Mais couvoiteus ont tel defaut
Que quant plus ont, plus leur deffaut,
85   Et quant plus sont puissant et riche,
Tant sont li plus aver et chiche
Qu'avarice ardant qui d'euls vist,
Com plus vivent, plus rajonnist.
Et de ce la vient la tempeste
90   Qui destruit le monde et tempeste,
Les merveilles et les fortunes
Qui au jour d'ui sont si communes
Qu'on n'oit de nulle part nouvelle
Qui soit aggreable ne belle;
95   Car il a plus grant difference
Dou temps que je vi en m'enfance
A cestui qui trop est divers
Qu'il n'ait des estés aus yvers.
Mais la chose qui plus me grieve
100   A souffrir, et qui plus m'est grieve,
C'est rendre a Dieu po reverence
Et ce qu'en riens n'a ordenance,
Et qu'au jour d'ui chascuns se pere
De ce qu'on claimme vitupere.
105   Pour ce en moy, plus que dire n'ose,
Estoit merencolie enclose.
Car qui le sceüst a demi
Assés meins en tenist de mi.

Et pour ce que merencolie
110   Esteint toute pensee lie,
Et aussi que je bien veoie
Que mettre conseil n'i povoie,
Et que, s'on sceüst mon muser,
On ne s'en feïst que ruser,
115   Laissay le merencolier
Et pris ailleurs a colier,
En pensant que se a Dieu plaisoit
Qui pour le milleur le faisoit.
Si cheï en autre pensee,
120   Pour ce que folie esprouvee
Est en tout homme qui se duet

To despoil brave men and cowards.
For avarice captures them
So no one escapes their grasp
Unless he's one of those with nothing to lose.
80   They have no desire to rob men like these,
For the man with nothing does not interest them.
Such men are never troubled,
But the greedy have a failing, which is that
The more they have, the more they want,
85   And the more powerfully rich they are,
They are that much more greedy and miserly,
For the burning avarice feeding on them
Grows younger the longer they live.
And from this comes the tempest
90   That destroys the world and rages on,
The strange events and misfortune
That today are so commonplace
No one hears news from anywhere
That might be agreeable or pleasant;
95   For there's a greater difference
Between the conditions I witnessed in my youth
And those that now are so unpleasant
Than there is between winter and summer.
But what grieves me more
100   To endure, and troubles me more too,
Is that God is accorded little reverence
And that there is no order to anything;
And today everyone ruins himself
With what is called vituperation.
105   Therefore, more than I dare say,
Melancholy had taken hold of me,
But whoever knew the half of it
Would think much less of me.

And because melancholy
110   Extinguishes every happy thought,
And also because I saw well
I could do nothing about this,
And because if anyone had discovered
My state of mind he'd only have mocked it,
115   I abandoned my sad meditations
And tried to concern myself with other matters,
Thinking that he pleases God
Who makes the best of things.
And then another thought occurred
120   To me because it is proven folly
For any man to be saddened

De chose qu'amender ne puet;
Et me pensai que se li temps
Estoit encore pires .x. temps,
125   Voire cent fois, voire cent mil,
N'i a il conseil si soutil
Comme de tout laissier ester,
Puis qu'on ne le puet contrester,
Et de faire selonc le sage
130   Qui dit et demoustre en sa page
Que, quant il a tout conceü,
Tout ymaginé, tout veü,
Esprouvé, serchié, viseté
Le monde, c'est tout vanité,
135   Et qu'il n'i a autre salaire
Fors d'estre liez et de bien faire.
Et tout einsi com je cuidoie
Laissier le penser ou j'estoie,
Il me sourvint une pensee
140   Plus diverse, plus effree,
Plus enuieuse la moitié
Et de plus grant merencolie.

Ce fu des orribles merveilles
Seur toutes autres despareilles
145   Dont homme puet avoir memoire,
Car je ne truis pas en histoire
Lisant nulles si mervilleuses,
Si dures, ne si perilleuses
De .iiij. pars, non de .x. temps
150   Comme elles ont esté de mon temps.
Car ce fu chose assez commune
Qu'on vit le soleil et la lune,
fol. 23v Les estoiles, le ciel, la terre,
En signefiance de guerre,
155   De doleurs, et de pestilences,
Faire signes et demoustrances.
Car chascuns pot veoir a l'ueil
De lune esclipce et de soleil
Plus grant et plus obscur assez
160   Qu'esté n'avoit mains ans passez,
Et perdre en signe de doleur
Longuement clarté et couleur.
Aussi fu l'estoile coumee
En samblance de feu couee
165   Qui de feu et d'occision
Faisoit prenostication.
Li ciel, qui de leur haut veoient

By something he cannot better;
And I determined that if the weather
Were even ten times worse,
125   Even a hundred times, or truly a hundred thousand,
There would be no counsel wiser
Than to let all this be
Since it cannot be changed,
And instead to act like the wise man
130   Who says and demonstrates in his writing
That, when he has considered everything,
Imagined everything, seen all there is,
Tested, examined, observed
The world, it is all vanity,
135   And there is no other course
But to be happy and do good.
And just as I was at the point of
Abandoning the reverie I was in,
A thought occurred to me
140   Even more bizarre and frightening,
More troubling by half
And much more filled with sadness.

This was of those horrible, uncanny events
Unlike the others
145   That anyone might remember,
Since in reading history I have not
Discovered any so unusual,
So hard to bear, or so threatening
By a fourth or even a tenth part
150   As these of my own time have been.
For it has been a rather common occurrence
That the sun and the moon, the stars,
The sky and earth have been seen
Displaying the signs of war,
155   Misery, and pestilence,
Offering tokens and manifestations,
For everyone could see with his own eyes
Eclipses of the moon and sun
Much fuller and darker
160   Than others had been for many years past,
And as a sign of misfortune these two bodies lost
For a long time their color and light.
Furthermore, there was a star with tresses
That seemed to be fire with a tail,
165   And it prognosticated
Murder and conflagration.
The heavens, which saw from their heights

Les meschiés qu'a venir estoient
Au monde, en pluseurs lieus plourerent
170   De pitié sanc et degouterent,
Si que de leur mervilleus plour
La terre trambla de paour
(Ce dient pluseurs qui ce virent)
Dont villes et citez fondirent
175   En Alemaingne, en Quarenteinne,
Assez plus d'une quaranteinne,
Dont je n'en say mie la somme.
Mais on le scet moult bien a Romme,
Car il y a une abeÿe
180   De Saint Pol qui en fu perie.
Mais li Sires qui tout a fait
Par experÿence de fait,
Com sires souvereins et dignes
Seur tous de ces mervilleus signes
185   Nous moustra la signefiance,
Et nous en mist hors de doubtance
Si a point et si proprement
Que chascuns le vit clerement.
Car les batailles et les guerres
190   Furent si grans par toutes terres
Qu'on ne savoit en tout le monde,
Tant comme il tient a la reonde,
Païs, regne, ne region,
Qu'il n'i heüst discention;
195   Dont .v.ᶜ mil hommes et femmes
Perdirent les corps et les ames
Se cils qui a tous biens s'acorde
Ne les prent a misericorde,
Et maint païs destruit en furent,
200   Dont encor les traces en durent.
Et des prises et des outrages
Et des occisions sauvages
De barons et de chevaliers,
De clers, de bourgois, d'escuiers,
205   Et de la povre gent menue
Qui morte y fu et confondue,
De rois, de duz, de bers, de contes
Seroit lons a faire li contes.
Car tant en y ot des perdus
210   Qu'on en estoit tous esperdus,
L'un par feu, l'autre par bataille.
Aprés ce, vint une merdaille
Fausse, traître, et renoïe:
Ce fu Judee la honnie,

The evil fortune to come
Into the world, wept in many places
170 And cried tears of blood from pity,
And because of the strange rain issuing from them,
The earth trembled with fear
(So said several who saw this),
Because of which villages and cities were destroyed
175 In Germany and Carinthia,
Somewhat more than forty altogether,
Although I cannot tell their exact number.
But the event is well known in Rome
Because an abbey there
180 Of St. Paul's was brought to ruin by it.
But the Lord who made everything
Through His direct intervention,
Like a sovereign gracious ruler
Over all things, showed us the meaning
185 Of these marvelous tokens
And dispelled our doubts
So directly and properly
That every man saw it clearly.
For the battles and the wars
190 Were so great throughout every land
That no one knew in all the world,
As much as it encompasses,
Any country, kingdom, or region
Where there was no strife;
195 For this reason five hundred thousand men and women
Would have lost their bodies and souls
If He who is in harmony with all good
Had not taken pity on them,
And many countries were destroyed by it,
200 And the results endure still.
The story would be long to tell
About captures and outrages,
The savage killings as well
Of noblemen and knights,
205 Of clerks, townspeople, squires,
And of poor people of little note
Who died as a result or were brought to ruin,
Of the kings, dukes, lords, and counts,
For so many of them perished in this way,
210 Some by fire, others in war,
That everyone was completely confounded by it.
After this appeared a group of scoundrels
Who were false, traitorous, and heretical:
This was shameful Judea,

215   La mauvaise, la desloyal,
       Qui het bien et aimme tout mal,
       Qui tant donna d'or et d'argent
       Et promist a crestienne gent
       Que puis, rivieres, et fonteinnes
220   Qui estoient cleres et seinnes
       En pluseurs lieus empoisonnerent,
       Dont pluseurs leurs vies finerent
       Car trestuit cil qui en usoient
       Asses soudeinnement mouroient
225   Dont, certes, par .x. fois cent mille
       En morurent, qu'a champ, qu'a ville
       Einsois que fust aperceüe
       Ceste mortel descouvenue.

       Mais cils qui haut siet et long voit,
230   Qui tout gouverne et tout pourvoit,
       Ceste traïson plus celer
       Ne volt, eins la fist reveler
fol. 24r Et si generaument savoir
       Qu'il perdirent corps et avoir.
235   Car tuit Juïf furent destruit,
       Li uns pendu, li autres cuit,
       L'autre noié, l'autre ot copee
       La teste de hache ou d'espee.
       Et meint crestien ensement
240   En morurent honteusement.

       En ce temps vint une maisnie
       De par leur dame Ypocrisie
       Qui de courgies se batoient
       Et adens se crucefioient
245   En chantant de la lopinelle
       Ne say quelle chanson nouvelle,
       Et valoient miex par leurs dis
       Que sains qui soit en paradis.
       Mais l'Eglise les entendi
250   Qui le batre leur deffendi,
       Et si condempna leur chanson
       Que chantoient li enfançon,
       Et tous les escommenia
       Dou pooir que Diex donné li a,
255   Pour itant que leur baterie
       Et leurs chans estoit herisie.

       Et quant Nature vit ce fait
       Que son oeuvre einsi se desfait,

215   The evil, the disloyal,
      Who hate good and love evil of all kinds,
      Who gave and promised so much
      Gold and silver to the Christian people
      That they in many places
220   Poisoned the wells, streams, and fountains
      That had been clear and healthy,
      And so many lost their lives
      Because all who used them
      Died quite suddenly, and in this way
225   Ten times a hundred thousand certainly
      Perished in the countryside and towns as well
      Before this deadly affliction
      Was taken notice of.

      But He who sits on high and sees far,
230   Who governs everyone and provides all things,
      Did not wish for this treason
      To be hidden any longer; instead He revealed
      And made it known so widely
      They lost their lives and goods.
235   For all the Jews were put to death,
      Some hanged, others burned alive,
      One drowned, another beheaded
      By the axe's blade or sword,
      And likewise many Christians
240   Died a shameful death because of this.

      At this time a company came together
      At the urging of Hypocrisy, their lady,
      And these people beat themselves with whips
      And crucified themselves flat on the ground
245   While singing to a catchy tune
      Some new song or other;
      And according to them they were worthier
      Than any saint in Paradise.
      But the Church dealt with them
250   By forbidding them to whip themselves
      And condemning their song,
      Which little children were singing,
      And by excommunicating all of them
      Through the power granted it by God
255   Because their self-abuse
      And song were heresy.

      And when Nature saw what was happening,
      That her work was in these ways destroying itself

       Et que li homme se tuoient
260   Et les yaues empoisonnoient
       Pour destruire humeinne lignie
       Par couvoitise et par envie,
       Moult en desplut la belle et gente,
       Moult se coursa, moult fu dolente.
265   Lors s'en ala sans atargier
       A Jupiter et fist forgier
       Foudres, tonnoirres, et tempestes
       Par jours ouvrables et par festes.
       Car ceste ouevre tant li tardoit
270   Que jour ne feste n'i gardoit.

       Aprés Nature commanda
       Aus .iiij. vens qu'elle manda
       Que chascuns fust aparilliés
       Pour tost courir, et abilliés,
275   Et qu'il issent de leurs cavernes
       Et facent leurs mervilleus cernes,
       Si qu'il n'i ait resne tenue,
       En ciel, en terre, er mer, n'en nue,
       Qu'il ne soient a l'air contraire;
280   Et facent pis qu'il porront faire.
       Car quant ses ouevres voit derompre,
       Elle vuet aussi l'air corrumpre.
       Et quant li vent orent congié,
       Et Jupiter ot tout forgié,
285   Foudres, tempestes, et espars,
       Qui lors veïst de toutes pars
       Espartir mervilleusement
       Et tonner tres horriblement,
       Vanter, gresler, et fort plouvoir,
290   Les nues, la mer esmouvoir,
       Bois trambler, rivieres courir,
       Et, pour doubtance de morir,
       Tout ce qui a vie seur terre
       Recept pour li garentir querre.
295   C'estoit chose trop mervilleuse,
       Trop doubtable et trop perilleuse.
       Car les pierres dou ciel cheoient
       Pour tuer quanqu'elles ataingnoient,
       Les hommes, les bestes, les fames;
300   Et en pluseurs lieus a grans flames
       Cheirent li temps et la foudre
       Qui mainte ville mist en poudre;
       N'au monde n'avoit si hardi
       Qui n'eüst cuer acouardi;

And men were killing each other
260   And poisoning the waters
In order to annihilate the human race
Because of greed and envy,
She, beautiful and noble, was much displeased,
Quite vexed, greatly pained.
265   So she made her way without delay
To Jupiter and had forged
Lightning, thunder, and storms
On working days and feasts.
Because she was so eager for the task,
270   She paid no mind to either weekday or holiday.

Afterward Nature ordered
The four winds over which she had command:
That each should make ready
And prepare to race off
275   And issue from their caverns
To give rise to raging cyclones
So that there should be no king's realm,
Nowhere in heaven, the earth, sea, or clouds
Where the air would not be troubled;
280   And they should do the worst they could.
For when she saw her works destroyed,
She wished the air corrupted as well.
And when the winds had taken their leave
And Jupiter had forged everything,
285   Lightning, storms, and turbulence,
Then one might have seen them
Marvelously disperse in all directions
And thunder quite horribly,
Blow in gusts, let fall hail and rain in torrents,
290   Disturb the clouds, the sea,
Shake the woods, make the rivers flood,
And force all things that live
On the earth to seek shelter
To save themselves because they feared death.
295   This turn of events was quite remarkable,
Terrifying, and filled with peril!
For stones fell from the sky,
Killing whatever they touched,
Men, beasts, women;
300   And in many places lightning and tempests
Descended with great flames
And turned a multitude of villages into dust;
Nor was there anyone in the world so brave
Who didn't then have a coward's heart;

305 Car il sambloit que decliner
   Vosist li mondes et finer.
   Mais nuls endurer ne peüst,
   S'auques durer cils temps deüst.
   Si que ces tempestes cesserent,
310 Mais tels bruïnes engendrerent,
   Tels ordures et tels fumees
   Qui ne furent gaires amees;
fol. 24v Car l'air qui estoit nés et purs
   Fu ors et vils, noirs, et obscurs,
315 Lais et puans, troubles et pus,
   Si qu'il devint tous corrompus;
   Si que de sa corruption
   Eürent les gens opinion
   Que corrumpu en devenoient
320 Et que leur couleur en perdoient.
   Car tuit estoient mal traitié,
   Descoulouré, et deshaitié:
   Boces avoient et grans clos
   Dont on moroit, et a briés mos,
325 Po osoient a l'air aler
   Ne de pres ensamble parler,
   Car leurs corrumpues alainnes
   Corrompoient les autres sainnes.
   Et s'aucuns malades estoit,
330 S'uns siens amis le visetoit,
   Il estoit en pareil peril
   Dont il en morut .v.ᶜ mil
   Si que li fils failloit au pere,
   La fille failloit a la mere,
335 La mere au fil et a la fille
   Pour doubtance de la morille.
   N'il n estoit nuls si vrais amis,
   Qui ne fust adont arrier mis
   Et qui n'eüst petit d'aïe,
340 S'il fust cheüs en maladie.
   Ne fusicien n'estoit, ne mire
   Qui bien sceüst la cause dire
   Dont ce venoit, ne que c'estoit
   (Ne nuls remede n'i metoit)
345 Fors tant que c'estoit maladie
   Qu'on appelloit epydimie.

   Quant Dieus vit de sa mansion
   Dou monde la corruption
   Qui tout partout estoit si grans
350 N'est merveilles s'il fu engrans

305   For it seemed that the world
     Was about to fall into ruin and end.
     But no one could have survived
     Had this weather lasted long,
     And so these storms came to an end,
310   But they gave rise to such haze,
     Such filth, and such vapors
     As were hardly loved;
     For the air that had been clear and pure
     Was now vile, black, and cloudy,
315   Horrible and fetid, putrefied and infected;
     And so it became completely corrupted;
     And about this corruption
     Men held the view
     It was corrupting them in turn
320   And they were thus losing their health.
     For everyone was badly afflicted,
     Discolored, and made ill;
     People had buboes and large swellings
     From which they died, and, to be brief,
325   Few dared to venture into the open air
     Or talk at close quarters with one another
     Because their infected breath
     Corrupted others who were healthy.
     And if anyone fell ill,
330   And some friend visited him,
     That man faced the same peril
     From which five hundred thousand died
     So that father failed son,
     Mother failed daughter,
335   Son and daughter failed mother
     From fear of this plague;
     And no one was so true a friend
     He was not thereupon ignored,
     The recipient of little help
340   If he fell ill with the disease.
     And there was no physician or healer
     Who knew enough to name the cause
     Of its appearance, or even what it was
     (And none of them applied any remedy),
345   Beyond that this was a disease
     One called an epidemic.

     When from His house God saw
     That the corruption in the world
     Was this great everywhere,
350   It is no wonder He was eager

De penre crueuse vengence
De ceste grant desordenance;
Si que tantost, sans plus attendre,
Pour justice et vengence prendre,
355   Fist la mort issir de sa cage,
Pleinne de forsen et de rage,
Sans frein, sans bride, sans loien,
Sans foy, sans amour, sans moien,
Si tres fiere et si orguilleuse,
360   Si gloute et si familleuse
Que ne se pooit saouler
Pour riens que peüst engouler.
Et par tout le munde couroit,
Tout tuoit and tout acouroit
365   Quanqu'il li venoit a l'encontre,
N'on ne pooit resister contre.
Et briefment tant en acoura,
Tant en occist et devoura,
Q'tous les jours a grans monceaus
370   Trouvoit on dames, jouvenceaus,
Juenes, viels, et de toutes guises
Gisans mors parmi les eglises;
Et les gettoit on en grans fosses
Tous ensamble, et tous mors de boces,
375   Car on trouvoit les cimatieres
Si pleinnes de corps et de bieres
Qu'il couvint faire des nouvelles.
Ci a mervilleuses nouvelles.
Et si ot meinte bonne ville
380   Qu'on n'i veoit, ne fil, ne fille,
Femme, në homme venir n'aler,
N'on n'i trouvoit a qui parler,
Pour ce qu'il estoient tuit mort
De celle mervilleuse mort.
385   Et ne gisoient que .iij. jours
Ou meins; c'estoit petis sejours.
Et maint en y ot vraiement
Qui mouroient soudeinnement;
Car ceuls meïsmes qui les portoient
390   Au moustier pas ne revenoient
(Souvent la vit on avenir),
Eins les couvenoit la morir.
fol. 25r   Et qui se vorroit entremettre
De savoir ou d'en escript mettre
395   Le nombre de ceuls qui moururent,
Tous ceuls qui sunt et ceuls qui furent
Et tous ceuls qui sont a venir

To take a cruel revenge
For the great disorder;
And so at once, waiting no longer,
In order to have His justice and vengeance,
355   From his cage He released Death,
Full of rage and anger
And lacked any check, bridle, or rein,
Any faith, love, or moderation,
So very proud and arrogant he was,
360   So gluttonous and famished
He could not be satisfied
By anything he could consume.
And he hastened throughout the world,
Killing and running down one and all,
365   Whomever he chanced upon,
Nor could he be resisted.
And, in short, he undid so many,
Struck down and devoured so great a multitude
That every day could be found
370   Huge heaps of women, youths,
Boys, old people, those of all degrees,
Lying dead inside the churches;
And they were thrown together
In great trenches, all dead from the buboes.
375   Because the cemeteries were found to be
So full of corpses and biers
It was necessary to lay out new ones.
These were strange new tidings.
And so there was many a fine town
380   Where no boy or girl, no man or woman
Was seen to come and go,
Nor was anyone found there to talk to
Because all of them had died
This unbelievable death.
385   And they lay ill no more than three days,
Sometimes less; the time was short.
And there were certainly many
Who died of it suddenly;
For those same men who bore them
390   To the church did not return
(This was often witnessed),
But instead were to die right there.
And whoever wished to undertake
Discovering or putting down in writing
395   The number of those who died,
Those who are still here and once were,
And all those to come,

Jamais n'i porroient venir,
Tant s'en sceüssent encombrer;
400   Car nuls ne les porroit nombrer,
Ymaginer, penser, ne dire,
Figurer, moustrer, ne escrire.
Car pluseurs fois certeinnement
Oÿ dire et communement
405   Que, mil .ccc. .xlix.,
De cent n'en demorroit que nuef,
Dont on vit par deffaut de gent
Que maint bel heritage et gent
Demouroient a labourer.
410   Nuls ne faisoit les chans arer,
Les blez soier, ne vingnes faire.
Qui en donnast triple salaire,
Non, certes, pour .i. denier vint
Tant estoient mort; et s'avint
415   Que par les champs les bestes mues
Gisoient toutes esperdues,
Es blez et es vingnes paissoient,
Tout partout ou elles voloient,
N'avoient signeur, ne pastour,
420   Ne homme qui leur alast entour,
N'estoit nuls qui les reclamast,
Ne qui pour siennes les clamast.
Heritages y ot pluseurs
Q'demouroient sans signeurs;
425   Ne li vif n'osoient manoir
Nullement dedens le manoir
Ou li mort avoient esté.
Fust en yver, fust en esté;
Et s'aucuns fust qui le feïst,
430   En peril de mort se meïst.
Et quant je vi ces aventures
Si diverses et si obscures,
Je ne fui mie si hardis
Que moult ne fusse acouardis.
435   Car tuit li plus hardi trambloient
De paour de mort qu'il avoient.
Si que tres bien me confessai
De tous les pechiez que fais ay
Et me mis en estat de grace
440   Pour recevoir mort en la place,
S'il pleüst a Nostre Signeur.
Si qu'en doubtance et en cremeur
Dedens ma maison m'enfermay
Et en ma pensee fermay

Never would he be able to compass it,
However hard he might labor.
400   For no one could count them,
Imagine, conceive, or tell of them,
Compute, make known, or record them.
And, to be sure, many times
I have heard it said and openly
405   That in thirteen hundred and forty-nine,
Only nine survived of every hundred,
And so one saw that, because people were lacking,
Many a fine, noble estate
Lay idle without those to work it.
410   No man had his fields plowed,
His grain sowed, or his vines tended
Though he'd have paid out triple wages,
No surely, not even for twenty times the rate,
Because so many had died; and thus it happened
415   The cattle lay about
The fields completely abandoned,
Grazing in the corn and among the grapes,
Anywhere at all they liked,
And they had no master, no cowherd,
420   No man at all to round them up;
And there wasn't anyone who might call them back,
No one to claim them as his own.
There were many estates
That remained without owners;
425   Nor did the living dare to stay
Any time at all inside the houses
Where the dead had been
Either in winter or summer.
And if anyone did so,
430   He himself then risked dying.
And when I witnessed these events
That were so strange and ominous,
I was not at all so brave
I did not become quite cowardly.
435   For all the most courageous trembled
From the fear of death that overcame them,
And so I quite thoroughly confessed myself
Of all the sins I had committed,
Putting myself into a state of grace
440   In order to accept death where I was
If it should please Our Lord.
Therefore with uncertainty and fear,
I closed myself up inside the house
And determined resolutely

445 Fermement que n'en partiroie
  Jusques a tant que je saroie
  A quel fin ce porroit venir;
  Si lairoie Dieu couvenir.
  Si que lonc temps, se Diex me voie,
450 Fui einsi que petit savoie
  De ce qu'on faisoit en la ville,
  Et s'en morut plus de .xx. mille,
  Cependant que je ne sceüs mie,
  Dont j'eüs meins de merencolie.
455 Car riens n'en voloie savoir,
  Pour meins de pensees avoir,
  Comment qu'assés de mes amis
  Fussent mors et en terre mis.

  Si qu'einsi fui lonc temps en mue,
460 Si comme un esprevier qu'on mue,
  Et tant qu'une fois entroÿ
  (Dont moult forment me resjoÿ)
  Cornemuses, trompes, naquaires,
  Et d'instrumens plus de .vij. paires.
465 Lors me mis a une fenestre
  Et enquis que ce pooit estre;
  Si que tantost me respondi
  Uns miens amis qui m'entendi
  Que ceuls qui demouré estoient
470 Einsi com tuit se marioient
  Et faisoient festes et noces.
  Car la mortalité des boces
fol. 25v Qu'on appelloit epydimie
  Estoit de tous poins estanchie;
475 Et que les gens plus ne moroient.
  Et quant je vi qu'il festioient
  A bonne chiere et liement
  Et tout aussi joliement
  Com s'il n'eüssent riens perdu,
480 Je n'os mie cuer esperdu,
  Eins repris tantost ma maniere
  Et ouvri mes yex et ma chiere
  Devers l'air qui si dous estoit
  Et si clers qu'il m'amonnestoit
485 Que lors ississe de prison
  Ou j'avoie esté la saison.
  Lors fui hors d'esmay et d'effroy,
  Se montai seur mon palefroy
  Grisart, qui portoit l'ambleüre
490 Moult souëf et de sa nature

445 In my mind I'd not leave
  Until the time when I should learn
  What conclusion this might come to;
  And I would leave it for God to decide.
  And so for a long time, may God help me,
450 There I remained, knowing little
  Of what was happening in the city,
  And there more than twenty thousand died,
  Though of this I knew nothing
  And so felt less sadness;
455 For I did not wish to know anything
  So that my sorrows would be fewer,
  Even though many of my friends
  Had died and been put in the ground.

  And so I remained long in hiding,
460 Just like a hawk in moult,
  Until at last one time I heard
  (Which made me greatly rejoice)
  Bagpipes, trumpets, kettledrums,
  And more than seven pairs of instruments.
465 Then I went to a window
  And asked what this might be,
  And at once one of my friends
  Who had heard me answered
  That those who remained were acting
470 Just as if all of them were getting married,
  Feasting, and celebrating weddings.
  For the deadly plague of the buboes
  That was called an epidemic
  Had completely ceased everywhere;
475 And people were no longer dying.
  And when I saw them celebrating
  Joyfully and with good cheer,
  And all just as merrily
  As if they had lost nothing,
480 I wasn't troubled in the least,
  But regained at once my composure,
  Turning my eyes and face
  To the air that was so sweet
  And clear it encouraged me
485 Then to leave the prison
  Where I had passed the season.
  At that moment, I was beyond grief and worry,
  And I mounted on my palfrey,
  Grisart, who moved at a pace
490 Quite calm, as was his nature.

S'alay aus champs isnellement
Chevauchier par esbatement,
Pour moy jouer et soulacier
Et la douceur a moy lacier
495   Qui vient de pais et de deduit
Ou cuers volentiers se deduit
Qui n'a cure de cusenson
Qui touche a noise, n'a tenson,
Mais bien vorroit cusensonner
500   Ad ce qui puet honneur donner.
En celle cusençon estoie
Pour honneur a quoi je tendoie.
Cusençon avoie et desir
Que je peüsse, a mon loisir,
505   Aucuns lievres a point sousprendre,
Par quoy je les peüsse prendre.
Or porroit aucuns enquester
Se c'est honneur de levreter.
A ce point ci responderoie
510   Que c'est honneur, solas, et joie;
C'est uns fais que noblesse prise,
Qui est de gracïeuse emprise,
Et tres honneste a commencier,
Dont il s'en fait bel avencier;
515   S'est en faisant plaisans a faire,
Et li honneurs gist ou parfaire,
Dont en celle perfection
Avoie si m'entention
Qu'a autre chose ne pensoie.
520   Et li bon levrier que j'avoie
Renforçoient si mon solas
Que je n'en peüsse estre las
Quant le les os mis en conroy,
Et je les vi de tel arroy
525   De courir a point sus les chans,
Et puis des oisillons les chans
Qui estoient melodïeus,
Et li airs dou temps gracïeus
Qui tout le corps m'adoucissoit.
530   On puet bien croire qu'einsi soit
Q'se pluseurs gens chevauchassent,
A fin que point ne m'araisnassent,
Et aucuns bien en congneüsse,
Que ja ne m'en aperceüsse,
535   Tant y avoie mis ma cure.
Se m'en avint une aventure
Qui me fu un petit doubteuse,

And I went quickly to the fields
In order to ride for pleasure,
To entertain and solace myself,
And to claim as my own the sweetness
495   That comes from the peace and from the enjoyment
In which the heart willingly delights
That feels no concern for the pain
Arising from either trouble or strife,
But would instead pursue
500   Whatever might bestow honor.
I was very excited about
The honorable thing I was bent on.
I had the desire and the urge
(If, in my good time, I could manage it)
505   To catch some hares by surprise
And then be able to hunt them down.
Now, someone might ask
If hare hunting is honorable.
My answer to this question would be
510   That it's an honor, diversion, and delight;
It's a sport that the nobility value,
Something of a gracious enterprise
And quite advantageous to undertake
Because it improves one nicely;
515   Certainly, the activity itself is pleasant enough,
And honor comes with accomplishing it,
So at this time I had so directed
My attention toward that end
And was thinking of nothing else.
520   And the good hare hounds I had
So multiplied my enjoyment
I could not have felt weary
After releasing them
And watching them run off
525   Just so in a pack across the fields,
And then there were the songs
Of birds, lovely to hear,
As well as the air of the mild weather
Soothing my whole body.
530   One could easily believe that if
Some people were to ride up
So that they might speak to me,
Even if I should benefit thereby,
I should indeed not notice,
535   So much had I to this sport devoted my attention.
It was then that an adventure befell me
Which frightened me somewhat,

        Mais briefment me fu gracïeuse,
        Si comme tantost le diray
540   Ci aprés; point n'en mentiray.

        Tandis que la m'esbanioie
        Que en moy oublié avoie
        Toutes autres merencoliés,
        Tant les dolentes, com les liés,
545   Une dame de grant noblesse,
        Bien acesmee de richesse,
        Venoit a belle compaingnie.
        Mais je ne les veoie mie,
        Car dou chemin estoie arriere,
550   Et, d'autre part, pour la maniere
        De ce que j'estoie entendus
        Et tous mes engins estendus
fol. 26r A ma queste tout seulement.
        Mais la dame premierement
555   Me vit eins que nuls me veïst,
        Ne que nuls samblant en feïst,
        C'est assavoir d'ycelle gent
        Qui conduisoient son corps gent.
        Lors .i. escuier appella
560   Et li dist: "Vois tu celui la
        Qui bel se deduit et deporte?
        Va a lui et si me raporte
        Qui il est, et revien en l'eure
        Sans la faire point de demeure."
565   Li escuiers n'en failli pas,
        Eins vint a moy plus que le pas
        Et hautement me salua.
        Mes propos de riens n'en mua.
        Si li dis: "Bien veingniés, biau sire."
570   S'il s'en retourna, sans plus dire,
        Au plus tost qu'il pot a la dame:
        "Dame," dist cils, "Foi que doi m'ame,
        C'est la Guillaumes de Machaut.
        Et sachiez bien qu'il ne li chaut
575   De riens fors que de ce qu'il chace,
        Tant est entendus a sa chace.
        Bien croy qu'il n'entent a nelui
        Fors qu'a ses levriers et a lui."

        Quant la dame ces mos oÿ,
580   Samblant fist de cuer esjoÿ,
        Nom pas samblant tant seulement,
        Mais de fait enterinement,

Yet quickly became pleasant enough,
Just as I will relate immediately
540   Hereafter; I'll not lie about it at all.

While I was disporting myself there —
I who had forgotten all
Those other melancholic thoughts,
As much the sad as the pleasant ones —
545   A lady of great nobility,
Nicely decked out with rich clothes,
Appeared with a beautiful company.
Yet I didn't see them at all
Because I was back from the road
550   And, moreover, because of how
I was attending to
And had concentrated all my attention on
My hunting alone;
But the lady was the first to take notice
555   Of me before anyone else spied me there
Or before anyone made a sign of doing so,
That is, from among the company
Escorting her noble person.
Then she summoned a squire
560   And said to him: "Do you see that man there
Pleasantly disporting and enjoying himself?
Go to him and then report to me
Who he is, and return quickly
Without delaying there at all."
565   At this the squire did not fail,
But came to me in some haste
And loudly said hello.
I didn't stop what I was doing,
And I said to him: "You're welcome, fair sir."
570   He returned, without saying any more,
As fast as he could to the lady:
"Lady," he said, "By the faith I owe my soul,
That's Guillaume de Machaut over there.
Know well that nothing interests him
575   Save what he is pursuing.
He is so involved with his hunting
I believe firmly he has no time for anything but
His hounds and himself."

When the lady heard these words,
580   She seemed to rejoice at heart,
And this was no simple outward show,
But the absolute truth,

De cuer joiant, a chiere lie,
Comme dame gaie et jolie.
585   Nom pourquant, ce ne di je point;
Eins y avoit .i. autre point,
Pour aucune cause certeinne
Dont sa volenté estoit pleinne.
Si le me voloit pronuncier
590   Pour li deduire et soulacier
Et moy mettre en merencolie.
A ce point ne failli je mie,
Car je fui de li galïes,
Ramposnes, et contralïez,
595   Aussi com se j'eüsse fait
Encontre li un grant meffait.

Quant li escuiers ot compté
De moy toute sa volenté,
La dame dist tout hautement:
600   "Or veons .i. petit, comment
Guillaumes est faitis et cointes.
Il m'est avis qu'il soit acointes
De trestoute jolieté
Apartenant a honnesté.
605   De nuit, en estudiant, veille,
Et puis de jours son corps traveille
En travail ou li bons s'atire
Qui a honneur traveille et tire.
Einsi va son corps deduisant
610   Toutes heures en bien faisant.
Si fais estas donne couleur
De maintenir homme en valeur.
Mais je li osterai briefment
Grant part de son esbatement,
615   Car je li donrai a ruser,
Pour li bonne piece muser.
Lonc temps a que je le desir:
S'en acomplirai mon desir.

Or t'en reva a li tantost,
620   Car je me merveil qui li tost
A ci venir. Si li diras
Par plus briés mos que tu porras
Qu'il veingne ci apertement.
Et se li di hardiement
625   Que ce soit sans querir essoingnes,
Non contrestant toutes besongnes,
Et que c'est a mon mandement."

Because her heart was joyful, her manner happy,
Like a woman gay and merry,
585   Not for my sake, I don't mean that at all,
But rather for another reason entirely,
Because of a particular matter
In which she took much interest.
And she was eager to bring to my attention
590   In order to delight and entertain herself
And, in turn, to sink me into melancholy.
This I did not fail to do,
For I was mocked by her,
Reproached and contradicted
595   Just as if I had sinned
Quite grievously against the woman.

After the squire related
All he wished about me,
The lady said in a loud voice:
600   "Now let's see just how
Agreeable and sharp Guillaume is.
As far as I know, he is knowledgeable
About all kinds of merriment
According with morality.
605   By night, he stays awake studying,
And then by day he labors his body
With the work the good man looks for,
Who seeks what brings and confers honor;
And so he goes around amusing himself
610   At all times by doing what is proper.
Such activities do cultivate the demeanor
To maintain a man in worthiness.
But shortly I will take from him
A large part of his enjoyment
615   Because I will have some fun at his expense
That will puzzle the man a good while.
I have been eager to do that for a long time;
So in this fashion I will fulfill my wish.

Now return to him as fast as possible
620   Because I am quite anxious
He be brought over here. So tell the man
In as few words as you can manage
To proceed here directly.
And say to him firmly
625   It must be with no excuse
And no matter what other business he has,
And it is at my command."

   "Dame, a vostre commandement,"
   Dist li escuiers, "Sans nul 'si,'
630 Je li vois dire tout einsi
   Com vous dites, ou au plus pres
   Que je porrai; j'en sui tous pres."

fol. 26v Lors li escuiers chevaucha
   Devers moy tant qu'il m'aprocha.
635 Et quant il me vint aprochant,
   Il m'appella en chevauchant,
   En galopant d'uns pas menuz
   Tant qu'il fu pres de moy venuz.
   Et si tost com j'oÿ sa vois,
640 Erraument devers lui m'en vois
   Car de lonc temps le congnoissoie.
   Et il, en signe de grant joie,
   Me salua de Dieu le pere
   Et de sa douce chiere mere.
645 Et je li respondi briefment
   En saluant courtoisement.
   Puis li demanday quels nouvelles
   Pour moy seront bonnes et belles,
   Se ma dame est preus et haitie,
650 En pais, sans estre courrecie.
   "Guillaume, de riens n'en doubtez,
   Car ma dame est de tous costez
   En pais, preus, et haitie, et seinne;
   Et que ce soit chose certeinne,
655 Assez tost savoir le porrez,
   Selonc ce que dire m'orrez.
   Il est bien voirs qu'elle vous mande,
   Nom pas qu'elle le vous commande,
   Mais d'un mandement par tel guise
660 Qu'il vaut auques pres commandise;
   Non prier et non commander.
   Einsi li plaist il a mander,
   Entre le vert et le meür.
   Mais tenez ceci pour seür:
665 Que c'est bien de s'entention
   Que, sans point d'excusation,
   Venrez a li moult liement;
   Elle le croit fiablement,
   Dont, s'il vous plaist, vous y venrez,
670 Ou vo plaisir responderez."

   Aprés ces mos li respondi:
   "Tres chiers amis, ytant vous di

"Lady, as you order,"
Said the squire, "Without any 'but,'
630   I will go tell him just what
You have said, or as close to it as
I am able; I am quite ready to do this."

Then the squire rode off
In my direction until he approached me
635   And as he drew near,
He called out to me while still riding,
Galloping at a quick pace
Until he came fairly close.
And as soon as I heard his voice,
640   I quickly went toward him
Because I had known the man a long time.
And as a token of his great joy,
He saluted me by God the Father
And by His sweet dear mother.
645   And I responded at once,
Greeting him courteously.
Then I inquired what news,
Good and pleasing, there might be for me,
If my lady were hale and happy,
650   At peace, not annoyed by anything.
"Guillaume, have no fear at all
Because my lady is in every way
At peace, in good health, happy, and well;
And that this is certain
655   You will be able to learn rather quickly
From what you'll hear me say.
For it's quite true she summons you,
Not really commanding you to go to her
But asking in such a fashion
660   It counts the same as an order,
Neither begging nor commanding.
Instead it pleases her to request,
Somewhere between 'green' and 'ripe.'
Yet mark this point for certain:
665   It is her intention beyond any doubt
For you to come to her willingly
Making no excuses;
She trusts you will do so,
And thus, if you please, you'll go to her
670   And there express your pleasure."

After these words, I answered him:
"My very dear friend, this much I will tell you,

Qu'a ma dame, ne quars, ne tiers
Ne sui, mais mes pooirs entiers
675   Est tous siens, sans riens retenir.
Se ne me porroie tenir
D'aler a li, ne ne vorroie,
Pour tant que de vray sentiroie
Que ma dame le penseroit.
680   Dont quant elle me manderoit,
Ce seroit bien folie a croire
Que point en vosisse recroire.
Mais un po vous vueil demander,
Afin qu'il n'i ait qu'amender:
685   Combien ma dame est loin de ci?"
"Guillaume, je respon einsi:
Qu'il n'i a pas bien trois journees.
Bel soient elles adjournees!"
Dis je: "Or alons sans sejour,
690   Si chevauchons et nuit et jour
Pour les bons ma dame acomplir.
Je ne me puis miex raemplir
De joie que son plaisir faire;
Se n'useray point dou contraire."

695   "Guillaume, j'ay bien entendu
Ce que vous avez respondu.
Je vous vueil un po apaisier
D'autre chose que de baisier.
Resgardez en celle grant pleinne
700   Un po dela celle versainne:
C'est ma dame a grant chevauchie
Qui pour vous s'est la adressie.
La vous atent, soiez certeins.
Or ne soit point vostres cuers teins
705   De paour pour trop loing aler;
Car la porrez a li parler."
A ces mos ma chiere dressay,
Et puis mon regart adressay
D'icelle part ou cils disoit.
710   Et quant je vi qu'einsi gisoit,
Que mes chemins yert acourciez,
Je n'en fui mie courreciez,
fol. 27r   Eins en fui liez; s'en pris a rire,
Et puis a celui pris a dire:
715   "Biaus amis, par merencolie
M'avez tenté de moquerie,
De bourde, et de parole voire,
Quant vous me donnastes a croire

Regarding my lady, neither a fourth nor even a third
Of what I am, but my entire being
675 Is completely hers, with nothing held back.
And I could not restrain myself
From going to her, nor would wish to,
Inasmuch as I would truly sense
What my lady would think about it.
680 And so when she sends for me,
It would surely be madness to believe
I would ever think twice about it.
But I do want to ask you about a small point,
Just so there will be nothing to remedy:
685 How far is my lady from this spot?"
"Guillaume, here is my answer:
It is not quite three days' travel.
And may those days dawn brightly!"
I said: "Let us go on now without delay,
690 And let us ride night and day
To do what is good for my lady.
I cannot better replenish myself
With joy than by doing her pleasure;
And so I will offer no resistance at all."

695 "Guillaume, I have listened attentively
To what you've said in response.
And I would like to appease you a little
With something other than a kiss.
Look toward the broad clearing
700 A bit below that fallow field:
That's my lady with a great troop,
And she has drawn herself up there for your sake.
At that spot she attends you; be certain of it.
Now let your heart be not at all troubled
705 By any fear of having to travel too far
Because you can speak to her over there."
At these words, my face brightened,
And I turned my eyes toward
The place he had indicated.
710 And when I saw her waiting there,
That my journey was shortened,
I was scarcely annoyed,
But pleased instead; and I began to laugh
And started to say to him:
715 "Good friend, you have nearly made me
Melancholy with your jokes,
Your trickery, and your true words
When you gave me to believe

    Ma dame long par bel mentir.
720 Y me plut moult bien a sentir
    Le vray de ce que vous mentites
    En ce qu'aprés le voir deïtes,
    Que ma dame estoit assez pres.
    Je m'en vois; or venez aprés,
725 Ou vous demourrez, s'il vous plaist."
    "Guillaume, bien heure de plait
    Est encor; ne vous hastez point.
    Vous y venrez assez a point
    Se ma dame y puet adrecier.
730 Se vous saviés un po tencier,
    Bon seroit et pour certein cas
    Ou vous devenez advocas;
    Car on vous porra bien sousprendre
    Se vous ne vous savez deffendre."
735 De si fais mos nous debatiens,
    Par gieu si nous en esbatiens;
    Dont tout en parlant chevauchames
    Que la gent la dame aprochames.
    Lors m'avansai, et quant je vi
740 Son gentil corps amanevi
    D'onneur, de grace, et de science,
    En signe de grant reverence
    Vos jus de mon cheval descendre;
    Mais tantost le me va deffendre.
745 En disant debonnairement:
    "Hola, Guillaume, nullement,
    Pour certein, n'i descenderez.
    A cheval a moy parlerez."
    Quant je l'oÿ, je m'en souffri,
750 Et si bel salu li offri
    Comme je pooie et savoie,
    Et comme faire le devoie,
    Einsi comme j'avoie apris
    A honnourer gens de tel pris.
755 Et elle aussi, sans contrefaire,
    Sceut moult bien le seurplus parfaire,
    En respondant par amisté,
    Gardant honneur et honnesté.
    Puis me dist moult rassisement:

LA DAME
760 "Guillaume, mervilleusement
    Estes estranges devenus.
    Vous ne fussiez pas ça venus,
    Se ce ne fust par mes messages,

Through a clever lie that my lady was far away;
720 It has pleased me much to realize
The truth of what you lied about
Because you afterward spoke the truth,
Namely that my lady was rather close by.
I'm on my way; come along now,
725 Or stay here as you please."
"Guillaume, there is still time
For a discussion; no need to hurry.
You will get there soon enough
If my lady can arrange it.
730 And if you have some skill in debating,
It will be good in this situation
Where you will play the lawyer's role;
For you could be taken by surprise
If you prove unable to defend yourself."
735 We bandied about these words
And with such game amused ourselves;
Thus absorbed in talk we rode on
Until nearing the lady's entourage.
Then I went on ahead, and seeing
740 Her noble person replete
With honor, grace, and learning,
As a sign of great reverence
I made to get off my horse.
But at once she started to forbid it,
745 Saying quite politely:
"Oh no, Guillaume, this will surely not do.
You must not dismount.
Speak to me from your horse."
And when I heard this, I obliged
750 And gave her as fine a greeting
As I could and knew how to,
And in the manner I should have,
Just as I had learned
To honor people of such rank.
755 And without dissembling, she in turn
Knew how to take care of the rest,
Responding in friendship,
Guarding her honor and integrity.
Then she spoke to me quite firmly:

THE LADY
760 "Guillaume, you have acted
Too much the stranger.
You would not have come here
Had it not been for my messenger.

Je croy que vous estes trop sages
765   Devenuz, ou trop alentis,
        Mausoingneus, et mautalentis,
        De vos deduis apetisiez,
        Ou trop po les dames prisiez.
        Quant je fu la dessus montee
770   En celle plus haute montee
        Mon chemin tenoie sus destre,
        Et je regardai vers senestre,
        Tout de plain vous vi chevauchier,
        Vos levriers siffler et huchier.
775   Tels ouevres faire vous ooie
        Tout aussi bien com je veoie
        Vous et vostre contenement.
        Dont je croy bien certeinnement,
        Guillaume, que vous nous veïtes.
780   Et pour quoy dont, quant vous oïtes
        Nos chevaus passer et hennir,
        Et se ne daigniés venir,
        Jusqu'a tant que je vous manday
        Einsi com je le commanday?
785   Dont je vous merci tellement
        Com je doy, et non autrement.”

GUILLAUME

        Lors li dis je: “Pour Dieu merci,
        Ma dame, ne dites ceci.
        Je respon, sauve vostre honneur,
790   Car foy que doy Nostre Signour,
fol. 27v Je ne vi riens, ne riens n'oÿ,
        Tant avoie cuer esjoÿ
        De ma chace a quoy je pensoie,
        Pour la fin a quoy je tendoie.
795   S'estoie einsi comme ravis.
        Ma dame, je feroie envis
        Riens encontre vostre voloir.
        Et que me porroient valoir
        A faire tels menuz despis?
800   Bien say que j'en vaurroie pis.
        Si m'en devez bien escuser.”

LA DAME

        “Guillaume, plus n'en vueil ruser.
        Puis qu'einsi va, mes cuers vous croit.
        Mais d'une autre partie croit
805   Moult durement une autre chose
        Encontre vous qui porte glose.

You have become, I think,
765 Too wise or too backward,
Inattentive and disagreeable,
Eager for your sport,
Or else you value ladies too little.
When I climbed the ground over there
770 On that highest rise,
I took the path on the right
And looked toward the left;
Quite clearly I saw you riding,
Whistling up and calling your hounds.
775 I heard you doing this
And likewise saw
You and your goings-on.
So I believe quite surely,
Guillaume, you must have seen us.
780 And why, then, when hearing
Our horses pass by and whinny
Did you not deign come forward
Until I gave you the order,
Just as if I made it a command?
785 So I thank you just as much for this
As I should and no more."

GUILLAUME

Then I said to her: "For God's sake,
My lady, don't say so.
I will reply to that, saving your honor,
790 For by the faith I owe our Lord
I saw nothing and heard nothing either,
So much was my heart enthralled
By the hunting I was intent on,
By the goal I wanted to attain.
795 And so I was spellbound.
My lady, only involuntarily would I do
Anything against your will.
And how would it profit me
To do something so petty and spiteful?
800 I know well I would be demeaned by this.
And so you should excuse me."

THE LADY

"Guillaume, I don't want to fool with this further.
Because it is so, my heart believes you.
But on the other hand a different matter
805 Has arisen — and very seriously —
To your discredit, and it needs explaining.

        Se vous donray assez a faire
        Et se vous ferai maint contraire
        Se pour confus ne vous rendez.
810   Guillaume, oëz et entendez:
        Vers les dames estes forfais,
        S'en avez enchargié tel fais
        Que soustenir ne le porrez
        Ne mettre jus quant vous vorrez."
815   Avec ces paroles diverses,
        En leurs diversetez perverses,
        Me moustra elle une maniere
        Aspre, crueuse, male, et fiere,
        En signe de grant mautalent
820   Pour moy faire le cuer dolent
        Et mettre ma pensee toute
        En effroy, en song, et en doubte.
        De ce se mettoit en grant peinne
        Qu'ele se tenoit pour certeinne
825   Que de tant bien la priseroie
        Q'son courrous moult doubteroie.
        Et si fis je; je le doubtay,
        Quant ces paroles escoutay,
        Nom pas pour cause de meffait
830   Qu'endroit de moy heüsse fait;
        Mais je doubtay pour mesdisans
        Qui sont aucunes fois nuisans
        Par fausseté et par envie
        Aus bons qui mainnent bonne vie.
835   Si doubtay si faite aventure.
        Mais seürs fui qu'enforfaiture
        N'avoie fait en ma vie onques
        Envers nulles dames quelsquonques.
        Se li respondi par avis.

GUILLAUME
840   "Dame, fait avez .i. devis
        Ou ma grant deshonneur moustrez,
        Mais li procés n'est pas outrez
        Ne mis en fourme justement.
        Pour faire certein jugement,
845   Vous me deüssiez dire en quoy
        J'ay forfait et tout le pourquoy
        Amener a conclusion.
        Or est en vostre entention
        Secretement mis en enclos.
850   S'il ne m'est autrement desclos,
        Je n'en saveroie respondre.

And I will keep you very busy
And offer much argument against you
If you do not admit your error.
810   Guillaume, listen and pay attention:
You have sinned against women,
And so you have taken on a burden
You will not be able to hold up under
Or put down when you would like."
815   With these strange words,
Perverse in their severity,
She showed me a manner
Bitter, cruel, hurtful, and haughty
As a sign of her great anger
820   In order to make my heart heavy,
And also to make fearful, hesitant,
And full of uncertainty my every thought.
She took pains in doing so
Because she was convinced
825   That, valuing her so highly,
I should fear her anger greatly.
And this I did; I started to fear her
When I heard these words,
Not because of any misdeed
830   I myself had supposedly committed;
Rather because I feared those gossip-mongers
Who are at times harmful
Because of their falseness and envy
To good people who lead decent lives.
835   And so I dreaded this turn of events.
Yet I was certain I had done
No harm in my whole life
To any woman whomsoever,
And with this in mind I answered her:

GUILLAUME
840   "Lady, you have brought up something
That heaps great dishonor upon me,
But the trial is not yet arranged
Or begun in proper form.
For a certain judgment to be rendered,
845   You must tell me how
I have erred and also explain in detail
All the facts of the matter.
At present your purpose here
Remains secret and hidden
850   If not divulged to me,
I will not be able to respond.

Or vueilliez, s'il vous plaist, espondre
Le fait de quoy vous vous dolez;
Et s'einsi faire le volez
855   Vous ensieurez la droite voie
De droit, ou je ne saveroie
Le fait congnoistre ne nïer.
Ce non, vous devez ottrïer
Que je m'en voise frans et quittes
860   De ce forfait que vous me dites;
J'en atenderoie bien droit."

LA DAME

"Guillaume, sachiés orendroit
N'en arez plus de ma partie.
Car la chose est einsi partie.
865   Se je le say, vous le savez,
Car le fait devers vous avez
En l'un de vos livres escript,
fol. 28r Bien devisié et bien descript.
Si regardés dedens vos livres.
870   Bien say que vous n'estes pas yvres
Quant vos fais amoureus ditez.
Dont bien savez de vos dittez,
Quant vous les faites et parfaites,
Se vous faites bien ou forfaites
875   Dés qu'il sont fait de sanc assis
Autant a un mot comme a sis.
S'il vous plaist, vous y garderez
Qu'autre chose n'en porterez
De moy, quant a l'eure presente.
880   Soiez certeins que c'est m'entente."

GUILLAUME

"Dame, qu'est ce que dit avez?
Selonc le bien que vous savez,
Trop mieus savez que vous ne dites:
J'ay bien de besongnes escriptes
885   Devers moy, de pluseurs manieres,
De moult de diverses matieres,
Dont l'une l'autre ne ressamble.
Consideré toutes ensamble,
Et chascune bien mise a point,
890   D'ordre en ordre et de point en point,
Dés le premier commancement
Jusques au darrein finement,
Se tout voloie regarder,
Dont je me vorray bien garder,

Now please, if you will, expound upon
That matter troubling you;
And if you agree to do so,
855   You will be following the proper path
Of the law, for otherwise I would not be able
To learn what the issue is and dispute it.
If not, you ought to grant
I should go free and clear
860   Of the allegation you have made against me.
I expect proper justice in this matter."

THE LADY

"Guillaume, you already know
And will hear nothing more from me.
Instead this is how things stand.
865   If I know about it, you know too,
Because the case against you is something
You have written down in one of your books,
Something well laid out and described therein.
So look through your books.
870   I know well you are not drunk
When you compose your love poems.
And so you know well, with regard to your own tales,
When you compose and complete them,
If you did right or wrong there
875   Because into these works you put your heart
As much in a single word as in six.
If you please, go look there
Because you will get nothing more
From me for the present.
880   Be sure this is my intention."

GUILLAUME

"Madam, what have you said?
As you are very well aware,
You know much more than you admit.
I have all sorts of written texts
885   In front of me, of various kinds,
Devoted to very different themes,
Each of which is quite unlike every other.
Examining all these at the same time,
And each one rather thoroughly,
890   Section by section and sentence by sentence,
From the beginning of the first
To the very end of the last
If I wished to look through all of them:
This I should indeed like to avoid,

895 Trop longuement y metteroie.
  Et d'autre part, je ne porroie
  Trouver ce que vous demandez
  S'a vos paroles n'amendez.
  Pour tel chose ne quier ja lire,
900 Dame, nom pas pour vous desdire,
  Mais ce n'est pas chose sensible
  Q'vostre pensee invisible
  Pëust venir a ma congnoissance,
  Fors que par la clef d'ordenance
905 Dont vostres cuers soit deffermiés,
  Et que si en soie enfourmés
  Que vostre bouche le me die.
  Lorsqu'a respondre contredie,
  Quant de bouche le m'arez dit,
910 J'en vueil moult bien, a vostre dit,
  Estre blamez et corrigiez.
  Dame, s'il vous plait, or jugiez
  Selonc la vostre opinion,
  Se j'ay tort a m'entention."

LA DAME
915 "Guillaume, puis qu'il est einsi,
  Je m'acort bien a ce point ci.
  Orendroit me rens je vaincue;
  Mais de vostre descouvenue,
  Qui est contre dames si grande,
920 Afferroit bien crueuse amende
  S'il estoit qui la vosist prendre.
  Or vueilles dés or mais entendre
  Ad ce que je diray de bouche,
  Car moult forment au cuer me touche.
925 Et quant dit le vous averay,
  En tel lieu le reprocheray
  Que vous en serez moult blasmez
  Et vers les dames diffamez.

  Une question fu jadis
930 Mise en termes par moult biaus dis,
  Belle et courtoisement baillie,
  Mais aprés fu trop mal taillie.
  Premierement fu supposé,
  Et en supposant proposé,
935 C'une dame de grant vaillance
  Par tres amiable fiance
  Ameroit .i. loial amant
  Si que toudis, en bien amant,

895   All this would take too long.
       And in addition I might not
       Come across what you are taking issue with
       If you do not tell me more.
       For I would never seek to read such a thing,
900   Madam, except to contradict you.
       Yet it is hardly to be expected
       That I would prove able to decipher
       A hidden thought of yours
       Except through the proper key
905   That might unlock your heart;
       And so I might be informed about this,
       Let your mouth tell it to me.
       If I refuse to respond
       After you have told me yourself,
910   Then I'd certainly agree to whatever
       Condemnation and reproof you utter.
       Madam, if you please, now decide
       If my view here is mistaken
       According to your own opinion."

THE LADY

915   "Guillaume, since this is how things stand,
       I agree completely with this point.
       At the moment I admit myself defeated;
       But this matter of your transgression,
       Which is so grave against women,
920   Would call for a severe punishment
       Should someone wish to exact it.
       So from this point listen carefully
       To what I will say from my own mouth
       Because the issue touches me right to the heart.
925   And after I have told you about it,
       I will reproach you in such a place
       Where you will be much blamed for this,
       Losing your reputation among ladies.

       One time an issue was
930   Advanced in a very pleasant poem,
       Prettily embellished and with refinement,
       But afterward quite unfortunately developed.
       At first it was supposed,
       And, in supposing, proposed
935   That a lady of great worthiness
       Through a very loving bond
       Did love a faithful lover
       So that at all times, in loving well,

Seroit de cuer loial amie.
940   Se il, en gardant courtoisie,
       Toudis de bon cuer l'ameroit
       Et son pooir estenderoit
       En li chierir et honnourer.
fol. 28v Et pour li miex enamourer
945   Il maintenroit toute noblesse:
       Honneur, courtoisie, et largesse.
       Biaus homs seroit, a grant devis,
       De membres, de corps, et de vis
       Renommez, de grace parfais,
950   Et si bien esprouvez par fais
       D'armes, comme nuls homs puet estre
       Qui a mis sa vie et son estre
       En sieuir joustes et tournois,
       Et tous amoureus esbanois.
955   Cependant qu'einsi s'ameront
       Et toudis bien se garderont
       Les courtois poins de loiauté
       En raison et en verité,
       Leur avenroit tele aventure,
960   Par violence ou par nature,
       Que li amans devieroit.
       Et celle, quant le saveroit,
       Demouroit lasse et esgaree,
       Loyal amie non amee.
965   Car ses cuers demorroit espris,
       Et li cuers de l'amant de pris
       Seroit selonc nature esteins,
       Dont li siens cuers seroit plus teins
       Pour cause de la departie.
970   Plus n'en di de ceste partie.
       Eins vorrai d'une autre compter
       Pour a ceste ci adjouster,
       En faisant ma comparison.
       Guillaume, or entendez raison:

975   Uns autres amans debonnaires,
       Aussi vaillans en ses affaires
       Comme cils de qui j'ay compté
       Tant en grace comme en bonté,
       Et de toutes autres parties
980   En honneur a point departies,
       Amera aussi une dame
       Sans mal penser et sans diffame,
       Et se li fera a savoir.
       Et quant elle en sara le voir,

She was at heart a loyal beloved.
940 And he, obedient to courtesy,
Always loved her with a good heart
And expended his energy
In cherishing and honoring her.
And in order to deepen her love
945 He upheld everything noble:
Honor, courtesy, and generosity.
He was a handsome man, strikingly so,
Renowned for his limbs, body,
And countenance, perfect in grace,
950 And as well proven in deeds of arms
As any man could be
Who had spent his life and energy
Devoted to tournaments and jousting,
As well as all other pursuits pertaining to love.
955 Though they loved each other in this fashion
And always closely observed
The courtly rules of faithfulness
In both reason and truth,
Such a chance befell them,
960 Whether through nature or violence,
That the lover did pass away.
And the lady, when she learned this,
Lived on sorrowful and abandoned,
A true beloved no longer loved.
965 Because her heart was still aflame
And the heart of the worthy lover
Had been undone by nature,
Her heart was the more afflicted
By the fact of his demise.
970 I will say no more about the matter.
Instead I would like to bring up another
In order to set it beside this one,
In order to make my comparison.
Listen now, Guillaume, and learn.

975 Another lover of high degree,
As worthy as the one
I have already mentioned in his deeds
In grace as much as in virtue,
And in all other respects
980 Rightly and honorably endowed,
Also loved a lady
With no thought of evil or infamy,
And this he made known to her,
And when she had learned the truth,

985   Volentiers le recevera
       Et s'amour li ottriera
       Liement, sans faire dangier.
       Pas ne vueil ce ci prolongier;
       Car cils l'amera loyaument
990   Et se la croira fermement
       Sans erreur et sans nulle doubte
       Car il cuidera s'amour toute
       Avoir acquis toute sa vie
       Sans jamais faire departie.
995   Mais il ira bien autrement.
       Quant il sera plus liement
       Conjoins a li et affermez
       En la fiance d'estre amez,
       Elle li jouera d'un tour
1000   Outreement sans nul retour,
       Ou il trouvera fausseté
       Contre lui, et desloiauté,
       Et se ne le porra nïer.
       Si doit bien celui anüer,
1005   Ce n'est mie moult grant merveille.
       Mais ce n'est pas chose pareille
       Au fait d'amours qui me remort,
       Qui se defenist par la mort.
       Guillaume, s'entendu m'avez,
1010   Assés legierement devez
       Vostre meffaçon recongnoistre
       Pour vostre deshonneur descroistre.
       Vous avez dit et devisié
       Et jugié de fait avisié
1015   Par diffinitif jugement
       Que cils a trop plus malement,
       Grieté, tourment, mal, et souffraite
       Qui trueve sa dame forfaite
       Contre lui en fausse maniere,
1020   Que la tres douce dame chiere
       Qui avera son dous amy
       Conjoint a son cuer, sans demy,
       Par amours, sans autre moien.
fol. 29r Puis le savera en loien
1025   De la mort ou il demourra
       Si que jamais ne le verra.
       Et comment l'osastes vous dire,
       Ne dedens vos livres escrire?
       Il est voirs qu'einsi l'avez fait,
1030   Dont vous avez griefment meffait.
       Si vous lo que vous tant faciez

985 She received him willingly
  And granted the man her love
  Joyfully, offering no refusal.
  I have no intention of drawing this out,
  But he loved her faithfully
990 And trusted her very much,
  Without any hesitation or doubt
  Because he thought he had acquired
  All her love for the rest of his life
  And would never have to share it.
995 Yet his path was quite different.
  When he was the most happily
  Joined to her and confident
  In the promise of being loved,
  She did him wrong,
1000 Outrageously and with no excuse,
  And in this he discovered her falseness
  Toward him, her disloyalty as well,
  And it could not be denied.
  If this gave him much pain,
1005 That's hardly much of a surprise.
  But it's not the same at all
  As what causes me to sorrow, the love affair
  That death brought to an end.
  Guillaume, if you have listened to me,
1010 You should very readily
  Acknowledge your misdeed
  In order to lessen your shame.
  You have stated and recounted,
  And also decided, advised of these facts,
1015 In a conclusive judgment
  That this man experiences much more misfortune,
  Grief, torment, ill, and suffering,
  — The one who found his lady false
  To him through her double dealing —
1020 Than does the gracious, dear lady
  Whose sweet lover had been joined
  Irrevocably to her heart
  Through love and not otherwise.
  Then she learned he was in the grasp
1025 Of death and should there remain
  So she will never see him again.
  And how did you dare say this
  Or write it down in your book?
  It's true that you have done so,
1030 And thus you have grievously erred.
  Therefore I advise you to do what you can

Que ce jugement effaciés,
Et que briefment le rapellez.
Guillaume, se vous tant valez,
1035   Vous le pouez bien einsi faire
Par soustenir tout le contraire.
Car li contraires, c'est li drois
En tous bons amoureus endrois."

GUILLAUME
"Dame, foi que doi Sainte Eglise,
1040   En qui ma foy est toute assise,
Pour nulle rien ne le feroie;
Eins iray tout outre la voie
Dou fait puis que j'y suis entrez.
Dés que mes jugemens outrez
1045   Est de moy, je le soustenray,
Tant que soustenir le porray.
Mais qui vorroit avant venir
Pour le contraire soustenir
Moult volentiers oubeïroie
1050   A quanqu'oubeïr deveroie.
Car je ne suis mie si fors,
Ne si grans n'est pas mes effors,
Ne de science mes escus,
Que je ne puisse estre vaincus.
1055   Mais se je puis, je veinqueray;
Se je ne puis, je soufferay.
Or voit einsi, qu'on puet aler;
Je n'en quier autrement parler.
Et nompourquant, ma dame douce,
1060   Q'vostres cuers ne se courrouce
A moy, nous ferons une chose
Ouvertement, nom pas enclose,
Ou vostre pais soit contenue
Et m'onneur y soit soustenue.
1065   Car ce seroit a ma grant honte,
Selonc vostre meïsme conte,
S'endroit de moy contredisoie
Le fait que jugié averoie,
De mon bon droit, tel et si fait
1070   Que tout par moy avroie fait.
Nous penrons un juge puissant,
De renommee souffissant,
Q'soit sages homs et discrez.
Se li soit comptés li secrez
1075   Entierement de la besongne
Qui a vous et a moy besongne.

Or soit einsi fait par acort;

To void this judgment
And overturn it at once.
If you are truly a worthy man, Guillaume,
1035   You could do so rather easily
By affirming exactly the opposite.
For the opposite view is the correct one
Wherever people esteem proper loving."

GUILLAUME
"Madam, by the faith I owe Holy Church,
1040   Where all my trust lies,
I would do so for no reason;
Instead, I will pursue the matter
To the very end now that I am involved.
Since my judgment was made public
1045   By me, I have upheld and will uphold it,
As long as I can.
Yet whoever might come forward
To defend the other side
Quite willingly I will submit
1050   To whatever I must submit.
For I am hardly powerful enough,
And my endurance is scarcely so great,
Or my storehouse of knowledge, for that matter,
That I could not be overcome.
1055   But if I can, I will prevail.
Should I prove unable, I will pay the price.
Let's look now to how we should proceed.
I don't want to banter more about the issue.
But nevertheless, my sweet lady,
1060   So your heart will not be cross with me,
We will deal with this matter
Openly, not in secret,
In a way that will preserve your peace of mind
And uphold my honor as well.
1065   For it would be to my great shame,
As you yourself have admitted,
If on my own I should reverse myself
About this case I judged,
As was my right, having done so in such a way
1070   That I accomplished it all alone.
We will find ourselves a powerful judge,
Someone of sufficient renown
Who would be a wise and discreet man;
And he shall be told from beginning to end
1075   The private details of this affair
Involving you and me.

Let it be done as we agree.

Mais vous en ferez le recort
Dou prendre tel que vous vorrez.
1080 Contredire ne le m'orrez,
Einsi y sui acordans dés ci
A vostre plaisir, sans nul 'si.'
Mes cuers y est ja tous entiers,
Car ce sera uns biaus mestiers
1085 De oïr les raisons repeter
Et les parties desputer
Soutilment, par biaus argumens
Q'vaurront auques jugemens."

LA DAME

A ces moz prist la dame a rire
1090 Et en riant tantost a dire:
"Guillaume, bien suis acordans
Ad ce qu'estes ci recordans;
S'en parlerai, comment qu'il aille.
Et nompourquant, vaille que vaille,
1095 Je nomme et pren celui qui rois
Est appellez des Navarrois.
C'est uns princes qui aimme honnour
Et qui het toute deshonnour,
Sages, loiaus, et veritables,
1100 Et en tous ses fais raisonnables.
Il scet tant et vaut, qu'a droit dire,
Nul milleur ne porroie eslire.
Li fais li sera savoureus
fol. 29v Pour ce qu'il est moult amoureus,
1105 Sages, courtois, et bien apris.
Il aimme l'onneur et le pris
Des armes, d'amours, et des dames.
C'est li roys par cui uns diffames
Ne seroit jamais soustenus.
1110 De toute villenie est nus
Et garnis de toute noblesse
Qui apartient a gentillesse.
Trop de biens dire n'en porroie,
S'ui mais tout adés en parloie."

1115 Einsi fumes nous acordé,
Comme devant est recordé.
Dont puis d'amors assés parlames,
Et en parlant tant chevauchames
Que nous entrames es drois las
1120 De pais, de joie, et de solas,
C'est a savoir en .i. dous estre

Yet you should assume the responsibility
For selecting such a man as you'd prefer.
1080   You will hear me voice no opposition,
Rather I am in agreement on this point from now on
With whatever pleases you and no 'buts' about it.
Truly, my heart is already in this,
Because it will be a pleasant task
1085   To hear the arguments rehearsed
And the parties dispute
With subtlety, with impressive reasoning
That will merit some kind of judgment."

THE LADY

At these words the lady began to laugh
1090   And at once, while laughing, to speak:
"Guillaume, I very much agree
With what you've just said;
And I will speak to it, no matter what.
And so, for whatever it's worth,
1095   I nominate and choose the man named
The king of Navarre.
He is a prince who loves honor
And hates dishonor of every kind,
A man wise, loyal, and truthful,
1100   Reasonable too in all his doings.
He knows so much, is so worthy
I could choose no one better, to speak the truth.
The case will appeal to him
Because he is quite romantically inclined,
1105   Wise, courteous, and well taught.
He loves the honor and the glory
Of arms, love, and ladies.
He is the king who would never
Support any kind of infamy.
1110   He is devoid of all uncouthness
And graced with all the nobility
Belonging to high rank.
I couldn't say enough of his virtues
If speaking of them all day long."

1115   In this way we came to an agreement,
Just as it is recorded above.
Then we spoke much about love
And, as we talked, rode on
Until we fell into the righteous bonds
1120   Of repose, joy, and solace,
Which means into a sweet state

Ou il faisoit si tres bel estre
Qu'on ne porroit miex, a mon gré:
C'estoit en souverein degré,
1125   A mon avis, de bon propos,
De deduit, et de bon repos,
Ou uns cuers se puet reposer
Qui a point se vuet disposer.
La avoit il un bel manoir
1130   Ou elle voloit remanoir.

Assés fu qui la descendi
Et qui entour li entendi;
Et, sans atendre, fu menee
Dedens une chambre aournee
1135   Si bien, si bel, si cointement
Et de tout si tres richement,
Qu'onques mais, dont j'eüs grant merveille,
N'avoie veu la pareille.
Et briefment tuit, grant et meneur,
1140   Li faisoient feste et honneur.
Mais bien sambloit estre maistresse,
Car elle fu par grant noblesse
Entre coussins de soie assise.
Mais moult estoit sage et rassise,
1145   Et fu d'aage si seür
Qu'entre le vert et le meür
Estoit sa tres douce jouvente,
Plus qu'autre simple, aperte, et gente.
Moult bien estoit acompaingnié
1150   De belle et bonne compaingnie.
N'i fu Margot ne Agnesot,
Mais .xij. damoiselles ot
Qui jour et nuit la norrissoient,
Servoient, et endoctrinoient.

1155   La premiere estoit Congnoissance,
Qui li moustroit la difference
D'entre les vertus et les vices
Et des biens fais aus malefices,
Par Avis, qui la conduisoit,
1160   Jusqu'a .i. miroir qui luisoit,
Si qu'onques plus cler miroir
Ne pot on tenir ne veoir.

Raisons le tenoit en sa destre,
Une balance en sa senestre,
1165   Si que la dame s'i miroit

Whose conditions were so pleasant
They could be no better, to my taste;
It was of the highest degree,
1125   Full of good sense, so I think,
Delight, and sweet leisure too,
Where a heart that seeks to act accordingly
Might discover peace.
A handsome manor stood at the spot
1130   Where she wished to halt.

Many there helped her dismount
And attended to the lady;
And, without delay, she was led
Inside a room decorated
1135   So well, so beautifully, so expertly,
And in all things so richly
That never before (which made me greatly marvel)
Had I ever laid eyes on anything similar.
And, quickly, everyone, high and low alike,
1140   Made her welcome and honored her.
And she very much seemed to be mistress there
Because in great nobility she was
Seated on cushions made of silk.
Yet she was very wise and self-contained,
1145   And of such a confident age
She was quite pleasantly youthful,
Being neither "green" nor "ripe."
More than any other, she was meek, friendly, and noble.
Very well attended the lady was
1150   By a virtuous and beautiful entourage.
None was a country girl;
Twelve damsels there were instead
Who attended to her day and night,
Served and instructed her as well.

1155   The first was Understanding,
Who showed her the difference
Between virtues and vices,
Between good deeds and evil ones as well,
With the help of Discretion, who escorted her
1160   To a mirror that gleamed so brightly
No one could ever grasp
Or gaze on a clearer reflecting glass.

Reason held this in her right hand,
A scale in her left,
1165   Where the lady looked at herself

Plus souvent qu'on ne vous diroit.
La veoit elle clerement,
Sans obscurté n'empecshement,
Quanque Diex et Nature donne
1170   A bonne eüreuse personne.
C'est le mal laissier et bien faire,
Et non voloir autrui contraire.
Car fols est qui autrui pourchace
Chose qu'il ne vuet qu'on li face.
1175   Et s'il heüst en son atour,
En son gentil corps, fait a tour,
Et en son cuer tache ne vice
Ou pensee d'aucun malice,
Ja ne fust si fort reponnue
1180   Qu'en miroir ne fust veue.
Et la veoit elle, sans doubte,
La guise et la maniere toute,
Comment Raison justement regle
fol. 30r   Par bele et bonne et loial regle.
1185   Si que la prenoit exemplaire
De tout ce qu'elle devoit faire.
Et aussi la juste balance
Li demoustroit signefiance
Qu'elle devoit en tous cas vivre
1190   Aussi justement com la livre,
Ou on ne puet, par nulle voie,
Mettre n'oster qu'on ne le voie.

La tierce avoit nom Attemprance,
Qui .i. chapelet de souffrance
1195   Avoit sus son chief par cointise;
Et avec ce, dont miex la prise,
Estoit de maniere seüre
Et, en parlant, sage, et meüre,
N'en fait, n'en port, n'en contenence
1200   N'ot vice, ne desordenance.

La quarte, se bien m'en recorde,
Estoit Pais, qui tenoit Concorde
Par le doy amiablement,
Et li disoit moult doucement,
1205   De cuer riant, a chiere lie:
"Ma douce suer, ma chiere amie,
Se nous volons vivre en leesse,
En pais, et repos, en richesse,
De tout ce qu'on puet faire et dire,
1210   N'en metons a nos cuers point d'ire,

More often than anyone could say.
There she saw clearly,
With no obscurity or impediment,
What God and Nature might grant

1170   A truly fortunate person.
And that is to abandon evil and do good,
And not to wish to cross anyone.
For the man is a fool who does something
To another he does not wish done to him.

1175   And if there might be in her person
Or noble body, of such beautiful shape,
Or in her heart any fault or vice,
Or malicious thought of any kind,
It could never be so well hidden that

1180   It could not be seen in the mirror.
And there without doubt she gazed on
The nature and manner of all things,
How Reason justly rules
Through fair, good, and loyal precept.

1185   And so there she found an example
Of everything she ought to do.
Moreover the scales of justice
Showed to her the truth
That she should in every instance live

1190   As correctly as the scales,
To which one in no way can add
Or take from and not have it noticed.

The third was named Temperance,
Who wore a garland of endurance

1195   On her head as an adornment;
And with this, to increase her worthiness,
She had a confident manner
And was wise in her speech, mature too,
Not in deed, or in her behavior, or her countenance

1200   Was there any vice or impropriety.

The fourth, and well I remember her,
Was Peace, who held Concord
By the finger out of friendship
And spoke to her quite sweetly,

1205   With a laughing heart, a happy face:
"My sweet sister, my dear friend,
If we intend to live in joy,
Peace, leisure, and wealth
In regard to all we say and do,

1210   Let us allow no anger into our hearts,

Et ne nous chaille dou dangier
Qu'on appelle contrevangier,
Car tels cuide vangier sa honte
Qui l'accroist et qui plus s'ahonte.
1215 Tenons les bons en amitié,
Et des mauvais aions pitié
Car onques homs ne fu parfais
Qui volt vangier tous ses tors fais."

La cincisme fu appellee
1220 Foy, qui richement endestree
Estoit de Constance la ferme,
Qui si l'affermoit et afferme
Que riens ne la bransle n'esloche;
Eins estoit com chastiaus sus roche,
1225 Fort et ferme et seürement,
Sans variable mouvement.

La setisme fu Charité,
Qui avoit si tres grant pité
Des besongneus qu'elle savoit
1230 Que leur donnoit quanqu'elle avoit.
Mais ja tant donner ne sceüst
Qu'assez plus a donner n'eüst.

Aprés Honnestez doucement
Se seoit moult honnestement,
1235 Qui paree par grant noblesse
Estoit d'un mantel de simplesse.
Mais nette estoit, sans nul reproche,
De cuer, de corps, de main, de bouche.

La .ix.ᵐᵉ estoit Prudence.
1240 En son cuer portoit Sapience,
Et si fermement la gardoit
Qu'aprés li d'amours toute adroit.
Bien savoit la cause des choses
Qui sont ou firmament encloses,
1245 Pourquoy li solaus en ardure
Se tient, et la lune en froidure;
Des estoiles et des planettes
Et des .xij. signes les mettes;
Pourquoy Diex par Nature assamble
1250 Humeur, sec, froit, et chaut ensamble;
Et pourquoy li .iiij. element
Furent ordené tellement
Qu'adés se tient en bas la terre,

And let us have no truck with the arrogance
Bearing the name of revenge,
For whoever intends avenging the shame done him
Makes it increase, further disgracing himself.
1215   Let us hold to good people in friendship,
And let us take pity on evildoers
Because no man ever attained perfection
Who was eager to avenge the wrongs done him."

The fifth among them was called
1220   Faith, who was escorted in grand style
By steadfast Constancy,
Who so strengthened and strengthens her
Nothing disturbs or worries the lady;
Instead she was like a castle built on rock,
1225   Strong and secure on its foundation,
Free from unpredictable change.

The seventh was Charity,
Who felt such great pity
For those she knew to be in need
1230   She gave them whatever she possessed.
But she could never give so much
She did not have much more to share.

Afterward Honesty seated
Herself quietly and with much politeness,
1235   And this lady was adorned in great nobility
With the mantle of simplicity,
For she was proper, beyond reproach
In her heart, body, hand, and speech.

The ninth was Prudence.
1240   In her heart she bore Wisdom,
Whom she guarded so closely
She burned with fierce love for her.
She knew well the reason why heavenly bodies
Are suspended within the firmament;
1245   Why the sun endures
In conflagration and the moon in ice;
All about the stars and the planets,
As well as the limits of the twelve signs;
Why God through Nature did assemble
1250   Wet, dry, cold, and hot together;
And why the four elements
Were ordered in such a fashion
That earth always remains below

Et l'iaue pres de li se serre,
1255   Li feus se trait haut a toute heure,
Et li airs en moien demeure.
Brief des oeuvres celestiennes
Et aussi des choses terriennes
Savoit tant qu'elle estoit experte,
1260   D'engin si vive et si aperte,
Q'nuls ne le porroit despondre.
Car a chascun savoit respondre
De quanqu'on voloit demander
Si qu'on n'i sceüst qu'amender.

fol. 30v   Aprés Prudence se seoit
1266   Largesse, qui riens ne veoit
Einsois donnoit a toutes mains,
A l'un plus et a l'autre mains,
Or, argent, destriers, oisiaus, terre,
1270   Et quanqu'elle pooit acquerre,
Contez, duchez, et baronnies,
A heritages et a vies.
De tout ce riens ne retenoit
Fors l'onneur. Ad ce se tenoit.
1275   Noblesse li avoit apris.
Et avec ce, dont miex la pris,
Elle reprenoit Advarice
Comme de tout le pieur vice.

L'autre, dont pas ne me vueil taire,
1280   Estoit Doubtance de Meffaire,
Qui tant se doubtoit de mesprendre
Qu'a peinne pooit elle entendre
A riens, fors estre sus sa garde.
En tous ses fais estoit couarde;
1285   Car Honte et Paour la gardoient,
Qui en tous lieus l'acompaingnoient.

La dousieme estoit Souffissance,
Qui de tres humble pacïence
Estoit richement aournee
1290   Et abondanment saoulee
Et pleinne de tous biens terriens.
Elle n'avoit besong de riens,
Ne li failloit chose nesune.
Hors estoit des mains de Fortune
1295   Et de son perilleus dangier.
De po se paissoit au mengier
Car plus refaite estoit d'un ouef

And water clings quite closely to it;
1255 Fire always rises to the heights,
And air remains in the middle.
In short, of celestial movements
And also of earthly matters
She knew so much she was a master,
1260 Possessed of such a lively and able wit
No one could explain it.
For she could answer
Any question a person might ask,
And no one could improve on what she said.

1265 Right next to Prudence sat
Generosity, who sees nothing
But rather gives with both hands,
More to one and less to another,
Gold, silver, chargers, hunting birds, estates,
1270 And whatever else she might acquire,
Counties, duchies, and baronetcies
In perpetuity and for life.
She has kept nothing from any of these
Save honor. This she has clung to.
1275 Nobility has so instructed her,
And furthermore, which increases her worthiness,
She condemned Avarice
As the worst vice of all.

The next, about whom I'll not be silent,
1280 Was Wariness of Misdeed,
Who was so afraid of error
She could hardly attend
To any matter save for being on her guard.
In all her doings she was a coward,
1285 But Shame and Fear protected her
And were everywhere her companions.

The twelfth was Sufficiency,
Who in quite humble tranquillity
Was richly turned out
1290 And gorged to overflowing,
Full too of all earthly goods.
There was nothing she needed,
Nor did she lack a thing.
She was beyond the grasp of Fortune
1295 And her most fearsome domination.
She ate little at her meals
Because she was more sated by an egg

          Que ne fust un autre d'un buef.
          Tant par estoit bonne eüreuse
1300   Et parfaitement vertueuse.
          Encor est et toudis sera,
          Tant com li mondes durera,
          Que c'est, a droit considerer,
          Li biens qu'on doit plus desirer.

1305   Mais aussi com pluseurs rivieres
          Arrousent, et pluseurs lumieres
          Radient et leur clarté rendent
          En tous lieus ou elles s'estendent,
          Ces .xij. nobles damoiselles,
1310   Qui de tous biens furent ancelles,
          Chascune selonc sa nature,
          En meurs, en maintieng, en figure,
          Embelissoient ceste dame
          De cuer, de corps, d'onneur, et d'ame.
1315   Car tant estoit d'elles paree,
          Arrousee et enluminee,
          Que chascune l'embelissoit
          De quanque de li bel issoit,
          Et chascune la repartoit
1320   De la vertu qu'elle portoit.
          Et encor des biens de Nature
          Avoit la noble creature:
          Gente maniere, loiauté,
          Faitis port, debonnaireté,
1325   Grace, douceur, et courtoisie,
          Dont elle estoit moult embellie.
          Mais sa souvereinne bonté
          De trop long passoit sa biauté.

          Quant je la vi si hautement
1330   Assise et si tres noblement
          De grans richesses acesmee,
          Et si servie et honnouree
          Chierement de tous et de toutes,
          Dedens mon cuer venirent doubtes
1335   Qui y entrerent par folie
          Et par droite merencolie.
          Car j'estoie trop esbahis
          Et aussi com tous estahis
          Et d'erreur telement temptés,
1340   Que je cuiday estre enchantés.
          Mais en si fait amusement
          Ne demourai pas longuement;

Than another might be by a cow.
She was as happy as could be
1300   And perfect in her virtue.
She still is and always will be
As long as the world endures,
For she is, to judge rightly,
The blessing one should most desire.

1305   But just as many rivers
Provide water and many lights
Glow and give off their brightness
To every place they reach,
These twelve noble damsels,
1310   Who were the servants of all good things,
Each one according to her nature,
In customs, manner, and appearance,
Embellished this lady's
Heart, body, honor, and soul.
1315   So adorned by them was she,
Nurtured and enlightened,
That each improved the lady
With whatever good flowed from her
And shared with the lady
1320   The virtue she bore within.
And the noble creature, in addition,
Possessed endowments from Nature:
A cultivated manner, loyalty,
Noble bearing, good breeding,
1325   Grace, pleasantness, and courtesy,
And these much improved her.
But her sovereign goodness
Surpassed by a great deal her beauty.

When I saw her enthroned
1330   In such exalted fashion and so very nobly
Adorned with great riches,
And, too, served and honored
With such affection by all the men and women,
My heart filled with doubts
1335   That made their way there through folly
And genuine melancholy.
For I was taken much aback,
And also struck completely dumb,
At the same time so tempted by error
1340   I thought I had been enchanted.
But in this state of bemusement
I did not long remain

        Car je usai dou conseil d'Avis,
        Qui fist retourner mon avis

fol. 31r   Justement par devers Raison,
1346   Qui est tout adés en saison
        Des loiaus cuers remettre a point
        Qui sont issu hors de leur point.
        Adont Raison me resgarda
1350   Si que depuis en sa garde a
        Mon cuer, mon sens, et mon penser,
        Pour resister et pour tenser
        Aus fausses cogitations
        Et oster les temptations
1355   Qui cuidoient avoir victoire
        A moy faire faussement croire.

        Or fui hors de celle pensee.
        Mais la dame bien apensee
        Moult sagement m'araisonna,
1360   Et en parlant scens me donna
        De respondre aprés son parler;
        S'en sceüs miex et plus biau parler.

LA DAME
        Se me dist: "Guillaume, biau sire,
        Au primes fust il temps de dire
1365   Ce que sus les champs avons dit.
        S'en rafreschissons nostre dit,
        Present ces .xij. damoiselles,
        Qui sont sages, bonnes, et belles,
        Et pluseurs gens qui y seront.
1370   Volentiers nous escouteront."

GUILLAUME
        Je ne fis pas longue demeure.
        Einsois m'agenoillai en l'eure.
        Et humblement li respondi:
        "Ma chiere dame, tant vous di:
1375   Pleüst a Dieu de Paradis
        Que cils qui doit oïr nos dis
        Fust ci endroit presentement,
        Li bons rois qui si sagement
        Saveroit oïr et entendre,
1380   Taire a point, et puis raison rendre,
        Quant il averoit escouté
        Ce qu'on li averoit compté.
        Bien saveroit examiner
        Et encor miex determiner.

Because I followed the advice of Discretion,
Who made my presence of mind return
1345   In the proper fashion through Reason,
Who is always ready at the right moment
To bring back to themselves the true hearts
Who have wandered too far off the mark.
Then Reason fixed me with a look
1350   And ever since has maintained in her keeping
My heart, senses, and thoughts,
So I could resist and struggle
Against misbegotten notions,
And, too, expel the temptations
1355   That intended to enjoy the victory
Of making me think incorrectly.

By then, I had gotten beyond this thought,
And the lady, her ideas well considered,
Addressed me quite wisely
1360   And, as she talked, inspired me
To respond after she finished talking;
Thus I could speak better and with more flourish.

THE LADY

And she said to me: "Guillaume, fair sir,
What we said out in the fields
1365   Is what we should discuss first.
So let's repeat our argument
In the presence of these twelve damsels,
Who are wise, good, and beautiful,
And also of the many good people who will be present.
1370   They will listen to us willingly."

GUILLAUME

I did not hesitate long at all,
But fell to my knees straightaway
And answered her humbly:
"My dear lady, I have already said enough.
1375   Would that it please God in Paradise
The man who is to hear our pleadings
Were in this place right now,
That is, the good king who will know how
To listen and pay attention quite intelligently,
1380   To keep silent, and then judge
After he has heard
What will be told him.
He will know well how to deliberate
And then, even better, what to decide.

1385   Et si croy bien qu'il jugeroit
        Selonc les parlers qu'il orroit.
        Et non pour quant, puisqu'il vous plait,
        Bien en poez dire hors plait,
        En supposant sans prejudice.
1390   Et je qui point n'i pens malice
        Volentiers vous escouteray,
        Et, se bon m'est, j'en parleray."

LA DAME
        "Guillaume, moult bel respondez.
        Mais .i. bien petit m'entendés.
1395   Levez vous, car il plaist a nous
        Que plus ne parlez a genous.
        Et se plus ci aprés parlez,
        Parlez einsi, com vous volez,
        Ou en seant, ou en estant,
1400   Car il nous souffist bien a tant."

GUILLAUME
        Lors me levay hastivement
        Pour faire son commandement
        Quant elle ot sa parole dite.
        Et puis tout droit a l'opposite
1405   De li m'en alai asseoir,
        Pour li en la face veoir.
        Car qui voit personne en la face
        Qui de parler doit avoir grace,
        Le parler trop miex en entent
1410   A quel fin sa parole tent.
        Lors prist la dame une maniere
        Able, diligent, et maniere
        De parler par si bel devis
        Qu'il estoit a chascun avis
1415   Qu'elle veïst tout en escript
        Ce qu'elle disoit et descript.
        Dont miex diter nuls ne porroit
        Nés que ses parlers atiroit.
        Elle ordena son parlement
1420   Dés le premier commancement,
fol. 31v Qu'elle m'avoit envoié querre,
        Et puis secondement requerre,
        Et comment j'alai devers li;
        Et comment elle m'assailli
1425   De parole cusensonneuse.
        Et comment elle fu crueuse
        De moy rudement ramposner

1385 And I believe firmly he will judge
   According to the testimony he should hear.
   Yet nevertheless, since it pleases you,
   You can certainly speak before the debate,
   Making suppositions without any prejudice.
1390 And I, intending no malice,
   Will listen willingly to you,
   And if I think it good, I will respond."

THE LADY

   "Guillaume, you answer quite eloquently;
   However, listen to me just a little.
1395 Get up now, for it pleases us
   That you say no more while kneeling.
   And if you have something else to say,
   Speak whatever way you please,
   Either seated or standing,
1400 For this much is all we require."

GUILLAUME

   Then I quickly got up
   To carry out her command
   Once she had spoken her mind.
   And then right opposite her
1405 I proceeded to sit down
   In order to face her directly.
   For whoever looks a person in the face,
   Intending his speech to find favor,
   He will hear much better what is said
1410 And the point being made as well.
   Then the lady assumed a manner
   That was forceful, assured, a way of
   Speaking with such pretty eloquence
   Everyone thought
1415 She was looking at the written text
   Of what she said and recounted.
   For no one could speak better
   Even if planning his words in advance.
   She organized her discussion,
1420 Starting from the very beginning
   When she sent to have me searched out
   And then, the second time, fetched;
   Also how I'd made my way to her and how
   She had attacked me
1425 With angry words;
   And how she'd been cruel,
   Reproaching me roughly,

        Pour moy seulement agoner
        Et en merencolie mettre,
1430   Dont bel se savoit entremettre.
        Que vous iroie je comptant?
        Elle y mist de biaus parlers tant
        Qu'elle mena l'entention
        Dou fait a declaration,
1435   De point en point, de tire a tire,
        Si bien qu'il n'i ot que redire,
        Par quoy les damoiselles toutes
        Furent tantost, sans nulles doubtes,
        Dou fait sages et avisees
1440   Et entierement enfourmees
        De quanqu'on avoit recordé
        Dessus les chams et acordé.

        Aprés ces paroles moustrees,
        Bien dites et bien ordenees,
1445   Eüs tantost le cuer esjoÿ,
        Car tant escoutay que je oÿ
        Chevaus venir et gens debatre,
        Dont en l'eure se vint embatre
        Devers nous cils bons rois de pris
1450   Que nous aviens a juge pris.
        Et la dame qui resgardoit
        Devers l'uis et ne s'en gardoit,
        Le vit et congnut a l'entree;
        Se s'est tantost en piez levee,
1455   S'ala a l'encontre de lui
        Et se n'i atendi nelui.
        Quant il la vit, il s'avansa
        Et .i. bien petit l'embrassa,
        Et elle lui moult humblement,
1460   En saluant courtoisement,
        Liement, et a bonne chiere.
        Et il li dist: "Ma dame chiere,
        Moult me poise quant sa venites.
        Pour quel cause ne vous tenistes
1465   En vostre siege toute coie?"
        "Tres chiers sires, se Diex me voie,
        Jamais ne l'eüsse einsi fait,
        Car trop pensasse avoir meffait.
        Car on dit — et c'est chose voire
1470   Qu'il est assez legier a croire —
        Qu'entre les grans et les meneurs
        A tous seigneurs toutes honneurs.
        Mais laissons ces parlers ester.

Only to make me squirm
And sink me into melancholy,
1430 Which she knew quite handily how to do.
Shall I go on telling you about it?
She expended so much fine talk
She brought out the facts
Of the matter fully in a declaration,
1435 Point by point, step by step,
So ably that nothing needed correction.
And in this way all the young ladies
Were quickly, and beyond any doubt, rendered
Knowledgeable and enlightened about this case,
1440 Completely informed as well
Of all that had been discussed
And concluded below in the fields.

After these explanatory words,
Which were ably spoken and well organized,
1445 My heart suddenly felt joy
Because, while listening, I heard
Horses come up and people talking;
For at that very hour the good and worthy king
Had come, for pleasure, into our presence,
1450 The man we had chosen for a judge.
And the lady, who was looking
At the door and was not slow to do so,
Saw and recognized him as he entered;
And she rose to her feet at once,
1455 Proceeding to greet him
And waiting for no one to do so.
Seeing her, he stepped forward
And embraced her lightly,
As she did him with much humility,
1460 Welcoming the man courteously,
Joyfully, and with a pleasant look.
And he said to her: "My dear lady,
I am quite unhappy you came forward.
Why did you not remain
1465 With propriety on your throne?"
"Dear sir, so God guide me,
I should never have done what
Would seem quite improper to me
But it is said — something true enough
1470 And rather easy to credit — that in the case of
Those of exalted rank and lesser persons,
All honor should be paid to every great lord.
But let's drop the matter.

Petit y devons arrester.
1475   S'alons en cest siege seoir.
La me vorrai je pourveoir
De vous compter une merveille
D'autres merveilles nom pareille.
Alez devant; je iray aprés,
1480   De vous me tenray assez pres."
"Par Dieu, ma dame, non ferai.
Aussi tost com je y monterai,
Tout d'encoste moy monterez.
Ja a ce point ne me menrez
1485   Qu'embedeus n'en alons ensamble.
Encor fais je trop, ce me samble."
De ce point si bien s'acorderent,
Si qu'ensamble tous .ij. monterent.
Et quant il furent haut monté,
1490   Encor, par grant humilité,
D'asseoir moult se debatirent.
Toutes voies il se seïrent.
Et quant il furent la assis,
La dame dist de sens rassis:
1495   "Sire, entendez un bien petit.
Et se prenez vostre apetit
A diligemment escouter
Ce que je vous vorray compter.
Vez la Guillaume de Machaut.
1500   C'est uns homs a cui il ne chaut
fol. 32r A tort ou a droit soustenir.
Tout aussi chier s'a il tenir
Vers le tort comme vers le droit,
Si com vous orrez orendroit.
1505   En un debat sommes entré
Dont nous devons de fait outré,
Sire, devant vous plaidïer,
Mais qu'il ne vous doie anuier.
Moy bien meüe et il meüs,
1510   Pour juges estes esleüs;
Dont c'est pour nous belle avenue,
Biau sire, de vostre venue.
Et vous en estes eüreus,
Se de riens estes amoureus.
1515   Car de cause avons nostre plest
Fourme qui aus amoureus plest
C'est d'amors, d'amant, et d'amie,
Et de leur noble signourie.
Guillaumes dit, tient, et afferme
1520   Pour vray, et que c'est chose ferme,

It should delay us but little.
1475   Instead, let us take our seats on the throne.
There I would like to see about
Telling you an extraordinary thing
Quite unlike other marvels.
Go on ahead; I'll follow along,
1480   Keeping quite close to you."
"By God, my lady, I shall not do so.
At the very moment I ascend
You will go up right by my side;
Never will you make me agree
1485   That we should not proceed together.
I believe I have already been too forward."
On this point they easily concurred
And then ascended together.
And after going up,
1490   Again, in their great humility,
They argued about sitting down.
But in the end they sat,
And once they were seated,
The lady spoke, her thoughts composed:
1495   "Sire, listen to me a little while
And take some pleasure
In attending diligently to
What I would like to tell you.
You see there Guillaume de Machaut.
1500   He's a man indifferent
To whether he upholds wrong or right.
In fact, he would just as soon defend
The wrong as the right,
As you will presently hear.
1505   We have entered into a debate
About an outrageous deed,
And this argument, sire, we should put before you,
But only if you would not be annoyed.
By his wish and my own,
1510   You were chosen to be the judge.
And so for us it is a happy chance,
Fair sir, that you have arrived here.
And you'll find this a happy chance
If you have any interest in love.
1515   For the issue of our disagreement concerns
Something that pleases the romantically inclined
Since it's about love, the lover, and the beloved,
And of their noble governance.
Guillaume says, maintains, and affirms
1520   As true and unassailable fact

Quant homs qui ha tout son cuer mis
En dame, tant qu'il est amis
Et celle s'amour li ottrie,
Si qu'il la tient pour vraie amie,
1525 Puis est de lui si esprouvee
Qu'il la trueve fausse prouvee,
Qu'il a de ce plus de grieté
C'une dame qui loyauté
En son vray ami trouvera;
1530 Et elle aussi tant l'amera
Comme dame puet homme amer,
Entierement, sans point d'amer.
Or avenra il que la mort,
Qui soutilment sus la gent mort,
1535 Torra a son ami la vie.
Et quant elle scet qu'il devie,
Ou qu'il est dou tout devïez,
Il est a la mort marïez,
Lors est finee leur querelle,
1540 Aroit cils aussi grief com celle?
Nennil! Il ne puet avenir;
Cils poins ne se puet soustenir,
Dont j'ay fait, et fais, et vueil faire
Protestation dou contraire.
1545 C'est auques nostres plaidïez.
Pour ce volons que vous soiez
Juges; si en ordonnerez
Selonc le plait que vous orrez."

LE JUGE

"Je vous respons, ma chiere dame,
1550 Par la foy que doy Dieu et m'ame,
Selonc la mienne entention,
Que d'estre en la perfection
De juge est moult noble chose,
Voire qui entrepenre l'ose
1555 Si hautement comme en Amours.
Mais pour les tres douces clamours
Qui y sont, j'entrepren l'office,
Sans mal penser et sans malice.
Se j'ay petit sens, j'apenray
1560 Parmi les parlers que je orray;
Et s'estre puis bien consilliez,
Je ne seroie pas si liez
D'avoir acquis .v.^{c} mars d'or.
Et pour tant vous dis je desor,
1565 Chiere dame, que j'esliray

That when a man has given all his heart
To a lady, thus becoming her lover,
And she grants him her affection,
And so he thinks the woman a true beloved,
1525 But then he has the experience
Of finding her proven false;
This man, he says, feels more pain
Than a lady who discovers
Faithfulness in her true lover,
1530 And she in turn loves him as much
As any lady can love a man,
Completely and without bitterness.
But then it chances that death,
Which with stealth stings mankind,
1535 Takes the life from her lover.
And when she learns he has passed away,
Has been completely undone,
Has been married to death,
And their affair has thus ended,
1540 Would that first man grieve like this woman?
Not at all! It could not happen.
This view is indefensible,
And so I have made, do make, and wish to make
A protest to the contrary.
1545 That is the gist of our dispute.
And we would like you to be its
Judge; thus you would decide
According to the disputation you'd hear."

THE JUDGE

"I will answer you, my dear lady,
1550 By the faith I owe God and my own soul,
From my own perspective
That to occupy the privileged position
Of a judge is a very noble thing,
Especially for someone who risks so much
1555 As to judge questions of Love.
But because the petitions offered here
Have greatly pleased me, I will undertake the office
Without improper thoughts or malice.
If I have but a little sense, I will learn
1560 From the speeches I hear;
And if I can be well counseled,
I would be much happier than if
I received five hundred marks of gold.
And yet I do inform you,
1565 Dear lady, I will choose

Tel conseil comme je vorray
De vostre bele compaingnie,
Qui a vous est acompaingnie.
Car a .i. bon juge apartient
1570 Qui jugemens en sa part tient
Qu'il ait conseil en tous endrois.
Prenons, qu'il soit ou non soit drois.
Se vous requier je qu'on le face,
Soit par courtoisie ou par grace.
1575 Et d'autre part, quoy que nuls die,
Bons drois a bon mestier d'aïe
Par quoy grace ait adés son cours
Pour aidier droit en toutes cours."

LA DAME

fol. 32v "Biau sire, de vostre recort,
1580 Que ce soit drois, bien m'i acort.
Or prenez cui que vous volez,
Par quoy de riens ne vous dolez."

LE JUGE

"Ma dame, je pren Congnoissance,
Qui est de bon conseil sustance;
1585 Avecques li sera Avis,
Li quels n'i sera pas envis
Pour ce que c'est sa bonne amie;
Volentiers li tient compaingnie.
Et se me plaist, qu'aussy y soit
1590 Raison, qui nelui ne deçoit,
Eins est adés en sa partie
De bon conseil apareillie.
Si entendra les parlemens
Pour raporter aus jugemens.
1595 La me sara bien consillier;
Pas ne m'en faurra resveillier.
Avec li sera Mesure;
Quar qui jugemens ne mesure,
Il ne puelent venir a point
1600 Afin qu'il soient en bon point
Pour les parties delivrer
Et chascune son droit livrer."
La Dame bien s'i acorda
Et hautement li recorda:
1605 "Biau sire, bien avez ouvré
D'avoir bon conseil recouvré!"

Such advisers as I desire
From among your splendid entourage,
Which has accompanied you.
Truly, it is fitting for a competent judge
1570 Weighing a decision
To take counsel from all sides.
We'll take it, whether this is correct or not.
So I ask you for this to be done,
Either with courtesy or grace.
1575 And yet, no matter what anyone says,
Proper justice most certainly needs help
So that it may at once proceed with grace
To assist the rendering of judgment in every court."

THE LADY

"Fair sir, concerning your request,
1580 I certainly agree it is proper.
Choose now whomever you wish,
And you will have nothing to complain about."

THE JUDGE

"My lady, I choose Understanding,
Who is the very substance of good counsel.
1585 Discretion will be at her side,
And he will not protest at all
Because she is his good friend;
Willingly he will accompany her.
And I should also be pleased for Reason
1590 To be present, who deceives no one
But instead is always for her part
Ready with good advice.
So she will listen to the testimony
In order to make it part of the judgment.
1595 She will know how to advise me well.
I will never need to review anything.
Moderation will stand by her;
For whoever does not moderate his judgment
Will not be able to proceed correctly
1600 And come to the proper point
Where he can release the parties
And deliver justice to each."
The Lady heartily agreed
And spoke to him enthusiastically:
1605 "Fair sir, you have done well
In obtaining such advisers!"

LE JUGE

       "C'est bon pour moy, ma dame gente;
       Dont a mon cuer bien entalente
       Que j'en soie einsi bien garnis.
1610 Qui n'est garnis, il est honnis.
       Juges sui par commun acort
       Especiaument d'un descort
       Qui est ci entre .ij. parties,
       Pour atendre droit de parties.
1615 Or est la court garnie et pleinne;
       Se puet on bien par voie pleinne,
       Ce m'est avis, aler avant.
       Dame, vous parlerez devant,
       Se fourmerez vostre demande,
1620 Nom pas pour ce que je demande
       Que li fais me soit refourmez,
       Car j'en suis assez enfourmez;
       Mais d'aucuns membres dou procés
       Me moustreroient les excés
1625 Qui vous en font doloir et pleindre;
       Et aussi pour Guillaume ateindre
       En son tort, se tort doit avoir;
       Autrement ne le puis savoir."

LA DAME

       "Sire, ceste raison me plait.
1630 Dés qu'entamé en avons plait,
       Mon fait moustrerai par figure
       Selonc les ouevres de Nature,
       Tout pour Guillaume, qui se tort
       De verité dont il ha tort.
1635 Vous savez que la turterelle,
       Qui est faitice, gente, et belle,
       Cointe, gaie, douce, et jolie
       Tant com ses males est en vie,
       Et s'il avient qu'elle le pert
1640 Par mort, on scet tout en appert
       Que jamais joie n'avera,
       Et par signes le moustrera.
       Tant est li siens cuers pleins d'ardeur,
       Jamais ne serra sus verdeur;
1645 Eins quiert tout adés obscurtez,
       Divers lieus et pleins de durtez,
       Aubres sés, verseinnes, et trieges.
       En tel lieus est souvent ses sieges
       Quant elle se vuet reposer.
1650 Autrement ne vuet disposer

THE JUDGE

"It will benefit me, my noble lady,
Because my heartfelt desire is
That I be well attended.
1610   For the man not so attended is shamed.
By their mutual agreement, I am now the judge
In the particular case of the dispute
Dividing these two parties
That awaits a just decision.
1615   Now the court is assembled and ready;
And the way is quite clear, I think,
For us to be able to proceed.
Lady, you will speak first
And formulate your complaint,
1620   Not because I ask that the details
Of the case be recounted to me,
Since I am already adequately informed,
But rather because the parties to this trial
Should explain to me what is so untoward
1625   It makes you sorrow and complain;
And also in order to charge Guillaume
With his wrongdoing, if he is indeed wrong.
Otherwise, I cannot know the situation."

THE LADY

"Sir, this point pleases me.
1630   Since we've begun the pleading,
I will formulate my complaint in a rhetorical figure
From the works of Nature,
All for Guillaume, who has turned from
The truth and has in this way erred.
1635   You know about the turtle dove,
Which is pretty, noble, and attractive,
Quiet, happy, sweet, and beautiful
While her mate is alive,
And if it happens she loses him
1640   Through death, it is readily apparent
She will never find joy,
For she demonstrates this through signs.
Her heart is so filled with passionate burning
She will never perch on greenery;
1645   Instead she always seeks out darkness,
Strange places full of misery,
Dead trees, fallow fields, and crossroads.
Her perch is often found in such locations
When she wishes to take her rest.
1650   She will permit her heart nothing

         Son cuer qu'en vie dolereuse,
         Tant est de son male grieteuse.
         Tout autel d'une dame di ge
         Qui est rendue a Amours lige.
1655   Quant elle ha son amy perdu
fol. 33r Par mort, le cuer si esperdu
         Ha que jamais n'avera joie,
         Eins quiert lieu, temps, et gens, et voie,
         Ou il ait tout adés tristece,
1660   Humble habit en lieu de richesse
         Tenebres en lieu de clarté,
         Et en lieu de joliveté
         Pour porter chapelés de flours,
         Ist de son chief larmes et plours.
1665   Et s'elle quiert aucun repos,
         Il est pris en humble propos.
         Einsi la dame se maintient
         Que le dueil de son amy tient,
         En cas qu'elle soit vraie amie.
1670   Or dirai de l'autre partie.

         Quant la secoingne se fourfait,
         Et ses males en scet le fait,
         Je croy bien que moult s'en aïre
         Et qu'il en ait au cuer grant ire.
1675   Mais trouver en puet aligence
         En ce qu'il en atent veingance.
         Car il s'en va tantost en serche.
         Par les nis des oisiaus reverche
         A ceuls qui sont de sa samblance
1680   Tant qu'il en ha grant habondance;
         Puis entour son nif les assamble,
         Et quant il sont la tuit ensamble,
         Il y tiennent .i. grant concire,
         Puis mettent celui a martire
1685   De mort qui l'a, ce dit, forfaite.
         La est devouree et deffaite.
         Or ha cils ses maus alegiés
         Qui en ce point en est vengiés.
         Tout autel di je que li homs
1690   Doit estre fiers comme uns lions
         Contre aucun tort, s'il li est fais.
         Et cils puet trouver moult de fais
         Aus quels il se puet encliner
         Pour son mal faire terminer,
1695   Par pluseurs manieres de tours.
         Mais la dame n'a nuls recours

But a sorrowful life,
So grief-stricken she is for her mate.
I say it is just the same for a lady
Who has sworn fealty to Love.
1655   When she has lost her lover
Through death, her heart becomes
So distressed she will never find joy;
Instead she seeks places, times, people, and paths
Where there is always total sadness;
1660   She chooses a simple habit instead of finery,
Shadows instead of sunlight;
And rather than the gaiety that comes
From wearing chaplets of flowers,
Weeping and tears flow from her face.
1665   And if she looks for any relief at all,
She does so modestly.
The lady who remains in mourning for her lover
Conducts herself this way,
That is, when she is a true beloved.
1670   Now I will speak to the other side.

When the stork is unfaithful
And her mate learns the facts of the matter,
I am convinced he is greatly upset
And feels much anger in his heart.
1675   But he can find relief
Because he can avenge himself.
And so he immediately begins to search.
Through the bird nests he looks for
Those of his own kind
1680   Until he finds a multitude of them.
Then he assembles these around his own nest,
And when he has them all together,
They hold a great council
And, afterward, make that one suffer
1685   Death who, so they say, has wronged him.
There she is undone and devoured.
The male has lightened the burden of his pain
After taking revenge in this fashion.
Similarly, I maintain that a man
1690   Must be fierce as a lion
In the face of any wrong done him.
And he can imagine many ways
He might consider
In order to end his trouble,
1695   Many different kinds of schemes.
But the lady has no recourse at all,

          Es quels elle se puist garir,
          Qui son amy verra morir.
          Dont elle sent pour .i. mal cent
1700   Que cils autres amans ne sent.
          Guillaume, aprés moy respondés;
          Se tort avez, si l'amendez."

GUILLAUME
          Aprés ces raisons me dressay
          Et mes paroles adressay
1705   Au juge, qui bien entendi
          Ce qu'elle ot dit et que je di.
          Et je li dis: "Sire, sans faille
          Ma dame a bien, comment qu'il aille,
          Son fait moustré, et sagement,
1710   Et de soutil entendement
          Bien baillié par vives raisons,
          Pour fourmer ses comparisons
          Bien faites et bien divisees
          Et si justement exposees
1715   Que qui amender y vorroit
          Je croy moult bien qu'on ne porroit.
          Et ce qu'elle en a devisé
          Vous l'avez tres bien avisé,
          Oÿ, senti, et entendu.
1720   Car de sa bouche est descendu
          En vostre cuer par escouter;
          Si ne le faut pas repeter.
          Et si croy bien certeinnement
          Que c'est de droit vray sentement,
1725   Ce qu'elle en a yci compté,
          Gardant sa grace et sa bonté,
          Sans point de vainne entention.
          Et j'ay une autre oppinion
          Qu'elle n'a; s'en dirai m'entente,
1730   S'il li plaist et il vous talente,
          Nom pas pour le sien fait punir,
          Mais pour ma cause soustenir.
          On puet bien sa cause prisier
          Sans autrui fait apetisier."

LE JUGE
fol. 33v "Guillaume, ne vueil contredire.
1736   Dites ce qu'il vous plaist a dire,
          Hastivement ou a loisir;
          Ouvrez en a vostre plaisir.

Nothing to heal her pain
Once she sees her lover die.
And she suffers a hundred times more misery
1700   Than that other lover ever feels.
Guillaume, find an answer now for this.
If you are wrong, then make amends."

GUILLAUME

After these arguments, I drew myself up
And addressed my words
1705   To the judge, who attended closely to
What she said and what I was saying.
And I told him: "Sir, without doubt
My lady, whatever the outcome,
Has stated her case wisely and well,
1710   And with a subtle understanding
Well supplied with lively arguments
So as to establish her comparisons,
Which are nicely developed and ably disposed,
So thoroughly expounded as well
1715   That whoever wished to offer improvements
Would find this impossible, I believe.
And what she has recounted
You have well remarked,
Heard, sensed, and understood.
1720   For from her mouth all this made its way
Into your heart as you listened;
And so there is no need to repeat it.
Furthermore I believe without question
That it comes from genuine feelings,
1725   What she has brought up, that is,
Maintaining her grace and goodness,
And it lacks vain intention of any kind.
And I hold an opinion that is different
From her own; and I will state my reasons why,
1730   If it pleases and interests you,
Not in order to undermine her point of view,
But rather to make my own case.
A man can quite well value his own position
Without belittling the contrary view."

THE JUDGE

1735   "Guillaume, I won't contradict you.
Say whatever it pleases you to say,
Either quickly or taking your time.
Work at this as you like.

Je vueil bien oïr et entendre,
1740   Et s'ay assez loisir d'atendre."

GUILLAUME

"Grant merci, sire. Je diray,
Et croy que point n'en mentiray.
Je vous di que la forfaiture
De dame est si aspre et si dure
1745   En cuer d'amant, et si perverse,
Que, quant elle y est bien aherse,
Jamais jour ne s'en partira.
Or ne scet cils quel part ira
Pour querir son aligement;
1750   Se prendre en voloit vengement
Par mort, et bien le peüst faire,
Il trouveroit tout son contraire
En la fourme de grant folour,
En l'attrait de toute dolour,
1755   .I. feu pour toute ardeur ateindre,
Une yaue pour douceur esteindre,
Norrissemens de tous meschiés;
Car dou faire seroit pechiés.
Et pechiez qui en cuer remort
1760   Est uns commencemens de mort,
De mort qu'on claimme mortel vie.
Car qui languist, il ne vit mie.
En mon fait que ci vous present
Maintenant, en vostre present,
1765   Ha plus de griés et plus d'ardure
Qu'en l'autre fait, et trop plus dure.
Dont je vous requier orendroit
Sus ce point ci que j'aie droit."

ATTEMPRANCE

Adont se leva Attemprance,
1770   Qui tenoit par la main Souffrance.
Si parla attempreement
En disant: "Guillaume, comment
Droit pour vous demander osastes?
Je me merveil que vous pensastes
1775   Quant vous en fustes si hastis:
Ou vostres scens est trop petis,
Ou outrecuidiers vous demeinne.
Ne savez vous pas bien qui mainne
Le droit quant parties y tendent
1780   Qui le desirent et attendent?
Je vueil moult bien que vous sachiez

I would very much like to listen and hear,
1740   And I have enough leisure to wait."

GUILLAUME

"Many thanks, sire. I will speak,
And I believe I'll say nothing false.
I tell you that unfaithfulness on the part of a lady
Is such a bitter and difficult thing
1745   For a lover's heart, so unnatural as well,
That, when the fact of it has taken firm hold,
It will never depart for a single day.
Now the man does not know where to go
In order to seek relief;
1750   If he thinks to avenge himself
Through murder (and well might he do so),
He should be firmly opposed
By the prospect of great madness
And a powerful, encompassing grief,
1755   A fire to afflict every passion,
A water to extinguish sweetness,
Nourishment for every mischance;
For to commit murder would be a sin.
And a sin that tortures the heart
1760   Is one way death can begin,
The death of what is called mortal life.
For whoever languishes thus is not alive at all.
In my case, the one I am presenting to you
Now in your presence,
1765   There is more grief and burning torment
Than in the other, and it is much harder to bear.
And so I ask now if
For this reason I might claim victory."

TEMPERANCE

Immediately Temperance arose
1770   Who was holding Endurance by the hand,
And she spoke in a temperate fashion,
Saying: "Guillaume, how
Dare you ask for the decision on your behalf?
I am amazed that you should consider this
1775   After offering only a brief argument:
Either your intelligence is quite limited
Or you are ruled by overconfidence.
Don't you know who determines
What is the right when parties argue,
1780   Desiring a decision and waiting for it?
I would like very much for you to know

Que Raisons en est li drois chiés
Et avec li sa compaingnie;
Chascune y a bonne partie
1785   D'entre nous damoiselles toutes.
De ce ne faites nulles doubtes,
Que drois ne se puet delivrer,
Se toutes ne sont au livrer,
Afin que fait soit bonnement,
1790   Se cils qui fist les drois ne ment.
Je meïsmes y ai office
Pour resister a tout malice
Qui maintes fois le droit destourne;
Et je d'office le retourne.
1795   Quant uns bons procés vient en fourme,
Et je perçoy qu'on l'en deffourme,
Je y puis bien tellement ouvrer
Qu'il puet sa fourme recouvrer.
Se trop y a, j'en puis oster,
1800   (Or vueilliez bien ce point noter),
Et se po y a, je y puis mettre
Quant je m'en vueil bien entremettre.
Et se la chose est en bon point,
Je la puis garder en ce point.
1805   C'est d'Atemprance li mestiers
Toutes fois qu'il en est mestiers.
Or vueil je dire d'autre chose
Qui contre vostre fait s'oppose.

Vous avez .i. point soustenu
1810   Dont po d'onneur vous est venu,
En ce que ma dame de pris
Avoit seur la segongne pris:
fol. 34r   Comment elle est a la mort traite
Quant envers son male est forfaite.
1815   Cuidiés vous qu'elle vosist dire
Qu'on meïst la dame a martyre
De la mort, qui se mefferoit
Envers celui qui l'ameroit?
Nennil! Voir, ce seroit folie.
1820   Ne ma dame ne maintient mie
Qu'il la face tuer ne tue.
Mais elle tient qu'il s'esvertue
Encontre les temptations
Des fausses cogitations
1825   Qui porroient en lui venir.
Encor s'el pooit avenir,
Qu'elle fust de bonne mort morte,

That Reason is in charge,
And along with her, her entourage;
Each of them holds a prominent position
1785   Among us other damsels.
Don't doubt this in the least.
For no decision can be rendered
If they all are not a part of its making
So that things might be done properly
1790   If the one who made the laws does not lie.
I myself have the responsibility
Of resisting any kind of malice,
Which many times diverts the right;
And by my efforts I put things back on track.
1795   When a proper trial takes shape,
And I see it going awry,
I can very well do what is needed
For it to be put right and returned to form.
If there is too much, I can remove something,
1800   And now please note this point well:
If there is too little, I can add something
Whenever I wish to make the proper effort.
And if everything is just right,
I can make certain it remains so.
1805   That is the office of Temperance
Anytime there is some need.
Now I wish to speak of something else
That contradicts your view.

You have defended an opinion
1810   That does you little honor,
And it concerns what my worthy lady
Maintained about the stork:
How she is put to death
After having proved unfaithful to her mate.
1815   Do you believe my lady meant
That the female who did wrong
To the male who loves her
Should be made to suffer death?
Not at all! Truly that would be folly.
1820   And my lady does not maintain in any way
He should kill her or have her killed.
Instead she advises he struggle
Against the temptations
Of those false ideas
1825   That might come into his mind.
Furthermore, although it might happen
That she die naturally,

Se vaurroit il miex (drois la porte)
Qu'elle demourast toute vive.
1830   Car tant com la personne vive
Qui se mefferoit par folour,
On n'en a peinne, ne dolour,
Grieté, souffrance, ne meschief,
Dont on ne veingne bien a chief.
1835   Quant il sent aucune grieté,
Il doit penser par verité,
Dés qu'il a loiaument servi,
Qu'il ne l'a mie desservi.
C'est une pensee valable,
1840   Pour lui conforter profitable.
Que vous yroie je comptant?
De remedes y a autant
En amours, com de griés pointures,
Soient aspres, pongnans, ou dures.
1845   Chascune son remede enseigne.
Or en fait bon querir l'enseigne.
Mais une dame qui verra
Que se tres dous amis morra
En cui en nul jour de sa vie
1850   N'ara trouvé que courtoisie,
Estre porra si fort ferue,
Si griefment, et si abatue,
Que jamais n'en porra garir;
Einsois la couvendra morir.
1855   En l'escripture est contenu
Que pluseurs fois est avenu.
S'en compteray .i. petit compte
Qui vous fera avoir grant honte
Et a ma dame grant honnour,
1860   Et grant clarté a mon signour,
Dont il verra plus clerement
Comment vous errez folement.

Il n'a pas lonc temps qu'il avint
Q'une grant dame a Paris vint,
1865   S'amena une sienne fille
Qui, sans penser barat ne guille,
Amoit .i. chevalier gentil,
Sage, courtois, gay, et soutil,
Preu aus armes, fort, et puissant,
1870   De toutes graces souffisant.
De lui nouveles li venirent
Q'forment au cuer la pongnirent,
Qu'il estoit a .i. tournoy mors.

It would be better (justice upholds it)
Had she remained alive.
1830 For as long as the person lives
Who sins in mad error,
One has no pain, no sorrow,
No grief, suffering, or mischance
That one cannot overcome.
1835 When feeling pain of some kind,
He must truly think,
Having served her faithfully,
That he has not deserved this at all.
This is a valid thought,
1840 Useful for comforting the man.
What else should I tell you?
There are as many remedies
In love as painful wounds,
However bitter, painful, or hard to bear.
1845 Each points to its proper remedy,
Teaches the man what is good to seek.
But a lady who witnesses
The death of her very sweet lover
In whom on no day of his life
1850 Was found anything but courtesy,
She could be so terribly stricken
And so grievously, beaten down so far as well
She will never prove able to recover;
Instead, she will not fail to die.
1855 Written tradition informs us
This has happened many times.
And so I will relate a short tale
That will bring great shame upon you
And great honor to my lady,
1860 As well as much clarity to my lord,
For he will see more distinctly
How foolishly you err.

Not long ago it happened
That a great lady came to Paris,
1865 And she brought along a daughter of hers
Who, intending neither deception nor trouble,
Fell in love with a noble knight,
A man wise, courteous, happy, and sophisticated,
Skilled at arms, strong and powerful,
1870 Possessing every grace.
News of him came to her
That greatly afflicted her heart,
For he had been killed in a tournament.

'Lasse!' dist elle, 'Quel remors
1875   Puis avoir de ceste nouvelle!'
       A cest mot cheÿ la pucelle
       A la terre, toute estendue.
       Adont sa mere y est venue
       Acourant moult dolentement;
1880   S'en prist a plourer tenrement
       Et la fist porter en .i. lit.
       La prist elle povre delit
       Car au cuer estoit fort atainte,
       Et eu viaire pale et tainte,
1885   Et si de son corps amatie,
       Et de ses membres amortie,
       Qu'einc puis ne s'en pot soustenir,
       Ne des mains nulles riens tenir.
       Et n'ot ainc puis tant de victoire
1890   Qu'elle peüst mengier ne boire.
       Fusicien furent mandé,
       Et la leur fu il demandé
fol. 34v S'elle averoit de la mort garde,
       Et que chascuns y prenist garde
1895   S'on li porroit donner santé,
       Et qu'il demandassent planté
       Hardiement de leur avoir,
       Tant comme il en vorront avoir.
       Et il en peinne s'en meïrent
1900   Et moult volentiers le feïrent
       Pour trouver son aligement,
       S'il peüssent, diligenment.
       Premiers, s'orine resgarderent,
       Et puis aprés si la tasterent;
1905   Li uns aprés l'autre tastoient
       Partout ou taster la devoient,
       Les piez, le pous, et puis les temples;
       Et puis si moustroient exemples
       Des cures qu'il avoient faites
1910   En pluseurs lieus et bien parfaites;
       Et que plus d'exemples moustroient,
       De tant plus esbahi estoient.
       L'orine la jugoit haitie,
       Et li tasters ne jugoit mie
1915   Cause froide, ne de chalour,
       En quoy il prenissent coulour
       D'ou ne de quoy cils maus venoit,
       Ne quel remede il couvenoit,
       Pour li un po assouagier
1920   Ou dou tout ses maus alegier,

'Alas!' she said, 'What grief
1875 This news brings me!'
With this word, the young girl
Fell to the earth in a heap.
Quickly her mother went over,
Running to her with great sorrow;
1880 And she began to cry softly
And had her carried to a bed.
There she found little comfort
Because her heart was so terribly afflicted,
And her face so pale and discolored,
1885 Her body so stricken,
And her limbs so withered
She could hardly stand
Or hold anything in her hands.
And she did not recover enough afterward
1890 To be able to eat or drink.
Physicians were sent for,
And it was asked of them
If she could be saved from death;
And that each should see about
1895 Bringing her back to health, if it could be done;
And that they should boldly demand
A great deal of what these people possessed,
As much as they desired to have.
And these men diligently applied themselves,
1900 As they quite eagerly and with care
Attempted to devise
A cure for her if they could.
First they examined her urine,
And then they palpated her.
1905 One after the other they touched her
Wherever palpation should be done:
The feet, the wrists, and then the temples.
And after this they discussed examples
Of the various cures they had brought about
1910 And successfully accomplished in many places;
But the more examples they discussed,
The more bewildered they were.
Her urine was judged healthy,
And the examination did not reveal
1915 Any symptoms of coldness or heat
From which they would have gotten indications
About where or what this illness came from,
Or what remedy was called for
In order to soothe her somewhat
1920 Or alleviate her ills altogether,

Fors tant que li uns s'avisa
Et sagement le devisa:
'Signeurs, j'ay veü en s'orine
Aussi comme un po de racine,
1925   Qu'elle est en l'esperit troublee.
Or nous est la science emblee
De ce point s'on ne s'en avise.
Et nous savons une devise
Que li bons philosophes dist;
1930   Il afferme, et je croy son dist,
Que les maladies quelconques —
Et qu'autrement il n'avint onques —
Sont curees par leur contraire.
Or ne poons a ce point traire
1935   De ceste maladie cy
Tant seulement que par un sy.
Car si hastives maladies
Puelent venir de .ij. parties:
C'est assavoir, se Diex me voie,
1940   De grant dueil ou de trop grant joie.
Et cause de joie desire
Qu'on la courresse et qu'on l'aïre,
Et celle de dueil autrement:
Faire couvenra liement,
1945   Present li, ce qu'elle vorra
Et quanqu'elle comandera;
Et qu'on li ait admenistres,
Pour faire feste, menestres.
Or couvenra il qu'elle die
1950   Dou quel li vient la maladie
Pour li donner certein conseil.
Je le lo einsi et conseil.
Se voit li uns tout simplement
Parler a li secretement.'
1955   Seur ce point furent acordans;
Dont li uns li fu demandans
Ce que devant avez oÿ.
Point n'en ot le cuer esjoÿ,
Eins en respondi moult envis,
1960   Et toute voie vis a vis
Pure verité l'en conta,
Si bien que point n'i arresta.
Lors li fist cils une requeste
Au mieus qu'il pot par voie honneste:
1965   'Fille, respondés moy d'un point
Que je vous dirai bien a point:
Vorriés vous de ci en avant

But in the end one of them took stock
And spoke these words of wisdom:
'Colleagues, I've seen in her urine
A little something of what's causing this,
1925 Namely that she is troubled in spirit.
Now our science casts little light
On this point unless one thinks it over.
For we are aware of a saying
The good philosopher affirmed:
1930 He states, and I believe what he says,
That illnesses of every kind —
And there are never exceptions —
Are cured by their contraries.
And so we cannot infer at this point
1935 That there is only one contrary
Side in regard to this particular illness.
For these sudden maladies
Can arise for two reasons:
That's to say, so God guide me,
1940 Great sorrow or overwhelming joy.
And as a cause joy requires
Her to be made angry and irritated,
And sorrow asks for just the opposite:
One should make merry
1945 In her presence, do what would please her
And whatever she asks for;
And minstrels too should be summoned
To entertain her.
Then it will be necessary for her to admit
1950 The cause of the illness
So she can be given certain advice.
This is what I advise and counsel.
So let one of us go very quietly
In order to speak to her privately.'
1955 They were agreed on this point;
And so one went to ask her
What you have already heard.
Her heart was hardly happy about this.
Instead she answered quite unwillingly,
1960 And yet still told him
Face to face the whole truth
So ably that she hesitated not at all.
Then he asked her this,
As ably as he could in all honesty:
1965 'Young lady, answer me one question
That I will now put to you;
Would you want from this moment on

Que vous le veïssiez vivant,
Mais que ce fust par tel maniere
1970 Q'jamais ne vous moustrast chiere,
Parole, ne samblant d'amy?'
Et elle respondi: 'Aymy!
fol. 35r Sire, se Diex me doint santé,
Que c'est bien de ma volenté
1975 Que volentiers le reverroie
Vivant, et fust par tele voie
Qu'il heüst fait une autre amie,
La quele fust de moy servie,
Mon vivant, jusqu'au deschaucier.
1980 Ne m'en vueilliez plus enchaucier;
Car tous li cuers de dueil me font
Si aigrement et si parfont
Toutes fois que j'en oy parole.
Si ne vueil plus qu'on m'en parole.'
1985 Aprés ce mot, cils s'en depart
Et s'en ala de celle part
Ou cil estient qui l'atendoient,
Qui desiroient et tendoient,
Savoir quel fin celle feroit.
1990 Et il leur dist qu'elle morroit:
'Je n'i puis veoir nul retour.
Ses cuers est fermez en la tour
D'Amour sous la clef de Tristesse,
Ou elle sueffre grant destresse,
1995 Si que morir la couvenra
Briefment; ja n'en eschapera.
Pour quoy nous nous departirons
De ci; plus n'i arresterons.'
En l'eure de la se partirent,
2000 Et puis a la mere deïrent:
'Ma dame, on n'i puet conseil mettre.
Mais vueilliez vous bien entremettre
De li garder et tenir pres.'
Euls departis, tantost aprés
2005 Elle cria a haute vois:
'Hé! Douce mere, je m'en vois.
A Dieu vous commant, douce dame!'
Et droit a ce point rendi l'ame.
Elle fu de la gent criee,
2010 Et sa mere en fu tourmentee.
De ce ne tieng je pas mon compte,
Car a mon propos riens n'en monte.

                    To see him alive,
                    Even if this were in such a way
1970   That he would never show you the demeanor,
                    The speech, the look of a lover?'
                    And she answered: 'Alas!
                    Sir, may God grant me health,
                    Such is indeed my wish,
1975   And I would willingly see him alive
                    Again even if it were
                    That he has taken another beloved,
                    Who would be served by me
                    All my life, even to taking off her shoes.
1980   Please press me no more about this;
                    For my heart breaks completely with sorrow,
                    A sorrow so bitter and deep
                    Every time anyone speaks of him to me.
                    So I do not want to hear about it anymore.'
1985   After this word, he left
                    And walked to the place
                    Where the others were awaiting him,
                    And they were eager and anxious
                    To learn what end she might come to.
1990   And he told them she would die:
                    'I see no recovery from this.
                    Her heart has been locked within the tower
                    Of Love by the key of Sadness,
                    Where she suffers great distress,
1995   And thus she shall die
                    Soon; she shall never escape.
                    Because of this we will depart;
                    We will remain here no longer.'
                    Within the hour they left the place,
2000   Saying to the mother:
                    'My lady, nothing can be done,
                    But please do your best
                    To watch over and stay close to her.'
                    After they left, she cried out
2005   All at once in a loud voice:
                    'Oh! Sweet mother, I'm dying.
                    I commend you to God, sweet lady!'
                    And just at that moment, she gave up the ghost.
                    The girl was lamented by the household,
2010   And her mother suffered terribly.
                    But of this I'll take no account
                    Because it adds nothing to my theme.

              Guillaume, ou porrés vous trouver
              Comment vous peüssiez prouver
2015   Qu'uns homs seroit a mort menez
              De ce point que vous soustenez,
              Dou forfait de sa bien amee,
              Et que ce fust chose prouvee
              Qu'elle heüst fait la villenie
2020   Et qu'adés demourast en vie?
              De la pucelle est chose voire,
              Mais ce seroit trop fort a croire
              Que plus grans fust li siens meschiés
              Que de celle. Bien le sachiez!"

GUILLAUME
2025   "Attemprance, moult bel parlez
              Toutes les fois que vous volez.
              Ci endroit especiaument
              Avez parlé moult sagement.
              Et quanqu'avez ci dit, je croy,
2030   Ne dou croire point ne recroy.
              Car c'est pour moy en aucun point
              Qui vient a mon propos a point
              Quant celle damoiselle gente
              Ot mis en chevalier s'entente,
2035   Et il estoit ses vrais amis
              Et puis se fu a la mort mis,
              Dont Amours si fort l'atrapa
              Que la mort tantost la hapa,
              Amours en fist pour li assez
2040   Car cils cops fu tantost passez.
              Aussi a morir avoit elle:
              Nuls contre ce point ne rebelle
              Cui la mort ne veingne haper;
              Nuls ne li porroit eschaper.
2045   Quant uns hons est grieteusement
              Tauxés a mort par jugement
              D'un bon juge sans mesprison,
              Et il le met en grief prison
              D'enfermeté en lieux divers,
2050   Ou estre puet mengiez de vers
              Et de planté d'autre vermine,
fol. 35v   Et il y est un lonc termine,
              Chargié col et les bras de fers
              Et les jambes — c'est bien enfers.
2055   La est il de foy en destour
              Pour renoier son creatour;
              Volentiers le renieroit

Guillaume, where will you discover
The proof you need to establish
2015   That a man would be compelled to die
As a result of the experience you describe,
Namely the betrayal of his dear beloved,
When it is already well established
That after she sinned so wickedly,
2020   He did in fact remain alive?
The case of the young girl is true,
But it would certainly be too hard to believe
That his misfortune was greater
Than hers. Well you know it!"

GUILLAUME
2025   "Temperance, you speak very prettily
Every time you wish to.
On this occasion especially
You have spoken quite wisely.
And whatever you have said here I affirm
2030   And do not shrink from believing.
But this has nothing to do
With my case in any way.
When this noble maiden
Granted her devotion to the knight
2035   And he became her true lover
And was afterward delivered so quickly to death,
For which reason Love held her so violently
That death presently struck her down without delay,
Love showed her great favor in this,
2040   For the blow passed quickly.
In any case, she did have to die;
No one contests this fact
Whom death does not come to seize.
No person might avoid it.
2045   When a man is unhappily condemned
To death by the sentence
Of a good judge without impropriety
And that judge puts him in a miserable prison
Enclosed within some horrible place
2050   Where he could be eaten by worms
Or by a host of other vermin,
And he serves a long sentence,
His neck and arms hung with irons
And his legs as well — that's hell for sure.
2055   There he's turned away from faith
In order to renounce his Creator;
Willingly he'd renounce Him

        Qui de la le delivreroit.

        Mais en celle heure qu'il est pris,

2060   Jugiés a mort par juste pris,

        Trop miex li vaut qu'on l'en delivre

        Par la mort qu'en tel doleur vivre.

        Einsi est il d'un vray amant

        Qui est trahis en dame amant,

2065   A tel fin com devant est dit.

        J'aferme et se di en mon dit

        Que nuls meschiés ne s'apartient

        Aus grietez que ses cuers soustient

        Tant come il dure et elle dure.

2070   Et si say moult bien que Nature

        Ha de son bon droit establi

        Qu'on mette celui en oubli

        Qui est mors et n'en puet ravoir

        Pour grant peinne, ne pour avoir.

2075   Seur ce point droit atenderoie;

        Miex estre jugiés ne vorroie."

PAIX

        Aprés ces mos s'est Pais levee

        Et dist, comme bien avisee:

        "Guillaume, assez souffissanment,

2080   Selonc le vostre entendement,

        Avez vostre propos baillié;

        Mais vous l'avez trop court taillié

        Pour avoir droit pour vous si tost.

        Car uns autres poins le vous tost.

2085   Vous avez de Nature trait

        Pour prouver .i. assez biau trait,

        Lequel on ha bien entendu.

        Mais j'ai un autre las tendu

        Contre celui, de plus grant pris,

2090   Par lequel vous serez sourpris,

        D'un exemple aucun de fait

        Qui bien a ramentevoir fait.

        Et pour ceci le vous propos,

        Car il sert bien a mon propos.

2095   Dydo, roïne de Cartage,

        Ot si grant dueil et si grant rage

        Pour l'amour qu'elle ot a Enee,

        Qui li avoit sa foy donnee

        Qu'a mouillier l'aroit et a femme.

2100   Et li faus l'appelloit sa dame,

        Son cuer, s'amour, et sa deesse,

For whoever might deliver him from that place.
But at the time he is arrested,
2060   Condemned to death in a just decision,
It avails him much more to be delivered
By death than to live on in such suffering.
So it is with the true lover
Who has been betrayed in loving a lady,
2065   With the same result as described above.
I affirm and state in my poem
That no misfortune compares to
The suffering his heart endures
As long as he and she live on.
2070   Also I know quite well that Nature
Has established by her proper right
That a person will be forgotten
Who dies and cannot be had back
Either through great trouble or for treasure.
2075   On this point I expect the decision for myself;
I could not wish to be judged by one better."

PEACE

After these words Peace rose up
And said, like one well schooled:
"Guillaume, you have buttressed
2080   Your argument rather sufficiently
According to your lights;
But you have cut it much too short
To gain the judgment for yourself so quickly.
For there is another point that deprives you of it.
2085   You have drawn on Nature
To prove your case, a fair enough point
That has been well understood.
But I have laid another trap
For this, a quite formidable one
2090   In which you shall be caught,
And it's contained in a true exemplum,
One quite useful to recall.
And so I offer it to you
Because it serves my purpose well.

2095   Dido, queen of Carthage,
Felt very great sorrow and anger
Because of the love she bore Aeneas,
Who had pledged her his faith
To take her as his woman and wife.
2100   And the traitor called her his lady,
His heart, his love, and his goddess,

Et sa souvereinne maistresse.
Puis s'en ala par mer nagent
En larrecin, lui et sa gent,
2105 Qu'onques puis Dydo ne le vit.
Oïez comment elle se chevit:
Quant failly li ot dou couvent
Que heü li avoit en couvent,
Einsi com pluseurs amans font
2110 Qui l'amant loial contrefont,
La desesperee, la fole,
Qu'amours honnist, qu'amours afole,
L'espee de Eneas trouva
Et en son corps si l'esprouva
2115 Qu'onques ne se pot espargnier
Qu'en soy ne la feïst baingnier.
Dont elle morut a dolour
Pour amer, et par sa folour.
Mais elle ne morut pas seule,
2120 Einsois a .ij. copa la gueule,
Car de Eneas estoit enceinte,
Dont moult fu regretee et plainte.
Mais einsois qu'elle s'oceïst,
Elle commanda qu'on feïst
2125 Un ardant feu en sa presence.
Et quant en sa desesperence
S'ocist, si forment s'envaÿ
Qu'avec le cop en feu chaÿ
Dont tantost fu arse et bruïe.
2130 Einsi fina Dydo sa vie.
fol. 36r Bien croy que ce fu chose voire,
Car einsi le truis en l'istoire.

Si que, Guillaume, vraiement,
Il me samble tout autrement
2135 Veües et considerees
Mes raisons devant devisees.
Car on puet veoir clerement
Que grieté, peinne, ne tourment
Ne se porroient comparer
2140 Ad ce que celle comparer
Volt pour le grief de son amy.
Et fust uns homs trestout enmy
Grant planté de ses annemis,
Qui tuit li heüssent promis
2145 La mort et tuer le porroient
A leur plaisir quant il vorroient,
Lui vivant en celle paour,

His sovereign mistress as well.
Then he sailed off across the ocean
Like a thief, he and his companions,
2105 So that Dido never saw him again.
Hear now what she did:
When he'd failed her by breaking the promise
He had agreed to make in good faith,
Just as many lovers do
2110 Who pretend to be loyal lovers,
That desperate and crazed woman,
Whom love had shamed, whom love had driven mad,
Found the sword of Aeneas
And tried it out on her own body,
2115 Not sparing herself
Until she made it bathe in her blood.
And so she died in pain
Because she loved and went mad.
Yet she did not die alone,
2120 But cut instead the throats of two,
For she was carrying the child of Aeneas,
And afterward she was much mourned and lamented.
But before she killed herself,
She ordered a blazing fire
2125 To be laid in her presence.
And when in her desperation
She killed herself, the woman struck so forcefully
That with the blow she fell into the fire
And was at once consumed and burned up.
2130 In this way Dido ended her life.
This is the truth, I firmly believe,
For so I found it in written history.

To conclude, Guillaume, truly
My view is just the opposite of yours
2135 In the light of and in view of
The reasons I've laid out above.
For it can be clearly seen
That misery, pain, and torment
Cannot be compared
2140 To what she was intent on paying in return
For the grief brought by her lover.
And if a man found himself among
A great horde of his enemies,
All of whom had promised him
2145 Death and indeed could kill him
As they wished whenever they liked,
Though living in this fear

Non obstant grieté ne freour,
Se trouveroit il reconfort.
2150   Encoy y a un point plus fort:
Qui le menroit aus fourches pendre
En celle heure, sans plus attendre,
Si seroit il reconfortez
Et soustenus et deportez
2155   En esperence d'eschaper;
Lors ne le porroient taper
Male errour, ne desesperence,
Tant comme il aroit Esperence;
Qu'Esperence le conduiroit
2160   Jusqu'a tant qu'il trespasseroit.

Aussi avez vous dit d'un point.
Encontre Amour trop mal a point:
C'est que Nature a commandise
Seur la gent d'Amour a sa guise,
2165   Et se Nature le commande,
Nuls n'obeïst a sa commande.
Elle comande qu'on oublie
Et mort d'amant et mort d'amie
Pour ce qu'on n'i puet recouvrer
2170   Par grant avoir, ne par ouvrer.
Commande; assez nous le volons.
De ce point pas ne nous dolons,
Que a moy riens n'en apartient.
Car Bonne Amour en sa part tient
2175   Un cuer d'amant tant seulement
Sans naturel commandement.
Qui ne vuet, nuls n'i est contrains;
Mais on est d'Amours si estrains,
Qu'obeïr y couvient par force;
2180   S'est fols qui contre li s'efforce.
Guillaume, se vous loeroie
A laissier ceste povre voie
De dire que Nature ait grace
Que propre commandement face
2185   En amours, qui soit de valeur,
Nature donne bien couleur
A amy d'un plaisant cuidier
Qui li fait folement cuidier
Acomplir ce qu'Amours desprise.
2190   Et par si faite fole emprise
Sont fait maint incouvenient
Qui valent trop meins que nient.
Plus desclairier ne m'en couvient

Disregarding the pain and terror,
Still he might find consolation.
2150   Yet there is an even stronger argument:
Whoever might take him to hang on the gibbet
At that very moment with no reprieve,
He would yet be comforted
And sustained and heartened
2155   By the hope of escaping:
And neither evil error nor despair
Might assault him
As long as he holds on to Hope;
For Hope will accompany him
2160   Right until the moment he dies.

You have also made a point
Against Love that's badly off the mark:
It is that Nature has control
Over the people of Love at her will,
2165   And thus if Nature commands,
No one would disobey that command.
She asks that one forget
The death of both lover and beloved
Because in this instance nothing can be restored
2170   By great treasure or by taking action.
Let her command; indeed we welcome it.
We do not have any worries on this score
Because this doesn't concern me at all.
For Good Love keeps for herself —
2175   And herself alone — a lover's heart
Without any command from Nature.
Whoever does not agree is not forced,
And yet one is so constrained by Love,
He must, feeling that power, obey.
2180   Anyone who resists is a fool.
Guillaume, I advise you therefore
To drop this unpersuasive argument
That maintains Nature has the ability
To enforce her own command,
2185   Whatever its value, in matters of love;
Nature lends a good appearance
To a lover's frivolous thought,
And this makes him foolishly determine
To do something Love hates.
2190   And because of such foolishness,
Much misfortune results
That is worth rather less than nothing.
I need discuss it no further

            Pour ce que point d'onneur n'en vient.

2195   Pais sui, qui volentiers feroie
            Adés bien et si defferoie
            Le mal; aussi feroit Concorde;
            Car quanque je vueil, elle acorde,
            Toutes heures, et soir et main.

2200   Pour ce la tien je par la main,
            Et pour faire ce qu'il li plait.
            Alés avant a vostre plait,
            Guillaume, par voie dehüe,
            Sans naturel descouvenüe.

2205   S'ensieuez d'Avis les usages,
            Par mon los, si ferez que sages."

GUILLAUME

            "Pais, damoiselle, pour vous croire
            Viennent tous biens, c'est chose voire.
            Si me garderay de mesprendre.

fol. 36v Mais je vueil ma cause deffendre

2211   Tant avant, comme je porray.
            Dont .i. exemple compteray
            Qui s'ensieut, a mon fait prouver
            Et a vostre tort reprouver.

2215   A Orliens ot .i. cler jadis
            Qui estoit renommez et dis
            Nobles clers, vaillans homs et riches,
            Et si n'estoit avers ne chiches,
            Sires de lois, et de decrez

2220   Maistres, et uns homs bien discrez
            De bien moustrer ce qu'il savoit
            Et la vaillance qu'il avoit.
            S'avoit esté nez en Prouvence,
            Et bien enlignagiez en France

2225   Estoit de princes et de contes
            Que veritables soit mes comptes.
            De gentils gens estoit servis,
            Preus et apers a grant devis,
            Et avoit en sa compaingnie

2230   De moult noble chevalerie,
            A qui riches robes donnoit.
            Cils poins moult bien li avenoit,
            Car pour sa grace desservir
            Se penoient de lui servir.

2235   Or estoit moult d'amer espris
            D'une damoiselle de pris
            Qui demouroit vers Montpeslier,

Because no point of honor is involved.
2195 I am Peace, who would willingly
Always do what's good and bring down
Evil; Concord would do the same,
For whatever I desire, so does she
At all times, both morning and night.
2200 Thus I hold her by the hand
In order to do what might please her.
Go on with your argument,
Guillaume, in the way you must,
Without being hindered by Nature.
2205 If, by my advice, you follow the principles
Of Discretion, you will do wisely."

GUILLAUME

"Peace, young lady, faith in you
Brings all good things, that is something true.
So I will guard myself from wrongdoing.
2210 But I wish to defend my opinion
As forcefully as I can.
In this regard I will relate an exemplum,
Which here follows, in order to prove my view
And refute your mistaken opinion.

2215 In Orleans there formerly was a clerk
Who was renowned and said to be
A noble cleric, a valiant and powerful man,
And so was neither miserly nor cheap,
A lord of laws, and of decrees
2220 The master, and a man quite discreet
In the demonstration of what he knew
And the valor that was his.
He had been born in Provence,
Though well connected by blood to princes
2225 And counts in France,
If indeed my story is true.
He was attended by noble people,
The competent and the learned in great number,
And had among his company
2230 Many well-born knights
To whom he would give rich robes.
This quality very well became him,
Because in order to merit his good will
They took pains to serve him.
2235 Now he was very much taken in love
With a worthy damsel
Who lived near Montpellier,

        Fille d'un vaillant chevalier,
        Attrait de moult noble lignie.
2240   S'estoit la besongne lignie
        D'entr'eus .ij. si entierement
        Qu'on ne peüst mieus autrement.
        Il s'estoient entrepromis,
        Il comme ses loiaus amis,
2245   Et elle comme vraie amie;
        A tousjours mais, toute leur vie
        Maintenroient en verité
        Les courtois poins de loiauté.
        Mais si loing devins leur loiens,
2250   Qu'il s'en vint manoir a Orliens
        Et elle en Prouvence manoit.
        Mais si bien, comme il couvenoit,
        Les secrez d'amours maintenoient
        Des lettres qu'il s'entr'envoioient
2255   Par leurs especiaus messages,
        Honnestes gens, secrez et sages.
        Einsi le feïrent grant piece.
        Mais Fortune, qui tost depiece
        Maint honneur aval le païs,
2260   Fist tant que cils fu esbahis,
        Plus que perdre .V.^{c} mars d'or,
        Si comme je diray dés or.

        Il avint a une journee,
        Male pour celui adjournee,
2265   Qu'a lui s'en vint uns messagiers
        De Prouvence, preus et legiers,
        Qui li aportoit lettres closes,
        En .i. petit coffret encloses.
        Il les prist, si les resgarda
2270   Et de haut lire se garda,
        Car pluseurs secrez devisoient.
        Et ou darrein point contenoient
        Que s'amie estoit mariee
        Au plus vaillant de la contree
2275   Et estoit ja grosse d'enfant.
        'Haro!' dist il, 'Li cuers me fent.
        Hé! Mors, que ne me viens tu prendre?
        A po que je ne me vois pendre!'
        Lors prist ses cheveus a tirer,
2280   Et puis sa robe a dessirer.
        Quant sa gent einsi le verrent,
        Isnelement avant saillirent,
        Dont chascuns forment l'agrapa.

The daughter of a valiant knight,
Descended from a very aristocratic line.
2240　And the relationship had been established
So firmly between these two
It could not have been better.
Each of them had committed to the other,
He as her loyal lover,
2245　And she as a loyal beloved;
And always, moreover, all their life
They upheld truly
The courtly rules of faithfulness.
But the distance between them became quite great,
2250　For he went to live in Orleans
And she remained in Provence.
Even so, quite ably, as it behooved them,
They maintained the secrets of love
With letters they sent to one another
2255　By their special messengers,
Honest men, discreet and wise.
They carried on in this fashion for some time.
But Fortune, who destroys quickly
Much of honor throughout the land,
2260　Saw to it that he had a terrible shock,
Much worse than losing five hundred marks of gold,
Just as I will now relate.

It happened one day,
Which dawned evilly for him,
2265　That a messenger arrived
From Provence, a man noble and adroit
Who was bringing him a sealed letter
Enclosed within a little chest.
This he took and looked over,
2270　Refraining from reading out loud,
For it contained many private things.
And at the very end the letter
Related how his beloved had been married
To the worthiest man of that region
2275　And was at that time big with child.
'Oh no!' he said, 'My heart is breaking.
Oh Death, why don't you take me now?
I'm almost ready to hang myself!'
Then he started pulling out his hair
2280　And, afterward, tearing his robe.
When his people saw him in such a state,
They moved quickly forward,
And each one tried to restrain him.

             Mais par force leur eschapa.
2285   Aval la ville se fuï.
             Il devint sours et amuÿ,
             Car des lors qu'il parti de la,
             Ainc puis de bouche ne parla
             Parole qu'entendre peüst
fol. 37r Homs vivans, tant le congneüst;
2291   Ne dés lors que ce li avint,
             Onques puis a li ne revint,
             Et ne dormoit que sus fumiers,
             Et de ce estoit coustumiers.
2295   Et quant si ami le prenoient
             Qui en aucun lieu le lioient,
             Jamais n'i beüst ne menjast.
             Eins est certein qu'il enrajast,
             Si qu'il le laissoient de plain
2300   A son voloir aler a plain.
             Mais il ne faisoit a nelui
             Nul mal, fors seulement a lui.
             En ce point fu .xx. ans tous plains;
             S'estoit moult regretez et plains
2305   De la gent qui le congnoissoient,
             Dont li pluseur forment plouroient.
             Si fu bien mis de haut au bas.
             Se nafferroit pas grans debas
             A jugier verité certeinne,
2310   Qu'il ot de grieté et de peinne
             Plus que cent dames n'averoient
             Qui leurs amis morir verroient.
             Quant il vous plaist, si resgardez,
             Et de mesjugier vous gardez!"

FOY
2315   Adont s'est Foy en piez drecié
             Comme sage et bien adrecié
             De droit, de coustume, et d'usage;
             S'a dit: "Guillaume, le musage
             Avez bien paié ci endroit,
2320   Par dehors la voie de droit,
             Au mains en aucune partie.
             S'en vorray faire departie,
             C'est assavoir, devision
             Par voie de distinction
2325   Des choses qui ne font a croire
             Et d'aucunes qui la victoire
             Puelent avoir d'estre creües
             Ou pour possible soustenues,

But he escaped them by force.
2285   Down to the town he fled.
He became deaf and dumb,
And from the time he left that place
He never spoke again with his mouth
A word that any living man
2290   Might understand, however well he knew him.
Nor from the time this happened
Did he ever return home;
Instead he slept on rubbish heaps,
Becoming accustomed to this.
2295   And when his friends would restrain him
And tie him up somewhere,
He would refuse to eat or drink.
Instead, and this is certain, he went mad.
And so they let him go free and clear
2300   To roam where he liked in the open.
But he never did any harm
To any man other than himself.
Twenty years altogether he remained in this state;
And he was grieved for and lamented
2305   By the people who knew him,
Many of whom wept bitterly.
So from up high he was pulled down low.
A long discussion is hardly needed
To establish a certain truth,
2310   Namely that he felt more misery and pain
Than any hundred ladies ever experienced
Who witnessed the deaths of their lovers.
When it pleases you, take this into consideration
And refrain from judging incorrectly."

FAITH
2315   Faith immediately got to her feet
Like someone wise and well schooled
In law, custom, and practical matters;
And she said: "Guillaume, you have certainly
Spent your time here foolishly,
2320   Straying from the path of justice,
At least in some respects.
And I intend to make a discrimination —
That is to say, a division
By way of a distinction —
2325   Between things that do not enforce belief
And those that are able to achieve
Being believed
Or considered possible,

Dont les unes essausseray
2330　Et les autres confonderay,
　　　Au los de m'amie Constance,
　　　Qui a tous mes contraires tense
　　　Et me soustient et fortefie
　　　Vers chascun qui en moy se fie.
2335　Que cils clers fust de grant vaillance,
　　　Gentils homs, et de grant puissance,
　　　Renommez de haute noblesse,
　　　Et de temporelle richesse
　　　Tres habundamment assasez,
2340　Espris d'amours et embrasez,
　　　Amis de cuer, amez d'amie,
　　　Et en l'estat de courtoisie
　　　Heüssent fait leur aliance
　　　Par tres amiable fiance,
2345　Si que les secrez garderoient
　　　D'amours, tant comme il viveroient;
　　　Qu'a Orlïens fust amainnagiez,
　　　En France bien enlinagiez
　　　De gens si honnourablement
2350　Qu'on ne peüst plus hautement —
　　　Ce sont toutes choses possibles.
　　　Et dou mal qui fu si horribles,
　　　Qui si soudennement li vint
　　　Qu'en lisant lettres li avint
2355　Et si grandement li dura,
　　　Que .xx. ans entiers l'endura —
　　　Encor di je qu'il pot bien estre.
　　　Car Diex en ce siecle terrestre
　　　A mains jugemens si enclos
2360　Qu'estre ne porroient esclos
　　　D'omme mortel par sa science.
　　　Aussi de vostre conscience
　　　Avez vous presentement dit
　　　De ces lettres par vostre dit
2365　Que plus secrez contenoient.
　　　Or ne scet on dont il venoient.
　　　Dont j'ay en droit .i. point trouvé
　　　Que vous n'avez mie prouvé,
fol. 37v　Que de s'amie li venist.
2370　Ceste raison ci defenist
　　　Qu'on n'en puet faire nullement
　　　A vostre profit jugement.
　　　Et se say bien des autres choses
　　　Qui seront, se je puis, escloses,

Of which I would prize the latter
2330   And put little stock in the former
At the urging of my friend Constancy,
Who argues in all my disputes
And supports my side, giving me strength
To uphold everyone who trusts in me.
2335   That this clerk was of great valor,
A noble man, and very powerful,
Renowned for his great gentility,
And, too, provided quite abundantly
With worldly goods,
2340   Smitten and burning with love,
A friend of the heart, loved by his beloved;
And, further, that in all courtliness
They had formed their liaison
Through a most loving bond,
2345   Keeping the secrets
Of love as long as they did live;
Also that he was living in Orleans,
Well connected by blood to people
In France with such honor
2350   It could not be greater —
All these things are possible.
Also, in regard to the quite horrible illness
That attacked him so suddenly that
It came upon him as he read the letter
2355   And then lasted quite long,
Enduring twenty years altogether —
Once again I say this could well be.
For God has ordained
So many secret things in this earthly life
2360   That could not be explained
Through the wisdom of mortal man.
Furthermore, from your own knowledge
You have just now said
By your own admission that this letter
2365   Contained even more secret matters.
Now no one knows whence they came,
And so I have truly found a point
You have not proved in the least:
That this was sent to him by his beloved.
2370   This reason makes it impossible
For anyone in any way to decide
The matter in your favor.
And I certainly know other things
That will be discussed, if I can bring it about,

2375   Pour vous dou tout suppediter,
        S'il est qui le sache diter."

GUILLAUME
        "Damoiselle, vueilliez laissier,
        S'il vous plaist, vostre menassier;
        Car ce ne vous puet riens valoir,
2380   Et il me fait le cuer doloir."

CHARITÉ
        Charitez adont s'avisa,
        Si a dit: "Foy, entendés sa!
        Je vous vueil dire une merveille."
        Lors li conseilla en l'oreille
2385   Ce qu'elle volt, secretement.
        De quoy Foy debonnairement
        Prist un bien petit a sousrire,
        Et en sousriant prist a dire:
        "Charité, damoiselle chiere,
2390   Liement, de bonne maniere,
        Ceste besongne conterez.
        Trop miex conter la saverez,
        Pour certein, que je ne feroie.
        Vous en estes ja en la voie;
2395   Car en vous en sentez le fait,
        Se vous pri qu'il soit einsi fait."

        "Foy, ma tres douce chiere amie,
        De ce ne vous faurai je mie,
        Eins en diray ce qu'il m'en samble.
2400   Car de .ij. personnes ensamble
        Les oppinions en sont bonnes,
        Quant loiaus sont les .ij. personnes.
        Si qu'a Guillaume en parleray
        Et tel chose li moustreray
2405   Qu'il se tenra pour recreans,
        S'il n'est trop fols ou mescreans.

        Guillaume, or entendés, amis:
        La puissance qui m'a commis
        A estre Charité nommee
2410   Fait que par ouevre sui prouvee,
        Dont on en voit les apparans
        En tous mes plus prochains parans.
        Ce sont li gentil cuer loial
        Qui entrent en la court roial
2415   De Bonne Amour qui n'a nul per.

2375 In order to defeat you utterly,
   If someone here can address them."

GUILLAUME
   "Young lady, kindly stop
   Your threatening, if you please,
   For it will profit you nothing
2380 And grieves my heart."

CHARITY
   Charity then reflected
   And said: "Faith, listen to this!
   I should like to tell you something extraordinary."
   And then she whispered in her ear
2385 Secretly what she had in mind.
   When she heard this, Faith demurely began
   To laugh a little
   And, smiling, started to say:
   "Charity, my dear young lady,
2390 This matter is something for you to bring up
   Cheerfully and in a pleasant fashion.
   You are better able to recount it,
   — And this is certain — than am I.
   Indeed, you have got a head start
2395 Because it is something you feel,
   And thus I beg you to do so."

   "Faith, my very sweet and dear friend,
   I will not fail you at all in this,
   But will make known my view,
2400 For the thoughts of
   Two people together are useful
   When the pair is trustworthy;
   And so I will speak to Guillaume about it,
   Demonstrating to him a particular point
2405 That will make him acknowledge defeat
   If he is not too foolish or malevolent.

   Now, friend Guillaume, listen to this:
   The power that has caused me
   To be called Charity
2410 Ordains I be proven so through my works,
   And the signs of this are seen
   In all those closest to me.
   They are the noble, faithful hearts
   Who enter the royal court
2415 Of Good Love, which has no peer.

Or entendez en quoy j'aper:
J'aper en souffissans promesses
Et en raisonnables largesses,
Especiaument par donner
2420 Et d'aucuns meffais pardonner;
Dont eüreus sont cil qui donnent,
Et aussi sont cil qui pardonnent.
Or regardons qu'Amours demande
Qu'on li doint, et plus ne commande:
2425 Elle demande expressement
Les cuers des bons entierement.
Se demande elle qu'on li doint,
Et se vuet aussi qu'on pardoint
Aucuns fais, selonc le propos
2430 Pourquoy ces raisons ci propos.
Se le moustreray par figure
Que Bonne Amour en moy figure,
Assés briefment, sans prolongier.
Uns riches homs ha .i. vergier
2435 Ou il a arbres grant planté.
Enseurquetout y a planté
Une moult tres gracïeuse ente
Qui au riche homme miex talente
Et li est trop plus avenans
2440 Que ne soit tous li remenans;
Et est einsi de lui amee,
Tant comme elle est ente clamee.
Or avient que li temps trespasse
Tant que li petis jouvens passe;
2445 Se montent ses branches au vent
Pour entrer en secont jouvent
fol. 38r Qui est moiens temps appellés;
S'estent ses branches de tous lés,
En eslargissant sa biauté
2450 Et en acroissant sa bonté
Pour traire a la conclusion
Qui est dite perfection,
Pour li deduire et deporter,
Fleurs, fueilles, et bon fruit porter.
2455 Or di je einsi qu'il avenra
Que li sires demandera
Comment celle ente se maintient
Et que qualité elle tient.
Li jardiniers puet dire: 'Sire,
2460 Pour verité, vous en puis dire,
Ce m'est avis, bonne nouvelle;
Ne demandez plus que fait elle,

Now note where I appear:
I am manifest in fulfilled promises
And reasonable generosity,
Especially in the bestowing of gifts
2420 And the pardoning of any wrongdoing:
For happy are those who give
And also those who forgive.
Let's examine what Love demands
One give her, and more she does not command.
2425 She expressly asks for the hearts
Of good people to be hers completely.
She demands this be granted her
And desires as well that some deeds
Be pardoned, according to the rule
2430 Whose justifications I here propose.
And I will demonstrate this through a figure
That Good Love embodies in my own person,
Doing so briefly and not drawing it out.
A prominent man owns an orchard
2435 In which there are a great many trees.
Most important, planted in that place
Is a very graceful grafting
That appeals more to the rich man
And pleases him much more
2440 Than do all the rest;
And he has loved her
As long as she has been called 'grafting.'
Now it happens that time passes
Until the youth of the little one ends;
2445 Into the wind her limbs reach
So that she enters into that second age
That is called the middle years,
As her branches extend on all sides
While they enlarge her beauty
2450 And increase her goodness
In order to draw toward the goal
That is termed perfection
So as to delight and amuse him
By bearing flowers, leaves, and fine fruit.
2455 At this moment, it will happen, I suggest,
That the lord will ask
How the grafting is doing
And what her condition is.
The gardener might then say: 'Sire,
2460 I can truly tell you
What seems to me good news about her;
Ask no longer how she is doing,

Mais demandez me bien qu'il fait,
Car vostre ente .i. arbre parfait,
2465   Et en tel guise se deporte
Que flours, fueilles, et bon fruit porte,
Dont perdu a d'ente le nom,
Et d'aubre a recouvré le nom,
Sous qui on se puet ombroier
2470   Plaisanment et esbanier.'
Or vueil je chanter et respondre
Pour miex m'entention espondre,
Dont je vueil faire une demande:
Se de la chose qui amende
2475   On doit avoir cuer esperdu,
S'elle a .i. petit nom perdu
Pour .i. plus grant nom recouvrer,
Par nature ou par bien ouvrer?
Je respon qu'einsi n'est il mie;
2480   Car ce seroit grant derverie.
Mais ce qu'on aimme chierement
Ou a acheté chierement,
Qui le verroit dou tout perir,
Si que ja ne peüst garir,
2485   Venir en porroit tel meschief
Qu'on y metteroit bien le chief
Et tout le corps entierement.
Je le say bien certeinnement
Que pluseurs einsi l'i ont mis,
2490   Tant amie com vrais amis.
Or vueil dou propre fait parler
Pour quoy j'ay meü mon parler.
Celle damoiselle jolie
Qui estoit a ce clerc amie.
2495   C'estoit li ente faitissette
Comme une douce pucelette
En grant vergier d'Amours plantee.
La pot estre si eslevee
Et de branches si estendue
2500   Et de fueilles si bien vestue,
De fleurs si cointement paree,
Comme estre aus milleurs comparee.
Si me vueil .i. po aviser
Pour les parties deviser:
2505   Branches de bonne renommee,
Fueilles d'estre bel emparlee,
Fleurs d'avoir la condition
D'onneste conversation,
Tant d'abit comme de maintien.

But rather how he does,
For your grafting is a perfect tree
2465 And in such estate takes great delight
In bearing flowers, leaves, and fine fruit,
And thus has lost the name of "grafting"
And gained that of "tree,"
Under which one can find shade
2470 And relax quite pleasantly.'
Now I will sing and respond as well
In order to make my meaning clearer,
And in this regard I will ask the following question:
Should one grieve at heart
2475 For that which improves,
If she has lost an insignificant name
Either through nature or good works
In order to gain a much greater title?
I answer no, not at all,
2480 For this would be terrible foolishness.
But whatever a man loves dearly
Or has bought at a high price,
Were he to see it completely perish,
And it were not possible to save it,
2485 Grievous misfortune might be his lot,
And he might lose his head,
Indeed his whole self.
I know this as a fact
Because some have done so,
2490 True lovers as much as beloveds.
Now I will say something about the issue
That has moved me to speak.
This beautiful maiden
Who was the clerk's beloved,
2495 Was the graceful scion
Planted like a sweet young girl
Within the magnificent orchard of Love.
There she could grow up so much,
Her branches extended so far,
2500 So finely clad with leaves,
So cunningly adorned with flowers
That she compared to the very best.
Now for a moment I wish to reflect
In order to describe these parts:
2505 The branches of good reputation;
The leaves of being well spoken of;
The flowers of having the ability
To conduct proper dealings with others,
In her appearance as much as in her actions.

2510   En cest estat dist: 'Amis, tien;
        Je te doing, pour toy deporter
        Grace dou fruit d'onneur porter.'
        Lors pluseurs pensees li viennent
        Qui de neccessité couviennent:
2515   Pour li entrer en mariage
        Par le conseil de son linage.
        S'elle le fait, ce n'est pas fais
        Dont cils doie enchargier tel fais
        Comme de lui desesperer.
2520   Eins doit penser et esperer
        Qu'elle y a profit et honneur
        Quant en la grace dou signeur
        Seroit de droit nommee dame.
        Ceste raison bon cuer enflame
2525   D'amer miex assez que devant.
        Pourquoy je di d'ore en avant
fol. 38v Que cils ne l'amoit pas pour bien.
        Vraiement, il y parut bien
        Quant Bonne Amour li volt souffrir,
2530   Son corps a tel martire offrir.
        Plus n'en di, Guillaume, biau sire.
        Dites ce qu'il vous plaist a dire."

GUILLAUME

        "Charité, se Diex me doint joie,
        Bien avez par soutille voie
2535   Pluseurs propos par biaus mos dis.
        Mais je ne voy pas en vos dis
        Que vous m'aiez de riens puny.
        J'ay mon procés aussi uny
        Comme devant et aussi ferme
2540   En son estat; par quoy j'afferme
        Que ja ne sera abatus,
        Se d'autres mos ne suis batus.
        .I. point y a qui gist en prueve,
        Par quoy il convenra qu'on prueve
2545   Le contraire de mes paroles,
        Ou je ne tenray qu'a frivoles
        Ce que devant avez compté,
        Nonobstant vostre grant bonté
        Et que pour grant bien l'avez fait,
2550   Pour auctorisier vostre fait
        Et pour le mien suppediter.
        Se vueil un petit reciter
        De ce clers qui fu vrais amis
        Et puis en tel grieté sousmis,

2510   In this condition, she says: 'Friend, take this.
        I give you for your enjoyment
        The favor of bearing the fruit of honor.'
        Then come to him many thoughts
        Born of necessity:
2515   To have her married
        According to the advice of her family.
        If she does so, he should not
        Worry about it so much that
        He begins to despair.
2520   Instead, he ought to wish and hope
        It profits and honors her
        When through a lord's favor
        She is rightfully called a lady.
        This reason encourages the virtuous heart
2525   To love far better than before.
        So from this point on I maintain
        He did not love her with a good intention.
        Surely this is quite apparent
        Since Good Love wants him to suffer,
2530   Offering his body to such torment.
        Guillaume, fair sir, I'll say no more about it.
        Say whatever you wish."

GUILLAUME
        "Charity, so God give me joy,
        You have ably and in a subtle fashion
2535   Brought up several points — and with pretty words.
        But I do not see that what you've said
        Has done me any damage at all.
        I have a brief as consistent
        And compelling as before
2540   In its evidence; and so I maintain
        I shall never be defeated
        Unless confronted with other arguments.
        One point remains established
        That makes it necessary for someone to prove
2545   The opposite of what I say;
        If not, I will consider only as inconsequential
        All you have brought up,
        Notwithstanding your great goodness
        And that you have done this in a worthy cause,
2550   To lend your opinion authority
        And denigrate my own.
        So I intend to say a little something
        About the clerk who was a true lover
        And then plunged into such misfortune

2555   Comme j'ay dit, .xx. ans entiers.
        Or prouvez seulement le tiers:
        Qu'onques nulle dame souffrist,
        Tant son corps a la mort offrist;
        Prouvez ce point tant seulement,
2560   Mais vous ne porriés nullement."

L'ACTEUR

        Charitez volt aprés parler,
        Et pour apointier son parler,
        Elle avoit ja la bouche ouverte.
        Mais Honnesté fu si aperte
2565   Que tantost fu aparillie
        Et dist: "Charité, douce amie,
        Que je die, mais qu'il vous plaise;
        Que je ne seray jamais aaise
        Se n'aie je dit mon talent
2570   Pour lui faire le cuer dolent."
        Charitez bien s'i acorda,
        Et puis Honnesté recorda
        S'entention par voie honneste,
        Dont toute la court fist grant feste.

HONNESTÉ

2575   S'a dit: "Guillaume, or entendez:
        Pour la fin a quoy vous tendez,
        Fondez estes petitement.
        Se vous dirai raison comment.
        Voirs est que grans grief li avint
2580   Et en petit d'eure li vint.
        Mais tantost, celle heure passee,
        Sa grant grieté fu trespassee.
        Car combien que lonc temps dura,
        Onques puis grieté n'endura
2585   Qui point fëist a son cuer touche.
        Et s'aucuns griés au cuer li touche,
        Il n'i a point de sentement,
        Dés qu'il n'i a consentement.
        C'est chose assez legiere a croire.
2590   Il avoit perdu sa memoire,
        Sens, maniere, et entendement;
        Dont on puet veoir clerement
        Qu'il n'avoit point de volenté,
        Fors que le cuer entalenté
2595   Des grans soties qu'il faisoit.
        Quant en .i. fumier se gisoit,
        C'estoit sa pais; c'estoit ses lis;

2555   For twenty full years, as I have related.
         Now prove to me only the third of these points:
         That any lady ever suffered
         So terribly she offered her body to death.
         Prove this point alone,
2560   But this you will not be able to do."

THE AUTHOR
         This Charity then wanted to say something,
         And she had her mouth already open
         To give shape to her speech.
         But Honesty was so quick
2565   She was ready even faster
         And said: "Charity, sweet friend,
         Let me speak, if you please;
         For I will never be satisfied
         If I do not speak my mind
2570   In order to trouble his heart."
         Charity was in complete agreement,
         And then Honesty presented
         Her view in an honest fashion,
         And this the court warmly welcomed.

HONESTY
2575   And she said: "Guillaume, now listen:
         You have laid little foundation
         For the point you're trying to establish.
         And I will tell you why.
         It is true enough he experienced
2580   A great misfortune that came suddenly on him.
         But immediately, that moment past,
         His terrible troubles were gone as well.
         Even though it may last long,
         A grief that pierces right to the heart
2585   Will never endure beyond its time.
         And if any sorrow touches his heart,
         There can be no emotion
         Unless there is consent.
         This principle is easy enough to credit.
2590   He had lost his memory,
         Reason, bearing, and understanding;
         Thus it can be clearly seen
         He had no will at all,
         Only a heart eager for
2595   The incredible foolishness he was doing.
         When he lay down on a dung heap,
         That was his peace, his bed.

        C'estoit de tous poins ses delis,
        Ou il dormoit a grant repos.
2600   Encor y a autre propos
        Que vous meïsmes dit avez.
        C'est certein, et bien le savez,
        Que, quant si amy le prenoient
fol. 39r Et en aucuns lieus l'enfermoient,
2605   Jamais n'i beüst ne mengast,
        Einsois trestous vis enragast,
        Qui le retenist malgré lui;
        Il n'en feïst rien pour nelui
        Et vivoit a plain comme beste.
2610   C'estoit vie trop deshonneste,
        Honteuse s'il en tenist conte;
        Mais point ne congnoissoit de honte.
        Dont j'ay assez mon fait prouvé
        Et vostre tort bien reprouvé
2615   Par .i. seul point qui me remort.
        De dame qui savera mort
        Son amy, sera plus cent tans
        En .i. jour que cils en cent ans,
        De grieté par .i. si fait trait
2620   Com ci devant avez retrait.
        Guillaume, se vous soufferrez,
        Ou d'un autre point parlerez
        Car de cestui estes vaincus,
        Ne vous y puet valoir escus."

GUILLAUME
2625   "Honesté, pour voir, non feray.
        Encor .i. po en parleray,
        Car je m'ay bien de quoy deffendre
        Mais que vous le vueilliez entendre.
        Quant tout le sens de lui perdi
2630   Pour le mal qu'a lui s'aërdi
        Qui dou tout le deshonnoura,
        Plus perdi, meins li demoura.
        Vous dites que mal ne sentoit,
        Pour ce que desvoiez estoit
2635   De maniere et d'entendement;
        Mais il est bien tout autrement:
        Car avant que homs son sens perde,
        Ne que forsens a lui s'aërde,
        Le prent et seurprent maladie
2640   Qui le trait a forcenerie.
        Si vueil faire .i. po d'argument
        Qui vous moustrera vivement

In every way, that was his delight,
A place where he slept deeply.
2600   There is yet another matter
You have yourself brought up.
It is certain — and well you know it —
That when his friends restrained him
And in different places locked him up,
2605   He never ate or drank,
But, instead, continually raged at
Whoever held him again his will;
He did nothing for anyone
And lived in the open like an animal.
2610   His was a quite disgraceful life,
Shameful had he taken account of it;
But he felt no shame at all.
So I have proved my point sufficiently
And reproved your wrong opinion
2615   By the single point I have brought up.
And a lady who comes to know
The death of her lover will find more than a hundred times
The suffering in a single day than will that man
In a century through such a blow
2620   As you have described here above.
Guillaume, you will either suffer
Or you will bring up another point
Because you are defeated in this one,
And it is not worth a penny to you."

GUILLAUME
2625   "Honesty, in truth, I will not do so.
I will speak a little more about this issue,
Since I have much with which to defend myself
If you would please hear me out.
When he lost all his senses
2630   Because of the pain that assailed him
And deprived him of all the honor he had,
He lost much more than what little he retained.
You say he did not feel any pain
Because he was disoriented
2635   In his behavior and understanding.
But it is certainly quite otherwise
Because, before a man can lose his mind
Or madness afflict him,
An illness grips and seizes him
2640   That drives him to madness.
Now I will argue this briefly
In order to demonstrate vividly to you

　　　　Comment m'entente prouveray
　　　　Dou droit que pour moy trouveray.
2645　Quant .ij. causes sont assamblees
　　　　Qui se sont a .i. corps fermees,
　　　　Celle qui vient premierement,
　　　　Elle attrait le commancement
　　　　Dés ce point par la premerainne,
2650　Pour ce que c'est la souvereinne.
　　　　Et qui la premiere osteroit,
　　　　La seconde s'en partiroit.
　　　　Or puelent dire tel y a:
　　　　'Guillaume, *verbi gracia,*
2655　A entendre si comme quoy?'
　　　　Vesci en l'eure le pourquoy:
　　　　Nous veons .i. chien qui enrage,
　　　　De quel cause li vient la rage?
　　　　D'un ver qui la langue li perse.
2660　Or est la cause si desperse
　　　　Qu'il pert le boire et le mengier,
　　　　Et puis le couvient enragier.
　　　　Or est dont li commencemens
　　　　De quoy vient li enragemens.
2665　Et quant il en pert l'abaier,
　　　　Adont se puet on esmaier
　　　　Dés ce point que la gent ne morde.
　　　　Et que de ce miex nous remorde,
　　　　Je vous en diray qu'il avint
2670　D'un chien qui enragiez devint,
　　　　Amez en l'ostel d'un riche homme.
　　　　Or entendez s'orrez la somme.
　　　　Li riches homs ot oÿ dire
　　　　Dont venoient si fait martire
2675　S'en volt veoir l'experience
　　　　Pour miex avoir en congnoissance.
　　　　Se fist son chien par force prendre,
　　　　Loier, bersillier, et estendre
　　　　Et sa langue sachier a plain,
2680　Tant qu'on vit le ver tout a plain.
　　　　Lors fu li vers fors esrachiez;
　　　　Et quant il fu a plain sachiez,
fol. 39v　Les mains celui prist a lechier
　　　　Cui il ot senti atouchier;
2685　Et fu la garis de tous poins.
　　　　Aussi di je que cils clers poins
　　　　Fu d'une maladie obscure;
　　　　Dont je vous di que la pointure
　　　　Dou grant mal que ses corps sentoit

What proof I can offer for my view
In order to gain the judgment for myself.
2645 When two causes are brought together
And manifest themselves within a single body,
The one that arises first
Sets things into motion
Because it has the first effect
2650 And therefore it is the chief cause.
And if someone removes the first cause,
Then the second disappears of its own accord.
Now some might say:
'Guillaume, *verbi gracia*,
2655 But what is your point?'
Here, right now, is the explanation.
We witness a dog going mad;
But what brings on this madness?
It's from a worm that pierces his tongue.
2660 Afterward the cause spreads so widely
He loses the ability to drink and eat,
And then must go mad.
This is then the first cause
From which the madness derives.
2665 And when for this reason the dog cannot bark,
That's the time to take care
He does not bite people.
Now to bring this point home better,
I'll talk about what happened to
2670 A dog that did go mad,
One that was loved in a rich man's home.
Listen now to the crux of the matter.
The rich man had heard spoken about
The cause of such a malady
2675 And wished to see it for himself,
The better to learn about it.
So he had his dog taken by force,
Tied up, tightly bound, and spread-eagled,
And then its tongue pulled completely out
2680 So that the worm could be plainly seen.
Then the worm was extracted;
And when it had been fully drawn out,
The dog began to lick the hands
Of the man he had felt touch him;
2685 And it was entirely cured.
And so I affirm that this was the obvious
Cause of an obscure malady;
Therefore I maintain that the attack
Of grievous illness the man's body suffered

2690 Le tenoit en point qu'il estoit.
    Dont mes drois est assez prouvez
    Et vostres grans tors reprouvez."

L'ACTEUR

    Aprés s'est Franchise levee
    Q'ne fu pas trop effraee;
2695 Et s'ot bon vueil et bonne chiere,
    Et tres gracïeuse maniere.
    Si encommensa a parler
    Et dist einsi en son parler:

FRANCHISE

    "On a veu generaument
2700 Toudis en amer loiaument
    Que les dames se sont portees
    Miex et plus loiaument gardees
    Que les hommes en tous endrois.
    Je le vueil prouver — and c'est drois —
2705 Par exemples que je vueil dire
    Pour ce qu'il font a ma matire.

    Quant cil d'Athennes eurent mort
    Androgeüs, si grant remort
    En ot Minos, li rois de Crete,
2710 Que par voie sage et discrete,
    Par force d'armes et de guerre
    Fist essillier toute leur terre.
    Et les mist tous pour cest outrage
    Minos en si mortel servage,
2715 Que tous les ans li envoient
    .I. homme; mais il sortissoient,
    Et cil seur qui li sors cheoit
    Trop mortelment li mescheoit.
    Car li rois Minos devourer
2720 Le faisoit la sans demourer
    Par un moustre trop mervilleus,
    Trop felon, et trop perilleus.
    Mais nuls ne se doit mervillier
    Se Minos volt ad ce veillier,
2725 Ne s'il en fu fort esmeüs,
    Car peres fu Androgeüs.
    Or avint que li sors cheï
    Seur Theseüs, qui esbahi
    Pluseurs; car il fu fils le roy,
2730 Preuz, vaillans, et de bel arroy.
    Mais pour la mort Endrogeüs

2690   Kept him in the condition he was in;
And so my point is quite adequately proved
And your grievous error corrected."

THE AUTHOR

After this, Frankness stood up
And was not very timid;
2695   She had good will and a pleasant expression,
And her manner was gracious.
Then she started to speak
And said the following in her remarks:

FRANKNESS

"It has been in most places — and always —
2700   Observed about true loving
That women have conducted themselves better
And have remained more faithful in it
Than men everywhere.
This I think to prove — and it's right to do so —
2705   With some instances I intend to relate
Because they are relevant to my theme.

When those of Athens had put Androgeus
To death, Minos, the king of Crete,
Felt such bitterness on this account
2710   That by wise and prudent means,
Through the force of arms and war,
He made desolate all their land.
And because of this outrage, Minos
Forced a deadly service upon them,
2715   That every year they were to send him
One man; but they were to cast lots
And for that man upon whom the lot fell
It was a quite fatal mischance.
For King Minos would have him
2720   Devoured there without delay
By a monster quite strange,
Very malevolent, and dangerous too.
But no one ought to wonder
If Minos wished to oversee all this,
2725   Or if he were strongly moved to do so,
Because he was the father of Androgeus.
Now it happened that the lot fell
On Theseus, and this dismayed
Many, for he was the son of the king,
2730   A noble man, valiant, and of fair appearance.
But because of the death of Androgeus,

Ala en Crete Theseüs
Pour lui faire estrangler au moustre
Se sa prouesse ne li moustre
2735   Si qu'envers lui se puist deffendre;
Autrement puet la mort attendre.
Et se Diex li donne victoire,
Il acquerra honneur et gloire,
Car ceuls d'Athennes franchira
2740   Et le servage acquitera.
Mais riens n'i vausist, fer ne fust,
Se belle Adriane ne fust,
Qui oublia Minos, son pere,
Et Androgeüs, son chier frere,
2745   Sa terre et ses charnels amis
Pour Theseüs, ou elle a mis
Son cuer, si qu'elle li moustra
Comment occis le fier moustre a
Pour lui delivrer dou servage;
2750   Et li donna son pucelage
Par si qu'a femme la penroit
Et qu'en son païs l'en menroit
Avec Phedra, sa chiere suer,
Qu'elle ne lairoit a nul fuer.
2755   Theseüs, qui se parjura
Ses diex et sa loy, li jura
Que jamais ne li fausseroit
Et qu'envers li loiaus seroit.
Il se menti, li renoiez.
fol. 40r   Pour quoy ne fu en mer noiez?
2761   Quant sa besongne ot assevie,
Il les charga en sa navie.
Mais vers li mesprist si forment
Qu'Adriane laissa dormant
2765   Seulette en estrange contree,
Lasse, dolente, et esgaree,
Et en mena la juene touse,
Phedra sa suer, s'en fist s'espouse.
Ci a trop mortel traïson.
2770   Aussi dirai je de Jason,
Qui conquist par l'art de Medee
En Colcos la toison doree,
Et sormonta, li bourdereaus,
L'ardant soufflement des toreaus,
2775   S'endormi le serpent veillable,
Seur toute beste espoventable,
Et desconfit les chevaliers
Armez, a cens et a milliers.

Theseus went to Crete
To have himself killed by the monster
If he should not manifest his prowess
2735 And prove able to defend himself against him.
Otherwise he could expect death.
And if God should grant him victory,
He would acquire honor and glory,
For he would free the Athenians
2740 And acquit them of their servitude.
Yet nothing would have availed him, wood or iron,
Had it not been for beautiful Ariadne,
Who forgot about Minos, her father,
And Androgeus, her dear brother,
2745 Her land, and her blood relations,
For the sake of Theseus, to whom she gave
Her heart, and so she showed him
How to kill the proud monster
In order to deliver himself from bondage.
2750 And she gave him her maidenhood
So he would make her his wife
And take her to his own country
Along with Phaedra, her beloved sister,
Whom she would leave behind on no account.
2755 Theseus, perjuring himself,
Swore to her by his gods and law
He would never prove false
And always be faithful to her.
He lied saying this, the traitor.
2760 Why wasn't he drowned in the sea?
After completing his mission,
He embarked them on his ships.
But he grievously betrayed her
When he left Ariadne asleep
2765 And all alone in a strange land,
Abandoned, sorrowing, and deceived,
And led off the young girl,
Her sister Phaedra, and made her his wife.
This betrayal was quite fatal.
2770 Also, I will talk about Jason,
Who took by force through Medea's arts
The golden fleece of Colchis,
And that trickster overcame
The fiery breath of the bulls,
2775 Put to sleep the guardian dragon,
More dreadful than any other beast,
And defeated the armed knights
In their hundreds and thousands.

         Mais nuls ce faire ne peüst
2780   Se Medea fait ne l'eüst.
         Son païs laissa et son pere,
         Et fit decoper son chier frere.
         Pelie occist a grant desroy,
         Et tout, pour Jason faire roy.
2785   Quanqu'elle ot, li abandonna;
         S'amour et s'onneur li donna.
         Mais Jason Medea laissa
         Pour Creusa, dont moult s'abaissa,
         Et mervilleusement mesprist
2790   Quant la laissa et autre prist.
         Et quant elle sot la nouvelle,
         Qui ne li fu plaisant ne belle,
         Elle fu si desesperee,
         Si hors dou sens, si forsenee,
2795   Que .ij. enfans qui sien estoient
         Pour ce que Jason ressambloient,
         Occist en despit de Jason,
         Puis mist le feu en sa maison.
         Aprés s'en ala la chetive
2800   O ses dragons par l'air fuitive.
         Mais puis en estranges contrees
         Furent roïnes coronnees.
         Car roys d'Athennes Egeüs
         Fu de Medee deceüs;
2805   Bacus Adriane honnoura
         Fort, car en li grant amour a.
         Cil dui les dames espouserent
         En leur païs et coronnerent.

         Si que, Guillaume, c'est la somme:
2810   On ne porroit trouver en homme
         Si grant loyauté comme en femme,
         Ne jamais d'amoureuse flame
         Ne seroient si fort espris
         Comme seroit dame de pris.
2815   Car quant il y a meins d'amour,
         Il y a tant meins de dolour
         Puis que ce vient a mal sentir.
         Ne je ne me puis assentir
         Qu'en endurant les maus d'amer
2820   Que homs ait tant com dame d'amer.
         Et si a de remedes cent
         Li homs tels que fame ne sent."

But no man could have accomplished all this
2780 Had Medea not done it for him.
She deserted her country and father,
Had her brother dear cut to pieces.
Because of her great foolishness, she killed Pelia.
And this all was to make Jason king.
2785 Whatever she owned, she gave him freely;
Her honor and love she bestowed upon him.
But Jason abandoned Medea
For Creusa, demeaning himself greatly
And sinning grievously
2790 When he left her and took up with the other woman.
When Medea learned the news,
Hardly pleasant or appealing to her,
She was so desperate,
So insane, so crazed,
2795 She killed her own
Two children to spite Jason
Because they resembled him;
And then she torched her own house.
Afterward the wretched woman fled
2800 Through the air with her serpents.
But later in foreign lands
These women were crowned queens.
For Aegeus, the king of Athens,
Was beguiled by Medea;
2805 Bacchus honored Ariadne
Greatly, for he dearly loved her.
These two married the women
In their own countries and crowned them.

And so, Guillaume, that is the gist.
2810 Loyalty as great as that of women
Cannot be found in any man,
Nor would men ever be as deeply
Inflamed by the spark of love
As a worthy lady would.
2815 For when there is less love,
There is that much less suffering
Because it comes from feeling pain.
And I cannot agree
That, enduring the ills of love,
2820 Any man would feel as much as a woman.
And the man has a hundred
Remedies unavailable to women."

GUILLAUME

   "Damoiselle, la traïson
   De Theseüs ne de Jason
2825 Ne fait riens a nostre matiere,
   Ne ce n'est mie la premiere
   Ne la darreinne fausseté
   Qui es amoureus ha esté,
   Autant es fames comme es hommes.
2830 Ne je ne donroie .ij. pommes
   De vostre entention prouver
   Par si fais exemples trouver.
   Car se mon fait prouver voloie
   Par exemples, j'en trouveroie
2835 Plus de .x., voire plus de .xx.
   Chascuns scet bien ce qu'il avint
   De l'amy a la Chasteleinne
   De Vergi: d'amours si certeinne
fol. 40v L'ama qu'il s'ocist sans demour
2840 Quant morte la vit pour s'amour.

   Li bons Lancelos et Tristans
   Eurent plus de peinne .x. tans
   Que femme ne porroit souffrir,
   Tant se peüst a peinne offrir,
2845 Et cent fois furent plus loiaus
   Que Jason ne fu desloiaus,
   Ne Theseüs, qui trop mesprist
   D'Adriane quant Phedra prist.
   Encor vueil d'un autre compter
2850 Se vous me volez escouter.

   Une dame sans villonnie
   D'un chevalier estoit amie,
   Si li donna .i. anelet
   Trop gent (ne fu villein ne let),
2855 Par si qu'adés le porteroit
   Et que jamais ne l'osteroit
   De son doy s'elle ne l'ostoit.
   Et li chevaliers, qui estoit
   Tous siens, bonnement li promist,
2860 Et la dame en son doy le mist.
   Or avint qu'elle avoit mari
   Qui ot le cuer triste et mari;
   Car l'anel a recongnëu
   Pour ce qu'autre fois l'ot vëu.
2865 Si l'ala tantost demander
   A la dame et li comander

GUILLAUME

"Young lady, the treason
Of either Theseus or Jason
2825   Has nothing to do with our issue,
And that was hardly the first
Or last betrayal
There's been with lovers,
As often with women as with men.
2830   And I wouldn't give two apples
For proving your point
By bringing up such examples.
For if I intended to establish my case
By examples, I would find
2835   More than ten, indeed more than twenty of them.
Everyone knows well what happened
To the lover of the Chatelaine
De Vergy: he loved her with a love
So certain he killed himself unhesitatingly
2840   When he saw her dead for the sake of his love.

Virtuous Lancelot and Tristan
Endured ten times more pain
Than any woman could suffer,
As much as she could subject herself to it,
2845   And they were a hundred times more loyal
Than Jason was disloyal,
Or Theseus either, who sinned greatly
Against Ariadne when he seduced Phaedra.
Still, I wish to tell of another
2850   If you are willing to listen to me.

A lady was loved
By a knight without any baseness,
And she gave him a ring that was
Quite beautiful (it was neither cheap nor ugly),
2855   On the condition he always wear
And never remove it
From his finger unless she did.
And the knight, who was
Hers completely, promised this in good faith,
2860   And then the lady put it on his finger.
Now it happened she had a husband
Whose heart was gloomy and vexed
Because he recognized the ring,
Having seen it another time.
2865   So he went at once to ask
The woman and command her

Qu'elle li baille en la place
Seur peinne de perdre sa grace.
La dame dist qu'elle l'avoit,
2870 Mais ou, pas bien ne le savoit.
Si fist samblant de l'aler querre
Et, en deffermant une serre,
Comme dame avisee et sage,
Dist a un sien privé message:
2875 'Va sans arrest a mon ami
Et se li di que mal pour my
Se mon anel ne me renvoie.
Et ne demeure pas seur voie,
Car mon signeur le vuet avoir
2880 Sans nul essoinne recevoir.
Di li bien qu'il n'en faille mie.
Car s'il en faut, je sui honnie
Et en peril de perdre honneur
Et la grace de mon signeur.'
2885 Li messages n'atendi pas,
Eins s'en ala plus que le pas
Au chevalier et tout li conte
Ce que devant ai dit en conte.
Quant li chevaliers l'entendi,
2890 A po li cuers ne li fendi,
Car il ot paour que sa dame
Honte pour li n'eüst ou blasme.
Si dist: 'Amis, foy que li doy,
Avuec l'anel ara mon doy,
2895 Car ja par moy n'en partira.'
Si que lors .i. coutel tira,
Son doi copa, et li tramist
Aveques l'anel qu'elle y mist.
Puet on faire plus loiaument
2900 Riens, ne plus amoureusement?
Certes, nennil! Ce m'est avis.
Car trop fu loiaus ses amis,
Si que bien oseroie attendre
Vray jugement sans plus contendre,
2905 Qu'on les doit plus auctorisier
Et en tous estas plus prisier
Que les dames, de qui parole
Tenez que je tien a frivole,
Qu'on dit — et vous le savez bien —
2910 Que par tout doit veincre le bien.
Et cil furent bon et loial
Tenu en toute court roial,
Comment que les dames feïssent

To furnish it on the spot
On pain of losing his favor.
The lady said she had it,
2870   But where, she did not really know.
So she made a show of going to look for it
And, opening a drawer,
Like a cunning and sharp woman
Spoke this secret message to one of her people:
2875   'Go directly to my lover
And tell him I am in for a bad time
Unless he sends my ring back;
And do not delay along the way,
For my master wishes to have it
2880   Without hearing excuses.
Make it clear he shouldn't fail me.
For if he does, I am shamed
And in danger of losing my honor
And the favor of my lord.'
2885   The messenger did not delay at all,
But proceeded faster than a walk
To the knight and told him everything
I related earlier in my tale.
When the knight heard this,
2890   His heart nearly broke
Because he feared his lady
Might be dishonored or accused on his account.
So he said: 'Friend, by the faith I owe her,
She will have my finger along with the ring,
2895   For I will not remove it.'
So then he took out a knife,
Cut off his finger, and sent it to her
Along with the ring she had put there.
Could anyone do something more loyal
2900   Than this, or more loving?
Surely, not at all. Such is my view.
For her lover was very trustworthy,
And so I should very much dare expect
A judgment of truth with no more debate,
2905   For men should have more respect
And in every case be counted superior
To women, whose words
You maintain that I consider frivolous,
Because as everyone says — and this you know well —
2910   Virtue should triumph everywhere.
And these men were considered
Virtuous and loyal in every royal court,
However much the ladies did for their lovers

Moult pour leurs amis et souffrissent.
2915 Mais on dit — et c'est veritez —
Qu'adés les .ij. extremitez,
C'est trop et po. Einsi l'enten ge:
Ne doivent recevoir loange;
fol. 41r Mais qui en l'amoureus loien
2920 Est loiez s'il tient le moien
Il ouevre bien et sagement.
Et li sages dist qui ne ment
Qu'adés li bonneüreus tiennent
Le moien partout ou il viennent."

PRUDENCE
2925 A ce Prudence respondi,
Qui riens n'enclot ne repondi
A la matiere appartenant,
Et dist: "Guillaume, maintenant
Voy je bien vostre entention;
2930 Mais j'ay contraire opinion
Qui de la vostre est trop lonteinne.
On scet bien que la Chastelainne
Fu morte pour .i. bacheler
Pour ce qu'il ne la sot celer.
2935 Car il dist toute leur besongne
A la Duchesse de Bourgoingne.
Et la Duchesse moult mesprist,
Qu'a une feste li reprist
Qu'elle savoit bien le mestier
2940 Dou petit chiennet affaitier.
S'en morut en disant 'aymi'
Par le deffaut de son ami.
Et quant li amis vit s'amie
Par sa gengle morte et perie,
2945 S'il s'ocist, il fist son devoir,
Qu'autre mort deüst recevoir,
N'il ne fist fors meins que justice.
S'il s'ocist pour punir son vice;
Qu'avoir le dehüssent detrait
2950 Chevaus enragiez pour ce trait.
Si m'est vis que la Chastelainne
Ot plus de meschief et de peinne
Quant sans cause reçut la mort,
Que n'ot cils qui se fu la mort
2955 Qui avoit desservi le pendre;
Et pour ce en fu sa dolour mendre.

And no matter how much they suffered.
2915   But people say — and true it is —
        It's always one extreme or the other,
        Too much or too little. This is how I see it:
        These extremes are not worthy of praise.
        However, anyone caught in the snares
2920   Of love who shows moderation
        Acts wisely and well.
        And the sage, a man who does not lie, says
        The fortunate hold to the middle path
        Wherever they go."

PRUDENCE
2925   Prudence responded to this,
        And she neither implicated nor involved herself
        In the issue at hand.
        And this lady said: "Guillaume, now
        I see well your intention.
2930   But I hold a contrary view,
        One very different from yours.
        It is well known that the Chatelaine
        Died for the sake of a young man
        Because he could not keep her secret.
2935   Instead, he related all their affair
        To the Duchess of Burgundy.
        And the Duchess did a terrible thing
        When at a feast she let it slip
        She knew all about the business
2940   Of the trickery with the little dog.
        So the Chatelaine died saying 'alas'
        Because of her lover's error.
        And when the lover saw his beloved
        Dead and undone because of his gossiping,
2945   If he killed himself, he did what he should,
        For he deserved to suffer another kind of death
        And did nothing but what was just
        When he killed himself to punish his misdeed;
        For they should have had wild horses
2950   Tear him to pieces for what he'd done.
        So it is my view the Chatelaine
        Suffered more misfortune and hurt
        When she had to die for no reason
        Than did the young man who killed himself
2955   And deserved to hang;
        For this reason his torment was less.

Et se Tristans ou Lancelos
Furent vaillans, bien dire l'os
Que leur vaillance et leur prouesse
2960   Leur fu gloire, honneur, et richesse;
N'il n'est homs qui peüst acquerre
Tels biens, sans avoir peinne en terre.
Si que, Guillaume, j'ose dire
Que plus de peinne et de martyre
2965   Cent fois les dames soustenoient
Que leurs amis qu'elles faisoient,
Qu'elles avoient les griés pensees
Et les paours desordenees,
Les paroles de mesdisans.
2970   Et s'il demourassent .x. ans,
Ja n'eüssent parfait joie;
Car qui atent, trop li anoie,
N'a cuer humain riens tant ne grieve
Com mesdis et pensee grieve.
2975   Ne autre bienfait n'en portoient
Que un po de joie qu'elles avoient.
Einsi est il de pluseurs dames
Qui mettent les cuers et les ames
Et quanqu'elles ont en leurs amis,
2980   Et quant tant chascune y a mis
Qu'il sont en vaillance parfait,
Apparent par ouevre et par fait,
Elles n'en ont autre salaire
Fors un petit de gloire au faire.
2985   Ils ont le grain; elles ont la paille;
Car l'onneur ont, comment qu'il aille.
Et s'aucune fois leur meschiet,
Tout premiers seur les dames chiet.
Certes, c'est mauvais guerredon.
2990   Quant pour bien ont de guerre don.

De l'autre qui son doy copa,
Vraiement fait .i. lait cop a.
Car Guillaume, quoy que nuls die,
Je le tien a grant cornardie,
2995   Si m'en pense po a debatre.
Car il y avoit .iij. ou .iiij.
Voies qui deüssent souffire,
Et il prist de toutes la pire.
fol. 41v   Et d'autre part, je ne croy mie
3000   Que celle qui estoit s'amie,
S'elle l'amoit d'amour seüre,
N'eüst trop plus chier l'aventure

And if Tristan and Lancelot
Were valiant, I dare well say
Their valor and prowess
2960 Meant glory, honor, and riches to them;
And no man might acquire
Such goods without suffering some earthly pain.
And so, Guillaume, I dare say
The ladies in question endured
2965 A hundred times more pain and torment
Than the lovers to whom they were committed,
For they suffered mournful thoughts,
Fears that confounded them,
As well as the words of slanderers.
2970 And if these men had waited ten years,
Never would they have found perfect joy;
For whoever waits is quite annoyed,
And nothing grieves the human heart so much
As slander and nagging thoughts.
2975 And the ladies found no benefit in all this
Except what little joy they received.
And so it is with many ladies
Who surrender their hearts and souls
And whatever they own to their lovers;
2980 And when each woman has given so much
That their men acquire knightly honor,
Which is manifest in word and action,
The women draw no other salary
Save a little glory from what they do.
2985 The men have the kernel; the women the chaff,
For the honor belongs to the men, whatever might happen.
And if misfortune is sometimes their lot,
The ladies are the first to suffer.
Surely this is an inadequate reward
2990 When for good they get strife in return.

In regard to the man who cut off his finger,
He struck an unfortunate blow in truth.
For Guillaume, whatever anyone might say,
I consider this quite foolish
2995 And intend to argue a little against this view.
For there were three or four
Paths that should have sufficed,
But he chose the worst of all.
And furthermore I do not believe at all
3000 That the woman who was his beloved,
If the love she felt had been faithful,
Would not have preferred the risky business

De son mari et son courrous,
Et deüst estre entre'eaus .ij. rous
3005 Li festus jusqu'a une piece,
Qu'oster de son ami tel piece,
Qu'a tous jours fu desfigurez,
Meins prisiés, et plus empirez."

GUILLAUME

"Certes, Franchise, vous avez
3010 Bien dit, que bien dire savez.
Mais je say sans nulle doubtance
Que c'est contre vo conscience,
Et que dit avez le contraire
De ce qui en vo cuer repaire.
3015 Mais je vous requier, s'il vous plest,
Que nous abregons nostre plet,
Car trop alongons la matiere
Qui meüe a esté premiere.
Il est certein — et je l'afferme —
3020 Qu'en cuer de femme n'a riens ferme,
Rien seür, rien d'estableté,
Fors toute variableté.
Et puis qu'elle est si variable
Qu'elle en rien n'est ferme n'estable
3025 Et que de petit se varie,
Il faut que de po pleure et rie,
Dont grant joie et grant tourment
N'i puelent estre longuement,
Car sa nature li enseingne
3030 Que tost rie et de po se pleingne;
Tost ottroie, tost escondit.
Elle a son dit et son desdit,
Et s'oublie enterinement
Ce que ne voit legierement.
3035 Et puis qu'elle ne puet ravoir
Jamais son ami pour avoir,
Pour pleindre, ne crier, ne braire,
Ne pour chose qu'elle puist faire,
Et aussi que de sa nature
3040 Oublie toute creature
Legierement quant ne la voit,
On puet bien penser, s'elle avoit
De ses amis damage ou perte,
Que briefment seroit si aperte
3045 Que d'un perdu .ij. retrouvez
Li seroit encor reprouvez.
Mais cuers d'omme est ferme et seürs,

Of her husband and his anger,
Even if it meant the bond ought to have been
3005 Broken between those two right at that moment,
Rather than depriving her lover of a finger
So he would always be disfigured,
Less esteemed, and quite impaired."

GUILLAUME

"Frankness, no doubt you have
3010 Spoken well, for you can speak ably.
But I know for certain
Your conscience says otherwise
And you have argued the opposite
Of what truly lies in your heart.
3015 But, I ask you, please
Let us focus our debate,
For we have moved too far from the question
Broached at its beginning.
It is indisputable, as I affirm,
3020 There is nothing stable in a woman's heart,
Nothing certain, no constancy of any kind
Save complete changeability.
And since she is so fickle
That she is firm about or convinced of nothing
3025 And alters for the slightest reason,
It follows she laughs or cries over trifles;
And so great joy and immense suffering
Cannot remain with her for very long
Because her nature leads her
3030 To laugh easily and cry over little things;
She agrees readily and demurs just as fast.
She has her say but then denies it,
And she forgets utterly
And easily what she does not see.
3035 Now since she cannot ever possess
Her lover again, for money,
For tears, moaning, lamentation,
Or for anything she might do;
And also since by her nature
3040 She forgets quite readily
Any person out of her sight,
One could well conclude that if she experienced
Loss and hurt because of her lover,
She would be ready again in such a short time
3045 'That for the one lost, two recovered'
Would be the reproach made to her.
In contrast, a man's heart is firm, secure,

      Sages, esprouvez, et meürs,
      Vertueus et fors pour durer,
3050 Et humbles pour mal endurer.
      Et quant de l'amoureuse ardure
      Est espris, tellement l'endure
      Qu'einsois morroit dessous l'escu
      Qu'on le veïst mat ne veincu.
3055 Ce que je di n'est pas contrueve,
      Car chascuns le dit et apprueve;
      Et pour ce que chascuns le dit,
      L'ai je recordé en mon dit.
      Se di en ma conclusion
3060 Que, vëu la condicion
      D'omme et de feme, nullement
      Feme ne puet avoir tourment,
      Tant braie ne se desconforte,
      Comme uns homs en son cuer le porte,
3065 Qu'estre ne puet en sa nature.
      Raison s'i acorde et droiture.
      Et aussi li maus qui termine
      Est mendres que cils qui ne fine
      Einsois dure jusqu'a la mort,
3070 Tant qu'il a son malade mort."

LARGESSE

      Largesse, qui aprés seoit,
      Parla, car moult bien li seoit,
      Et dist: "Guillaume, vraiement,
      Je sui mervilleuse comment
3075 Vous osez des dames mesdire,
      Car ce ne deüssiez pas dire.
fol. 42r Et de ce qu'avez dit, li blames
      Est plus seur vous que seur les dames.
      Vous avez dit en vostre dit —
3080 Dont, certes, vous avez mal dit —
      Que chascuns tient pour veritable
      Que toute dame est variable,
      Et que ce n'est de leur couvent
      Nés que d'un cochelet au vent.
3085 Mais toute ceste compaingnie
      Tient le contraire et le vous nie.
      Et pour ce bien dire pouez
      Que vous n'estes pas avouez;
      Si devez paier la lamproie.
3090 De ce plus dire ne saroie,
      Qu'on ne puet bon argüement
      Faire seur mauvais fondement."

Wise, experienced, and mature,
Virtuous and strong in endurance,
3050   But humble in suffering adversity.
And when all aflame
With amorous burning, his heart is so committed
It would rather die behind its shield
Than be seen beaten down or vanquished.
3055   What I maintain is hardly arguable,
For everyone says so and agrees
And since everyone says the same
I have written it in my poem.
So I say in conclusion
3060   That, considering the nature
Of men and women, no woman
Can suffer as much torment,
However much she moans and carries on,
As any man's heart can bear,
3065   For it is simply not in her nature.
Reason and good custom concur.
In any case, the misfortune that ends
Is less severe than the one that does not,
But rather endures right to death,
3070   Killing whoever suffers the ill."

GENEROSITY

Generosity, who was sitting nearby,
Then spoke up, for it suited her well to do so,
And she said: "Guillaume, truly,
I am astonished how
3075   You dare to malign women,
For you should not talk this way.
And any blame in what you have said
Falls more on you than on women.
You have said in your poem
3080   (And surely you are wrong)
How everyone considers it the truth
That all women are fickle,
And their word is worth no more
Than a weathercock in the wind.
3085   But this entire company
Believes the opposite and is against you.
So for this reason you can certainly say
You are not endorsed
And must pay the piper.
3090   I don't know what more to say,
For no one can construct a valid
Argument on a faulty premise."

DOUBTANCE

     "Et je ne m'en porroie taire,"
     Ce dist Doubtance de meffaire,
3095 "Eins en diray ce qu'il m'en samble,
     Car tous li cuers me frit et tramble
     Quant einsi sans cause blamer
     Oy les dames et diffamer.
     Or entendez a ma demande:
3100 Biau Guillaume, je vous demande,
     Se celle change ne varie
     Qui est tous les jours de sa vie
     Loial amie, sans fausser,
     N'en fait, n'en desir, n'en penser?"

GUILLAUME

3105 "Certes, damoiselle, nennil!
     Mais je croy qu'entre .v.ᶜ mil
     N'en seroit pas une trouvee;
     Car tel greinne est trop cler semee."

DOUBTANCE

     "Mon biau sire, se Diex me gart,
3110 Moult avez estrange regart,
     Et s'avez diverse parole!
     Et s'avez esté a l'escole,
     Si com je croy, d'aler en change;
     Et pour ce que li cuers vous change,
3115 Vous cuidiez que chascuns le face
     Si com vous; mais ja Dieu ne place!
     Car je prouverai le contraire
     De fait, cui qu'il doie desplaire."

GUILLAUME

     "Damoiselle, ne vous desplaise,
3120 Se je vous resgarde a mon aaise,
     Car pas ne vous hé si forment
     Com je vous regart laidement;
     Et se ma parole est diverse,
     Bons cherretons est qui ne verse.
3125 Mais je cuide verité dire,
     Comment que m'en vueilliez desdire;
     Si me sui ci mal embatus
     Se pour voir dire sui batus."

SOUFFISSANCE

     Adont se leva Souffissance
3130 Et dist: "Guillaume, sans doubtance,

WARINESS

"I cannot hold my peace,"
Declared Wariness of misdeed,
3095   "Rather I will speak what is on my mind,
For all my heart shakes and quivers
When for no reason I hear
Ladies maligned and defamed.
Now listen to my question.
3100   Fair Guillaume, I ask you
If that woman alters or changes
Who is all the days of her life
A loyal beloved, never betraying
In deed, desire, or thought?"

GUILLAUME

3105   "Surely, damsel, not at all!
But I believe not one such would be found
Among five hundred thousand,
For this seed is too thinly sown."

WARINESS

"My fair sir, may God preserve me,
3110   Your point of view is quite strange
And your words amaze me!
You must have been to the school
Of constant change, or so I believe;
And because your own heart is fickle,
3115   You believe everyone is the same
As you. But, please God, it is not so!
For I will prove the contrary
In fact, whomever it should displease!"

GUILLAUME

"Damsel, I hope you won't be dismayed
3120   If I look at you in a friendly way,
For I do not dislike you enough
To frown at you.
And if my words are unwelcome,
It's a good cart that never overturns.
3125   But I believe I speak the truth,
However much you would like to dispute it.
So I am quite badly treated here
If for speaking the truth I am beaten down."

SUFFICIENCY

And then Sufficiency rose to her feet
3130   And said: "Guillaume, without a doubt,

Vous estes or mal emparlez.
Resgardez coment vous parlez;
Car nuls homs qui vueille voir dire
Ne porroit des dames mesdire,
3135   Qu'en elles est, ce scet on bien,
Tout quanqu'on puet dire de bien.
Si que je vous lo et conseil
Que plus ne parlez sans conseil;
Car vous estes trop juenes homs
3140   Pour dire si faites raisons."

GUILLAUME
Lors entroÿ une murmure,
Que chascune d'elles murmure
De ce que si fort soustenoie
Ce que des dames dit avoie;
3145   Et vi que chascune faisoit
Samblant, qu'il li en desplaisoit.
Et quant j'aperçu la maniere
De leur parler et de leur chiere,
Et que meües furent toutes
3150   Pour bouter le feu es estoupes,
fol. 42v Au juge fis une requeste
Qui me sambloit assez honneste,
Et humblement li depriay
Et requis en mon depri ay
3155   Qu'elles parlassent tout a fait,
Si averoient plus tost fait.
Si firent elles, ce me samble;
Qu'elles parloient tout ensamble;
Dont li juges prist a sousrire
3160   Qui vit que chascune s'aïre.
Et certes, j'en eus moult grant joie,
Quant en tel estat les veoie.
Mais li juges, qui sagement
Voloit faire son jugement,
3165   Tantost leur imposa silence,
Fors seulement a Souffissance
Et a Doubtance de meffaire.
Et lors prist Doubtance a retraire
.I. conte propre a sa matiere,
3170   Et commensa par tel maniere.

DOUBTANCE
"Que fist Tysbé pour Piramus?
Quant elle vit que mors et nus
Estoit pour li, sans nul retour,

You have now misspoken.
Look to what you are saying!
For no man who wishes to speak the truth
Would be able to defame women
3135   Or what they are (this is well known)
Since so much good can be said;
And so I advise and enjoin you
Not to say, without counsel, any more,
For you are a very young man
3140   To make arguments like these."

GUILLAUME

Then I heard a murmuring,
For each lady was whispering
About how forcefully I was upholding
What I had said about women;
3145   And I saw each was giving the impression
She was displeased.
And taking note of how
They were speaking and the looks on their faces,
And that all were eager
3150   To add fuel to the fire,
I made a request to the judge,
Who seemed fairly honest to me,
And I begged him humbly
And stated in my proposal
3155   That they should speak at once
And thus have done more quickly.
For so they were doing, it seemed to me,
Talking all at once, that is;
And at this the judge started to smile,
3160   For he saw they were all growing angry.
And, to be sure, I felt quite great joy
Seeing them in such a state.
But the judge, who was intent on
Making a wise judgment,
3165   Immediately imposed silence on them,
With the exceptions of Sufficiency
And Wariness of misdeed as well.
And Wariness began to rehearse
A story that reflected her viewpoint,
3170   And she began in this fashion.

WARINESS

"What did Thisbé do for Pyramus?
When she saw him naked and dead
Because of her, without any recourse,

A doloir s'en prist par tel tour,
3175 Que d'une espee s'acoura
Seur le corps et la demoura;
Car aprés li ne volt pas vivre,
Eins fina s'amour et son vivre
En pleins, en plours, et en clamours.
3180 Certes, ce fu parfaite amours;
Car il n'est dolour ne remort
Qu'on puist comparer a la mort.
Ne nuls ne me feroit entendre
Q'nuls homs vosist son cuer fendre
3185 Si crueusement, n'entamer,
Comme Tysbé fist pour amer.
Et qui diroit uns homs est fors
Pour souffrir d'amours les effors,
Et s'a cuer plus dur qu'aÿmant
3190 Ou que ne soit .i. dÿamant,
Je ne donroie de sa force
Le quart d'une pourrie escorce,
Ne je ne pris riens sa durté,
Sa vertu, ne sa mëurté,
3195 Ne chose qu'il endure aussi.
Mais quant une dame a soussi
Qu'en son cuer secretement cuevre,
Par tel guise le met a ouevre
Qu'elle y met le corps et la vie.
3200 Mais, Guillaume, je ne croy mie
Que on veïst onques morir
Homme par deffaut de merir
Et qui tost ne fust confortez,
Tant fust ses cuers desconfortez;
3205 N'il n'est doleur qui se compere
A mort, com grieve qu'elle appere,
Ne que li feus, fais en peinture,
Encontre le feu de nature.
Car Nature ne puet pas faire,
3210 Tant soit a corps humein contraire;
Ne cuers ne puet riens endurer
Qu'on peüst a mort comparer."

SOUFFISSANCE

"Doubtance, laissiez le plaidier,
Car .i. petit vous vueil aidier,
3215 Pour mettre nostre entention
A plus vraie conclusion,
Comment qu'aiez si bien conclus
Selonc raison, qu'on ne puet plus.

She became so grief-stricken
3175 She ran herself through with a sword,
Right through the body, and left it there.
For she would not live on after him,
But instead put an end to her love and life
With laments, tears, and wailing.
3180 Surely this was a perfect love.
For there is no pain or suffering
That can be compared to death;
Nor could anyone convince me
That any man's heart could break
3185 So cruelly, or that he could injure himself
As did Thisbé for love.
And whoever would say a man is strong
In suffering the hardships of loving,
With a heart stronger than adamant
3190 Or any diamond might be,
I would not give for his strength
A bit of putrid peel,
Nor do I value highly his fortitude,
His virtue or maturity either,
3195 Or anything he endures.
But when a woman suffers pain
She conceals in her heart,
She proceeds to
Give herself to it body and soul.
3200 But, Guillaume, I don't believe at all
That any man has ever been seen
Who died from a lack of reward
Or who was not quickly comforted,
However disconsolate his heart might have been;
3205 Nor is there any pain comparable
To death, however grievous it may seem,
No more than fire depicted in a painting
Can be compared to fire in nature.
For Nature cannot produce anything,
3210 No matter how contrary to the human body,
Comparable to death,
Nor can a heart endure anything like it."

SUFFICIENCY

"Wariness, stop your arguing,
For I wish to help you a bit
3215 In bringing your point
To an even truer conclusion,
Although you've developed it quite well
And reasonably, better than others could.

         Adont commensa Souffissance
3220   Et dist ainsi en audiance:

         "Leandus, li biaus et li cointes,
         D'une pucelle estoit acointes
         Qui bele Hero fu nommee;
         N'avoit en toute la contree
3225   Nulle si cointe damoiselle,
         De trop si gente, ne si belle;
         N'en Abidois n'avoit, n'en Crete
         Nulle amour qui fust si secrete,
fol. 43r Car nuls ne savoit leur couvine,
3230   Fors seulement une meschine
         Qui belle Hero norrie avoit;
         Celle seulement le savoit.
         De moult parfaite amour s'amoient;
         Mais a grant peinne se veoient,
3235   Qu'entre Hero et Leandus
         Fu un bras de mer espandus
         Qui estoit larges et parfons,
         Si qu'on n'i preïst jamais fons;
         Et ce leur faisoit trop d'anuis.
3240   Mais Leandus toutes les nuis
         Passoit le bras de mer au large,
         Tous nus, seuls, sans nef et sans barge.
         Belle Hero au gent atour
         Ot en sa maison une tour
3245   Ou toutes les nuis l'atendoit,
         Et .i. sierge ardant la tendoit,
         Auquel Leandus se ravoie
         Souvent quant la mer le desvoie.
         Or avint que la mer tourbla
3250   Pour le fort vent qui y souffla
         Si qu'elle en devint toute tourble
         Pour le vent qui l'esmuet et trouble.
         Leandus se tient a la rive,
         Qui fort contre son cuer estrive;
3255   Qu'Amours li enjoint et commande
         Et ses cuers, qu'a passer entende,
         Et la plus belle de ce mont
         Voit d'autre part qui l'en semont;
         Si que li las ne sot que faire,
3260   N'il ne voit goute en son affaire.
         Car il voit la mer si orrible
         Que de passer est impossible.
         Et de sa tempeste et son bruit
         Toute la region en bruit.

Sufficiency then began by saying
3220   The following for all to hear:

"Leander, that handsome and clever man,
Was friendly with a young girl
Named Hero the beautiful;
In all the land there was no
3225   Damsel so attractive,
None so noble by far or so lovely;
Nor was there in Abydos or Crete
Any love affair as secret,
For no one knew of their bond
3230   Save a serving woman
Who had raised beautiful Hero.
She alone was in the know.
They loved each other with a quite perfect love.
It was very hard for them to meet,
3235   For between Hero and Leander
Extended an arm of the sea
That was so wide and deep
No one had ever found its bottom.
And this troubled them greatly.
3240   But every night Leander
Passed over that arm of the sea in the open
Completely naked, alone, with no boat or barge.
Beautiful Hero of the noble appearance
Had a house with a tower
3245   Where every night she waited for him,
Keeping a candle burning
Toward which Leander often directed himself
When the sea threw him off course.
Now it happened that the sea, troubled by
3250   A strong wind, rose high,
And it became roiled by the wind
That disturbed and roused it.
Leander stayed on the shore,
Struggling mightily against his heart,
3255   For Love enjoined and commanded him,
As did his heart, that he should determine to cross.
And on the other side, summoning him,
He saw the most beautiful woman in the world;
And so the miserable man did not know what to do,
3260   Nor could he figure a way out of the fix,
For the sea, he saw, was so threatening
It was impossible to traverse.
And all the region was in an uproar
With storm and thundering.

3265   Mais finalment tant l'assailly
        Amours, que en la mer sailli,
        Dont briefment le couvint noier,
        Car a li ne pot forsoier.
        Et certes, ce fu grans damages,
3270   Car moult estoit vaillans et sages.

        Bele Hero ne scet que dire;
        Tant a de meschief, tant a d'ire,
        Qu'en nulle riens ne se conforte.
        Elle vorroit bien estre morte
3275   Quant son dous amy tant demeure.
        Dou cuer souspire, des yex pleure;
        La nuit ot plus de mil pensees,
        Par .v.ᶜ mille fois doublees.
        Elle ne fait que reclamer
3280   Nepturnus, le dieu de la mer,
        Et li promet veaus et genices,
        Oblations et sacrefices
        Mais que la mer face cesser
        Par quoy Leandus puist passer.
3285   Einsi toute nuit se maintint
        Et l'ardant sierge en sa main tint
        Jusqu'a tant qu'il fu adjourné.
        Mais mar vit pour li ce jour né,
        Qu'entre les flos vit Leandont,
3290   Qui floteloit a abandon.
        Et quant de pres le pot veoir,
        Seur le corps se laissa cheoir
        Au piet de sa tour droitement;
        Si l'embrassoit estroitement,
3295   Forcenee et criant: 'Haro!'
        Einsi fina belle Hero,
        Qui de dueil fu noïe en mer
        Avec son ami pour amer.
        Si qu'il n'est doleurs ne meschiés
3300   Dont cuers d'amant soit entechiez
        Qui soit de si triste marrien
        Com celle qui n'espargna rien,
        Que Hero ne meïst a mort
        Pour son amy qu'elle vit mort,
3305   Ne nuls n'en porroit par raison
        Faire juste comparison,
        Ne que de fiel encontre baume.
        Et pour ce je vous lo, Guillaume,
fol. 43v Que cils debas soit en deport,
3310   Car vraiement, vous avez tort."

3265 But in the end Love so inspired him
He leapt into the water,
Where he quickly drowned,
For he could not make his way to her.
And, surely, this was a great loss,
3270 For he was a man quite valiant and wise.

Beautiful Hero did not know what to say;
So much anguish and anger did she feel
She could find consolation in nothing.
She wished very much to be dead
3275 When her lover was so delayed.
From the heart she sighed; from the eyes she cried.
That night she had more than a thousand thoughts,
Multiplied some five hundred thousand times.
All she could do was call upon
3280 Neptune, the god of the sea,
And she promised him calves and heifers,
Oblations and sacrifices
If only he would calm the sea
So Leander might cross it.
3285 She continued all night doing so
And held the burning candle in her hand
Until a new day dawned at last.
But this day brought her ill luck,
For in the waves she spied Leander,
3290 Who was floating aimlessly.
And when she could see him close up,
She threw herself upon his body
Right at the foot of her tower;
And she held him close,
3295 Crazed as she was, and cried out: 'Alas!'
Beautiful Hero met her end in this way,
Drowned in the sea from grief
Along with her lover because of love.
And so there is no pain or misfortune
3300 That might afflict a lover's heart
And bring on such grievous pain
As that which spared nothing,
Which made Hero die
For the sake of the lover she saw dead.
3305 Nor could anyone with reason
Make a true comparison to anything else,
No more than bitterness set against balm.
And so, Guillaume, I counsel you
To suspend this debate,
3310 For truly you are mistaken."

GUILLAUME

      "Damoiselle, se tort avoie,

      Bien say que condempnez seroie

      Nom pas par vous; car l'ordenance

      Ne doit pas de ceste sentence

3315   Estre couchié en vostre bouche,

      Pour ce que la chose vous touche.

      Eins la doit pronuncier le juge,

      Qui a point et loyaument juge.

      Mais j'ay le cuer moult esjoÿ

3320   De ce que j'ay de vous oÿ;

      Car c'est tout pour moy, vraiement."

SOUFFISSANCE

      "Pour vous, biau Guillaume? Et comment?"

GUILLAUME

      "Damoiselle, or vueilliez entendre,

      Et je le dirai sans attendre;

3325   Quant Amours si fort enlassoit

      Leandus, que la mer passoit

      A no, sans batel n'aviron,

      A la minuit ou environ,

      Li fols qui tant y trespassa

3330   Que d'amer en mer trespassa,

      Il fist trop plus et plus souffri

      Que Hero, qui a mort s'offri,

      Considerés les grans peris

      Ou il fu en la fin peris,

3335   Que ne fist Hero pour s'amour,

      Non contrestant mort ne clamour.

      Car cils qui fait premierement

      Honneur, on dit communement

      Qu'il a la grace dou bien fait,

3340   Nom pas cils a qui on le fait.

      Et plus va a Amour tirant

      Cils qui preste que cils qui rant.

      Einsi est il de tous services,

      Et aussi de tous malefices:

3345   Car qui d'autrui grever se peinne,

      Certes, il doit porter la peinne.

      Si que, ma chiere damoiselle,

      Qui moult amez honneur la belle,

      Vous devez bien, a dire voir,

3350   De ce cop ci honneur avoir.

      Car bien et bel et sagement

GUILLAUME

"Young lady, if I am in the wrong,
I know well I shall be condemned,
But not by you; for the passing
Of this sentence ought not
3315   To come from your mouth
Since you are involved.
Instead it must be pronounced by the judge,
Who will decide fittingly and truthfully.
But my heart greatly rejoices
3320   In what I have heard you say;
For truly it all helps my case."

SUFFICIENCY

"Helps yours, fair Guillaume? How so?"

GUILLAUME

"Young lady, now please listen,
And I will tell you without delay.

3325   When Love so tightly snared
Leander, who was swimming across the sea
Naked, without boat or oar,
At midnight or thereabouts,
The fool who erred terribly
3330   In crossing the sea for the sake of love,
Did more and suffered worse
Than did Hero, who gave herself to death,
If one considers the great perils
That in the end destroyed him,
3335   Since Hero did not do the same out of love for him,
Notwithstanding her death and lamentation.
For he who first does
Something honorable is commonly said
To get the grace from the good deed,
3340   Not the one for whom it is done.
And he is truer to Love who bestows
Than he who gives in return.
So it is with all kinds of service,
And likewise with every kind of mistreatment.
3345   For whoever troubles himself to hurt another
Ought surely to bear the punishment for it.
Thus, my dear damsel, you
Who are very keen to honor the beautiful lady,
To speak the truth, you should certainly
3350   Have the honor of this encounter.
For you have discoursed ably,

L'avez dit; et certeinnement,
Diex pour moy dire le vous fit,
Car j'en averai le profit.

3355   Si que, gentils dame de pris,
        Je croy que bien avez compris
        L'entention des .ij. parties.
        Et se celles qui ci parties
        Sont contre moy vuelent plus dire,
3360   Ce ne vueil je pas contredire,
        Mais j'en ay dit ce qu'il m'en samble,
        Present elles toutes ensamble,
        Et tant, que je ne doubte mie
        Que n'aie droit de ma partie."

LA DAME
3365   Adont la dame souvereinne,
        Des .xij. droite cheveteinne
        Qui avoient parlé pour li,
        Dont au juge moult abelly,
        Prist a dire tout en oiant;
3370   "De riens ne me va anoiant
        Ce qui est fait de nostre plait,
        Mais moult souffissanment me plait,
        Et bien m'en vueil passer atant.
        Sires juges, jugiez atant
3375   Que sentence sera rendue.
        Je suis de moult bonne attendue
        Pour attendre vostre jugier
        Quant il vous en plaira jugier.
        Bon conseil avez et seür,
3380   Bien attempré et bien meür.
        S'alez, s'il vous plaist, a conseil,
        Je le lo einsi et conseil.
        Et vous conseilliez tout a trait.
        Faire ne pouez plus biau trait
fol. 44r Que de traitablement attraire
3386   Bon conseil et puis de retraire
        Les articles dou jugement,
        Selonc le nostre entendement,
        En gardant toudis nostre honneur.
3390   Faire le devez, mon signeur.
        Et vous estes bien si vaillans
        Que point n'en serez defaillans."

Skillfully, and wisely; but surely
God made you speak for my sake,
For I am the one who will profit from it.

3355   And so, noble and worthy lady,
I think you understand quite well
The opinions of the two parties.
And if the ladies who have here sided
Against me wish to say something more,
3360   I will offer no protest,
But I have said what I think
In the presence of the ladies here assembled,
And it is sufficient, I do not doubt at all,
To win the debate for me."

THE LADY
3365   And then the sovereign lady,
True leader of the twelve
Who had spoken on her side
(And this pleased the judge greatly),
Said this so all could hear:
3370   "I find nothing that has happened
In our debate displeasing;
Instead I am quite well satisfied
And wish to be done with it now.
Sir judge, render your decision
3375   So that sentence may be passed.
I have very high hopes
For the judgment I expect from you.
When it pleases you to decide,
You have competent and assured counselors
3380   Who are cool-headed and quite mature.
So proceed, if you please, to deliberate;
I so advise and recommend,
And take this matter under advisement at once.
You could do no better
3385   Than to request in a fitting way
Some good advice and afterward rehearse
The issues that bear on the judgment,
According to our understanding,
Preserving our honor at all times.
3390   This you ought to do, my lord,
For you certainly are so competent
You shall not be found wanting in any way."

LE JUGE

        Li juges, qui bien l'escouta
        Ses paroles, si bien nota
3395   Qu'a entendre pas ne failly.
        Tantost son conseil acueilly,
        Et puis de la se departirent.
        Or ne sceus je pas qu'il deïrent
        En leur secret quant ad present,
3400   Mais assez tost m'en fist present.
        Uns amans qui tant bien m'ama
        Que de tous poins m'en enfourma,
        Non pas par favourableté,
        Mais de sa debonnaireté,
3405   Afin que point ne variasse
        Et que de riens ne m'esmaiasse,
        Par quoy je preïsse maniere
        Uniement toudis entiere;
        Qu'autel samblant devoie faire
3410   Dou droit pour moy com dou contraire.
        Or me fonday seur ce propos;
        S'en fu mes cuers plus a repos.

        Quant a conseil se furent mis,
        Li juges dist: "Je suis commis
3415   A estre bons juges fiables,
        Aus .ij. parties amiables
        Justement a point sans cliner.
        Si doy moult bien examiner
        Trestout le fait par ordenence
3420   Qui appert en notre audience
        Afin que loiaument en juge.
        Einsi doivent faire bon juge.
        Et vous vous devez travillier
        De moy loyaument consillier.
3425   S'en die chascuns son plaisir,
        Tandis com nous avons loisir."
        Dont Avis dist tantost aprés,
        Qui fu de Congnoissance pres:

AVIS

        "Avis sui qui doy bien viser
3430   Comment je vous puisse aviser,
        Car on puet faire trop envis
        Bon jugement sans bon avis.

        Je vous avis que bien faciés
        Et que le contraire effaciés.

THE JUDGE

        The judge, listening closely
        To her words, paid such good attention
3395   He did not fail to understand them.
        His advisers he assembled at once,
        And then they retired.
        Now I did not know at the moment
        What they said in private.
3400   But quite soon afterward a lover
        Who was very fond of me did me the favor
        Of telling me about everything,
        Not through favoritism on his part,
        But because of his good breeding,
3405   So that I would not disagree at all
        Or be surprised by anything
        And thus could assume a manner
        Of complete composure and assurance;
        For I was obliged to react the same
3410   To a decision for me as to one against.
        And so I set myself upon this course;
        Therefore my heart was put more at ease.

        When they had disposed themselves in council,
        The judge said: "I have been commissioned
3415   To be a competent and trustworthy judge,
        Amicable toward the two parties
        To the same degree and without bias.
        Thus I must examine quite carefully
        All the evidence as it was presented
3420   To us while we listened
        So I can judge faithfully.
        This is what good judges should do.
        And you all should exert yourselves
        To advise me in good faith.
3425   So let everyone say what she wishes
        Because we have time for it."
        And immediately afterward Discretion,
        Who was at the side of Understanding, said:

DISCRETION

        "I am Discretion, who must attend carefully
3430   To how I should advise you,
        For someone might be quite unwilling
        To judge without good advice.

        I advise you to do what is good
        And undo what is wrong.

3435 S'il vient par devant vostre face,
Afin que point ne se parface,
En avisant seur .iiij. choses
Qui ne sont mie si encloses
Qu'on ne les puist assez veoir,
3440 Qui un po s'en vuet pourveoir.
Ce jugement avez a rendre,
Premierement devez entendre
De savoir quels est li meffais
Et a qui il a esté fais.
3445 Et si devez aussi savoir
Et enquerir, par grant savoir,
Quant vous saverez le forfait
Et a cui cils l'avera fait,
Que vous sachiez dou tout l'affaire,
3450 Quel cause l'esmuet ad ce faire.
Or avez de .iiij. les trois.
Et li quars est li plus estrois
Au quel on doit bien regarder
Comment on le puist bien garder:
3455 C'est que vous metés vostre cure
A sieuir les poins de nature
Ou coustume attraite de droit.
Se jugerez en bon endroit.
Plus n'en di. Qui vuet, si en die.
3460 J'en ay assez dit ma partie."

CONGNOISSANCE

Congnoissance, qui avisa
Les poins qu'Avis bien devisa,
Dist en haut: "Avis, mes amis,
fol. 44v Ha orendroit en termes mis
3465 Aucuns poins qu'il a devisé,
Les quels j'ay moult bien avisé,
Pour quoy dont je sui Congnoissance,
Qui donne a bon Avis substance
Pour deviser ce qu'il devise,
3470 De quoy la bonne gent avise.
Je fais le scens d'Avis congnoistre,
Et il fait Congnoissance croistre
Par le courtois avis qu'il donne
De son droit a mainte personne.
3475 Juges se vous apointerez
Comment seürement tenrez
D'Avis les poins et les usages.
Faites le, si ferez que sages.
Et de moy qui sui sa compaingne

3435   And thus it is your task,
       So nothing may lack perfection,
       To attend to four things
       That are not so troublesome
       A man cannot see to them properly
3440   If he wishes to spend some time on them.
       As for this judgment you must render,
       You must undertake first
       To learn what the wrong might be
       And against whom it has been done.
3445   And then you must also come to learn
       And seek out with great wisdom,
       Having already discovered the wrong
       And the injured party as well,
       In order to understand the matter entirely —
3450   Namely what moved the man to do it.
       Now of the four things you have three.
       And the fourth is the most difficult
       And you must carefully attend to it
       In whatever way it can be best seen to:
3455   And that is you should pay attention
       To following the principles of nature
       Or of custom related to law.
       In this way, you will judge on a sound basis.
       Now I will say no more. Whoever wishes, let her speak.
3460   For my part, I have said enough."

UNDERSTANDING
       Understanding, who paid attention
       To the points Discretion had well developed,
       Said loudly: "Discretion, my friend,
       Has just given voice to several issues
3465   He has described,
       And these I have noted well
       Because I am Understanding,
       Who lends good Discretion the substance
       To devise what he devises,
3470   With which he advises this good company.
       I make understood the meaning of Discretion,
       And he makes Understanding increase
       Through the courtly advice he gives
       Many a person by his right.
3475   Judge, please make plain
       How closely you will hold
       To the terms and customs of Discretion.
       Do so and you act wisely.
       And as for me who am his companion,

3480   Entendez que je vous enseingne.
        On a ci ce plait demené
        Tant qu'on l'a par poins amené
        Jusques au jugement oïr.
        Resgardez qui en doit joïr.
3485   Jugiez selonc le plaidïé
        Qu'on a devant vous plaidïé.
        Par ce point ne poez mesprendre;
        Car s'on vous en voloit reprendre,
        Li plaïdiers aprenderoit
3490   Le scens qui vous deffenderoit.
        Jugiez einsi hardiement
        Et le faites congnoissanment
        Au condempné bien amender.
        Vous le pouez bien commander.
3495   Je, Congnoissance, m'i acort.
        Et s'en preng aussi le recort
        De Mesure, qui la se siet
        Lez Raison, et moult bien li siet,
        Et Raison aussi en dira
3500   Ce qui bon li en semblera."

MESURE

        Adont s'est Mesure levee,
        En disant: "Ma tresbien amee
        Congnoissance, dire ne vueil
        Riens qui soit contre vostre vueil,
3505   Eins sui moult tres bien acordans
        Ad ce qu'estes ci recordans.
        S'en parleray a vostre honneur
        Au juge, ce noble seigneur
        Qui est courtois et amiables,
3510   Sages, vaillans, et honnourables."
        Lors tourna devers li sa chiere
        De si amoureuse maniere,
        Qu'il ne s'en pot tenir de rire.
        Et Mesure li prist a dire:
3515   "Biau sire, bien eüreus fustes
        Dou conseil que vous esleüstes.
        Vous avez tout premierement
        A Avis si bel commencement,
        Qu'on faurroit bien en court roial
3520   D'avoir conseil aussi loial.
        Je ne di pas qu'aucune gent
        Ne moustrassent bien aussi gent
        Conseil et aussi bien baillié,
        Et d'aussi bel parler taillié.

3480   Listen to how I instruct you.
        This debate has been here conducted,
        Proceeding through its different stages
        Until the point of hearing a judgment.
        Look to who shall be pleased with it.
3485   Judge according to the testimony
        That has been offered before you.
        In this way you cannot go wrong;
        For if anyone wished to fault you,
        The pleadings would demonstrate
3490   The rationale to justify you.
        Be bold in your judgment
        And require that with full understanding
        The condemned party pay the price.
        You have the right to command him.
3495   I, Understanding, am in agreement.
        And I accept also the opinion
        Of Moderation, who is seated there
        At the side of Reason, and this suits her well,
        And Reason will also say
3500   Whatever she deems appropriate."

MODERATION

        Then Moderation rose,
        Saying: "My highly esteemed friend
        Understanding, I wish to say nothing
        You might find objectionable;
3505   Instead I very much agree
        With what you have been saying here.
        And in your honor I will speak of it
        To the judge, this noble lord
        Who is courteous and friendly,
3510   Wise, valiant, and honorable."
        Then toward him she turned her face
        In such a flirtatious fashion
        He could not refrain from laughing.
        And Moderation began to say to him:
3515   "Fair sir, you have been fortunate
        In the counsel you sought out.
        At first you had a quite good
        Beginning with Discretion,
        For one assuredly should in a royal court
3520   Receive advice as trustworthy as this.
        I do not say another company
        Would not proffer advice
        As proper and as well considered,
        Fittingly dressed out with proper speech.

3525　Mais veons la condition
　　　　D'Avis selonc s'entention:
　　　　Il donne conseil franc et quitte
　　　　Et n'en attent autre merite
　　　　Fors ce que li juges tant face
3530　Qu'il en ait pais, honneur, et grace.
　　　　Et Congnoissance, sa compaingne,
　　　　A tel salaire s'acompaingne,
　　　　Sans demander nulle autre chose;
　　　　Dont loiaus juges se repose
3535　Qui de tels gens est consilliez.
　　　　Sire, s'en devez estre liez.
　　　　Comment qu'il aient dit a point,
　　　　Se passerai je oultre d'un point
　　　　Qu'Avis avoit bien avisé —
3540　Et se ne l'a pas devisé —
　　　　Et Congnoissance congnëu.
　　　　Mais il s'en sont en cas dëu
fol. 45r　Pour moy porter honneur, souffert;
　　　　Dont de moy vous sera offert,
3545　Pour ce que j'ay bien entendu
　　　　Qu'il s'en sont a moy attendu.
　　　　Mais einsois averai ditte
　　　　D'un petit de ma qualité.

　　　　Je suis Mesure mesuree,
3550　En tous bons fais amesuree,
　　　　Et aussi sui je mesurans,
　　　　Ferme, seüre, et bien durans
　　　　A ceuls qui vuelent sans ruser
　　　　Justement de mesure user;
3555　Et qui non, aveingne qu'aveingne.
　　　　De son damage li souveingne.
　　　　Dont uns maistres de grant science
　　　　Et de tres bonne conscience
　　　　A un sien deciple enseingne
3560　Et li moustre de moy l'enseingne,
　　　　Disant; 'Amis, je te chastoy;
　　　　Se tu ne mes Mesure en toy,
　　　　Elle s'i mettra maugré tien.
　　　　Ceste parole bien retien:
3565　S'elle s'i met, tu es peris;
　　　　Se tu l'i mes, tu es garis.'
　　　　Or vueil passer les poins tout outre
　　　　Qu'Avis et Congnoissance moustre.
　　　　Il ont servi courtoisement
3570　De leur bon conseil largement,

3525   But let us look to the nature
           Of Discretion as he himself understands it.
           He provides counsel free and clear,
           Expecting no reward at all in return
           Except that the judge might do
3530   What would bring peace, honor, and thanks.
           And Understanding, his companion,
           Accompanies him for the same salary,
           Without demanding anything further;
           And so a trustworthy judge rests easy,
3535   One advised by such as these.
           Therefore, sire, you ought to be happy about it.
           Although they have spoken ably,
           I will say something more about a point
           Discretion has taken notice of —
3540   And yet has not described at length —
           And that Understanding has understood.
           Now in this case they have been obliged
           To exert themselves to honor me;
           And so I will offer it to you
3545   Because I have certainly noticed
           They have paid me due heed.
           Even so, I will go ahead and say
           Some things about my nature.

           I am moderated Moderation,
3550   Temperate in all good deeds,
           And also I am moderating,
           Firm, stable, and strong in endurance
           For all who wish without trickery
           To make proper use of moderation;
3555   And whoever does not, what will be, will be.
           And let him be mindful of his own hurt.
           In this regard, a master of great wisdom,
           Who had a very virtuous conscience,
           Was instructing his disciple
3560   And explaining the teachings about me,
           Saying: 'Friend, I admonish you.
           If you do not acquire Moderation yourself,
           She will make herself felt in you regardless.
           Remember this saying well:
3565   If she comes to you, you are done for.
           But if you welcome her, you will be all right.'
           Now I would like to review thoroughly all the points
           Discretion and Understanding raise.
           They have served out generously
3570   And courteously their good advice,

Si comme on sert a un mengier,
Sans rien d'especïal jugier.
Et de ce qu'il ont bien servi,
Dont il ont grace desservi,
3575 J'en vorray l'escot assener,
Et a chascun son droit donner.
Guillaumes, qui en ses affaires
Soloit estre si debonnaires,
Si honnestes et si courtois,
3580 Enclins aus amoureus chastois,
A attenté contre Franchise,
Et tout de sa premiere assise,
Quant ma dame a point l'aprocha
Dou fait qu'elle li reprocha,
3585 Et il s'en senti aprochiez
A juste cause et reprochiez.
Il ala avant par rigueur,
Et se mist tout sa vigueur
Pour lui deffendre encontre li.
3590 Cils poins fort me desabeli,
Pour ce qu'il se desmesura:
Par ces raisons de Mesure ha
Les regles et les poins perdus,
Dont il sera moult esperdus
3595 Quant a moy le retourneray;
Car d'onneur le destourneray
Quant Congnoissance li dira
Le meffait que fait avera.
Il deüst avoir mesuré
3600 L'estat dou gent corps honnouré
De celle dame souvereinne;
Qu'en tout le crestien demainne
N'a homme, s'il la congnoissoit,
— C'est bon a croire qu'einsi soit —
3605 Qui hautement ne l'onnourast
Et qui de li ne mesurast
Humble et courtoise petitesse
Au resgart de sa grant noblesse.
Dont Guillaumes est deceüs
3610 Quant il ne s'en est perceüs.
Car trop hautement commensa,
Dont petitement s'avansa.
Pour bien sa cause soustenir;
Eins est assez pour li punir.
3615 Or veons au fait proprement
Dés le premier commencement,
Pour bien deviser les parties,

Just as one serves at a meal,
Without judging the particulars of the case.
And since they have served well,
They have earned thanks.
3575   I would like to add up the bill
And give everyone his due.
Guillaume, who once was
So well mannered in all his actions,
So honest and courteous as well,
3580   Conforming to the chastisements of love,
Launched an attack against Frankness
And all those of her high rank
When my lady properly approached him
About the deed she reprimanded him for,
3585   And he felt himself upbraided
For just case and reproached as well.
He then proceeded forcefully,
Putting every effort into it,
To defend himself against her.
3590   This fact distresses me a great deal
Because he acted immoderately.
For these reasons, he has abandoned
The rules and principles of Moderation,
And this will trouble him greatly
3595   When I bring him back to me;
For I will turn him away from honor
When Understanding informs him
Of the misdeed he has committed.
He should have properly measured
3600   The station of the gentle, honored person
Of that sovereign lady;
For in all the Christian realm
There is no man who, if he knew her
— And it is good to believe it would be so —
3605   Would not honor her highly
And would not measure himself
As humble and of lesser courtliness
In regard to her great nobility;
And so Guillaume was deceived
3610   When he did not perceive this.
For he began much too haughtily,
And so has advanced himself but little
In the competent presentation of his case.
And this is quite enough to have him punished.
3615   Now let us look to the issue itself
From its proper commencement
In order to distinguish between the parties,

Comment elles sont departies,
A savoir la quele se tort.
3620　Je di que Guillaumes a tort,
Car de tous les crueus meschiés
La mort en est li propres chiés;
fol. 45v　A dire est que tous meschiés passe,
Et pour ce que nuls n'en respasse.
3625　Car on se puet trop miex passer
De ce dont on puet respasser.
Plus de vueil de ce fait espondre,
Car j'ay assez, pour lui confondre,
D'autres choses trop plus greveinnes,
3630　Simples, foles, vuides, et veinnes.

Sires juges, or m'entendez;
Pour la fin a quoy vous tendez,
De rendre loial jugement,
Je vueil un po viser comment
3635　On a alligué de ce plait.
Et vous meïsmes, s'il vous plait,
.I. petit y resgarderez
Si que miex vous en garderez
De jugier autrement qu'a point.
3640　Car vous congnoisterez le point
De quoy justice est a point pointe
Quant juges sus bon droit s'apointe.
Je vueil que vous soiez certeins
Que Guillaumes doit estre attains
3645　De son plait en celle partie
Ou sa cause est mal plaidoïe,
Non obstant ce qu'en tous endrois
Par tout est contre lui li drois;
Dont ma dame a tout sormonté,
3650　Tant dou plait com de la bonté
De sa querelle, qui est toute
Mise en clarté et hors de doubte.
Ma dame, par ses damoiselles,
A alligué raisons tres beles
3655　Et toutes choses veritables,
Fermes, seüres, et estables,
Toutes traites de l'escripture
Et ramenees a droiture.
Mais qui tout vorroit deviser,
3660　Trop y averoit a viser.
Et, d'autre part, chose est certeinne:
Que la court en est assez pleinne
De tout ce qu'on a volu dire

How they are divided,
In order to learn which one is in error.
3620 I say Guillaume is wrong,
For of all cruel misfortunes,
Death is the absolute worst;
Which is to say, it surpasses all miseries,
And that is because no one recovers from it.
3625 For a person can suffer more easily
What he can recover from.
I do not wish to go on further,
For to condemn him I have enough
Evidence, much more grievous things that are
3630 Simpleminded, foolish, inane, and vainglorious.

Sir judge, now listen to me;
For the sake of the goal at which you aim,
Namely the rendering of a faithful judgment,
I wish to consider somewhat
3635 How this trial was conducted.
And if you please, look
Into this a little yourself
So you can the better refrain
From judging in any but the proper fashion.
3640 For you will recognize the point
On which justice is properly fixed
When a judge aims at true justice.
I want you to be certain
That Guillaume is to be reproached
3645 For the part of his argument
That has been badly presented,
Notwithstanding that in every way
And in everything the law is against him;
And so my lady is completely victorious,
3650 As much in the debate as in the correctness
Of her complaint, which has been completely
Clarified and put out of doubt.
My lady has through her damsels
Alleged quite pertinent reasons
3655 And facts that are all true,
Firm, assured, and unassailable,
All drawn from written tradition
And connected to the law.
But whoever might want to recount all this
3660 Would have too much to consider here.
And, furthermore, one thing is certain:
The court has been sufficiently provided
With all that anyone wished to say

      De par ma dame sans mesdire;
3665 Si que de ma dame me tais.
      Et de Guillaume, qui entais
      A esté d'alliguer s'entente,
      Parleray — car il me talente —,
      De son plaidïé seulement.
3670 Et se m'en passerai briefment,
      Foy que devez tous vos amis.
      Veons qu'il a en terme mis:
      Dou clerc qui hors dou sens devint,
      A il prouvé dont ce li vint,
3675 Que ce li venist de sa dame?
      Sires juges, foy que doi m'ame,
      Il n'en a nulle riens prouvé;
      Se li doit estre reprouvé.
      Et dou chevalier qui par ire
3680 Pour ce qu'il ne se volt desdire
      Copa son doi a tout l'anel,
      Il fist en s'onneur .i. crenel
      De honte pleinne de sotie
      Avec tres grant forcenerie
3685 Quant a sa dame l'envoia.
      Car bien croy qu'il li enuya;
      Au mains li dut il ennuier
      D'un si fait present envoier.
      Car quant dame son amy aimme,
3690 Dou droit d'Amours pour sien le claimme
      Et puet clamer, ce m'est avis.
      Or resgardons sus ce devis
      Comment li chevaliers meffist:
      Ce qu'elle amoit, il le deffist,
3695 Q'estoit sien dou droit d'Amour;
      Dont je fais ci une clamour
      Contre Guillaume de ce fait,
      Que avis m'est qu'il n'a riens fait,
      Car cils poins qu'il a mis en prueve
3700 Sa cause punist et reprueve.
      Et aussi de la Chastelainne
      De Vergi, a petite peinne
fol. 46r Assez reprouver le porray
      Par les raisons que je diray:
3705 Li fais que Guillaumes soustient,
      Sire, vous savez qu'il contient
      Qu'amans, garnis de loiauté,
      Truist en sa dame fauss
eté.
      Et sus ceste devision
3710 Il fait une allegation,

On my lady's behalf with no infamy;
3665   And so I will be silent about my lady.
And concerning Guillaume, who has been
Intent on arguing his case,
I will say something — for I wish to do so —
But only in regard to his pleading.
3670   And I will pass over this quickly
By the faith you owe all your friends.
Let us see what he has brought up.
Concerning the clerk who went mad,
Has he proved what caused this,
3675   That it was something his lady did?
Sir judge, by the faith I owe my soul,
He has proved nothing of the kind;
And so he ought to be reproved.
And concerning the knight who in his anguish
3680   Not to violate his pledge
Cut off his finger with the ring still on it,
He erected in her honor a monument
Full of shame and madness
When in a fit of great craziness
3685   The man sent it on to his lady.
For I certainly believe she found it troubling,
Or at least it should have troubled her
To have sent her such a thing as a present.
For when a lady loves her lover,
3690   By the law of Love she claims him as her own
And has the right to claim an injury, so I think.
Now let us consider how in regard
To this principle the knight erred.
The thing she loved he harmed,
3695   And it was hers by the law of Love;
And so I lodge a complaint
Against Guillaume on this point
Because I think he has accomplished nothing.
For this instance he has presented as evidence
3700   Damages and undermines his case.
And also, in regard to the Chatelaine
Of Vergy, I can refute this example
Sufficiently with only a little trouble,
Using the reasons I will here rehearse.
3705   The evidence that Guillaume adduces,
Sire, you know contends
That the lover, filled with loyalty,
Found falseness in his lady.
And beginning with this assumption,
3710   He makes an allegation

Pour prouver par .i. fait contraire.
La chasteleinne debonnaire
N'avoit son ami riens meffait.
Mais il meïsmes fist le fait
3715   Pour quoy elle se mist a mort.
Quant il le sceut, il se remort
Et se mist en la congnoissance
Qu'il y apartenoit vengence;
Dont il meïsmes se juga,
3720   Punist dou tout et corriga,
Dont Guillaumes a par son dit
Pour son profit meins que nient dit.
Plus n'en di; mais Raisons dira
Ci aprés ce qu'il li plaira."

L'ACTEUR
3725   A ces mos s'est Raison drecié
Comme sage et bien adrecié,

RAISON
Disant: "Raions en consistoire.
La porrons par parole voire,
Ce m'est vis, bon jugement rendre,
3730   S'il est qui bien le sache entendre."
Atant de la se departirent.
Es propres lieus se rasseïrent
Ou il avoient devant sis.
Lors dist Raisons par mos rassis:
3735   "Sire juges, certeinnement
Chose n'a sous le firmament
Qui ne tende a conclusion:
Les unes a perfection
Pour pluseurs cas de leur droit tendent;
3740   Et si a autres qui descendent
De haut ou elles ont esté
En declinant d'un temps d'esté
En l'iver qu'on dit anientir.
Dont cils plais desire a sentir
3745   De droit conclusion hastive
Par sentence diffinitive,
Pour ce qui est bien pris parfaire
Et ce qui est mal pris deffaire.
Et il est temps, bien le savez,
3750   Que desormais dire en devez,
Ou ordener qu'on en dira."

To be proven by a contrary fact.
The respectable chatelaine
Did not wrong her lover in any way.
Instead, he himself did
3715   What caused her to kill herself.
When he found out, he felt remorse
And came to the recognition
That vengeance was required;
And so he passed judgment on himself,
3720   Punished and corrected himself for everything,
And thus Guillaume, with all he has said,
Has said less than nothing to his profit.
I will say no more; rather Reason will say
Whatever she wishes."

THE AUTHOR

3725   At these words, Reason stood up
In the manner of one well schooled and wise,

REASON

Saying, "Let us return to the council room.
There we can with truthful speech
Render a truthful judgment, I think,
3730   If there is any man capable of understanding it."
At once they left that place.
And they again sat down in their own seats
Where they had sat earlier.
With measured words, Reason then said:
3735   "Sir judge, certainly
There is nothing beneath the firmament
That does not seek its proper end:
Some things tend toward perfection
For various reasons pertaining to their own laws;
3740   And there are yet others that descend
From on high where they have been,
Declining from a season of summer
Into the so-called winter of destruction.
Just so, this pleading is tending to arrive at
3745   A speedy conclusion according to the law
Through a definitive sentence,
So as to perfect what has been done well
And remedy what has been done badly.
And the moment has arrived, as well you know,
3750   When you must speak of it
Or command that it be spoken of."

LE JUGE

      "Raison, dame, ne m'avenra
      Que j'en die, quant ad present.
      Mais je reçoy bien le present
3755 D'ordener. Et de m'ordenance,
      Mais qu'il soit a notre plaisance,
      Dites en et tant en faciez
      Que le tort dou tout effaciez
      Et metez le droit en couleur
3760 De toute honnourable honneur,
      Qui savez en tels couleurs teindre
      Ou nuls fors vous ne puet ateindre."

GUILLAUME

      Lors Raisons .i. po s'arresta
      Et puis sus destre s'acota,
3765 En regardant devers senestre,
      Pour miex aviser de mon estre.

RAISON

      Se me dist: "Guillaume, biaus sire,
      Vous avez piessa oÿ dire
      Que c'est folie d'entreprendre
3770 Plus que pooirs ne puet estendre.
      Et toute voie, s'on emprent
      Aucun fait de quoy on mesprent,
      S'on s'en repent au moien point,
      Encor y vient il bien a point.
3775 Mais qui son forfait continue
      Et dou parfaire s'esvertue
      Jusqu'a tant qu'il vient au darrain,
fol. 46v Et a ce point ne trueve rien
      Fors que son dueil et son damage,
3780 Se lors recongnoist son outrage,
      Il vient trop tart au repentir.
      Guillaume, sachiez sans mentir,
      Qu'ensement avez vous ouvré.
      S'en avez un dueil recouvré
3785 Q'vous venra procheinnement,
      Et se vous durra longuement,
      Voire, se ne vous repentez.
      Mais je croy que vous estes, telz
      Que vous ne le deingneries faire.
3790 Car trop fustes de rude affaire,
      Quant la dame vous aprocha
      D'un fait qu'elle vous reprocha
      Que fait aviés en temps passé.

THE JUDGE

"Lady Reason, it is not fitting for me
To speak at this present time.
But I receive well the notion
3755   Of deciding. And concerning my decision,
So that it may be to our liking,
It is up to you to say and do
Enough to efface everything wrong
And restore the right to the hue
3760   Of every honorable honor,
You who can paint in such colors
As no one else save you can manage."

GUILLAUME

Then Reason halted a little
And leaned toward her right,
3765   While glancing to her left
In order to see better how I was doing,

REASON

And she said to me: "Guillaume, fair sir,
You have just now heard said
It is madness to take on
3770   More than ability can compass.
And yet when a man undertakes to do
Something that gives offense,
If he repents in the middle,
Then he will still make out all right.
3775   But he who persists in his error
And exerts himself to see it through
Until he comes right to the very end,
And at that point he finds nothing
Except his own grief and harm,
3780   If then he acknowledges his own misdeed,
He comes too late to repentance.
Guillaume, be sure — and it's no lie —
This is how you have carried on,
And so you have merited some unpleasantness
3785   That will soon fall to your lot,
And it will long endure,
Truly, if you do not repent.
But I believe you are the kind of man
Who will not deign to do so,
3790   For you were quite rude in your behavior
When the lady approached you
About the deed for which she reproached you,
Something you did some time ago.

       Se vous heüssiez compassé
3795 En vous aucune congnoissance
       Qui fust signes de repentence
       De ce que vous aviez mespris
       Contre les dames de haut pris,
       Vous heüssiez fait moult que sages.
3800 Car d'Amours est tels li usages
       Que s'aucuns des dames mesdit,
       S'il ne s'en refreint et desdit,
       Amender le doit hautement
       Ou comparer moult chierement.
3805 Or de ce meffait premerein
       Vous di de par le souverain
       Amours, q'est maistres et sires,
       Des plaies amoureuses mires:
       Jugemens en est ordenez
3810 Dou quel vous estez condempnez.
       Si qu'amender le vous couvient;
       Hastivement li termes vient.
       Encor vous puis je commander
       Si qu'il vous couvient amender
3815 Un autre fait qui me desplait,
       De ce q'vous prenistes plait
       Contre dame de tel vaillance
       Et de si tres noble puissance,
       Que je ne say haute personne,
3820 Tant com li siecles environne,
       Prince ne duc, conte ne roy,
       Qui osast faire tel desroy,
       Guillaume, comme vous feïstes
       Dou plait qu'a li entrepreïstes.
3825 Et meïstes force et vigueur
       En aler avant par rigueur;
       Einsi l'avez continué;
       S'avez vostre sens desnué
       De courtoisie et d'ordenance.
3830 Se ce ne fust la pacience
       Qui est en li, vous perdissiez
       Tant qu'a meschief le portissiez."

GUILLAUME

       Quant j'oÿ ce, je fui dolens;
       Mais je ne fui feintis ne lens
3835 De li demander humblement
       Qu'elle me devisast briefment
       De la dame la verité
       D'un petit de sa poësté.

  If you had shown in yourself
3795 Any recognition of this at all,
  Which would have been a sign of repentance
  For having committed this wrong
  Against ladies of great worthiness,
  You would have acted very much the wise man.
3800 For the custom of Love is such
  That when any man vilifies women,
  If he does not recant and henceforth refrain
  From so doing, he must make great amends
  Or pay a very high price.
3805 Now concerning this initial misdeed
  I tell you on behalf of sovereign
  Love, who is master and lord,
  The physician for the wounds of love,
  Namely that a judgment has been rendered
3810 Condemning you in this matter.
  And so it is necessary you make amends;
  The time for this quickly approaches.
  In addition, I am empowered to order
  You to make amends
3815 For another deed that displeases me,
  In that you undertook to debate
  A lady of such worthiness
  And of such very noble authority
  That no highborn person I know of,
3820 So far as the world extends,
  No prince or duke, count or king,
  Would dare commit such an outrage,
  Guillaume, as the one you did
  In the dispute you undertook against her.
3825 And you put into this force and vigor
  As you proceeded aggressively;
  And you've continued in the same vein.
  In this way, you have stripped your mind
  Of courtesy and respectfulness.
3830 And if she did not have the patience
  That she does, you would have lost so much
  You would have come to grief."

GUILLAUME

  Hearing this, I was distressed;
  But I was neither abashed nor hesitant
3835 To ask her humbly
  If she would briefly explain to me
  The truth about the lady
  And something about her powers.

RAISON

              Lors dist: "Guillaume, volentiers.
3840   Mais je n'en dirai hui le tiers,
              Non mie, par Dieu, le centisme.
              Car dés le ciel jusques en bisme
              Ses puissances par tout s'espandent,
              Et de ses puissances descendent
3845   Circonstances trop mervilleuses,
              Et sont a dire perilleuses,
              Qui s'apruevent par leur contraire.
              Par ces raisons s'en couvient taire
              Pour les entendemens divers
3850   Qui sont aucune fois pervers.
              La dame a nom Bonneürté,
              Qui tient en sa main Seürté
              En la partie de Fortune.
              Car il n'est personne nesune
3855   Cui Fortune peüst abatre,
fol. 47r Se la dame le vuet debatre.
              Et quant elle vuet en Nature
              Ouvrer par especial cure,
              La la voit on sans nul moien
3860   Voire li astronomien
              Qui congnoissent les nations
              Parmi les constellations,
              C'est assavoir és enfans nestre
              De quel couvine il doivent estre.
3865   Dont, quant la chiere dame regne
              Et uns enfés naïst en son regne,
              Se Bonneürtez l'entreprent,
              Nature point ne l'en reprent,
              Eins l'en laist moult bien couvenir,
3870   Comment qu'il en doie avenir.
              Voirs est que Nature norrit
              Par quoy li enfés vit et rit.
              Et Bonneürtez le demeinne
              Tout parmi l'eüreus demainne,
3875   Tant qu'il est temps qu'en lui appere
              Que de Bonneürté se pere.

              Or sont celle gent si parent,
              Dont elle est en euls apparent
              Parmi le bien qu'il en reçoivent,
3880   Afin que ne lui n'en deçoivent.
              Or vous vueil je dire en appert
              En quels manieres elle appert,
              En aucunes, non pas en toutes;

REASON

   Then she said: "Guillaume, willingly.
3840 But today I will not describe even a third,
   No, not even a hundredth part.
   For from the sky down to the pit of hell,
   Her powers extend through all things,
   And from these powers flow
3845 Quite marvelous results,
   Things that are dangerous to utter
   And show this through their contraries.
   For these reasons, it is well to pass them over in silence
   Because of faulty understandings,
3850 And these sometimes are perverse.
   The lady's name is Happiness,
   And she holds Security by the hand
   Among the company of Fortune.
   For there is no person
3855 Whom Fortune can bring down
   If the lady wishes to contest it.
   And when she intends to work through Nature
   Because she has some special concern
   She can be seen there readily
3860 In truth by the astrologers
   Who recognize the different nations
   Among the constellations,
   That is to say, in the birth of infants,
   To what sign they will belong.
3865 And so when the dear lady is regnant
   And an infant is born into his sign,
   If Happiness takes charge of him,
   Nature does not take him back from her,
   But instead very much lets her do her will,
3870 No matter how it is to turn out.
   It is true that Nature takes care of
   How the infant lives and laughs.
   And Happiness leads him
   Into the domain of good luck
3875 Until the time has come for it to show
   That Happiness is caring for him.

   Now these people are all around us,
   And in them the lady makes herself manifest
   Through the benefits they receive,
3880 As long as they do not betray her somehow.
   Now I want to tell you specifically
   In what different ways she manifests herself,
   In some, but not in all.

              Et si ne faites nulles doubtes
3885   Des paroles que j'en diray,
              Car de riens ne vous mentiray.
              Elle appert en prosperité
              Et en issir de povreté;
              Elle appert en acquerre amis
3890   Et en punir ses anemis
              Par victoire, sans nul tort faire.
              Elle appert en tout bon affaire,
              Et quant elle appert en amours,
              C'est quant amans, par reclamours,
3895   Par servir ou par ses prieres
              Et en toutes bonnes manieres,
              Puet en pais de dame joïr
              Dou droit especial joïr,
              Qu'Amours donne de sa franchise.
3900   La est Bonneürtés assise
              Entre ami et loial amie
              Qui ne vuelent que courtoisie
              Et ont par certeinne affiance
              Li uns a l'autre grant fiance.
3905   La les tient elle en moult grant point.
              Elle est a tous biens mettre a point.
              S'en est moult plus gaie et plus cointe.
              Elle est de tous les biens acointe.
              Elle appert en mains esbanois,
3910   Tant en joustes comme en tournois,
              Pour chevalerie essaucier
              Et les fais des bons avancier
              A la congnoissance des dames.
              La croist honneur; la chiet diffames.
3915   Car tels a esté diffamez
              Qui puis est chieris et amez
              De ceuls qui ains le diffamoient,
              Pour ce qu'apertement veoient
              Qu'il met son corps en aventure;
3920   Dont tels fois est qu'il aventure
              Dou fait d'armes qu'il a empris,
              Tant qu'il vient au souverein pris.
              Einsi Bonneürtez avance
              Les siens de sa haute puissance.

3925   Se Bonneürtez par nature,
              Par fortune ou selonc droiture,
              Appert en la chevalerie,
              Elle appert aussi en clergie.
              La tient elle honneur en ses mains.

And have no doubt of any kind
3885   About the words I will speak,
For in no way will I lie.
She appears in prosperity
And in the leaving behind of poverty.
She is there in the making of friends
3890   And in the punishment of enemies
Through a victory, without any wrongdoing.
She appears in every good deed,
And when she is present in love,
It is that the lover, through his demands,
3895   Through his service and pleadings,
And because of proper deeds of all kinds,
Is able to enjoy his lady in peace,
To take pleasure in the special privilege
Love grants in her generosity.
3900   There Happiness sits
Between the lover and loyal beloved,
Those who wish for only what is courtly
And who have by an explicit pledge
Placed great trust in one another.
3905   She sustains them in a quite grand style.
All goods are hers to bestow properly.
And so she is much more gay and friendly.
She is acquainted with all good things.
She appears in many diversions,
3910   In jousts as much as in tourneys,
In order to exalt chivalry
And advance the deeds of good men
In the understanding of women.
There honor grows; there infamy falls away.
3915   For the man who has been maligned
Is afterward cherished and loved
By those who spoke ill of him
Because they see openly
That he puts his life at risk;
3920   And so the time comes when he takes his chance
In a trial of arms he embarks upon,
Until in the end he rises to the highest rank.
In this way Happiness advances
Her own through her great power.

3925   If Happiness through Nature,
Or by fortune, or according to custom
Does appear in chivalry,
She also appears in learning.
There she holds honor in her hands.

3930 A l'un plus et a l'autre mains
   En fait ses larges departies;
   S'en donne les plus grans parties
   A ceuls qui tiennent miex l'adresse
   Ou Bonneürtés les adresse.
3935 Aussi appert elle en science,
fol. 47v Et se s'enclot en conscience,
   Pour garder ceuls aucune fois
   En cui est pais et bonne fois,
   Qui n'ont pas par voie autentique
3940 Mis leur scens en fourme publique,
   Eins sont sage secretement.
   La se tient elle closement;
   La li tiennent grant compaignie
   Loiaus Secrez et Bonne Vie.
3945 La se vuet elle reposer
   Et les cuers a point disposer
   En la vie contemplative.
   Or revient par la voie active
   Pour esmouvoir ceuls de parler
3950 Qui tiennent volentiers parler
   Des biens de contemplation;
   Dont maint, par bonne entention,
   S'enclcinent si a sa doctrine
   Que chascuns par soy se doctrine
3955 D'estre diligens et hastis
   De devenir contemplatis.
   Que vous iroie je contant?
   En Bonneürté a de biens tant
   Que jamais n'aroie compté
3960 Le centisme de sa bonté.
   Dont au monde n'a grant signeur
   Ne dame, tant aient d'onneur,
   Qu'il ne leur fust et bel et gent,
   S'estre pooient de sa gent.
3965 Atant m'en tais; je n'en di plus,
   Mais que venir vueil au seurplus
   Des .ij. poins dont condampnés estes.
   Et s'ay mes raisons toutes prestes
   Dou tiers point que je vous diray,
3970 Dou quel je vous condempneray.

   Il est bien veritable chose
   Que s'aucuns a .i. plait s'oppose
   S'il se trait a production
   Et il vient a probation,
3975 Se s'entention bien ne prueve,

3930   More to one and less to another
        She makes her generous distribution;
        And she gives out the greatest shares
        To those who obey better the summons
        Happiness issues them.
3935   She is also manifest in knowledge
        And encloses herself within the mind
        In order to safeguard at times those
        In whom are peace and good faith,
        Those who have not in any acknowledged fashion
3940   Put their wisdom into a public form,
        But rather are wise in secret.
        In them she keeps herself hidden;
        And in them Faithful Secrets and Good Living
        Afford her good companionship.
3945   And there she wishes to rest
        And appropriately turn those hearts
        Toward the contemplative life.
        Then by the active path she returns
        To encourage those to speak
3950   Who willingly hold discussion
        About the virtues of contemplation.
        And therefore many, with good intentions,
        Then incline themselves to her teachings,
        So they each teach themselves on their own
3955   How to be diligent and eager
        To become contemplative.
        Why should I go on speaking about this to you?
        Happiness possesses so many goods
        Never might I have related
3960   The hundredth part of her virtue.
        So in the world there is no great lord,
        No lady, however much honor they might possess,
        For whom it would not be pleasing and noble
        If they could be among her company.
3965   Now I will be silent. I will say no more about her,
        But deal instead with what remains
        Of the two counts on which you have been condemned.
        And I have my thoughts in order
        For what I intend tell you about the third count
3970   On which I shall condemn you.

        It is certainly an indisputable fact
        That if someone opposes a complaint,
        Busies himself with producing evidence,
        And then comes to the test,
3975   Yet fails to prove his view adequately,

    Verité de droit li reprueve
    Qu'il en doit estre condempnez.
    Cils drois est de si lonc temps nez
    Qu'il n'est memoire dou contraire.
3980 Or veons a quoy je vueil traire,
    Et s'entendez bien a mon dit:
    De quanque la dame vous dit
    De son fait, vous vous opposastes
    Et dou prouver vous avansastes.
3985 Mais vous avez si mal prouvé
    Qu'il vous doit estre reprouvé
    A vostre condempnation,
    Selonc la mienne entention.
    Vous n'avez ci dit que paroles
3990 Qui sont aussi comme frivoles.
    Belles sont a conter en chambre,
    Mais elles ne contiennent membre
    Dont pourfis vous peüst venir
    Pour vostre prueve soustenir.
3995 Et si avons si bien gardé
    Com nous poons, et regardé,
    Pour querir loyal jugement.
    S'il vous plaist a savoir comment,
    On vous en dira les parties,
4000 Comment elles sont departies.
    Et de vostre erreur tous les poins.
    Et se vous veez qu'il soit poins
    Qu'on vous die vostre sentence,
    Se nous dites que vos cuers pense.
4005 Qu'il vous en plaist, on le fera
    Si a point que bien souffira."

GUILLAUME

    "Dame, bien vous ay entendu,
    Et s'ay bonne piece attendu
    Que je fusse sentenciez.
4010 Se vous pri que vous en soiez
    Diligens de moy delivrer,
    Quant a ma sentence livrer.
    Dés que mes fais est si estrois
    Que je doy des amendes trois
fol. 48r Et qu'autrement ne puet aler,
4016 Je n'en quier plus faire parler."

RAISON

    "Guillaume, soiez tous certeins
    Que de droit y estes ateins;

The truth of the law then reproves him
And he must be condemned.
This legal principle arose so long ago
There is no memory of its contrary.
3980   Now let us see what I wish to recount,
So listen carefully to what I say.
Whatever the lady told you
About her evidence, you opposed,
And you tried to offer proof for your view.
3985   Yet you have so badly failed to prove it
You ought to be reprimanded
And, as a consequence, condemned
In my opinion.
You have said nothing here save
3990   Words that are frivolous.
They are pretty to mouth in private,
But they contain no substance
To afford you an advantage
In sustaining the proof of your case.
3995   And so we have looked into and
Examined this case as best we could
In order to seek out a faithful judgment.
If it pleases you to know the particulars,
You will be told about the different opinions,
4000   And how they are distributed to those involved,
And also all aspects of your error.
And if you see it might be time
For your sentence to be pronounced,
Then tell us what you think in your heart.
4005   For whatever pleases you, it will be done
Thoroughly enough to satisfy you."

GUILLAUME

"Lady, I have listened to you quite well
And have waited some time
To be sentenced.
4010   So I beg you to be diligent
About delivering me to it,
That is, about granting me my sentence.
Since what I did is so serious,
Three amends are required,
4015   And since things cannot go otherwise,
I do not wish to discuss the matter further."

REASON

"Guillaume, be completely assured
That you have received justice here.

          Se n'en serons point negligens.
4020   Or soiez aussi diligens,
          Et puis maintenant vous levez
          Pour faire ce que vous devez
          Vers celui qui pour juge siet.
          S'en fera ce que bon l'en siet.
4025   Dés or mais a lui appartient,
          Car tout le droit en sa main tient."

GUILLAUME
          A ce mot au juge en alay
          Et d'un genouil m'agonouillay.
          La li presentai je mon corps
4030   Par si couvenable recors,
          Comme je peüs et li sceüs dire;
          Dont il prist un petit a rire.
          Lors pris mes gans, si li tendi;
          Dont il qui bien y entendi
4035   Les prist, et puis si les laissa.
          Aprés .i. po se rabaissa,
          Si que secondement les prist,
          Puis les laissa, puis les reprist,
          En signe de moy moustrer voie
4040   Que troie amendes li devoie.
          Moult bien le me signefia,
          Et pour verité m'affia
          Qu'il les me couvenroit paier.
          Lors me dist il, sans delaier,
4045   Que je me ralasse seoir,
          Car il se voloit pourveoir
          Quel penitence il me donroit,
          Et que brief m'en delivreroit.

          Lors pres de la dame se trait,
4050   Et Raison aussi, tout attrait,
          A leur secret conseil se mist
          Et de bas parler s'entremist.
          Mais a leur parler bassement
          Pris un petit d'aligement,
4055   Pour ce que je bien percevoie
          Que leurs consaus estoit de joie,
          Car d'eures en autres rioient,
          Et a ce droit point qu'il estoient
          Au plus estroit de leur conseil,
4060   Avis me dist: "Je vous conseil
          Que ceste dame resgardez
          Et songneusement entendez

And we will not be negligent in any way.
4020   But now you should be just as diligent.
So get on your feet at this time
To do what you should do
In the presence of that man who sits as judge.
And then he will do what he thinks right.
4025   From now on the matter rests with him
Since he holds in his hands all the legal power."

GUILLAUME

At this word, I went over to the judge
And got down on one knee.
There I offered my person to him
4030   In as appropriate a speech
As I was able and knew how to deliver.
And it made him smile a little.
I then took my gloves and tendered them to him.
And he who paid this close attention
4035   Seized and then dropped them.
In a moment, he leaned down again
And took them up a second time,
Then letting them drop, then taking them up once more
As a sign to demonstrate to me how
4040   I owed him three payments for damages.
Quite well he signified this to me,
Assuring me in truth
That I would have to pay them.
Then without hesitation he told me
4045   I should go back and sit down,
For he wished to look to
What penance he would assign me,
And to this he would shortly deliver me.

Then he drew up close to the lady,
4050   As did Reason, quite demurely,
And he counseled privately with them,
Taking care to speak softly.
But in their whispering
I found some relief,
4055   Because I saw well
Their council was a pleasant one,
For from time to time they laughed,
And just at that moment when they were
Most seriously deliberating,
4060   Discretion said to me: "I advise you
To look at this lady
And attend carefully to

Aus drois poins de sa qualité.
La verrez vous grant quantité
4065 De sa grace et de son effort.
S'en averez le cuer plus fort
Pour endurer et pour souffrir
Ce que drois vous vorra offrir."
Lors li dis je: "Biaus dous amis,
4070 Mais vous m'en faites le devis
Qui congnoissez de moult de choses
Les apparans et les encloses.
Souvent en estes a l'essay,
C'est une chose que bien say."

4075 Adont dist Avis: "Ce vaut fait.
Or entendez bien tout a fait:
Quant aus parties deviser,
Se bien vous volez aviser,
Elle ot vestu une chemise
4080 Qui est appellee Franchise
Pour secrés amans afranchir
Et de Sobreté enrichir
En la partie de Silence
Parmi l'acort de Congnoissance.
4085 Car pour tant qu'elle n'est veüe
Sa cause doit estre teüe.
Et sa pelice, c'est Simplesse
Si souëf que point ne la blesse,
Car elle est de Beniveillance,
4090 Orfroisié de Souffissance,
A pelles de Douce Plaisance
Qui bons cuers en tous biens avance.
fol. 48v   Et li changes qu'elle a vestu
Par tres honnourable vertu
4095 Fu fais de Loial Acointance
Et ridez de Continuance
A pointes de Perseverence
Egalment, sans desordenance.
Or est cils changes biaus et lés,
4100 Et est de son droit appellés
Pour certainne condition
Honneste Conversation.
Et la sainture qu'elle ha sainte
N'est pas en amours chose fainte,
4105 C'est propre loial Couvenance,
Cloee de ferme Fiance.
Quar qui couvenances affie,
Necessité est qu'on s'i fie.

The rightful aspects of her estate.
There you will see a great deal
4065   Of her grace and power.
And in this way you will have a much stronger heart
For enduring and for suffering
Whatever justice she will render you."
Then I said to him: "Dear sweet friend,
4070   You describe these things to me,
You who know the obvious
And hidden details of so many things.
Often you take on such a task;
That's something I know well."

4075   Discretion said then: "This merits doing.
Now pay quick attention:
As far as describing the parts is concerned,
If this is something you wish to mark well,
She has put on a shift
4080   That is called Frankness
In order to liberate secret lovers
And enrich them with Seriousness
On behalf of Silence,
With Understanding in agreement.
4085   For until she has been seen
Her cause should be kept silent.
And her fur tunic, that is Simplicity,
So soft it does not wound her,
For it comes from Goodwill,
4090   Gilt-edged by Sufficiency,
With the pelts from Sweet Pleasure,
Who moves good hearts toward every good.
And the robe with linen sleeves that she wears
In very honorable virtue
4095   Was crafted by Loyal Friendship,
Pleated by Steadfastness
Tipped with ribbons from Perseverance,
Neatly, without any disorder.
Now this robe is beautiful and flowing,
4100   And by proper right it is called,
Because of its special status,
Honest Familiarity,
And the belt she has girded herself with
Is no insignificant thing in regard to love,
4105   For it is properly called Loyal Promise,
Studded with Stable Commitment,
For whoever makes promises,
It is necessary they be trusted.

Et li mordans, pour ce qu'il poise,
4110   Sert d'abaissier tençon et noise,
Si que jusqu'a ses piez li bat.
Et si piet deffont maint debat
Entre amie et loial amy,
Quant aucuns amans dit: 'Aimy!
4115   De ma dame sui refusez;
Mais mes drois n'est pas abusez,
Car je croy bien qu'elle le fit
A s'onneur et a mon profit.'
Einsi si piet la gent demainne,
4120   Cui elle tient en son demainne;
Car il sont chaucié d'Aligence,
Lacié a laz de Diligence.
Et s'a mis blans gans en ses mains,
Li quel sont fait ne plus ne mains
4125   Entre Charité et Largesse,
Dont elle depart la richesse
D'Amours qu'on ne puet espuisier
Ne par nul jour apetisier.
Plus en prent on, plus en demeure
4130   De jour en jour et d'eure en heure.

Dou mantel vous vueil aviser
Comme il est biaus a deviser,
Et mieudres que biaus qui s'en cuevre
Par dit, par maintieng, et par ouevre.
4135   Lainne de bons Appensemens
Avecques courtois Parlemens,
Scienteuse Introduction,
Et amiable Entention
Furent ensamble compilees,
4140   De Bonté proprement drapees;
Et de ses choses asamblant
Fu fais li dras de Bon Samblant,
Tains en une gaie couleur
De tres honnourable valeur
4145   Qui est appellee Noblesse,
Et est fourrez de Gentillesse.
Or est Bonneürtez couverte
Dou mantel, et est chose aperte
Que par dessous tous biens enclot.
4150   Mais veritablement esclot
Quanqu'il a sous sa couverture
Li apparans de sa figure,
Si comme en sa fisonomie
Li bien de toute courtoisie

And the belt medallion, because it is heavy,
4110   Serves to beat down dissension and discord,
And thus it hangs down all the way to her feet.
And her feet prevent many an argument
Between the beloved and loyal lover
Whenever any lover cries 'Alas!
4115   I have been refused by my lady;
But my right has not been abused,
For I believe she has done so
To my profit and to her honor.'
And so her feet keep this company in line,
4120   Whomever she holds in her domain;
For they are shod with Relief,
Laced with the cord of Diligence.
And she has put white gloves on her hands,
Which have been equally made
4125   By both Charity and Generosity,
With which she shares out the riches
Of Love, which cannot be exhausted
Or reduced as time goes by.
The more that is taken, the more remains
4130   From day to day and hour to hour.

I would like to tell you about the mantle,
Which is so handsome to describe,
And he who wears it finds it better than handsome
In words, demeanor, and deeds.
4135   The wool of Good Reflection
Along with Courtly Speech,
Knowledgeable Introduction,
And Friendly Intention
Were woven there together,
4140   Properly felted by Goodness.
And the cloth of Good Appearance
Was made by assembling these things,
Dyed a merry color
Of most honorable worthiness
4145   That is called Nobility,
And it was lined with Gentility.
Now Happiness is covered
With the mantle, and it is obvious
That all good things are therein enclosed.
4150   But it reveals, in truth,
No matter what she is beneath her covering,
The appearance of her face,
Which is such that in her features
The benefits of courtesy of every kind

4155   Tres souffissanment y apperent,
        Dont ses damoiselles se perent.
        Et elle est aussi bien paree
        D'elles, sans estre separee
        D'elles et de leur bon arroy.
4160   Car elles souffissent pour roy
        Et pour souvereinne roÿne.
        Pour ces raisons vous determine
        Que Bonneürtez dou tout passe
        Toutes roÿnes et trespasse.
4165   Se je voloie sa coronne
        Deviser, qui est belle et bonne,
        Trop longuement vous en tenroie;
        Car je voy bien la droite voie
        Que leur consaus va a declin.
4170   Atant pais de ce vous declin."

GUILLAUME
        Quant leur consaus fu affinez,
fol. 49r Li juges s'est vers moy tournés,

LE JUGE
        En disant: "Guillaume, par m'ame,
        Ytant vous di de par ma dame
4175   Et de par Raison ensement,
        Et je sui en l'acordement,
        Que de .iij. amendes devez
        Devisees, et eslevez,
        Lesqueles vous devez sans faille
4180   Par jugement, comment qu'il aille.
        Il vous couvient, chose est certeinne,
        Faire .i. lay pour la premereinne
        Amiablement, sans tenson;
        Pour la seconde une chanson
4185   De .iij. vers et a un refrein
        — Oëz, comment je le refrein —
        Qui par le refrein se commence,
        Si comme on doit chanter a dance;
        Et pour la tierce, une balade.
4190   Or n'en faites pas le malade,
        Eins respondez haitiement
        Aprés nostre commandement
        De tous poins vostre entention.
        Je fais ci ma conclusion."

4155   Appear there in abundance,
          With which her damsels are adorned.
          And she is as well adorned
          As they, without being set apart
          From them and their beautiful array.
4160   For they are fine enough for a king,
          And for a sovereign queen as well.
          For these reasons I put it to you
          That Happiness completely surpasses
          And is of higher estate than all queens.
4165   If I wished to describe
          Her crown, which is beautiful and becoming,
          I would detain you too long;
          For I readily see, and there can be no doubt,
          That their council is drawing to a close.
4170   And so I will spare you its description."

GUILLAUME

          When their council ended,
          The judge turned my way,

THE JUDGE

          And said: "Guillaume, by my soul,
          I will tell you this on my lady's behalf
4175   And on behalf of Reason as well,
          And I am in agreement with them,
          That you owe three compensations,
          As these have been determined and decribed,
          And for these you are responsible
4180   According to the judgment, without fail.
          You must — the thing is certain —
          Compose a lay for the first
          And agreeably, without resisting;
          For the second, a song
4185   Of three stanzas and a refrain
          — Listen how I qualify this —
          Which begins with the refrain,
          Just like the ones sung at dancing;
          And for the third, a ballade.
4190   Now do not make as if this sickens you
          But rather respond happily
          In regard to our command,
          About your intentions on all these points.
          I make here an end."

GUILLAUME

4195   Et pour ce que trop fort mespris,
        Quant a dame de si haut pris
        M'osay nullement aastir
        De plait encontre li bastir,
        Je, Guillaumes dessus nommez,
4200   Qui de Machau sui seurnommez,
        Pour miex congnoistre mon meffait,
        Ay ce livret rimé et fait.
        S'en feray ma dame present,
        Et mon service li present,
4205   Li priant que tout me pardoint.
        Et Diex pais et honneur li doint
        Et de paradis la grant joie
        Tele que pour moy la voudroie.
        Mais pour ce que je ne vueil mie
4210   Que m'amende ne soit paié.
        Pour la paier vueil sans delay
        Commencier .i. amoureus lay.

Explicit *le Jugement le Roy de Navarre contre le Jugement dou Roy de Behaingne.*

GUILLAUME

4195   And because I so grievously erred
        When I dared to make trouble
        With a lady of such high estate
        In that I attempted to dispute with her,
        I, the Guillaume named above,
4200   Who has the surname de Machaut,
        In order the better to acknowledge my fault,
        Have composed and rhymed this little book.
        And of it I will make my lady a present,
        Offering her my service and
4205   Begging her to pardon me for everything.
        And may God grant her peace and honor
        And the great joy of Paradise
        Such as I would wish for myself.
        But because I do not want in any way
4210   That my fine should remain unpaid,
        I wish to retire the debt without delay
        By beginning work on a lay whose theme is love.

Here ends *The Judgment of the King of Navarre* against *The Judgment of the King of Bohemia*.

LE LAY DE PLOUR, MUSIC EDITED BY URI SMILANSKY

Ci commence le lay de plour

Qui bien aim-me a tart ou - bli - e, Et cuers
Quar plai - sen-ce si me li - e Que ja -

qui ou - blie a tart Res-sam - ble le feu qui
mais l'a - mou-reus dart N'iert hors trait, a tiers n'a

art Qui de le - gier n'es-teint mi - e. Aus-
quart, De moncuer, quoy que nuls di - e, Car

si qui ha ma-la - di - e Qui plaist en - vis
tant m'a fait com-pai - gni - e Que c'est ni - ant

se de - part. En ce point, se Dieus me gart,
dou de - part, Ne que ja-mais, par nul art,

Me tient A - mours et mais - tri - e,
Soit sa poin - tu - re ga - ri - e,

II.

Qu'en-vis puet on des - ra - ci - ner Un grant ar -
Cer - tes, ein - si est il d'a - mer. Car quant uns

330

bre sans de-mou - rer De la ra - ci - ne,
cuers se vuet en - ter En a-mour fi - ne,

Qu'on voit puis flou-rir et por - ter Et ses bran-ches croi -
En - vis puet s'a-mour ou-bli - er; Ein-sois a - dés par

stre_et ge - ter En brief ter - mi - ne.
ra - mem - brer A li s'en - cli - ne.

III.

Car l'iau - e qui chiet des - seu - re La ra - ci - ne
Et c'est ce qui me de - veu-re. C'est ce qui mon

qui de - meu - re Fait renn-ver - dir et flo - rir Et por - ter
vis es - pleu-re. C'est ce pour quoi je sou - pir. A ce me

fruit. Tout ein - si mes cuers, qui pleu-re Par - fon - de-ment
duit Vraie A - mour, qui me court seu-re, Et Bon - té, qui

a tou - te_heu-re, A - croi - stre mon sou - ve - nir Fait
l'as - sa - veu - re, Qu'en moy ne puis-sent ve - nir. Ce

jour et nuit.
me des - truit.

IV.

Rai-sons et Droi - tu - re, Plai-sen - ce et Na -
Et je m'as-se - u - re Que, tant com je

tu - re Font par leur po - oir Tou-te cre-a -
du - re, Ne por-ray ve - oir A-mour si se -

tu - re De vo - len-té pu - re Ten-dre a
u - re, Bon-té si me - u - re, N'a tant

mieus va - loir.
de sa - voir.

V.

Aus - si voit on cle - re - ment Que li cuer qui
Or say je cer - tein-ne - ment Que mien-ne es-toit

loy-au - ment Et sans fo - lour Aim-ment de tres fi - ne a -
li - ge - ment La droi-te flour De ceaus qui ont plus d'on -

mour Cui - dent sou - vent Qu'en mil - leur et en plus
nour. Quar tou - te gent Di - soi - ent com - mu - ne -

gent Ai - ent se - jour. Car plai-sen-ce et sa ri - gour Ce
ment, Et li mil - lour, Qu'il a - voit tou - te va - lour En-

leur a - prent.
tie - re - ment.

VI.

Et quant si bon ne mil - lour ne plus coin - te
Qu'en mon cuer est si tres fer - me et si join - te

N'est, ne si bel, ne d'on - neur si a - coin - te, A droit ju -
L'a - mour de li qu'es - tre n'en puet des - join - te. Car cuer en -

gier, Mer - vil - lier Ne se doit Nulz se ne vueil par l'a - mou - reu - se
tier Qui tri - chier Ne sa - roit Par sou - ve - nir vuet que dou tout m'a -

poin - te Nou - vel - le - ment d'au - tre a - mour es - tre poin -
poin - te Si qu'au - tre a - mour n'en - tre - prein - gne, n'a - coin -

te. Pour ce chan - gier Ne me quier, Et j'ay droit.
te, Qu'au - tre a - coin - tier Em - pi - rier Me fe - roit.

VII.

Dont le bon re - cort Qui de li re - cort
"A - mis, mi con - fort, Mi joi - eus de - port,

Fait qu'a ce m'a - cort Que ja ne soie en a - cort
Ma pais, mi res - sort, Et tuit mi a - mou - reus sort

IX.

La sous - pi - re, La s'a - i - re Mes cuers qui tant
La se em - pi - re Ti - re a ti - re; La ne fait que

a mar - ty - re Et de mor - tel pein - ne Et tant
fon - dre et fri - re; La son dueil de - mein - ne; La sans

de i - re, Qu'a voir di - re Son mal ne por - roit des -
ri - re Se mar - ti - re; La se mour - drist; la de -

cri - re Cre - a - tu - re hu - mein - ne.
si - re Qu'il ait mort pro - chein - ne.

X.

Dous a - mis, tant ay gre - ven - ce, Tant ay grief souf -
En toy es - toit m'es - pe - ran - ce Tou - te et ma fi -

fran - ce, Tant ay dueil, tant ay pe - sen - ce, Quant ja -
an - ce, Ma joi - e, ma sous - te - nan - ce. Las - set -

mais ne te ver - ray Que do - leur me point et lan - ce
te! Or per - du les ay. Bien pert a ma con - te - nen - ce

De si mor - tel lan - ce Au cuer qu'en des - es - pe - ren - ce
Et a ma lo - quen - ce, Car ma - nie - re ne puis - san - ce

Pour toy mes jours fi - ne - ray.
N'ay, tant me dueil et es - may.

XI.

A cuer pen - sis Re-gret et de - vis
Mes es - pe - ris Et mes pa - ra - dis

Ton haut pris Que tant pris. Ein - si le cou - vient. Et
Es - tient mis Et as - sis En toy; s'a - par - tient Que

vis a vis Te voy, ce m'est vis, Dous a - mis,
soit fe - nis Mes cuers est pe - ris, Qu'est che - tis

Et tou - dis De toy me sou - vient.
Et re - mis, Quant vi - e le tient.

XII.

A - mis, je fus - se moult li - e S'e-us -
Ta mort tant me con-tra - li - e Et tant

ses cuer plus cou - art; Mieux vau - sist a mon es -
de maus me re - part, A - mis, que li cuers me

gart Que vo - len - té si har - di - e. Mais
part. Mais ein-sois que je de - vi - e, Hum -

hon - neur, che - va - le - ri - e, Et tes re - nons
ble - ment mes cuers sup - pli - e Au vray Dieu qu'il

qui s'es - part Par le mon-de_en main - te part
nous re - gart De si a - mou - reux re - gart

Ont fait de nous de - par - ti - e.
Qu'en liv - re soi - ens de vi - e."

Explicit le lay
de plour

LE LAY DE PLOUR

Ci commence le lay de plour

I

Qui bien aimme a tart oublie,
Et cuers qui oublie a tart
Ressamble le feu qui art
Qui de legier n'esteint mie.
5   Aussi qui ha maladie
Qui plaist envis se depart.
En ce point, se Dieus me gart,
Me tient Amours et maistrie,
Quar plaisence si me lie
10   Que jamais l'amoureus dart
N'iert hors trait, a tiers n'a quart,
De mon cuer, quoy que nuls die,
Car tant m'a fait compaignie
Que c'est niant dou depart,
15   Ne que jamais, par nul art,
Soit sa pointure garie.

II

Qu'envis puet on desraciner
Un grant arbre sans demourer
        De la racine,
20   Qu'on voit puis flourir et porter
Et ses branches croistre et geter
        En brief termine.
Certes, einsi est il d'amer.
Car quant uns cuers se vuet enter
25   En amour fine,
Envis puet s'amour oublier;
Einsois adés par ramembrer
        A li s'encline.

338

THE LAY DE PLOUR

Here begins *The Lay de Plour*

I

1   Whoever loves well forgets slowly,
And the heart that slowly forgets
Is like the fire that burns
But cannot easily be put out.
5   And whoever suffers an illness
That pleases unwillingly recovers.
In such a state, so God give me help,
Love restrains and commands me,
For Pleasure has me so snared
10   That the arrow of loving
Will never be drawn out, not even a little,
From my heart, whatever anyone might say,
For it's been in me so long
That there's no question of its leaving,
15   Nor ever, by any art,
Will that wound be healed.

II

A huge tree can hardly be
Uprooted without leaving behind
      Some of its roots,
20   And so in a short time it is seen
Bearing flowers and fruit, its branches
      Growing and spreading.
Surely, it's the same with love,
For when a heart's bent on
25   A noble love affair,
It can hardly forget its loved one,
Rather, always, through memory
      Inclines toward him.

III

       Car l'iaue qui chiet desseure
30   La racine qui demeure
       Fait rennverdir et florir
           Et porter fruit.
       Tout einsi mes cuers, qui pleure
       Parfondement a toute heure,
35   A croistre mon souvenir
           Fait jour et nuit.
       Et c'est ce qui me deveure.
       C'est ce qui mon vis espleure.
       C'est ce pour quoi je soupir.
40   A ce me duit,
       Vraie Amour, qui me court seure,
       Et Bonté, qui l'assaveure,
       Qu'en moy ne puissent venir.
           Ce me destruit.

IV

45   Raisons et Droiture,
       Plaisence et Nature
       Font par leur pooir
       Toute creature
       De volenté pure
50   Tendre a mieus valoir.
       Et je m'asseüre
       Que, tant com je dure,
       Ne porray veoir
       Amour si seüre,
55   Bonté si meüre,
       N'a tant de savoir.

V

       Aussi voit on clerement
       Qui le cuer qui loyaument
           Et sans folour
60   Aimment de tres fine amour,
           Cuident souvent
       Qu'en milleur et en plus gent
           Aient sejour.
       Car plaisence et sa rigour
65   Ce leur aprent.

III

       For the water flowing down
30   To the root that remains
       Makes it green again and flourish,
            Bearing fruit:
       Just the same, my heart, weeping
       Bitterly all the time,
35   Makes my memory grow
            Both day and night.
       And this drives me mad;
       This covers my face in tears;
       This is the reason I cry out;
40   True Love
       Drives me to it, assaulting me,
       And Goodness finds it sweet:
       But they cannot enter me,
            And I am destroyed.

IV

45   Reason and Justice,
       Pleasure and Nature,
       Create by their power
       All that lives
       Through pure will
50   To incline toward greater worthiness.
       And I console myself,
       For, as long as I endure,
       I'll never see
       A love so certain,
55   A goodness so well grown,
       Nor so much wisdom.

V

       And more, it is obvious
       That the hearts which loyally
            And without madness
60   Love with a quite noble love
            Often think
       To find a relief that's better
            And more noble;
       For pleasure in its insistence
65   Suggests this to them:

Or say je certeinnement
Que mienne estoit ligement
La droite flour
De ceaus qui ont plus d'onnour,
70   Quar toute gent
Disoient communement,
Et li millour,
Qu'il avoit toute valour
Entierement.

VI

75   Et quant si bon ne millour ne plus cointe
N'est, ne si bel, ne d'onneur si acointe,
A droit jugier,
Merveillier
Ne se doit
80   Nulz se ne vueil par l'amoureuse pointe
Nouvellement d'autre amour estre pointe.
Pour ce changier
Ne me quier,
Et j'ay droit.
85   Qu'en mon cuer est si tres ferme et si jointe
L'amour de li qu'estre n'en puet desjointe.
Car cuer entier
Qui trichier
Ne saroit
90   Par souvenir vuet que dou tout m'apointe
Si qu'autre amour n'entrepreingne, n'acointe,
Qu'autre acointier
Empirier
Me feroit.

VII

95   Dont le bon recort
Que de li recort
Fait qu'a ce m'acort
Que ja ne soie en acort
D'avoir autre amy.
100   Mais en desconfort
Sans nul reconfort
De tout mon effort
Vueil pleindre et plourer sa mort,
En disant einsi:

Now I know for sure
That my lover, without doubt,
      Was the rightful flower
Of those men with the greatest honor:
70   For everyone
Says this everywhere,
      And the best people in fact,
That his alone was complete
      Worthiness.

VI

75   And since there's none better, more genteel,
None more handsome, so familiar with honor,
      No one,
      To judge truly,
      Should wonder
80   If I don't wish to be wounded
By the shaft from another lover.
      I don't want
      To change this,
      And I'm right;
85   For my love for him is so implanted, so firm
In my heart it cannot be removed;
      For a heart undivided
      Which cannot
      Be false
90   Intends that I spur myself on through memory
To never undertake a new love, or meet with one;
      For to take up with some other man
      Would do
      Me harm.

VII

95   For the beautiful memory
      That recalls him to me
      Makes me determined
Never to agree
      To have another lover;
100   Rather in misery,
      With no relief,
      But with all my strength
I intend to lament and weep over his death,
      Saying this:

105   "Amis, mi confort,
       Mi joieus deport,
       Ma pais, mi ressort,
Et tuit mi amoureus sort
       Estoient en ty.
110   Or ay un remort
       De toy qui me mort
       Et point si tres fort
Que o toy sont tuit mi bien mort
       Et ensevely.

VIII

115   Dous amis, tant fort me dueil,
         Tant te plaint,
      Tant te complaint
      Le cuer de moy,
Tant ay grief que, par ma foy,
120   Tout mal recueil:
        Dont mi oueil
      Que souvent mueil,
      Et cuer estreint,
Viaire pali et taint,
125   Garni d'effroy
        Et d'anoy,
      Sans esbanoy
      Moustrent mon dueil.
Dous amis, seur ton sarcueil
130   Sont mi plaint
      Et mi complaint.
      La m'esbanoy;
Par pensee la te voy;
      Plus que ne sueil
135   La me vueil;
      La sont mi vueil;
      La mes cuers maint.
Le mort pri que la me maint,
      Car la m'ottroy.
140   La, ce croy,
      De la mort doy
      Passer le sueil.

105   "Lover, my comfort,
     My joyous pleasure,
     My peace, my refuge,
   And all my loving destiny
     Were in you.
110   Oh I'll have pain again
     To tear at me on your account,
     Wounding me so terribly,
   For all my goods died with you
     And were put in the ground.

     VIII

115 Sweet love, I grieve so hard;
      My heart
     Mourns you so much,
     Laments you so much,
   My grief's so great, by my faith,
120   I reap all ills;
      Thus my eyes
     Are very often wet,
     My heart quite anguished,
   My face pale, tear-stained,
125   Wracked by troubles,
      And pain,
     Lacking comfort;
     These show my sorrow.
   Sweet lover, on your bier
130   Lie my laments,
     And all my weeping;
     There I find pleasure,
   Seeing you in my thoughts;
     More than I was wont
135   I wish to be there.
     There lie my desires.
     My heart remains there.
   I beg for the death that leads me there.
     For there I offer myself.
140   There, I believe,
     I ought pass over
     Death's threshold.

IX

La souspire,
La s'aïre
145   Mes cuers qui tant a martyre
Et de mortel peinne
Et tant de ire,
Qu'avoir dire
Son mal ne porroit descrire
150   Creature humeinne.
La se empire
Tire a tire;
La ne fait que fondre et frire;
La son dueil demeinne;
155   La sans rire
Se martire;
La se mourdrist; la desire
Qu'il ait mort procheinne.

X

Dous amis, tant ay grevence,
160   Tant ay grief souffrance,
Tant ay dueil, tant ay pensence,
Quant jamais ne te verray
Que doleur me point et lance
De si mortel lance
165   Au cuer qu'en desesperence
Pour toy mes jours fineray.
En toy estoit m'esperance
Toute et ma fiancé,
Ma joie, ma soustenance.
170   Lassette! Or perdu les ay.
Bien pert a ma continence
Et a ma loquence,
Car maniere ne puissance
N'ay, tant me dueil et esmay.

XI

175   A cuer pensis
Regret et devis
Ton haut pris
Que tant pris.
Einsi le couvient.

IX

My heart
Sighs there
145 Grows angry there, there suffers martyrdom.
Feels such deadly pain
And so much regret,
That to tell the truth
No person alive could even
150 Describe it.
There my heart grows worse
Without stopping;
There it can only tremble and burst;
There it manifests grief;
155 There, hardly laughing,
It suffers;
There it kills itself; there it wishes for
A death that's on its way.

X

Sweet lover, my grief's so great,
160 My suffering so terrible,
I feel such pain, worrying so much,
Since I never will see you,
And so sorrow stabs and wounds me
With such a deadly lance
165 In the heart that despairing
For you I'll end my days.
All my hope was in
You, my trust as well,
My joy, my nourishment.
170 Sorrowful one! Now I've lost them.
It's readily apparent in my look
And in my speech,
For I've no strength or direction,
So much do I sorrow and grieve.

XI

175 With a heavy heart
I mourn and recall
Your great worthiness
Which I prized so much.
It must be so;

180   Et vis a vis
          Te voy, ce m'est vis,
                    Dous amis,
                    Et toudis
          De toy me souvient.
185   Mes esperis
          Et mes paradis
                    Estient mis
                    Et assis
          En toy; s'apartient
190   Que soit fenis
          Mes cuers et peris,
                    Qu'est chetis
                    Et remis,
          Quant vie le tient.

                    XII

195   Amis, je fusse moult lie
          S'eüsses cuer plus couart;
          Mieux vausist a mon esgart
          Que volenté si hardie.
          Mais honneur, chevalerie,
200   Et tes renons qui s'espart
          Par le monde en mainte part
          Ont fait de nous departie.
          Ta mort tant me contralie
          Et tant de maus me repart,
205   Amis, que lie cuers me part.
          Mais einsois que je devie,
          Humblement mes cuers supplie
          Au vray Dieu qu'il nous regart
          De si amoureux regart
210   Qu'en livre soiens de vie."

          Explicit *le Lay de Plour*

180   And I see you
         Face to face, so I think,
                Sweet lover,
             And always
         I remember you.
185   My soul
         And my paradise
             Were placed
            And set
         In you; and so it follows
190   That my heart
         Is finished and done for,
             For it is wretched
             And brought to nothing,
         While life clings to it.

XII

195   Lover, I would have been quite happy
         If you had had more the coward's heart;
         This would have been worth more to me
         Than a will so hardy.
         But honor, chivalry,
200   And your renown, spreading
         Throughout the world in many places,
         Have brought us to an end.
         Your death does trouble me so much,
         And so much ill comes upon me,
205   Lover, that the heart goes out of me;
         But before I do die,
         My heart humbly begs
         The True God to look upon us
         With such a loving countenance
210   That in a book we'll find life."

         Here ends *The Lay de Plour*

⚜ EXPLANATORY NOTES

ABBREVIATIONS: *BD*: Chaucer, *Book of the Duchess*, ed. Benson; *DMF: Analyse et Traitement Informatique de la Langue Française Dictionnaire de Moyen Français*; *LGW*: Chaucer, *Legend of Good Women*, ed. Benson; *CA*: Gower, *Confessio Amantis*; **Hassell**: Hassell, *Middle French Proverbs, Sentences, and Proverbial Phrases*; *JRB*: Machaut, *Le Jugement dou Roy de Behaingne*; *JRN*: Machaut, *Le Jugement dou Roy de Navarre*; *OM*: *Ovide Moralisé*, ed. Cornelis de Boer; *RR*: *Roman de la Rose*, trans. Dahlberg; *TC*: Chaucer, *Troilus and Criseyde*, ed. Benson.

LE JUGEMENT DOU ROY DE BEHAINGNE

1–40   *Au temps pascour . . . . ne le porroire.* This section draws explicitly on *RR*, in which the archetypal Lover similarly falls prey to the enticements of springtime. Here, however, Machaut radically transforms the structure by rejecting allegorical personages in favor of a confrontation between two human characters.

27   *"Ocy! Oci!".* "Ocy" is not a sound that birds were, at least conventionally, thought to make in Middle French. The word, however, is the imperative form of the verb *kill*. Perhaps here the springtime birds sing out "Kill! Kill!" in acknowledgment of Love's proverbial destructiveness, but it is difficult to pin down the precise meaning of the word in this context. It is also used in a number of sung *virelais* of this period that imitate birdsong (so-called "realistic" *virelais*).

28ff.   *Qu'en .i. destour* . . . In Machaut's hands, the idealized pastoral landscape familiar from *RR* becomes, as Ardis Butterfield explains, "a place of carefully defined seclusion" ("Pastoral," p. 11). As in his other *dits*, Machaut's "landscape is an isolated, wild area, difficult of access but placed within a courtly, civilized enclosure. Such a conjunction between the courtly and the wild is a characteristic pastoral relation and one exploited to the full by Spenser, for example, in his Bower of Bliss or in Froissart's *Paradys d'amours* ("Pastoral," p. 11).

41–1223   *Mais tout einsi . . . . de ma partie.* At this point, the narrator is displaced from his role as main character of the developing story and becomes, if only for a time, a clerkly witness (not himself of noble birth) to the debate between the two aristocratic figures. As part of a wider discussion connecting sight, power, and authorship, Jacqueline Cerquiglini-Toulet describes the position of clerkly witness as passive, or impotent. She explains that it is the ear of the author that overhears conversations, the mouth of the author that relates

351

them, and the hand of the author that records them, but the poet is denied sight, the most noble of the five senses. For a further discussion of the theme of a clerk listening from a concealed position, see Cerquiglini-Toulet, "L'ecriture louche,"pp. 25–27. It may be of interest to note that Jean de Luxembourg, himself was blind.

56ff.   *Mais quant amis . . . .* This "first confrontation between the sorrowing knight and the equally distraught lady . . . leads to a second encounter scene between them and the poet, who finally brings about a third between them and the king as judge. In each situation the balance of social decorum subtly alters as the equally matched pair of grieving courtly lovers gives way first to the ingenuity of the clerical poet and then to the superior courtly authority of the king himself" (Butterfield, "Pastoral," p. 10).

125   *vij. ans ou .viij. entiers.* The seven years marks the completion of the lover's apprenticeship; the eighth year would start a new beginning, this time into rewards. Compare *BD*, lines 37–38, where the protagonist has suffered sickness for "this eight yere" [eighth year], yet his "bote is never the nere" [unfulfilled].

125–205   *Sire il a . . . . je me dueil.* The debate proper begins at this point, with the lady's long account of her experience with love.

126   *sers et rentiers.* The lady describes herself as the "serf and vassal," a theme which frequently recurs in the poem (e.g., the knight's description of himself as his lady's "vassal" in line 279) and also in other works.

130–32   *Cuer, corps, povoi . . . . En son servage.* Compare Alceone's vow to sacrifice herself "with good wille, body, herte, and al" (*BD*, line 116) to Juno for word of the missing king, Ceyx. Her sacrifical pledge of thralldom to Love is repeated by the Black Knight in, line 768, "with good entente" (line 766).

148–76   *Et je l'amoie . . . . En nos amours.* As William Calin notes, the lady and her lover's relationship was "successful, honest and genuine . . . [and] could only be destroyed by powers beyond human control" (*Poet at the Fountain*, p. 44). Compare her story to the description of the knight's account of his love affair, where we hear mainly of "frustration, anguish and protracted love-service"(p. 44).

156–59   *Tous mes confors . . . . mes ressors.* Compare Chaucer's *TC* 3.477–81: he was "a wal / Of stiel and shald from every displesaunce, / . . . she was namore afered."

169–76   *Tuit d'un acort . . . . en nos amours.* Compare *BD*, lines 1288–97, on the lovers being so well-matched a pair. They suffered "oo blysse and eke oo sorwe bothe" (line 1293) and were both glad and upset as a single being.

177–208   *Lasse, dolente . . . . Cheï com morte.* Here, the sickness and longing for death caused by disappointed love is described in detail. It also recurs elsewhere in the poem (e.g., in line 719) and in other works, such as *RR*.

220–30   *Qu'elle est pasmee . . . . par loiaument amer.* In this section, the lady faints and the knight sprinkles dew on her face to revive her. Perhaps this implies a courtly "baptism," especially considering the implications of love's capacities of restoration. Such fainting scenes are common in courtly literatures for both women and men. Compare *TC* 3.1086–92 (Troilus' swoon) and 4.1150–80. (Criseyde's swoon).

259–880   *Dont vous diray . . . . qui me martyre.* Here the lover offers his account of the suffering inflicted by his faithless ladylove. James Wimsatt, *Chaucer and His French Contemporaries*, suggests that "in presenting a perfidious lady and stating that the knight suffered more . . . than the lady whose gentle lover had died, Machaut evidently stimulated a protest from at least one great lady, perhaps Bonne of Luxembourg" (p. 161), which prompted him to write *JRN*. The name of Bonneürté from *JRN* is "particularly suggestive" (p. 323n19). This problem is similar to that which Chaucer had with some noble ladies in his audience's criticism of his portrayal of Criseyde (p. 161). For another explanation see Wimsatt's "Preface" to this volume (pp. ix–xv).

As Katherine Heinrichs, *Myths of Love*, remarks that the formal structure of the poem is "odd." Heinrichs accounts for this structural asymmetry by suggesting that it is here and in Reason's later response to the knight (lines 1755–84) that the "real *matière*" of the poem is located: "Machaut's emphasis is not really upon [the lovers] or the *jugement*, [they] merely furnish . . . the witty pretext for a discussion of the causes and consequences of misplaced spiritual allegiance" (pp. 184–88).

286–452   *Si en choisi . . . . son dous viaire.* The long portrait of the lady's appearance, her dancing, laughter and song follow a love poetry convention, as much illustrative of the lover's devotion as of the charms possessed by the object of his desire. As J. J. Anderson, "Man in Black," makes clear, the description of White in Chaucer's *BD* draws heavily on this passage. See *BD*, lines 847–54.

302–95   *Car si cheveus . . . . maintien estoit paree.* The lady is described in a "head-to foot- portrait," a traditional rhetorical device in medieval descriptions of ideal beauty (Kibler and Wimsatt, "Question of His Personal Supervision").

305   *Blanc et poly.* Compare the extrametrical riddling on the countenance of "the good faire White" in *BD*: "Hyt was whit, smothe, streght . . ." (line 942) and she "was whit, rody, fressh and lyvely hewed" (line 905).

319–35   *Tous pleins de . . . . il cheoit proprement.* Here love is described using the language of hunting, a trope that recurs several times throughout the poem (e.g., lines 428–35, 517–20, and 1237–39), as well as a reminder of the call of the birds in the opening stanza (line 27).

321–35   *Et s'estoient clungnetant . . . . il cheoit proprement.* On the piercing potential of the beloved's eyes, see the opening lines of Chaucer's "Merciles Beaute": "your yen two wol slee me sodenly; / I may the beautee of hem not sustene." The idea is echoed in lines 433–34. See *RR*, lines 1688–1718, where love's darts pierce Amans through the eye, and strike deep into his heart.

409–27   *Si que, dame . . . . plaire li deüsse.* In this section, the knight claims that his lady's beauty has left a physical impression on his heart. *TC*, *RR* and *CA* also describe wounds as a physical effect of love.

421   *Othevien.* Grandnephew of Julius Caesar, Octavian (63 BCE–14 CE), is better known as Augustus Caesar, the name he took after becoming the first emperor of Rome. His reign was marked by lavish expenditures on public buildings and the road system of the empire. Octavian was also a generous patron of the arts.

422   *Galien.* Galen, who lived c. 130–200, was the most noted physician of the ancient world. Born of Greek parents in Asia Minor, he moved in his early thirties to Rome, where he eventually became court physician to the emperor Marcus Aurelius. A remarkable polymath, Galen was the author of more than five hundred writings, mostly on human physiology, but on other topics as well, including philosophy.

457–82   *Et d'autre part . . . . me faisoit esperer.* In this passage, the knight refers to a number of allegorical figures, including Fair Welcome and Sweet Hope. However, unlike those who appear in the trial scene (see note to line 1484), they do not interact with other characters. Instead, "the Knight evokes these figures only to proceed to other matters . . . they serve but to underscore the Knight's anguish" (Calin, *Poet at the Fountain*, p. 46). When drawing attention to the links between Machaut and John Gower, Peter Nicholson, shows how these figures are part of the heritage of the conventions of *RR*. Poets such as Machaut and Gower who were self-consciously departing from the tradition nonetheless retained elements such as these figures, the setting of the garden and so on. For more details, see Nicholson, *Love and Ethics*, pp. 3–40.

671–83   *Et elle aussi . . . . et li rois.* A euphoric interlude of mutual joy in new love before Fortune turns her wheel further. Compare *TC* 3.450–83.

684   *Fortune.* The figure of the goddess Fortune (Fortuna) derives from one of the best-known works of the Middle Ages, Boethius' *Consolation of Philosophy* (c. 525). The ancient Roman worshiped Fortuna, the personification of luck, but Boethius assigns her a more important role in human affairs, making her responsible for the apparently random and capricious distribution of goods to human beings. Those she favors climb up on the wheel she holds as a symbol of her power, but the wheel, ever turning, eventually throws them off into the mud, depriving them of the benefits that they had previously enjoyed.

725–860   *Car il m'est . . . . D'ore en avant.* See note to lines 457–82 above. Again, allegorical figures are mentioned but only in passing.

745–54   *Chascun deçoit et . . . . seur li commandement.* Instead of blaming his lady for his unhappiness, the knight chooses to blame Fortune who appears in this section as an allegorical character. The classic presentation of the jealous lover is Jean de Meun's (*RR* lines 8425–9462), who is more violent than Machaut's lover. Gower's Amans is more akin to Machaut in the subtleties of his disappointment in *CA* 3.865–930; Gower's Genius defines Jealousy in *CA*

5.455–578.

749–822   *Le ferai je . . . . dolours ne doy.* The lover demonstrates both his virtue and his intellectual finesse in his extended meditation on the cause of his suffering. Should he blame Love or his lady? He decides that neither is actually at fault, thereby showing his loyalty to both the divinity and his beloved.

881–928   *Certes, sire, pas . . . . Selonc nature.* Here the dialogue resumes and the lady responds to the knight's story, explaining that she is more tormented than he is because there is the possibility that he can win his lover back, whereas for her, this is impossible.

963   *Nés que feroit .i. estuef seur .i. toit.* A tennis reference. The medieval game was played on indoor courts with roofed galleries. Balls hit on the roof that rolled back down were still in play.

1000–01   *Car nourreture . . . . et passe nature.* Proverbial; see Hassell N35. Also referred to by Froissart in *Le trésor amoureux* (lines 2649–53) and in Christine de Pizan's *Mutacions de fortune* (lines 5801–02).

1002–03   *Et toudis va . . . leux au bois.* Proverbial. See Hassell L101. Also referred to by Froissart in *Le joli buisson de jonece* (lines 1380–87).

1007   *serai matez en l'angle point.* Literally "caught in the sharp angle . . ." This is a metaphor from chess.

1071   *Et n'arreste ne que fueille de tramble.* A very popular proverbial phrase. See Hassell F75.

1074   *au feu, a la table.* As Kibler and Wimsatt, "Question of His Personal Supervision," note, this image "suggest[s] the conventional presentation of the month of January in medieval picture calendars, in which the dining table and the fire are the foci of activity" (p. 486).

1081–87   *Einsi est il . . . . tost se part.* The lover, understandably, here charges his lady with fickleness and instability, two of the conventional "truths" about women in the misogynistic traditions.

1185–98   *Et quant je . . . . j'iroie a eaus.* Long a silent witness to the debate between two people of higher rank, the narrator now feels summoned to action by the difficulty they are experiencing in finding a judge to decide between them. See Andreas Capellanus, *The Art of Courtly Love*, as a model for love debates requiring a judge. The literary genre is discussed in the introduction to this volume (pp. 14–17).

1204–13   *Le petit chien . . . . paour son abay.* Kibler and Wimsatt, "Question of His Personal Supervision," point out that" there are very few small domestic dogs in medieval fiction. Tristan's *Petitcreu* is one, but he is a fairy dog, quite unreal, whereas Machaut's dog, as Chaucer's after him, acts in a naturalistic manner" (p. 486). Compare the dog's behavior to the bird in lines 25–32 who leads the narrator onto the solitary path where he overhears the conversation between the lady and the knight.

1267–84   *Et je li dis . . . . chief en chief.* Here, as Kevin Brownlee, *Poetic Identity*, notes, the re-telling of the beginning of the poem functions as "a process of textual self-authentification . . . The main narrative thread of the *Behaingne* thus becomes, in summary form, a secondary narrative embedded in itself. The process of what might be called narrative doubling will be repeated several times in the course of the poem" (pp. 161–62). See the introduction for further discussion on this point (pp. 29–30).

1293   *.I. chevalier qui moult fait a amer.* This laudatory portrait of Jean de Luxembourg, king of Bohemia, is one of several in Machaut's works. See the extended passage devoted to Jean in Machaut's *Prise d'Alixandre*, lines 989–1058 in Volume 6 of *Guillaume de Machaut: The Complete Poetry and Music*.

1297   *Alixandre.* Alexander the Great (356–323 BCE) was king of Macedon and conqueror of much of Asia Minor in the Middle East.

           Hector. Hector, the son of Priam, king of Troy, is one of the principal characters of Homer's *Iliad*, and in the tradition of Virgil, Godfrey of Monmouth, and Anglo-Norman literature, the hero of the poem.

1327   *Ovides.* Publius Ovidius Naso (43 BCE–18 CE), usually known as Ovid, was one of the most celebrated poets of ancient Rome. His works on love, particularly *Ars Amatoria* (*The Art of Love*), a guidebook for prospective lovers, exerted a great influence on the writers of the Middle Ages.

1337   *roys de Behaingne.* For further discussion of Jean de Luxembourg, king of Bohemia, see the introduction (pp. 3–4).

1362–442   *Je respondi . . . . dist qu'il iroit.* In this section the narrator switches back and forth between the clerkly witness of the story and an individual with "an explicitly extradiegetic dimension" (Brownlee, *Poetic Identity*, p. 162), where Machaut's intimate knowledge of Jean, his habits, and his residence overlap with the story. Here, the speaking "I" is "simultaneously within and without . . . the narrative he recounts" (p. 164): the narrator is a participant as he leads the knight and the lady up to the castle door, but speaks as Machaut when he describes the customs of castle life.

1366   *Durbui.* Durbuy, one of Jean's favorite residences, is now a small city in the Belgian province of Luxembourg. See also note to lines 1379–92 and 1394 below.

1379–92   *Et quant il . . . . En la contree.* The castle mentioned here had just been reconstituted by Jean when this poem was composed during the 1330s. The site, on an outcropping of limestone, was first fortified in the 900s and had been completely destroyed in local warfare in 1317, requiring Jean to rebuild it. The castle still stands and was thoroughly refurbished in 1882.

1394   *iaue.* The reference here is to the Durthe, which flows through the city of Durbuy, granted its charter by Jean in 1331.

1443   *Mais tout einsi com de nou se partoit.* At this point, the narrator ceases to play an active role in the plot and returns to his previous position of clerkly witness.

1474   *.i. clerc que nommer ne saroie.* Both Brownlee, *Poetic Identity*, pp. 165–66, and Kibler and Wimsatt, "Question of his Personal Supervision," pp. 8–10, draw attention to the anonymous clerk in Jean's entourage who is reading out loud to the king. Almost as soon as the narrator draws attention to him, he is immediately dismissed, which must be a self-referential and ironic moment of awareness on Machaut's part.

1475   *Qui li lisoit la bataille de Troie.* Poets, such as Christine de Pizan, Froissart, and Machaut himself saw themselves as "advisors of princes and sages," not as entertainers; the creators of "books, not performances." Cerquiglini-Toulet, *Color of Melancholy*, reminds us of the status of books as texts to be read, as well as "beautiful objects" which were bought and collected by princes (pp. 40–41).

1484   *Cil .xvj.* Sylvia Huot compares these allegorical figures to those who appear in the *JRN*, lines 1152–54: "from a self-indulgent idealization of aristocratic life in terms of chivalric prowess, youthful pleasures, wealth, and leisure, we have moved to the arena of moral and spiritual virtues. In this context, what is valorized is not the persistence of desire in the face of rejection, but rather the constancy of love and devotion in the face of death ("Patience in Adversity," p. 232).

1509–608   *Ci pres a . . . . Vous en prions.* Here is another example of narrative doubling. This time, the knight is summarizing the plot of the poem for the benefit of the king. See note to lines 1267–84.

1595–96   *Si comme il . . . . Y ci dessus.* The nobleman's playful and, in the context, nonsensical reference to the "written" text of his encounter with the lady, calls attention to the poem's fictionality, to the fact that it does not represent "real" experience. Later, Reason makes much the same kind of metafictional reference in line 1782.

1626–59   *Cils chevaliers qui . . . . bien le savez.* Another example of narrative doubling. Now the king is re-telling the story of the knight and the lady to his allegorical jury. See note to lines 1267–84.

1668–69   *Si com la . . . se degaste et empire.* Proverbial. See Hassell C209.

1698–99   *je ne donroie . . . une pomme porrie.* Proverbial. See Hassell P232.

1665–723   *je di que . . . . fuer la dolour.* Reason's argument to this point may be readily summarized: (1) because the lady's lover is beyond recovery, Reason will work to make her forget him, an attachment to the dead being an unreasonable state; (2) Youth, preoccupied with jollity and the pleasures of the present, will also push the lady toward forgetfulness; and (3) there is no love without sexual attraction and, in the absence of a body to love, it will disappear, especially since the soul is always ambivalent about the emotion, which is inherently sinful to some degree.

1724–79   *Mai cils amis . . . . vous avez oÿ.* Unlike the lady, so Reason argues, the lover is forced by Youth, Companionship, Beauty, Love, and Loyalty to continue in his affection for his faithless beloved, the constant sight of whom fills him with pain. And there is no relief possible since, even if his beloved took him back, he would no longer be able to trust her.

1782   *Car en escript l'ay ci dessus trouvé.* See note to line 1595–96 above.

1786–1811   *Amours parla qui . . . . le fait doloir.* Love agrees with Reason's assessment of the lover's suffering, but finds nothing extraordinary in the man's inability to find secure happiness, for it is the fate of all lovers to serve without the expectation of meriting the reward of the lady's favor.

1821–47   *Loiauté se retrait . . . . dame a tort.* Offended by the lady's faithlessness, Loyalty sides with the nobleman, accepting Reason's explanation of why his suffering is greater.

1848–91   *Et quant Juenesse . . . . porte et soustient.* At this point in the dispute, the question for which the court has been convened has been forgotten completely. Youth addresses instead the issue of the nobleman's situation and finds, much like Love, that it is hardly desperate or regrettable.

1892–1928   *Lors s'avisa . . . . com moy samble.* Though he himself admonishes Youth to allow the nobleman to abandon his attachment to an undeserving woman, the king reminds the court that they have other business to consider.

1929–56   *Or estes vous . . . . Et de grevance.* The knight is judged the winner in the debate, an indication, perhaps, of the greater power of male reasoning and discernment. It could be argued that the author who has created a fiction that so obviously favors men over women has insulted the gentler sex. Whether Machaut is guilty of this charge is the question that, with no little humor and irony, is debated in the *JRN*.

1968–88   *Adont li rois . . . . de leur vie.* After passing judgment, the king advises both the knight and the lady to avoid giving in to their grief. Wallowing in pain, he tells them, can lead to the death of the heart, as well as the self.

2012–43   *Car Courtoisie . . . . gentil ne virent.* The king's entertainment of the knight and the lady has a number of points in common with King Sarpedoun's hospitality to Pandarus and Troilus, and their leave taking in Chaucer's *TC*, 5.435–48.

2040–51   *Si se partirent . . . . a Durbui retournerent.* The lady and the knight return to their homes after an eight-day stay with Jean. Although they both agree to accept the king's judgment, Machaut leaves the question of whether they take his advice unanswered.

2052–54   *Ci fineray . . . . a rimer ay.* Here, for the first time, the narrator steps outside the poem to reveal himself as the poet, rather than as the character of a clerkly witness.

2055–66   *Mais en la . . . . ne m'en prisera.* Characteristically, Machaut signs his poems with an anagram to be solved by rearranging the letters of a verse or pair of verses. The solution to the anagram contained, as Machaut tells us, in the poem's last line, is not straightforward. Once the required letters are removed to spell the invariable form *Machaut*, the ones which remain cannot spell *Guillaume*. However, as Ernest Hœpffner ("Anagramme," p. 405) notes, the anagram can be successfully solved. He proposes the well-attested by-form *Guillemin* as a solution. In his article, he goes on to demonstrate that this same form is necessary to solve the similar anagram that closes Machaut's *Remede de Fortune*.

Machaut makes his authorship part of the text, difficult either to ignore or to delete when copying or reading. For a similar example of an author riddling his name into the text, see John Gower's *Prologue* to Book I of *Vox Clamantis*, lines 1.19–24, a device conceivably learned from Machaut.

LE JUGEMENT DOU ROY DE NAVARRE

1–458   *Au departir dou . . . . en terre mis*. Instead of evoking the springtime setting that is such a conventional element of love poetry, this section takes place during the autumn and describes the events surrounding the outbreak of the Black Death. For further discussion, see the introduction to this volume (p. 21).

9   *hoqués*. The term *hoqués* is interestingly ambiguous here since its two commonly attested senses, a musical form and a musical style characterized by rapid alternation of fragments of melody between the voices, giving a hiccuping effect, are each meaningful here. In the *Prologue* Machaut uses the term to denote a kind of musical work, so I have translated with that sense in mind here. But the line could alternatively be rendered: "held their service with notes and rests."

62   *Jehans li Ermites*. Likely a reference to St. John the Silent (d. 558), who was appointed bishop of Colonia in his native Armenia at age twenty-eight. After serving in that office for nine years, he retired to a monastery where he eventually had himself walled up, there to live as a recluse. Later, for some years, he lived as a hermit in the desert.

109–42   *Et pour ce . . . . plus grant merencolie*. The reference to the Book of Ecclesiastes is a commonplace element in the *topos mundus senescit* or "the world grows old." Machaut's pessimism and world-weariness here are thoroughly conventional.

151–80   *Car ce fu . . . . en fu perie*. The astrological and meteorological events mentioned here are attested in the various chronicles of the period. Machaut is likely following one of them closely. See also lines 214–56.

158–62   *De lune esclipce . . . . clarté et couleur*. The most notable of the heavenly signs, including various astrological configurations, and seen as predicting the coming epidemic, was the lunar eclipse on 17 January 1348.

172   *La terre trambla de paour*. This devastating earthquake occurred on 25 January 1348.

175   *Quarenteinne*. Carinthia or Kärnten is the southernmost province in Austria.

189–228   *Car les batailles . . . . ceste mortel descouvenue.* Machaut's point about human destructiveness is a general one, but he is also likely to be referring in particular to the depredations of the ongoing struggle between France and England known to modern historians as the Hundred Years' War (1337–1453).

212–28   *une merdaille . . . . Ceste mortel descouvenue.* By the early fourteenth century a population of Jews numbering at least 100,000 had settled in northern France, with an especially strong and vibrant community in Machaut's native Champagne. Persecutions and expulsions followed the spreading of rumors that the Jews, secretly in the service of the Muslim ruler of Granada, were plotting to poison the wells and murder the Christian population. At the outbreak of the plague in 1348, these rumors of a Jewish plot were revived and credited by many in the Christian community, including educated men like Machaut. Persecution and murder followed, and in 1394 the Jewish community in France was again expelled, this time definitively for some centuries.

241–56   *En ce temps . . . . chans estoit herisie.* The flagellant movement, a distortion of a more widespread Christian practice, did not begin, as Machaut suggests, at the time of the plague's outbreak. Originating in thirteenth-century northern Italy, this group, which amounted to a rival Christian sect with its own preachers and devotions, was officially condemned by Pope Clement IV in 1349. By that time, it had spread northward across the Alps to Germany, Bohemia, and Poland. With the outbreak of the epidemic, itinerant bands of adherents made their way from the east to northern France and traveled from town to town. In public places they would strip down and beat themselves and each other bloody with, among other instruments, leather whips studded with small nails designed to tear the flesh. Their preachers would exhort the townspeople to repent of their sins, which, they maintained, had brought down God's wrath, like many at the time endorsed. Those devotions included the singing of hymns, as Machaut indicates.

406   *De cent n'en demorroit que nuef.* Modern historians estimate that between a quarter and a half of the population died from the disease in northern France. As Machaut indicates, "scientific" explanations for the epidemic ranged from the poisoning of the wells to meteorological conditions (a deadly "miasma") to unusual astrological conjunctions.

431–58   *Et quant je . . . . en terre mis.* If this part of the poem is accurate autobiography, then Machaut is probably referring to his residence in Reims as the "house" where, far from the rest of the city, he sat out the ravages of the epidemic. See Bowers, "Canonry of Reims," for a different view.

459   *Si qu'einsi fui lonc temps en mue.* Here, the historical Machaut makes way for his textual counterpart, the bumbling and ungracious Guillaume who resembles the real-life poet only in some particulars. As Calin notes, the timidity and misogyny displayed by Guillaume are "traditionally ascribed to the clergy." He continues that it is "appropriate that a canon at Reims should be afflicted with them, but incongruous that a master in the doctrine of love and potential

lover should fear or dislike the object of love" (Calin, *Poet at the Fountain*, p. 117).

480   *Je n'os mie cuer esperdu.* At this point, the poem leaves behind history, with its sadness, death, and political turmoil, for the conventional setting of love poetry, as a new springtime appropriately turns the narrator's thoughts to the outdoors and, after some coaxing, to matters of love.

507–19   *Or porroit aucuns . . . . chose ne pensoie.* Hare-hunting in the courtly texts of the period is often a slyly oblique way of referring to the pursuit of women (based on an obscene double entendre). Machaut does not reproduce the double entendre here, so it is not certain whether he meant the passage to be read in other than a literal sense. It is known from other sources that he did possess a horse named Grisart (line 489) and owned some hunting dogs; this means that a literal, autobiographical meaning may well be intended here.

611–12   *Si fais estas . . . homme en valeur.* The grammar of these lines is very obscure. The translation offered here is not certain, hardly more than an educated guess.

760–68   *Guillaume, mervilleussement . . . . les dames prisiez.* After the extended opening section discussing the plague and Guillaume's encounter with the lady, this is the first mention of the main subject matter of the poem.

779–801   *Guillaume, que vous . . . . devez bien escuser.* Note that the gender politics of the failed-greeting motif from *JRB* are reversed here. In the earlier poem, it was the lady who, lost in grief, ignored the nobleman's salute, while here it is Guillaume, preoccupied with his hunting, who does not acknowledge the lady's presence. See *JRB*, lines 56–74. Perhaps Guillaume protests too much about his innocence of the lady's initial charge of failing to pay her proper attention. In *JRB*, the lady is overcome with grief when she first crosses paths with her nobleman, but here Guillaume's excuses are weaker: preoccupation with his pursuit of hares and the unlikeliness that he would deliberately wish to offend her.

811   *Vers les dames estes forfais.* As this line indicates, the infidelity versus death debate is quickly forgotten and the dispute becomes one of men against women: a battle of the sexes to decide who loves best (Calin, "Contre la fin'amor," pp. 76–77).

827–34   *je le doubtay . . . . mainnent bonne vie.* Guillaume's overconfidence about his own innocence is evidenced by his admission here that he fears only the malevolence of lying gossips, not any error he might have made. Yet his failure to notice the presence of his lady suggests that the poet's monitoring of his own behavior, particularly toward women whom he should respect, might be less than reliable.

844–47   *Pour faire certein . . . Amener a conclusion.* Another indication of the main theme of the poem.

884–95   *J'ay bien de . . . . longuement y metteroie.* "Behind the humor of this passage we can clearly see Machaut's pride in the number and diversity of his poetic works. At the same time, the entire discussion stresses that these disparate works are united as the work of a single individual. Properly arranged, they would create a coherent composite picture of his poetic craft and his doctrine of love" (Huot, *From Song to Book*, p. 248). Huot goes on to discuss Machaut's possible involvement with manuscript production as part of the creation of a larger corpus, and draws a parallel between the sentiments of the fictional Guillaume and those of the real-life poet (pp. 248–59).

929–1030   *Un question fu . . . . avez griefment meffait.* Though it is not named, it is clear from the summary that this is *JRB*, where the king's decision about who suffers more, a betrayed man or a bereaved woman, becomes the issue debated by Guillaume and the lady, later revealed as Happiness. See note to *JRB*, lines 1267–84, for more on narrative doubling.

1037   *Car li contraires, c'est li drois.* Guillaume, as it turns out, never embraces the "opposite view," as his lady puts it, but simply acknowledges that he has been defeated in the debate and, impressed by the great nobility of his erstwhile opponent, agrees to complete the assigned penance.

1071–88   *Nous penrons un . . . . Q'vaurront auques jugemens.* Note that Guillaume, rejecting the lady's accusation of his shortcomings, demands that their case be presented to a man for judgment. Appropriately enough, he gets his wish when the King of Navarre agrees to decide the question. Ironically, though, the king chooses as advisers three of the lady's female courtiers: Discernment, Moderation, and Reason, who are hardly predisposed to Guillaume's point of view.

1096–114   *Navarrois . . . adés en parloie.* This very flattering description of Charles de Navarre can be compared to that of Jean de Luxembourg in *JRB*, lines 1291–348. The laudatory portrait was an essential part of the patronage system.

1151   *N'i fu Margot ne Agnesot.* The literal translation here is "there was no Maggie or Agnes present."

1155–328   *La premiere estoit . . . . passoit sa biauté.* Here follows a long catalogue and "characterization" of twelve allegorical figures who embody different aspects of the lady's character. Compare those introduced in lines 1476–85 in the *JRB*. Just what the twelve are varies somewhat, though the idea comes mainly from Aristotle's *Nicomachean Ethics* 4.2–5, which had strong bearing on Aquinas and most medieval analyses of moral behavior. Machaut's twelve figures that define the character of his lady are: 1) Understanding manifesting with Discretion; 2) Reason; 3) Temperance; 4) Peace with Concord; 5) Faith; 6) Constancy; 7) Charity; 8) Honesty; 9) Prudence, with Wisdom in her heart; 10) Generosity, who condemns Avarice; 11) Wariness of Misdeed, being perpetually on guard, protected by Shame and Fear (compare *RR*, see Intro, pp. 16–17); and 12) Sufficiency, who places her beyond Fortune's grasp. Aristotle's catalogue, defining virtue as consciousness of choice, is as follows: 1) Courage; 2) Temperance manifesting self control; 3) Liberality or generosity; 4) Magnificence; 5) Magnanimity or high-mindedness; 6) Ambition, modified by balance toward the mean; 7) Gentleness or mansuetude; 8) Friendship and Courtesy; 9) Honesty or truthfulness about oneself; 10) Wittiness and Jocularity; 11) Modesty, with a sense of shame; 12) Justice and Fairness, righteous indignation that deserves a separate chapter unto itself. Spenser initially appears to have planned *The Faerie Queene* to be in twelve books, each defined by one of the virtues (see his Prologue), though he completed only six: Holiness, Temperance, Chastity, Friendship, Justice, and Courtesy.

1374–92   *Ma chiere dame . . . . j'en parleray.* Once again, Guillaume fails here to be guided by his lady's pleasure, preferring to wait until the (male) judge arrives rather than presenting his case to her female courtiers.

1385–89   *Et si croy . . . . supposant sans prejudice.* Here, as throughout the debate, the technical language of scholastic debate is invoked to describe the proceedings, creating an ironic disjunction between the formality of the language (and the intellectual procedure it is meant to control) and the often comic tone of the disputation.

1462–91   *Ma dame chiere . . . . moult se debatirent.* The mini-debate between the King of Navarre and the lady is filled with class humor, satirizing the fine points of polite behavior and distinctions in rank that hardly seem significant, a perhaps excessive concern on the part of these noble characters.

1515–44   *Car de cause . . . . protestation dou contraire.* Again the story of *JRB* and the lady's subsequent displeasure is repeated.

1565–66   *que j'esliray / Tel conseil, comme je vorray.* Navarre's decision to use consultants in making his choices is admirable, especially if he were "to take counsel from all sides" (line 1571). However, they all come from the lady's entourage, such as Understanding (line 1583), Discretion (line 1585), Reason (line 1589), and Moderation (1597), which may not work much to Guillaume's advantage. He should be accompanied by the same virtues which are, of course, not gender specific.

1619–28   *Se fourmerez vostre . . . . le puis savoir.* Setting the tone of the trial, the King of Navarre suggests that each party should air their general concerns, rather than once again describing the specific details of the case in *JRB*. In the section that follows, the lady's speech (lines 1629–1702) follows the king's command by setting out the terms of the debate with considerable rhetorical flourish in the form of an extended metaphor: the turtle dove and the stork are both birds conventionally associated with faithfulness and loyalty to a single mate. In her opinion, they are a fitting description of the feminine experience of love. With the lady's formal presentation of her complaint, the debate — or perhaps the trial — begins here.

1696–1700   *Mais la dame . . . . amans ne sent.* The lady's point is that men, with more control over their lives than women, have at their disposal many courses of action to remediate romantic sorrow, including that caused by a lover's betrayal.

1809–25   *Vous avez . . . . en lui venir.* Surely Temperance is correct in pointing out that Guillaume is arrogant to claim victory, having only proven that, when faced with a lover's betrayal, a man cannot claim his lot by surrendering to violence, a mortal sin.

1857ff.   *S'en compteray .i. petit compte . . . .* In order to argue their cases, Guillaume and the allegorical prosecution use a series of exemplary stories which illustrate the points that they are attempting to make. Thus, the narrative turns away from the original catalyst for the trial: "the *Jugement Navarre* [sic] moves very quickly beyond the parameters of the earlier poem [*JRB*], becoming an extended meditation on the intertwined phenomena of love and pain, as experienced by men, on the one hand, and women, on the other" (Huot, "Consolation of Poetry," p. 180). In contrast to the tales in the *Confort d'ami* (see volume 2), which are biblical and classical, the stories in this text include some which are specifically French and seem near-contemporary. See also the episode of the clerk from Orleans (lines 2215–314) and that of the Chatelaine de Vergy (lines 2836–38).

1863–2010 *Il n'a pas . . . . en fu tourmentee.* This first story told by Temperance outlines the feminine response to suffering that will be upheld by the lady and her counselors throughout the debate. Huot describes this reaction as "characterized by bodily reactions of illness or death, whether by suicide or simply from the effects of grief and emotional trauma" ("Consolation of Poetry," p. 180).

1903   *Premiers s'orine resgarderent.* Examination of the patient's urine is the first diagnostic step in matters of internal medicine, picked up frequently in literature to indicate a doctor's competence. Compare the Ellesmere drawing of Chaucer's Physician holding a urine flask on high even as he rides his horse, with the mockery of such a gesture by the Host in the prologue to the Pardoner's Tale: "God so save thy gentil cors, / And eek thyne urynals and thy jurdones" (*CT* VI [C] 304–5). See also *The Croxton Play of the Sacrament*, where, when another Jonathas is sorely afflicted, those in attendance call "the most famous phesycyan / That ever sawe uryne" (lines 535–36).

1929   *li bons philosophes.* The "good philosopher" is likely Galen, the Greek thinker and physician (c. 130–200) whose opinions of medicine and human physiology were rarely challenged during the Middle Ages.

1933   *Sont curees par leur contraire.* According to Hippocrates, "Diseases caused by repletion are cured by depletion; those caused by depletion are cured by repletion, and in general contraries are cured by contraries" (Hippocrates, *Aphorisms* section 2, ch. 22). The concept became proverbial; see Whiting C414, and Hassell C287.

2055–58   *La est il . . . . la le delivreroit.* The meaning of these lines is fairly clear, but the relevance of the ideas contained therein is questionable. This may well be another example of Guillaume's "ineffective" argument. See lines 1750–62 and the corresponding note above for a similar lapse of good rhetoric.

2095–132   *Dydo roïne de Cartage . . . truis en l'istoire.* The Middle Ages knew the tragic story of the love affair between the Trojan Aeneas and his beloved Carthaginian Dido from Virgil's epic poem, the *Aeneid*, and from the writings of Ovid. Machaut may have drawn on the long twelfth-century romance based on Virgil's epic, the *Roman d'Eneas*, but it seems more likely that his main source was the monumental early-fourteenth-century French translation of Ovid's works, the *Ovide Moralisé*, for the details of the story, including Dido's pregnancy, which is not mentioned in Virgil. After the murder of her husband Sychaeus, Dido has fled her native Phoenica for Carthage, where, remaining faithful to the dead man, she establishes a powerful kingdom. When the shipwrecked Aeneas makes his way to her palace, Dido is seduced into loving him by the man's divine mother, the goddess Venus. This love affair shames her in the eyes of her people and neighboring rulers. Summoned by the gods to reestablish the Trojan kingdom in Italy, Aeneas abandons Dido, who commits suicide rather than face the wrath of the gods and the ignominy of this betrayal. See *OM* 14.302–602. In this context, the story serves to highlight the depths of feminine grief when a woman's love has been betrayed. For other reworkings of this story, see Chaucer, *LGW*, lines 924–1367, and Gower, *CA*, 4.77–137. Machaut's extensive borrowings from *OM* are discussed in more detail in the introduction to Volume 2 of *Guillaume de Machaut: The Complete Poetry and Music*.

2215–314   *A Orliens . . . . mesjugier vous gardez.* The story of the clerk from Orleans is an example of the masculine response to suffering, according to Huot. Here the clerk "escape[s] it entirely through the amnesia of madness" ("Consolation of Poetry," p. 180). It is interesting that the protagonists of this story are neither members of the nobility, nor are they drawn from classical sources, but come from Machaut's own social and economic milieu.

2362–76   *Aussi de vostre . . . . le sache diter.* Faith's counter-argument.

2377–80   *Damoiselle vueilliez laissier . . . . le cuer doloir.* Guillaume's defensiveness seems humorously out of proportion to the "threatening" to which he suggests he has been subjected.

2434–532   *Uns riches homs . . . . plaist a dire.* Machaut also draws upon the story of the nobleman and the tree in the *Lay de Plour*, lines 33–37.

2434–70   *Un riche homs . . . . Plaisanment et esbanier.* This passage plays on the fact that French has grammatical gender; *ente* is feminine, while *arbre* is masculine. The French term for a "graft" has multiple resonances — scion, offshoot, flowering branch, new growth and fruitfulness (see *DMF, ente* (n.1), sense B). Figuratively, it can mean descent or "stock," which might apply here too. The grafting as she matures proclaims a rich and worthy descent, that appeals to her lord and those who love her.

2561   L'ACTEUR. Here, the authorial speaker narrates the actions of two characters, rather than speaking as the character, Guillaume. The speech heading here is from the base MS (as are all the speech headings). These speech markers may have been copied for *in vivo* reading to an audience, so "l'acteur" can be understood as either author or performer (reader).

"L'acteur" appears twice more as a speech heading, at lines 2693 and 3725.

2654   *verbi gracia*. That is, "thanks for the words."

2699–706   *On a veu . . . . a ma matire*. As in *JRB*, the debate here widens in scope from the agreed-upon question of relative suffering to the more general issue of whether it is men or women who love more faithfully and deeply.

2707–822   *Quant cil d'Athennes . . . . fame ne sent*. Like that of Dido and Aeneas, the story of Theseus was well known to the Middle Ages, especially through the writings of Ovid. Machaut's source for the legend is here again *OM* (7.1681–2038). Minos, King of Crete, is married to Pasiphaë, who has borne him a son, Androgeus, as well as two daughters, Ariadne and Phaedra. Because of a slight to his dignity, the god Poseidon causes the woman to develop a fatal passion for a bull; the result of their coupling is the Minotaur, a monster with the head of a bull and the body of a man. King Aegeus of Athens kills Androgeus, and Minos then imposes a deadly yearly tax on the citizens of the city of seven young men and seven young maidens, who are sacrificed to the Minotaur. Theseus is chosen by lot to be one of those sacrificed, but he proves able to win the affections of Ariadne who provides him with a ball of thread with which to escape from the labyrinth where the monster lives. Theseus then kills the beast and escapes from Crete with Ariadne and her sister, Phaedra. Stopping at the island of Naxos, he leaves Ariadne behind and makes his way to Athens with Phaedra, whom he subsequently marries. Ariadne, however, does not fail to prosper; the god Dionysus falls in love with and then marries her, and she is made immortal by Zeus. Though Frankness narrates the myth in detail, it is the story of Ariadne's desertion by Theseus that is most relevant to her argument. A popular theme in art and literature; for other examples, see Ovid, *Heroides* letter 10 and Chaucer, *LGW*, lines 1886–2227.

2770–800   *Aussi dirai je . . . . par l'air fuitive*. The story of Jason's pursuit of the Golden Fleece, though treated in Greek epic, was better known in the Middle Ages in the Roman poet Ovid's shortened version. Machaut's sources, as for all the classic tales retold in *JRN*, is *OM* (7.8–682), though he may also have known a Latin version of the Troy story in which the tale of Jason appears, the *Historia Destructionis Troiae* of Guido delle Colonne. Jason and his companions, the Argonauts, journey to Colchis to obtain a great treasure, the Golden Fleece. Medea, the king's daughter, falls in love with Jason and helps him to obtain the fleece. After several harrowing adventures, in which Medea's command of the black arts figures significantly, the two establish themselves in Corinth, there to rule together until Jason attempts to divorce Medea so that he can marry Creusa. Medea sends the unfortunate woman a poisoned robe that delivers her to a horrible death and, to gain further vengeance on her betraying husband, murders their children, afterwards escaping the city in a chariot drawn by dragons. For other examples of a sympathetic portrayal of Medea, see Chaucer, *LGW*, lines 1580–1671 and, especially, Gower, *CA* 5.3247–4237.

2810–11   *On ne porroit . . . . comme en femme*. These classical exempla, of course, also provide histories of well-known faithless, conscienceless men: Jason and Theseus.

2836–40   *Chascuns scet bien . . . . vit pour s'amour.* The reference is to the thirteenth-century French romance, *La Chatelaine de Vergy*, which traces the misery and pain that result from, first, a young wife's betrayal of her husband and, second, a jealous woman's betrayal of her husband's trust. The chatelaine's lover is approached by the Duchess of Burgundy, his lord's wife, and he refuses her love, protesting that he loves another, although no one knows of their affair. The knight has promised the chatelaine never to reveal their relationship, but he is forced to break his word when the duchess complains to her husband that the man has insulted and lied to her. Only by telling the duke of his affair, his meetings arranged by the little dog the chatelaine lets into the garden to signal she is alone, does he free himself from his lord's anger and probable exile. The duke promises never to reveal the knight's secret, but he in turn breaks the promise when the duchess extorts the truth from him, though he does enjoin her on pain of death never to reveal the secret. The jealous woman does so, however, causing the deaths of the chatelaine and her lover, who stabs himself when a servant tells him the truth. The duke exacts a terrible revenge on his wife, killing the woman, and then he departs on a crusade. It might be pointed out that this is a particularly inept example for Guillaume to adduce, since the story involves the betrayal of a sworn trust by two otherwise morally irreproachable men, the lover and the duke. A translation of this work is included in Palmer, *Medieval Epic and Romance*, pp. 799–824.

2841   *Lancelos et Tristans.* These famed lovers were involved in tragic relationships with the wives of their sovereigns, Tristan with Iseut, the wife of King Marc, and Lancelot with Guinevere, the wife of King Arthur. As incorporated within Arthurian legend in the thirteenth century, Tristan's story ends with the young man, estranged from his beloved, dying on a battlefield of his wounds and despair. Iseut finds his body and dies herself from grief. In that same tradition, likely known to Machaut, the illicit affair between Lancelot and Guinevere leads in part to the destruction of Arthur's kingdom. "Virtuous" Lancelot and Tristan, of course, are both involved in adulterous affairs with the wives of their lords — perhaps yet another instance of Guillaume's inattention to detail in the case he makes in support of men. Machaut also points to Tristan and Lancelot as examples of ideal lovers in *Confort*, line 2803 and *Lyon*, line 1321. For other references to this story, see Oton de Granson's «J'ay tout perdu; le festu est rompu», «A Dalida, Jhezabel, et Thays» and *Le Livre Messire Ode* (*Poems*, ed. Nicholson and Grenier-Winther, pp. 54, 60–62, 212–326 respectively).

2851–98   *Une dame sans . . . . qu'elle y mist.* According to Huot, the story of the knight who cut off his finger stages "a masculine response to suffering" by transforming it into a heroic gesture ("Consolation of Poetry," p. 180). See the story of the clerk from Orleans (lines 2215–314) for a masculine response to emotional turmoil.

2920–95   *Est loiez s'il . . . . po a debatre.* The theme of moderation reflects the advice that the narrator gives Charles in lines 1675–78 of the *Confort*. However, Guillaume makes himself an unintended butt of humor by praising the power of moderation after telling the story of a man who cuts off his own finger to demonstrate his obedience to his lover's commands.

3009–10   *Certes Franchise vous . . . . bien dire savez.* Guillaume here responds to Franchise, pointedly ignoring what Prudence had just said.

3019–46   *Il est certain . . . . seroit encor reprouvez.* Guillaume's description of the fickleness of a woman's heart is a common topos in misogynist literature, in which the voice is that of a frustrated male. See, for example, the Chaucerian lyric "Against Women Unconstant" (Benson, *Riverside Chaucer*, p. 657). The motif is prominent in Jean de Meun's treatment of a jealous husband and his dissatisfaction with women who are disobedient to his wishes (*RR* lines 8425–9462).

3055–89   *Ce que je . . . . paier la lamproie.* In the course of returning the debate to its original issue — who suffered more, the man or the woman — Guillaume manages as well to broaden it, introducing by way of defense the anti-feminist view that women are more fickle and changeable than men. He thereby ensures that he will lose the debate, providing strong evidence that he does harbor misogynist thoughts even if, technically speaking, he buttresses his "published" view that the betrayed nobleman is in more pain than the bereaved lady, for her "fickleness" will ensure that her grief will soon end.

3112–13   *Et s'avez esté a l'escole . . . d'aler en change.* The meaning here is somewhat obscure, perhaps a confusing reference to the stereotypical anti-feminist of the late Middle Ages, the university scholar.

3141–67   *Lors etroÿ une . . . . Doubtance de meffaire.* The debate shifts. Although many of the characters have had their say, Guillaume remains stubbornly unconvinced, and they are beginning to get angry.

3170   *Et commensa par tel maniere.* Offended by Guillaume's obstinate declaration that women are fickle and hence do not suffer long in love, the female courtiers offer a series of classical exempla to prove the persistence unto death of women in love.

3171–212   *Que fist Tysbé . . . . a mort comparer.* The story of Pyramus and Thisbé has likely also been borrowed by Machaut from *OM* (4. 219–1169). The two grow up as neighbors in the city of Babylon, prohibited by their parents from communicating with one another. But they find a crack in the wall that divides their two houses and, one day, make plans to meet outside the city, close to the tomb of Ninus. Thisbé arrives before the young man and, as she waits for him, is frightened by a lion. She flees in haste, dropping her veil, which the beast, its jaws bloody from a recent kill, mouths before dropping. When Pyramus arrives, he finds the bloody veil, thinks that his lover has been killed because of his negligence, and stabs himself. Thisbé returns to find him dead and, wishing to live no longer, kills herself with the same sword.

3221–307   *Leandus li biaus . . . . fiel encontre baume.* The story of Hero and Leander is also taken from *OM* (4.3150–731). In Greek mythology, Hero is the priestess of Aphrodite (Venus) in Sestos, with whom Leander, who lives across the Hellespont in Abydos, falls in love. At night he swims across the watery passage to visit her, but one night during a storm the light that Hero holds for him as a guide blows out. Leander loses his way and drowns. Discovering his body the next day, Hero, despairing, throws herself into the sea and is drowned as well.

3365–69   *Adont la dame . . . . tout en oiant.* Here the lady returns to the debate.

3398–412   *Or ne sceus . . . . plus a repos.* Machaut inserts a strikingly plausible explanation of how Guillaume was able to find out about the Judge's private deliberations. According to Nicholson, Machaut's later *dits* show a shift to an increasingly realist setting and tone, of which this is a good example. See Nicholson, *Love and Ethics*, pp. 15–18.

3414–26   *Je suis commis . . . . nous avons loisir.* The Judge, like a wise man, calls upon counselors — both male and female — to accord with his deliberations. Compare Prudence's advice in Chaucer's Tale of Melibee (*CT* [B²] 2191–203). Here, unlike Melibee who demands advice from flatterers, enemies and false counselors, the lady's judge invokes advice from Reason's company — Discretion, Understanding, and Moderation — who weigh Guillaume's arguments objectively, without personal bias.

3441–4001   *Ce jugement avez . . . . tous les poins.* In summing up the case (which is another example of the type of narrative doubling that frequently occurs in this text), Moderation and Reason outline the reasons why Guillaume should be condemned. Calin identifies four different points in their argument: Guillaume has pleaded his case badly using inappropriate evidence and false reasoning, he has spoken out against ladies and Love, he has not shown the lady proper courtesy and, finally, that it is wrong to view jealousy as worse than grief. Calin's main point is that condemning Guillaume on the basis of carelessness and his poor rhetorical skills means that Machaut's own argument put forth in *JRB* remains intact (*Poet at the Fountain*, pp. 111–13).

3609–14   *Dont Guillaumes est . . . . pour li punir.* The point is that Guillaume offended against the dignity of the noble lady by arguing with her when she rightly upbraided him for his insults against women.

3649–838   *Dont ma dame . . . . de sa poësté.* In addition to arguing with a lady whose views he should accept unconditionally, Guillaume is convicted for both advancing an incorrect opinion (death is the worst of all human misfortunes) and conducting himself incompetently. Guillaume, we learn, would have been made to suffer a more dire punishment had it not been for the mercy shown him by the lady, whom Guillaume, lost in his self-concern, has failed to identify properly or even inquire about. Abashed and ashamed, Guillaume now asks Reason who his benefactress is.

3851   *Bonneürté.* Meaning, happiness. This is the first time that the lady is referred to as *Bonneürté.* An alternative translation of the name would be Good

Fortune, and indeed the lady, with her metaphysical powers and presence, partakes of some of the qualities conventionally assigned to the goddess Fortuna in the Middle Ages, following the influential portrayal in Boethius' *Consolation of Philosophy*, one of the central texts of the era and an important source for Machaut. At the same time, the lady, in her humanity and good humor, undoubtedly recalls as well Bonne ("Good") de Luxembourg, daughter of Jean de Luxembourg, King of Bohemia, and Machaut's generous patroness before her death during the plague.

4093   *li changes*. The *DMF* defines *chainse* (n., sense a) as "longue tunique de femme, à manches, robe faite de toile de lin ou de chanvre" [a long tunic for women, with sleeves; or a dress made of linen or hemp].

4177–89   *de .iij. amendes . . . . une balade*. This judgment, punishing the author by demanding more writing, provides a reasonable conclusion to the debate. See, for example, Chaucer's Prologue to *LGW*, where the poet must go back to his library and write more (lines F.548–77).

4182   *.i. lay*. Of the three assigned lyric penances, only a lay seems to have been composed, and this piece follows directly *JRN* itself in three early manuscripts of Machaut's works, but (except for E) not in the later ones that are generally regarded as more authoritative by modern scholars because the poet likely supervised their production. It may be that some years after writing the poem Machaut decided not to include the lay.

LE LAY DE PLOUR

1ff.   *Ci commence le lay de plour*. This text, first referenced in line 4182 of *JRN*, is likely to be the *Lay de Plour*, which is included in this volume. The lay is the most complicated of all lyric forms, composed as it is of twelve stanzas of varying length and meter, with no pattern of rhyme repeated from one stanza to the next. Confusingly, the term *lai* is also used in the Middle Ages to refer to short narrative poems, e.g., the *Lais* of Marie de France.

TEXTUAL NOTES

ABBREVIATIONS: B: Paris, Bn,F fr. 1585; **C**: Paris, BnF, fr. 1586; **D**: Paris, BnF, fr. 1587; **E**: Paris, BnF, fr. 9221; **F**: Paris, BnF, fr. 22545; **G**: Paris, BnF, fr. 22546; **H**: *Oeuvres de Guillaume de Machaut*, ed. Ernest Hœpffner; **J**: Paris, Arsenal 5203; **K**: Berne, Burger-bibliothek 218; ***JRB***: Machaut, *Le Jugement dou Roy de Behaingne*; ***JRN***: Machaut, *Le Jugement dou Roy de Navarre*; **M**: Paris, BnF, fr. 843; **MS**: Paris, BnF, fr. 1584 [base text]; **P**: Paris, BnF, fr. 2166; **Pm**: New York, Pierpont Morgan Library, M. 396; **R**: Paris, BnF, fr. 2230; **Vg**: Cambridge, Parker Library, Ferrell 1 (formerly Vogüé Ferrell).

The *JRN* is found together with the *JRB* in eight Machaut manuscripts that contain only the works of the poet. These are, together with their customary sigla: Vg, B, D, E, F, M, MS, Pm. The *JRB* is found without the *JRN* in an additional twelve manuscripts (a complete listing can be found in Earp, *A Guide to Research*, p. 207). For a variety of reasons, one of these is an excellent, if early, witness to the *JRB*: C.

For reasons set out at some length in the introduction, this edition takes A (here MS) as an authoritative text for Machaut's works, including the two *dits* and the *lay* included in this volume. Because of the unique authority of MS the practice has been to deviate from its readings only in clear cases of spelling error, scribal misinterpretation, and omissions or miswritings of various kinds (such as diplographies). In these cases, the reading of MS simply been corrected. In the case of the *JRB*, there are several passages of some length that have been neatly excised in MS's version of the text; this "editing" can hardly be interpreted as other than deliberate, and since there is good reason to think that Machaut himself might have been involved in the preparation of this text (of the fair copy that was its basis), these lacunae, if that is what they are, have been supplied from C. In keeping with the minimal variant policy of this series, only semantically significant variants are here noted. Spelling variations or slight changes in word order are ignored. All deviations from the readings of MS, however, are accounted for here.

LE JUGEMENT DOU ROY DE BEHAINGNE

55	*embuschiez*. MS: *embunschiez*, due to spelling error.
61	*que*. MS: *qui*, due to spelling error.
114	*avant*. MS: *avent*, due to spelling error.
126	*rentiers*. MS: *renties*, due to spelling error.
187	*durté*. MS: *dutte*, due to spelling error.
202	*Eimy*. MS: *einmy*, due to extra nasal stroke.
287	*solaus*. MS: *solans*, due to spelling error.
323	*pointure*. MS: *poiture*, due to missing nasal stroke.
382	*Que d'nature*. MS: *Quature*, due to spelling error.

497	*requerre.* MS: *requerir,* due to spelling error.
525	*annuy.* MS: *anny,* due to spelling error.
627	*qu'un.* MS: *cun,* due to spelling error — homonym.
675	*regnay.* MS: *resnay,* due to spelling error.
688	*Einsi.* MS: *Eins,* due to spelling error.
742	*qu'uns.* MS: *cuns,* due to spelling error — homonym.
852	*ç'a.* MS: *sa,* due to spelling error — homonym.
933	*ne pooie.* So MS. M, C, B, D: *ne savoie.*
980–83	*Quant je li . . . ne me marvoy.* These verses are supplied from C.
994	*venir.* MS: *veinr,* due to spelling error.
1000–47	*Car nourreture. . . pasmer me couvient.* MS: omitted. These verses are supplied from C.
1065	*espoir.* MS: *esporr,* due to spelling error.
1158	*pooir.* MS: *poir,* due to spelling error.
1183	*dites.* MS: *ditos,* due to spelling error.
1187	*refais.* MS: *refaie,* due to spelling error.
1271	*vraiement.* MS: *vraiemnt,* due to spelling error.
1380	*s'arrestoient.* MS: *arrestoient,* due to spelling error.
1383	*disoient.* MS: *disoiet,* due to missing nasal stroke.
1402	*Et l'aiue.* MS: *Etiaue,* due to spelling error.
1437	*aussi.* MS: *ossi,* due to spelling error.
1453	*aussi.* MS: *assi,* due to spelling error.
1483	*Jeunesse.* MS: *largesse,* due to eyeskip. Reading supplied from C.
1530	*c'iere.* MS: *siere,* due to spelling error — homonym.
1538	*durement.* So MS. D, E: *doucement.*
1667	*aimment.* MS: *amment,* due to spelling error.
1682	*Qu'une.* MS: *Cune,* due to spelling error — homonym.
1816–19	*Et qui vous. . . son guerredon pert.* MS: omitted. These verses are supplied from C.
1831	*haute game.* So MS. F: *fausse game.*
1835	*autrement.* MS: *autremnt,* due to spelling error.
1861–84	*N'iert ja partis. . . Qu'Amour ma dame.* MS: omitted. These verses are supplied from C.
1899	*n'amoit.* So MS. C, B, D, E: *avoit.*
1906	*recours.* MS: *recoues,* due to spelling error.
1908	*Car.* MS: *Ca,* due to spelling error.
2015	*durement.* So MS. C, E: *doucement,* but gives inferior sense.
2043	*Qu'eins.* MS: *Quenie,* due to spelling error.

LE JUGEMENT DOU ROY DE NAVARRE

235	*furent.* MS: *furent furent,* due to diplography.
386	*sejours.* MS: *secours,* due to spelling error.
391	*la.* So MS. F: *le* also gives good sense.
461	*qu'une.* MS: *cune,* due to spelling error — homonym.
485	*lors.* So MS. F: *hors.* Either gives good sense. *Hors* would render the line's sense as "so that I went out of that prison."

667	*Venrez.* MS: *Verrez,* due to spelling error.
756	*parfaire.* So MS. F, M, B, D, E: *faire.*
870	*yvres.* MS: *yures,* due to spelling error.
874	*forfaites.* So F. MS repeats *parfaites* from previous line.
894	*Dont je me vorray bien garder.* Line missing in MS, which repeats line 893. Line supplied from F.
902	*invisible.* So MS. F, M, B: *nuisible,* giving an interesting reading here. *Nuisible* would render the line's sense as "your annoying thought."
1078	*ferez.* MS: *feirs,* due to spelling error.
1081	*Einsi.* MS: *Eins,* due to spelling error.
1149	*accompaingnié.* A: *accompaignie,* due to missing nasal stroke.
1214	*s'ahonte.* MS: *lahonte,* due to spelling error.
1227	*setisme.* MS: *sisieme,* due to miswriting.
1257	*oeuvres.* MS: *ouvres,* due to spelling error.
1265	*Aprés Prudence se seoit.* Line missing in MS, which repeats line 1264. Line supplied from F.
1372	*m'agenoillai.* So F. MS: *agelongnai,* due to miswriting.
1421	*m'avoit.* MS: *mavoit mavoit,* due to diplography.
1487	*si.* MS: *ci,* due to spelling error — homonym.
1493	*assis.* So F. MS: *rassis,* the rhyme word of the next line. Eyeskip error.
1564	*tant vous.* So F. MS: omits *tant.*
1630	*avons.* MS: *avos,* due to missing nasal stroke.
1640	*on scet.* So MS. F, M, B, D, E: *ou soit.*
1647	*trieges.* MS: *rieges,* due to spelling error.
1734	*LE JUGE.* So F. MS omits heading.
1813	*Comment.* MS: *commene,* due to spelling error.
1821	*face.* MS: *facent,* due to spelling error.
1846	*querir.* So H, who emends *metri causa.* MS: *querre,* due to spelling error.
1891	*Fusicien.* MS: *Fusitien,* due to spelling error.
1913	*jugoit.* MS: *jugent,* due to spelling error.
1929	*philosophes.* MS: *philophes,* due to spelling error.
1983	*oy.* MS: *jos,* due to spelling error.
2014	*prouver.* So F, H. MS: *trouver,* repeated from line 2013 due to eyeskip error.
2045	*est.* MS: *en,* due to spelling error.
2108	*Que heü.* So F. MS omits *heü.*
2151	*fourches.* MS: *fouches,* due to spelling error.
2161	*Aussi.* MS: *Iussi,* due to spelling error.
2162	*point.* MS: *poit,* due to missing nasal stroke.
2170	*par.* MS: *par par,* due to diplography.
2173	*Que a moy.* So MS. All manuscripts except M give *Qu'ami,* which also gives good sense.
2189	*qu'Amours.* So MS. F, M, B, D, E: *qu'amis,* which gives inferior sense.
2195	*Pais.* MS: *Pas,* due to spelling error.
2213	*prouver.* So all other manuscripts. MS: *premier.*
2276	*fent.* MS: *fant,* due to spelling error.
2330	*confonderay.* MS: *confimderay,* due to spelling error.
2341	*Amis.* MS: *Ainis,* due to spelling error.

2349   *honnourablement.* MS: *honnourablemmt,* due to spelling error.

2371   *nullement.* MS: *nullemet,* due to missing nasal stroke.

2381   *s'avisa.* So MS, B, D. All other manuscripts give *savanca,* which also gives
                good sense.

2448   *S'estent.* MS: *se sent,* due to spelling error.

2465   *Et en.* MS: *Est en,* due to spelling error.

2476   *S'elle.* MS: *Celle,* due to spelling error — homonym.

2573   *par voie.* MS: *pa voie,* due to spelling error.

2628   *le.* So MS. All other manuscripts, *me,* which renders the line's sense as "listen
                to me."

2674   *martire.* So MS, E. All other manuscripts give *matire,* which also gives good
                sense.

2688   *Dont je vous di que la pointue.* MS repeats this line.

2695   *vueil.* MS: *voult.* The grammar of the sentence requires a noun form.

2700   *loiaument.* MS: *loiament,* due to spelling error.

2785   *Quanqu'elle.* MS: *Quenquelle,* due to spelling error.

2924–25   *L'ACTEUR.* MS: omits heading here, which is supplied from F, per H.

2932   *Chastelainne.* MS: *chastolainne,* due to spelling error.

2982   *Apparent.* MS: *appernt,* due to spelling error.

3045   *retrouvez.* So MS. F, B, D, E: *recouvrez.*

3172   *nus.* MS: *mus,* due to spelling error.

3214   *aidier.* MS: *aididier,* due to spelling error.

3215   *nostre.* So MS. All other manuscripts give *vostre.* Either reading gives good
                sense.

3249   *tourbla.* So MS. All other manuscripts give *senfla,* which gives good sense and
                yields a richer rhyme.

3315   *couchié.* So MS. F, M, D, E: *touchié,* which gives inferior but possible sense.

3386   *de retraire.* So H. MS: *le contraire,* which gives poor sense. F, M, B, D, E: *le
                retraire,* which also gives poor sense.

3389   *nostre.* So MS, B. All other manuscripts give *vostre.* Either reading gives good
                sense.

3420   *notre.* So MS. All other manuscripts give *vostre.*

3426   *Tandis com.* MS: *toudis.*

3435   *s'il vient.* MS: *il bien,* due to spelling error.

3475   *Juges.* MS: *Jugiez,* due to spelling error.

3590   *poins fort me.* So F. MS: *poins ci me,* which as H points out, gives inferior
                sense.

3749   *bien le savez.* So MS. All other manuscripts give *vous le,* which gives equally
                good sense.

3887, 3889   *Elle.* MS and all manuscripts give *Il.* These masculine pronouns to the lady
                must be miswritings.

3891   *nul tort.* So all manuscripts except MS. MS: *accort,* probably due to a
                miswriting.

3913   *des dames.* So all manuscripts except MS. MS: which was *des des* due to
                diplography.

3914   *honneur.* MS: *bonneur,* due to spelling error.

3948   *la voie.* MS: *la vie,* due to spelling error.

3984	*dou prouver*. So all manuscripts except MS. MS: *dou premier*, a miswriting.
4058	*estoient*. MS: *estioient*, due to spelling error.
4089	*Beniveillance*. MS: *bniveillance*, due to spelling error.
4121	*chaucié*. MS: *chauciet*, due to spelling error.
4124	*sont*. MS: *son*, due to spelling error.
4127	*espuisier*. MS: *espursier*, due to spelling error.
4134	*oeuvre*. MS: *ouevre*, due to spelling error.
4155	*apperent*. MS: *apperet*, due to spelling error.
4185	*a un*. MS: *aa un*, due to spelling error.

Notes to the Music by Uri Smilansky

Abbreviations: see Textual Notes.

As detailed in the introduction (p. 36), the following comments do not contain a list of variants, but discuss the problems presented by the readings in **MS A** (henceforth MS) and the way they were solved in this edition. A complete list of music variants can be found in Volume 10: *The Lays*.

The *Lay de Plour*

The *Lay de Plour (Lay of Weeping)* is intimately connected with the *Navarre*, at the end of which the narrator promises to compose exactly such a lay as part of his punishment. (For the relationship between the two works and the particular issues raised by its positioning in the various manuscripts see the introduction to this volume, pp. 27–33.) Current thinking (based on its position and notational style in C) places this work in the early 1350s.[1] C, which presents this song in the music section where each lay is accompanied by an opening miniature, begins the *Lay* with an image of a man and woman debating (C102 according to Earp's system).[2] While more complex interpretations of the program of lay-illuminations in C have been suggested,[3] this might be a simple link of association, affiliating this work with the two judgment (or debate) poems. J, the only manuscript to place the *Lay* immediately after the *JRB*, uniquely opens with an illumination (J4) depicting the main theme of the work — a woman dressed in black sitting in front of a coffin covered in black drapery.[4] No other manuscript couples this song with a miniature.

The *Lay* follows Machaut's preferred lay structure of twelve strophes; the last reproduces the text structure, rhyme scheme, and music (transposed a fifth higher) of the first. In comparison with the lay incorporated into the *Remede*, this text is shorter and has a simpler line-structure. Its rhyme scheme, however, is more complex, and the *Lay* is notated in note-shapes more typical of the up to date *Ars nova* style than the *Remede* lay, which in its use of longer note-values conforms better to the more archaic notational

---

[1] See Earp, *Machaut: A Guide to Research*, pp. 365–66, where other opinions also appear.

[2] To view image C102, see http://gallica.bnf.fr/ark:/12148/btv1b8449043q/f380.item.

[3] See Huot, *From Song to Book*, pp. 263–70.

[4] To view image J4, see http://gallica.bnf.fr/ark:/12148/btv1b550058905/f95.item.

habits of the *Ars antiqua*. Like most lays, it has a wide vocal range: this time spanning the interval of a twelfth.

Music manuscripts: Text only manuscripts:

C 187r–189r in music section   **M** 48v–49v   after *JRN*
Vg 87v–89v   after *JRN*   and 221v–222v in Lay section
B 87v–89v (new 104v–106v) after *JRN* **K**   42r–42v fragment, after *JRB*
A 410v–412v in music section   **J** 45r–46r   after *JRB*
E 57r–58r   after *JRN*

Text structure: Letters indicate single rhyme endings. Numbers indicate the syllable count of the line in question. Apostrophes indicate an unstressed appendage syllable not included in the syllable count.

1. a b b a | a b b a || a b b a | a b b a ||
        7 7' 7' 7 7 7 7' 7' 7   7 7' 7' 7 7 7' 7' 7

2. c c d | c c d || c c d | c c d ||
        8 8 4' 8 8 4'   8 8 4' 8 8 4'

3. e e f g | e e f g || e e f g | e e f g ||
        7' 7' 7 4   7' 7' 7 4   7' 7' 7 4   7' 7' 7 4

4. h h i | h h i || h h i | h h i ||
        5' 5' 5 5' 5' 5   5' 5' 5 5' 5' 5

5. j j k k j j k k j || j j k k j j k k j ||
        7 7 4 7 4 7 4 7 4   7 7 4 7 4 7 4 7 4

6. l l m m n | l l m m n || l l m m n | l l m m n |
        10' 10' 4 4 3 10' 10' 4 4 3   10' 10' 4 4 3 10' 10' 4 4 3

7. o o o o p | o o o o p || o o o o p | o o o o p ||
        5 5 5 7 5   5 5 5 7 5   5 5 5 7 5   5 5 5 7 5

8. q r r s s q q r r s s s q || q r r s s q q r r s s s q ||
        7 3 4 4 7 4 3 4 4 7 4 3 4   7 3 4 4 7 4 3 4 4 7 4 3 4

9. t t t u | t t t u || t t t u | t t t u ||
        3' 3' 7' 5' 3' 3' 7' 5' 3' 3' 7' 5' 3' 3' 7' 5'

10. v v v w | v v v w || v v v w | v v v w ||
        7' 5' 7' 7   7' 5' 7' 7   7' 5' 7' 7   7' 5' 7' 7

11. x x x x y | x x x x y || x x x x y | x x x x y ||
    4 5 3 3 5 4 5 3 3 5   4 5 3 3 5 4 5 3 3 5

12. a b b a | a b b a || a b b a | a b b a ||
    7 7' 7' 7 7 7' 7' 7   7 7' 7' 7 7 7' 7' 7

Comments on the readings in MS

m. 1–2	There is no dot after first brevis, but it is clear from spacing and repetition (m. 18–19).
m. 3–4	While the given underlay also works, underlay lines show the original intention here (elision of '-me' and 'a', and placement of 'ou-').
m. 8	'-bli-' was added faintly by a different hand. Its underlay is not entirely clear.
m. 11	A fa-sign (flat) added perhaps by a corrector's hand.
m. 20–21	The second text 'm'a' is written at the beginning of a new line rather than at the end of the old one, which creates alignment problems between the two lines of text.
m. 128	The second text '-te' ends a line rather than begin the next. Adjusted according to the first text underlay.
m. 165	The second text '-port' was wrongly copied at the beginning of the next line, disrupting the alignment of the texts. Corrected according to the first text.
m. 176–77	There are some erasures here.
m. 186	There are more erasures or other damage here.
m. 211–13	No dot appears here. One can stay closer to the notational rules and add an extra measure here:

But the previous line and rhythmic structure of this section suggests not to.

m. 225	There is some small erasure or damage here.
m. 250	The fa-sign may be the work of a different hand.
m. 258	There is some erasure or damage affecting also the text above.
m. 281	A rest (or dot) is missing after the brevis, but the spacing and the repetition make it clear an imperfection was not intended here.
m. 298–301	The underlay is not entirely clear. Adjusted according to the first strophe.

❧ BIBLIOGRAPHY

EDITIONS OF GUILLAUME DE MACHAUT'S WORKS

Cerquiglini, Jacqueline, ed. and trans. *Le Livre de la Fontaine Amoureuse*. Paris: Stock, 1993.

Chichmaref, V., ed. *Guillaume de Machaut: Poésies lyriques*. 2 vols. Paris: Honoré Champion, 1909.

Earp, Lawrence, Domenic Leo, and Carla Chapreau, eds. *Ferrell-Vogüé Machaut Manuscript: Facsimile and Introductory Study*. 2 vols. Oxford: Digital Image Archive of Medieval Music Publications, 2014.

Froissart, Jean. *"Dits" et "Débats": Introduction, édition, notes, glossaire. Avec en appendice quelques poèmes de Guillaume de Machaut*. Ed. Anthime Fourrier. Geneva: Droz, 1979.

Gaudet, Minnette, and Constance B. Hieatt, eds. and trans. *The Tale of the Alerion*. Toronto: University of Toronto Press, 1994.

Hœpffner, Ernest, ed. *Œuvres de Guillaume de Machaut*. 3 vols. Paris: Firmin-Didot, 1908–21.

Imbs, Paul, and Jacqueline Cerquiglini-Toulet, eds. *Le Livre du Voir Dit*. Paris: Librairie Générale Française, 1999.

Leech-Wilkinson, Daniel, ed. *Le Livre dou Voir Dit (The Book of the True Poem)*. Trans. R. Barton Palmer. New York: Garland Publishing, 1998.

Ludwig, Friedrich, ed. *Guillaume de Machaut: Musikalische Werke*. 4 vols. Leipzig: Breitkopf and Härtel, 1954.

Mas Latrie, M. L. de, ed. *La Prise d'Alexandrie ou Chronique du roi Pierre 1er de Lusignan*. Geneva: Jules-Guillaume Fick, 1877.

Palmer, R. Barton, ed. and trans. *The Judgment of the King of Bohemia (Le Jugement dou Roy de Behaingne)*. New York: Garland Publishing, 1984.

———, ed. and trans. *The Judgment of the King of Navarre (Jugement deu roy de Navarre)*. New York: Garland Publishing, 1988.

———, ed. and trans. *Le Confort d'ami (Comfort for a Friend)*. New York: Garland Publishing, 1992.

———, ed. and trans. *The Fountain of Love (La Fonteinne Amoureuse) and Two Other Love Vision Poems*. New York: Garland, 1993.

———, ed. and trans. *La Prise d'Alixandre (The Taking of Alexandria)*. New York: Routledge, 2002.

Paris, P., ed. *Le Livre du Voir-Dit de Guillaume de Machaut*. Paris: Société des Bibliophiles François, 1875.

Plumley, Yolanda, Uri Smilansky, and Tamsyn Rose-Steel, eds. *The Works of Guillaume de Machaut: Music, Image, Text in the Middle Ages*. University of Exeter, 2016. Web. Accessed May 2016. Online at http://machaut.exeter.ac.uk/.

Schrade, Leo, ed. *The Works of Guillaume de Machaut*. Monaco: L'Oiseau–Lyre, 1956.

Shirley, Janet, trans. *The Capture of Alexandria*. Burlington, VT: Ashgate, 2001.

Wilkins, Nigel, ed. *La Louange des Dames*. Edinburgh: Scottish Academic Press, 1972.

Wimsatt, James I., ed. *The Marguerite Poetry of Guillaume de Machaut*. Chapel Hill, NC: University of North Carolina Press, 1970.

Wimsatt, James I., and William W. Kibler, eds. *Le Jugement du roy de Behaingne and Remede de Fortune*. Athens, GA: University of Georgia Press, 1987.

Young, Karl, ed. "The *Dit de la Harpe* of Guillaume de Machaut." In *Essays in Honor of Albert Feuillerat*. Ed. Henri M. Peyre. New Haven, CT: Yale University Press, 1943. Pp. 1–20.

OTHER SOURCES

Albritton, Benjamin. "Moving Across Media: Machaut's Lais and the Judgement Tradition." In McGrady and Bain. Pp. 119–42.

Alexander, Jonathan J. G. *Medieval Illuminators and Their Methods of Work*. New Haven, CT: Yale University Press, 1992.

Allen, Graham. *Intertextuality*. Second edition. Abingdon and New York: Routledge, 2011.

Altmann, Barbara K. "Reopening the Case: Machaut's *Jugement* Poems as a Source in Christine de Pizan." In *Reinterpreting Christine de Pizan*. Ed. Earl Jeffrey Richards. Athens, GA: University of Georgia Press, 1992. Pp. 137–56.

———. "Guillaume de Machaut's Lyric Poetry." In McGrady and Bain. Pp. 311–32.

Altmann, Barbara K., and R. Barton Palmer, eds. and trans. *An Anthology of Medieval Love Debate Poetry*. Gainesville, FL: University Press of Florida, 2006.

Amon, Nicole. "Le Vert: Guillaume de Machaut, Poète de l'Affirmation et de la Joie." *Revue du Pacifique* 2 (1976), 3–11.

Amtower, Laurel. *Engaging Words: The Culture of Reading in the Later Middle Ages*. New York: Palgrave, 2000.

Anderson, J. J. "Criseyde's assured manner." *Notes and Queries* 236 (1991), 160–61.

———. "The man in black, Machaut's knight, and their ladies." *English Studies* 73.5 (1992), 417–30.

Areford, David S. "The Passion Measured: A Late-Medieval Diagram of the Body of Christ." In *The Broken Body: Passion Devotion in Late-Medieval Culture*. Ed. A. A. MacDonald, H. N. B. Ridderbos, and R. M. Schlusemann. Groningen: Egbert Forsten, 1998. Pp. 211–38.

Ariès, Phillipe, and Georges Duby. *Histoire de la vie privée*. Paris: Seuil, 1985.

Aristotle. *Nicomachean Ethics*. Trans. Martin Ostwald. Indianapolis: Bobbs-Merrill, 1962.

Arlt, Wulf. "Donnez signeurs — Zum Brückenschlag zwischen Ästhetik und Analyse bei Guillaume de Machaut." In *Tradition und Innovation in der Musik. Festschrift für Ernst Lichtenhahn zum 60. Geburtstag*. Ed. Christoph Ballmer and Thomas von Gartmann. Winterthur: Amadeus, 1993. Pp. 39–64.

———. "Machaut in Context." In Cerquiglini-Toulet and Wilkins. Pp. 147–64.

L'Art au temps des rois maudits: Philippe le Bel et ses fils, 1285–1328. Paris: Réunion des musées nationaux, 1998. Exhibition Catalog.

Attwood, Catherine. *Dynamic Dichotomy: The Poetic "I" in Fourteenth- and Fifteenth-Century French Lyric Poetry*. Amsterdam: Rodopi, 1998.

———. "The Image in the Fountain: Fortune, Fiction and Femininity in the *Livre du Voir Dit* of Guillaume de Machaut." *Nottingham French Studies* 38 (1999), 137–49.

Aubailly, Jean-Claude, Emmanuèle Baumgartner, Francis Dubost, Liliane Dulac, Marcel Faure, and René Martin, eds. *Et c'est la fin pour quoy sommes ensemble: Hommage à Jean Dufournet professeur à la Sorbonne*. 3 vols. Paris: Honoré Champion, 1993.

Auerbach, Erich. *Scenes from the Drama of European Literature*. New York: Meridian, 1959.

Avril, François. *Manuscript Painting at the Court of France: The Fourteenth Century, 1310–1380*. Trans. Ursule Molinaro with Bruce Benderson. New York: George Braziller, 1978.

———. "Les manuscrits enluminés de Guillaume de Machaut: essai de chronologie." In Chailley, ed. *Poète et compositeur*. Pp. 117–33.

———. *L'art au temps des rois maudits: Philippe le Bel et ses fils, 1285–1328*. Paris: Réunion des musées nationaux, 1998. Exhibition Catalog.

Avril, François, Philippe Chapu, Danielle Gaborit-Chopin, and Françoise Perrot, eds. *Les Fastes du gothique: le siècle de Charles V, Les*. Paris: Galeries nationales du Grand Palais, 1981. Exhibition Catalog.

Badel, Pierre-Yves. "Le débat." In *La littérature française aux XIVe et XVe siècles*. Heidelberg: Carl Winter, 1988. Ed. Daniel Poirion. Pp. 95–110.

Bain, Jennifer. "'. . . et mon commencement ma fin': Genre and Machaut's Musical Language in His Secular Songs." In McGrady and Bain. Pp. 79–102.

Bakhtin, Mikhail M. *The Dialogic Imagination: Four Essays*. Trans. Caryl Emerson and Michael Holquist. Austin, TX: University of Texas Press, 1981.

Basso, Hélène. "Relier, relire: des poèmes courtois faits *galanteries*." *Babel: Littératures plurielles* 16 (2007), 185–208.

Baumgartner, Emmanuèle, and Laurence Harf-Lancner, eds. *Progrès, réaction, décadence dans l'Occident médiéval*. Geneva: Droz, 2003.

Bec, Pierre. "Note musico-philologique sur l'orgue et l'*aile* chez Guillaume de Machaut." In Aubailly et al. Pp. 149–61.

Beer, Jeanette M. A. "The Ambiguity of Guillaume de Machaut." *Parergon* 27 (1980), 27–31.

———. *Narrative Conventions of Truth in the Middle Ages*. Geneva: Droz, 1981.

Bennett, Philip E. "The Mirage of Fiction: Narration, Narrator, and Narratee in Froissart's Lyrico-Narrative *Dits*." *Modern Language Review* 86.2 (1991), 285–97.

———. "Rhetoric, Poetics and History: Machaut's *Prise d'Alixandre* and the anonymous *Geste des ducs de Bourgogne*." *Reading Medieval Studies* 34 (2008), 53–75.

Bent, Margaret. "The Machaut Manuscripts *Vg, B* and *E*." *Musica Disciplina* 37 (1983), 53–82.

Bétemps, Isabelle. *L'Imaginaire dans l'œuvre de Guillaume de Machaut*. Paris: Honoré Champion, 1998.

———. "La figure du poète dans le *Voir Dit*: du cœur d'amant au testam(a)nt." *Littératures* 45 (2001), 5–22.

———. "Les *Lais de plour*: Guillaume de Machaut et Oton de Granson." In Cerquiglini-Toulet and Wilkins. Pp. 95–106.

Biblia Sacra Iuxta Vulgatam Clementinam, eds. Alberto Colunga and Laurentio Turrado. Madrid: Biblioteca de Auctores Cristianos, 1977.

Bibliothèque nationale de France. Web. Accessed May 2016. Online at http://gallica.bnf.fr.

Biezen, Jan van, and J. P. Gumbert. *Two Chansonniers from the Low Countries: French and Dutch Polyphonic Songs from the Leiden and Utrecht Fragments (Early 15th Century)*. Amsterdam: Vereniging voor Nederlandse Muziekgeschiedenis, 1985.

Blamires, Alcuin. *Woman Defamed and Woman Defended: An Anthology of Medieval Texts*. Oxford: Oxford University Press, 1992.

———. *The Case for Women in Medieval Culture*. Oxford: Oxford University Press, 1997.

Blanc, Odile. "From Battlefield to Court: The Invention of Fashion in the Fourteenth Century." In *Encountering Medieval Textiles and Dress: Objects, Texts, Images*. Ed. Désirée G. Koslin and Janet E. Snyder. New York: Palgrave, 2002. Pp. 157–72.

Blumenfeld-Kosinski, Renate. *Reading Myth: Classical Mythology and Its Interpretations in Medieval French Literature*. Stanford, CA: Stanford University Press, 1997.

Boenig, Robert. "Musical Instruments as Iconographical Artifacts in Medieval Poetry." In *Material Culture and Cultural Materialisms in the Middle Ages and Renaissance*. Ed. Curtis Perry. Turnhout: Brepols, 2001. Pp. 1–15.

Boethius. *The Consolation of Philosophy*. Trans. Richard Green. Indianapolis: Library of Liberal Arts, 1962.

———. *Fundamentals of Music*. Ed. Claude V. Palisca. Trans. Calvin M. Bower. New Haven, CT: Yale University Press, 1989.

Boogaart, Jacques. "*Folie couvient avoir*: Citation and Transformation in Machaut's Musical Works — Gender Change and Transgression." In Plumley, Di Bacco, and Jossa. Pp. 15–40.

Bordonove, Georges. *Jean le Bon et son temps*. Paris: Ramsay, 1980.

Boswell, John. *Christianity, Social Tolerance and Homosexuality: Gay People in Western Europe from the Beginning of the Christian Era to the Fourteenth Century*. Chicago: The University of Chicago Press, 1980.

Boudet, Jean-Patrice, and Hélène Millet, eds. *Eustache Deschamps en son temps*. Paris: Publications de la Sorbonne, 1997.

Boulton, Maureen. "The Dialogical Imagination in the Middle Ages: The Example of Guillaume de Machaut's *Voir Dit*." *Allegorica* 10 (1989), 85–94.

———. "Guillaume de Machaut's *Voir Dit*: The Ideology of Form." In Busby and Kooper. Pp. 39–47.

———. *The Song in the Story: Lyric Insertions in French Narrative Fiction, 1200–1400*. Philadelphia:

University of Pennsylvania Press, 1993.

Bowers, Roger. "Guillaume de Machaut and His Canonry of Reims, 1338–1377." *Early Music History* 23 (2004), 1–48.

Brewer, Derek. "Chaucer's Knight As Hero, and Machaut's *Prise d'Alexandrie*." In *Heroes and Heroines in Medieval English Literature*. Ed. Leo Carruthers. Brewer, 1994. Pp. 81–96.

Brothers, Thomas. "Musica Ficta and Harmony in Machaut's Songs." *The Journal of Musicology* 15.4 (1997), 501–28.

Brown, Cynthia J. *Poets, Patrons and Printers: Crisis of Authority in Late Medieval France*. Ithaca, NY: Cornell University Press, 1995.

Brownlee, Kevin. "The Poetic Œuvre of Guillaume de Machaut: The Identity of Discourse and the Discourse of Identity." In Cosman and Chandler. Pp. 219–33.

———. "Transformations of the Lyric 'Je': The Example of Guillaume de Machaut." *L'Esprit Créateur* 18.1 (1978), 5–18.

———. *Poetic Identity in Guillaume de Machaut*. Madison, WI: The University of Wisconsin Press, 1984.

———. "Metaphoric Love Experience and Poetic Craft: Guillaume de Machaut's *Fonteinne amoureuse*." In *Poetics of Love in the Middle Ages: Texts and Contexts*. Ed. Moshe Lazar and Norris J. Lacy. Fairfax, VA: George Mason University Press, 1989. Pp. 147–55.

———. "Guillaume de Machaut's *Remede de Fortune*: The Lyric Anthology as Narrative Progression." In *The Ladder of High Designs: Structure and Interpretation of the French Lyric Sequence*. Ed. Doranne Fenoaltea and David Lee Rubin. Charlottesville, VA: University Press of Virginia, 1991. Pp. 1–25.

———. "Pygmalion, Mimesis, and the Multiple Endings of the *Roman de la Rose*." *Yale French Studies* 95 (1999), 193–211.

———. "Fire, Desire, Duration, Death: Machaut's Motet 10." In Clark and Leach. Pp. 79–93.

Brownlee, Kevin, and Sylvia Huot, eds. *Rethinking The Romance of the Rose: Image, Text, Reception*. Philadelphia: University of Pennsylvania Press, 1992.

Bullock, Alison. "The Variant Musical? Readings of the Machaut Manuscripts." Ph.D. Dissertation: University of Southampton, 1998.

Buren, Anne H. van, and Roger S. Wieck. *Illuminating Fashion: Dress in the Art of Medieval France and the Netherlands, 1325–1515*. New York: The Morgan Library and Museum, 2011.

Burger, Glenn, and Steven F. Kruger, eds. *Queering the Middle Ages*. Minneapolis, MN: University of Minnesota Press, 2001.

Burke, Mary Ann. "A Medieval Experiment in Adaptation: Typology and Courtly Love. Poetry in the Second Rhetoric." *Res Publica Litterarum* 3 (1980), 165–75.

Burkholder, J. Peter, Donald Jay Grout, and Claude V. Palisca. *A History of Western Music*. New York: Norton, 2006.

Burrow, John. *Ricardian Poetry: Chaucer, Gower, Langland and the* Gawain *Poet*. London: Routledge and Kegan Paul, 1971.

———. "Poems without Contexts: The Rawlinson Lyrics." *Essays in Criticism* 29.1 (1979), 6–32.

———. "The Poet and the Book." In *Genres, Themes, and Images in English Literature*. Ed. Piero Boitani and Anna Torti. Tübingen: Gunter Narr Verlag, 1988. Pp. 230–45.

Busby, Keith. *Codex and Context: Reading Old French Verse Narrative in Manuscript*. 2 vols. Amsterdam: Rodopi, 2002.

Busby, Keith, and Erik Kooper, eds. *Courtly Literature: Culture and Context*. Amsterdam: John Benjamins, 1990.

Butterfield, Ardis. "Interpolated Lyric in Medieval Narrative Poetry." Ph.D. Dissertation: University of Cambridge, 1988.

———. "Lyric and Elegy in *The Book of the Duchess*." *Medium Ævum* 60.1 (1991), 33–60.

———. "Pastoral and the Politics of Plague in Machaut and Chaucer." *Studies in the Age of Chaucer* 16 (1994), 3–27.

———. *Poetry and Music in Medieval France: From Jean Renart to Guillaume de Machaut*. Cambridge: Cambridge University Press, 2002.

———. "Articulating the Author: Gower and the French Vernacular Codex." *Yearbook of English Studies* 33 (2003), 80–96.

———. "Chaucer's French Inheritance. In *The Cambridge Companion to Chaucer*. Second edition. Ed. Piero Boitani and Jill Mann. Cambridge and New York: Cambridge University Press, 2003. Pp 20–35.

———. "*Confessio Amantis* and the French Tradition." In *A Companion to Gower*. Ed. Siân Echard. Cambridge: Brewer, 2004. Pp. 165–80.

Calin, Françoise, and William Calin. "Medieval Fiction and New Novel: Some Polemical Remarks on the Subject of Narrative." *Yale French Review* 51 (1974), 235–50.

Calin, William. "A Reading of Machaut's 'Jugement dou Roy de Navarre'." *Modern Language Review* 66.2 (1971), 294–97.

———. *A Poet at the Fountain: Essays on the Narrative Verse of Guillaume de Machaut*. Lexington, KY: Kentucky University Press, 1974.

———. "The Poet at the Fountain: Machaut as Narrative Poet." In Cosman and Chandler. Pp. 177–87.

———. "Problèmes de technique narrative au Moyen-Age: *Le Roman de la Rose* et Guillaume de Machaut." In *Mélanges de langue et littérature françaises du moyen-âge offerts à Pierre Jonin*. Paris: Honoré Champion, 1979. Pp. 125–38.

———. "Le *Moi* chez Guillaume de Machaut." In Chailley, ed. *Poète et compositeur*. Pp. 241–52.

———. *A Muse for Heroes: Nine Centuries of the Epic in France*. Toronto: University of Toronto Press, 1983.

———. *In Defense of French Poetry: An Essay in Revaluation*. University Park, PA: Pennsylvania State University Press, 1987.

———. "Medieval Intertextuality: Lyrical Inserts and Narrative in Guillaume de Machaut." *The French Review* 62.1 (1988), 1–10.

———. "Contre la *fin'amor*? Contre la femme? Une relecture de textes du Moyen Age." In Busby and Kooper. Pp. 61–82.

———. *The French Tradition and the Literature of Medieval England*. Toronto: University of Toronto Press, 1994.

———. "Machaut's Legacy: The Chaucerian Inheritance Reconsidered." In Palmer, *Chaucer's French Contemporaries*. Pp. 29–46.

Calvez, Daniel. "La Structure du rondeau: mise au point." *French Review* 55.4 (1982), 461–70.

Camille, Michael. *The Gothic Idol: Ideology and Image-Making in Medieval Art*. Cambridge: Cambridge University Press, 1989.

———. "Gothic Signs and the Surplus: The Kiss on the Cathedral." In "Contexts: Styles and Values in Medieval Art and Literature." Ed. Daniel Poirion and Nancy Freeman Regalado. Special issue, *Yale French Studies* (1991), 151–70.

———. *The Medieval Art of Love: Objects and Subjects of Desire*. New York: Harry N. Abrams, 1998.

———. "'For Our Devotion and Pleasure': The Sexual Objects of Jean, Duc de Berry." *Art History* 24.2 (2001), 169–94.

Campbell, Anna. *The Black Death and Men of Learning*. New York: Columbia University Press, 1931.

Campbell, Thomas P. "Machaut and Chaucer: *Ars Nova* and the Art of Narrative." Chaucer Review 24.4 (1990), 275–89.

Capellanus, Andreas, *The Art of Courtly Love*. Trans. John Jay Parry. New York: Frederick Ungar, 1960.

Cappelli, Adriano. *Cronologia, Cronografia e Calendario Perpetuo*. Third edition. Milan: Hoepli, 1969.

Carré, Yannick. *Le Baiser sur la bouche au Moyen Âge: Rites, symboles, mentalités, à travers les textes et les images, XIᵉ-XVᵉ siècles*. Paris: Le Léopard d'Or, 1992.

Cattin, Guilio, and Francesco Facchin. *French Sacred Music*. Monaco: L'Oiseau-Lyre, 1991.

Caviness, Madeline H. *Visualizing Women in the Middle Ages: Sight, Spectacle, and Scopic Economy*. Philadelphia: University of Pennsylvania Press, 2001.

Cayley, Emma, and Ashby Kinch, eds. *Chartier in Europe*. Cambridge: D. S. Brewer, 2008.

———. "Machaut and Debate Poetry." In McGrady and Bain. Pp. 103–18.

Caylus, M. le Comte de. "Premier Mémoire sur Guillaume de Machaut, poëte et musicien dans le XIVe siècle." *Mémoires de littérature, tirés des registres de l'Académie Royale des Inscriptions et Belles-Lettres* 20 (1753), 399–414.

Cazelles, Raymond. *Société, Politique, noblesse et couronne sous Jean le Bon et Charles V*. Geneva: Droz, 1982.

———. *Etienne Marcel, champion de l'unité française*. Paris: Tallandier, 1984.

Cerquiglini, Bernard, and Jacqueline Cerquiglini-Toulet. "L'écriture proverbiale." *Revue des Sciences Humaines* 163 (1976), 359–75.

Cerquiglini, Jacqueline. See Cerquiglini-Toulet, Jacqueline.

Cerquiglini-Toulet, Jacqueline. "Le clerc et l'écriture: Le *Voir dit* de Guillaume de Machaut et la définition du *dit*." In *Literatur in der Gesellschaft des Spätmittelalters*. Ed. Hans Ulrich Gumbrecht. Heidelberg: Carl Winter, 1980. Pp. 155–63.

———. "Ethique de la totalisation et esthétique de la rupture dans le *Voir-Dit* de Guillaume de Machaut." In Chailley, ed. *Poète et compositeur*. Pp. 253–62.

———. "Le Clerc et le louche: Sociology of an Aesthetic." Trans. Monique Briand-Walker. *Poetics Today* 5.3 (1984), 479–91.

———. "L'écriture louche. La voie oblique chez les Grands Rhétoriqueurs." In *Les Grands Rhétoriqueurs. Actes de Ve Colloque International sur le Moyen Français. Milan, 6–8 Mai 1985*. Vol. 1. Milan: Pubblicazioni della Università Cattolica del Sacro Cuore, 1985. Pp. 21–31.

———. *"Un Engin si soutil": Guillaume de Machaut et l'écriture au XIVe siècle*. Paris: Honoré Champion, 1985.

———. "Écrire le temps. Le lyrisme de la durée aux XIVe et XVe siècles." In *Le temps et la durée dans la littérature au Moyen Âge et à la Renaissance*. Ed. Yvonne Bellenger. Paris: Nizet, 1986. Pp. 103–14.

———. "Le Dit." *Grundriss der romanischen Literaturen des Mittelalters* 8 (1988), 86–94.

———. "Le *Voir Dit* mis à nu par ses éditeurs, même. Étude de la réception d'un texte à travers ses éditions." In *Mittelalter-Rezeption. Zur Rezeptionsgeschichte der romanischen Literaturen des Mittelalters in der Neuzeit*. Ed. Reinhold Grimm. Heidelberg: Carl Winter, 1991. Pp. 337–80.

———. *The Color of Melancholy: The Uses of Books in the Fourteenth Century*. Trans. Lydia G. Cochrane. London and Baltimore, MD: Johns Hopkins University Press, 1997.

———. "'Ma fin est mon commencement': The Essence of Poetry and Song in Guillaume de Machaut." In McGrady and Bain. Pp. 69–78.

Cerquiglini-Toulet, Jacqueline, and Nigel E. Wilkins, eds. *Guillaume de Machaut: 1300–2000*. Paris: Presses Paris Sorbonne, 2002.

Cerquiglini-Toulet, Jacqueline, René Pérennec, and Uwe Grüning. *Guillaume de Machaut: Lob der Frauen. Gedichte altfranzösisch und deutsch*. Leipzig: Reclam, 1987.

Chailley, Jacques. "Du cheval de Guillaume de Machaut à Charles II de Navarre." *Romania* 94 (1973), 251–58.

Chailley, Jacques, ed. *Guillaume de Machaut: Poète et compositeur. Colloque-table ronde organisé par l'Université de Reims (19–22 avril 1978)*. Paris: Klincksieck, 1982.

Chastelaine de Vergi, La. Ed. René Ernst Victor Stuip. The Hague: Mouton, 1970.

Chaucer, Geoffrey. *The Riverside Chaucer*. Ed. Larry D. Benson et al. Third edition. Boston: Houghton Mifflin, 1987.

Chérest, Aimé. *L'Archiprêtre: Episodes de la guerre de cent ans au XIVe siècle*. Paris: A. Claudin, 1879.

Chism, Christine. "Romance." In *The Cambridge Companion to Middle English Literature: 1100–1500*. Ed. Larry Scanlon. Cambridge: Cambridge University Press, 2009. Pp. 57–69.

Clark, Alice V. "Machaut Reading Machaut: Self-Borrowing and Reinterpretation in Motets 8 and 21." In Clark and Leach. Pp. 94–101.

———. "The Motets Read and Heard." In McGrady and Bain. Pp. 185–208.

Clark, Suzannah, and Elizabeth Eva Leach, eds. *Citation and Authority in Medieval and Renaissance Musical Culture: Learning from the Learned*. Woodbridge and Rochester: Boydell Press, 2005.

Cohen, Gustave. *La poésie en France au Moyen-Âge*. Paris: Richard-Masse, 1952.

Coldwell, Maria V. "*Guillaume de Dole* and Medieval Romances with Musical Interpolations." *Musica*

Disciplina 35 (1981), 55–86.

Coleman, Joyce. *Public Reading and the Reading Public in Late Medieval England and France*. Cambridge: Cambridge University Press, 1996.

———. "The Text Recontextualized in Performance: Deschamps' Prelection of Machaut's *Voir Dit* to the Count of Flanders." *Viator* 31 (2000), 233–48.

———. "Authorizing the Story: Guillaume de Machaut as Doctor of Love." In *Telling the Story in the Middle Ages: Essays in Honor of Evelyn Birge Vitz*. Ed. Kathryn A. Duys, Elizabeth Emery, and Laurie Postlewate. Cambridge and Rochester, NY: D. S. Brewer, 2015. Pp. 141–54.

Connery, William J. "The Poet and the Clerk: A Study of the Narrative Poetry of Guillaume de Machaut." Ph.D. Dissertation: Yale University, 1974.

Contamine, Philippe. "Les compagnies d'aventure en France pendant la guerre de cent ans." *Melanges de l'Ecole Française de Rome* 87 (1975), 365–96.

Cosman, Madeleine Pelner, and Bruce Chandler, eds. *Machaut's World: Science and Art in the Fourteenth Century*. New York: Academy of Sciences, 1978.

Courcelle, Pierre Paul, and Jeanne Courcelle. *Lecteurs païens et lecteurs chrétiens de l'Enéide*. Paris: Gauthier-Villars, 1984.

Cropp, Glynnis M. "Les manuscrits du 'Livre de Boece de Consolacion'." *Revue d'Histoire des Textes* 12–13 (1982–83), 263–352.

———. "The Medieval French Tradition". In *Boethius in the Middle Ages: Latin and Vernacular Traditions of the Consolatio Philosophiae*. Ed. Maarten J. F. M. Hoenen and Lodi Nauta. Leiden: Brill, 1997. Pp. 243–65.

———. "Boethius and the *Consolatio Philosophiae* in XIVth and XVth-century French writing." *Essays in French Literature* 42 (2005), 27–43.

The Croxton Play of the Sacrament. Ed. John T. Sebastian. Kalamazoo, MI: Medieval Institute Publications, 2012.

Dalglish, William E. "The Hocket in Medieval Polyphony." *Musical Quarterly* 55.3 (1969), 344–63.

D'Angiolini, Giuliano. "Le son du sens: Machaut, Stockhausenn. Le ballade 34 et le Chant des Adolescents." *Analyse Musicale* 9 (1987), 43–51.

Davenport, W. A. *Chaucer: Complaint and Narrative*. Cambridge: Brewer, 1988.

Davis, Steven. "Guillaume de Machaut, Chaucer's 'Book of the Duchess,' and the Chaucer Tradition." *Chaucer Review* 36.4 (2002), 391–405.

De Boer, Cornelis. "Guillaume de Machaut et *l'Ovide moralisé*." *Romania* 43 (1914), 335–52.

———. *L'Ovide moralisé*. Amsterdam: Müller, 1915–38.

De Fréville, E. "Des Grandes Compagnies au XIVe siècle. I." *Bibliothèque de l'Ecole de Chartres* 3 (1841–42), 258–81, 606.

De Fréville, E. "Des Grandes Compagnies au XIVe siècle. II." *Bibliothèque de l'Ecole de Chartres*, 5 (1843–44), 232–53.

Delachenal, Roland. *Histoire de Charles V*. 3 vols. Paris: Picard, 1909–16.

———. *Chronique des Règnes de Jean II et de Charles V*. Vol. 2. Paris: Renouard, 1916.

Delogu, Daisy. *Theorizing the Ideal Sovereign: The Rise of the French Vernacular Royal Biography*. Toronto: University of Toronto Press, 2008.

———. "'Laisser de mal, le bien eslire': History, Allegory, and Ethical Reading in the Works of Guillaume de Machaut." In McGrady and Bain. Pp. 261–76.

De Looze, Laurence. "Guillaume de Machaut and the Writerly Process." *French Forum* 9.2 (1984), 145–61.

———. "'Mon nom trouveras': A New Look at the Anagrams of Guillaume de Machaut — the Enigmas, Responses, and Solutions." *Romanic Review* 79 (1988), 537–57.

———. "From Text to Text and from Tale to Tale: Jean Froissart's *Prison amoureuse*." In *The Centre and Its Compass: Studies in Medieval Literature in Honor of Professor John Leyerle*. Ed. Robert A. Taylor and John Leyerle. Kalamazoo, MI: Medieval Institute Publications, 1993. Pp. 87–110.

———. "'Pseudo-Autobiography' and the Body of Poetry in Guillaume de Machaut's *Remede de Fortune*." *L'Esprit Créateur* 33 (1993), 73–86.

————. *Pseudo-Autobiography in the Fourteenth Century: Juan Ruiz, Guillaume de Machaut, Jean Froissart, and Geoffrey Chaucer*. Gainesville, FL: University Press of Florida, 1997.

Denifle, Henri. *La Désolation des Eglises, Monastères et Hopitaux en France pendant la Guerre de Cent Ans*. 2 vols. Brussels: Culture et Civilisation, 1965. Originally published in Paris: Alphonse Picard, 1899.

Deschamps, Eustache. *Œuvres complètes de Eustache Deschamps*. Ed. Auguste de Queux de Saint-Hilaire and Gaston Raynaud. 11 vols. Paris: Firmin Didot, 1878–1903.

————. *L'Art de Dictier*. Ed. and trans. Deborah M. Sinnreich-Levi. East Lansing, MI: Colleagues Press, 1994.

Delsaux, Olivier. "L'humaniste Simon de Plumetot et sa copie des poésies d'Eustache Deschamps. Une édition génétique au début de XVe siécle? (Partie I)" *Revue d'histoire des textes* 9 (2014), 273–439.

————. "L'humaniste Simon de Plumetot et sa copie des poésies d'Eustache Deschamps. Une édition génétique au début de XVe siécle? (Partie II)" *Revue d'histoire des textes* 10 (2015), 141–95.

Desmond, Marilynn, and Pamela Sheingorn. "Queering Ovidian Myth: Bestiality and Desire in Christine de Pizan's Epistre Othea." In Burger and Kruger. Pp. 3–27.

Desportes, Pierre. *Histoire de Reims*. Toulouse: Privat, 1983.

Deuchler, Florens. "Looking at Bonne of Luxembourg's Prayerbook." *Metropolitan Museum of Art Bulletin* 29.6 (1971), 267–78.

Deviosse, Jean. *Jean le Bon*. Paris: Librairie Fayard, 1985.

DIAMM. Digital Image Archive of Medieval Music. University of Oxford, 2015. Web. Accessed May 2016. Online at http://www.diamm.ac.uk/.

Dictionnaire du Moyen Français (1330–1500). Analyse et Traitement Informatique de la Langue Française, Université de Lorraine, 2015. Web. Accessed May 2016. Online at http://www.atilf.fr/dmf.

Diekstra, F. N. M. "Chaucer's Digressive Mode and the Moral of *The Manciple's Tale*." *Neophilologus* 67.1 (1983), 131–48.

Dömling, Wolfgang. "Zur Überlieferung der musikalischen Werke Guillaume de Machauts." *Die Musikforschung* 22.2 (1969), 189–95.

————. "Aspekte der Sprachvertonung in den Balladen Guillaume de Machauts." *Die Musikforschung* 25.3 (1972), 301–07.

Douce, André. *Guillaume de Machaut: Musicien et poète rémois*. Reims: Matot-Braine, 1948.

Downes, Stephanie. "After Deschamps: Chaucer's French Fame." In *Chaucer and Fame: Reputation and Reception*. Ed. Isabel Davis and Catherine Nall. Cambridge: D. S. Brewer, 2015. Pp. 127–42.

Drobinsky, Julia. "*Peindre, Pourtraire, Escrire*. Le rapport entre le texte et l'image dans les manuscrits enluminés de Guillaume de Machaut (XIVe–XVe siècles)." Ph.D. Dissertation: Université de Paris IV- Sorbonne, 2004.

————. "Eros, Hypnos et Thanatos, ou les stratégies de mise à distance de la mort dans la *Fontaine Amoureuse* de Guillaume de Machaut." In *La mort écrite, rites et rhétoriques du trépas au Moyen Âge*. Ed. Estelle Doudet. Paris: Presses de l'Université Paris Sorbonne, 2005. Pp. 71–83.

————. "Recyclage et création dans l'iconographie de Guillaume de Machaut (quatorzième-quinzième siècles)." In *Manuscripts in Transition: Recycling Manuscripts, Texts, and Images*. Ed. Brigitte Dekeyzer and Jan van der Stock. Leuven: Peeters Publishers, 2005. Pp. 217–33.

————. "La narration iconographique dans *l'Ovide moralisé* de Lyon (BM ms. 742)." In *Ovide métamorphosé: Les lecteurs médiévaux d'Ovide*. Ed. Laurence Harf-Lancner, Laurence Mathey-Maille, and Michelle Szkilnik. Paris: Presses Sorbonne Nouvelle, 2009. Pp. 223–38.

————. "Amants péris en mer. Transmission textuelle, transmission visuelle de la légende de Héro et Léandre." In *L'Antiquité entre Moyen Age et Renaissance: l'Antiquité dans les livres produits au nord des Alpes entre 1350 et 1520*. Ed. Chrystèle Blondeau and Marie Jacob. Paris: Presses Universitaires de Paris Ouest, 2011. Pp. 139–58.

————. "L'Amour dans l'arbre et l'Amour au cœur ouvert. Deux allegories sous influence visuelle dans les manuscrits de Guillaume de Machaut." In *L'Allégorie dans l'art du Moyen Age: Formes et fonctions. Héritages, créations, mutations*. Ed. Christian Heck. Turnhout: Brepols, 2011. Pp. 255–72.

Duhamel, Pascale. "Le *Livre dou Voir Dit* de Guillaume de Machaut et la transition de la tradition orale vers la tradition écrite en musique." *Cahiers de recherches médiévales et humanistes* 26 (2013), 129–51.

Dwyer, Richard A. *Boethian Fictions: Narratives in the Medieval French Versions of the Consolatio Philosophiae.* Cambridge, MA: The Medieval Academy of America, 1976.

Dynes, Wayne. "Orfeo without Eurydice." *Gai Saber* 1 (1978), 267–73.

Eagleton, Terry. *Criticism and Ideology: A Study in Marxist Literary Theory.* London: Verso, 1976.

Earp, Lawrence. "Scribal Practice, Manuscript Production and the Transmission of Music in Late Medieval France: The Manuscripts of Guillaume de Machaut." Ph.D. Dissertation: Princeton University, 1983.

———. "Machaut's Role in the Production of Manuscripts of His Works." *Journal of the American Musicological Society* 42.3 (1989), 461–503.

———. *Guillaume de Machaut: A Guide to Research.* New York: Garland, 1995.

———. "Declamatory Dissonance in Machaut." In Clark and Leach. Pp. 102–22.

———. "Declamation as Expression in Machaut's Music." In McGrady and Bain. Pp. 209–40.

Easton, Martha. "The Wound of Christ, The Mouth of Hell: Appropriations and Inversions of Female Anatomy in the Later Middle Ages." In *Tributes to Jonathan J. G. Alexander: The Making and Meaning of Illuminated Medieval and Renaissance Manuscripts, Art and Architecture.* Ed. Susan L'Engle and Gerald B. Guest. London: Harvey Miller Publishers, 2006. Pp. 395–414.

Ehrhart, Margaret J. "Guillaume de Machaut's *Jugement dou roy de Navarre* and Medieval Treatments of the Virtues." *Annuale Mediaevale* 19 (1979), 46–67.

———. "The 'Esprueve de fines amours' in Machaut's *Dit dou Lyon* and Medieval Interpretations of Circe and Her Island." *Neophilologus* 64 (1980), 38–41.

———. "Machaut's *Dit de la fonteinne amoureuse*, the Choice of Paris, and the Duties of Rulers." *Philological Quarterly* 59 (1980), 119–39.

———. "Machaut's *Jugement dou roy de Navarre* and the Book of Ecclesiastes." *Neuphilologische Mitteilungen* 81.3 (1980), 318–25.

———. *The Judgment of the Trojan Prince Paris in Medieval Literature.* Philadelphia: University of Pennsylvania Press, 1987.

———. "Machaut and the Duties of Rulers Tradition." *French Forum* 17.1 (1992), 5–22.

———. "Only Connect: Machaut's Book of Morpheus and the Powers of the Weak." In Palmer, *Chaucer's French Contemporaries.* Pp. 137–62.

Eichelberg, Walter. *Dichtung und Wahrheit in Machauts "Voir Dit."* Frankfurt: Düren, 1935.

Einhorn, Jürgen W. *Spiritualis Unicornis: Das Einhorn als Bedeutungsträger in Literatur und Kunst des Mittelalters.* Munich: Wilhelm Fink Verlag, 1976.

Eisenberg, Michael. "The Mirror of the Text: Reflections in *Ma fin est mon commencement*." In *Canons and Canonic Techniques, 14th–16th Centuries: Theory, Practice and Reception History.* Ed. Katelijne Schiltz and Bonnie J. Blackburn. Leuven: Peeters, 2007. Pp. 83–110.

Enders, Jody. "Music, Delivery, and the Rhetoric of Memory in Guillaume de Machaut's *Remède de Fortune*." *PMLA* 107.3 (1992), 450–64.

———. "Memory, Allegory, and the Romance of Rhetoric." *Yale French Studies* 95 (1999), 49–64.

Everist, Mark. "The Horse, the Clerk and the Lyric: The Musicography of the Thirteenth and Fourteenth Centuries." *Journal of the Royal Musical Association* 130.1 (2005), 136–53.

———. "Machaut's Musical Heritage." In McGrady and Bain. Pp. 143–58.

Fallows, David. "Guillaume de Machaut and the Lai: A New Source." *Early Music* 5.4 (1977), 477–83.

Faral, Edmond. *Recherches sur les sources Latines des contes et romans courtois du moyen age.* Paris: Honoré Champion, 1913.

Fasseur, Valérie. "Apprendre l'art d'écrire: Sens de la relation didactique dans le *Voir Dit* de Guillaume de Machaut." *Romania* 124 (2006), 162–94.

Favier, Jean. *La Guerre de Cent Ans.* Paris: Fayard, 1980.

Fenster, Thelma S., and Clare A. Lees. *Gender in Debate from the Early Middle Ages to the Renaissance.* New York: Palgrave Macmillan, 2002.

Ferrand, Françoise. "Le Mirage de l'image: de l'idole à l'icône intérieure chez Guillaume de Machaut." In *Le Moyen Age dans la modernité: Mélanges offerts à Roger Dragonetti*. Ed. Jean R. Scheidegger, Sabine Girardet, and Eric Hicks. Paris: Honoré Champion, 1996. Pp. 203–20.

———. "Au delà de l'idée de progrès: La pensée musicale de Guillaume de Machaut et le renouvellement de l'écriture littéraire dans le *Voir Dit*." In Baumgartner and Harf-Lancner. Pp. 231–49.

Ferster, Judith. *Fictions of Advice: The Literature and Politics of Counsel in Late Medieval England*. Philadelphia: University of Pennsylvania Press, 1996.

Friedman, John Block. *Orpheus in the Middle Ages*. Syracuse, NY: Syracuse University Press, 2000.

Froissart, Jean. *Oeuvres de Froissart: Poésies*. Ed. Auguste Scheler. Vol 2. Brussels: Victor Devaux, 1872.

———. *Voyage en Béarn*. Ed. A. H. Diverres. Manchester: Manchester University Press, 1953.

———. *Chronicles*. Ed. and trans. Geoffrey Brereton. Harmondsworth: Penguin, 1968.

———. *L'Espinette amoureuse*. Ed. Anthime Fourrier. Paris: Klincksieck, 1972.

———. *Le Joli Buisson de Jonece*. Ed. Anthime Fourrier. Geneva: Droz, 1975.

———. *The Lyric Poems of Jean Froissart: A Critical Edition*. Ed. Rob Roy McGregor, Jr. Chapel Hill, NC: University of North Carolina, 1975.

———. *La Prison Amoureuse (The Prison of Love)*. Ed. and Trans. Laurence de Looze. New York: Garland, 1994.

Fuller, Sarah Ann. "Machaut and the Definition of Musical Space." *Sonus* 12.1 (1991), 1–21.

———. "Guillaume de Machaut: De toutes flours." In *Models of Musical Analysis: Music Before 1600*. Ed. Mark Everist. Cambridge, MA: Harvard University Press, 1992. Pp. 41–65.

Galderisi, Claudio. "'Ce dient nobles et bourjois': La Destinée poétique de Canens / Caneüs dans *Le Livre du Voir Dit*." *Le Moyen Français* 51–53 (2002–03), 291–303.

Gallo, Franco Alberto. *Trascrizione di Machaut: "Remede de Fortune" — "Ecu bleu" — "Remede d'Amour."* Ravenna: Longo, 1999.

Gaudet, Minnette. "Machaut's *Dit de l'alerion* and the Sexual Politics of Courtly Love." *RLA: Romance Languages Annual* 4 (1993), 55–63.

———. "Machaut's Use of Repetition: Signification as Enigma in the *Dit de l'alerion*." *RLA: Romance Languages Annual* 8 (1996), 35–40.

Gaullier-Bougassas, Catherine. "Images littéraires de Chypre et évolution de l'esprit de croisade au XIVe siècle." In Baumgartner and Harf-Lancner. Pp. 123–35.

Gauvard, Claude. "Portrait du prince d'après l'œuvre de Guillaume de Machaut: étude sur les idées politiques du poète." In Chailley, ed. *Poète et compositeur*. Pp. 23–39.

Geiselhardt, Jakob. *Machaut und Froissart: Ihre literarischen Beziehungen*. Jena: Thomas and Hubert, 1914.

Geoffrey of Vinsauf. *Poetria Nova*. Trans. Margaret F. Nims. Toronto: Pontifical Institute, 1967.

Germain de Maidy, Léon. *L'Erection du Duché de Bar*. Nancy: Crepin-Leblond, 1885.

Glénisson, Jean. "La seconde peste: l'épidémie de 1360–1362 en France et en Europe." *Annuaire-bulletin de la Société de l'Histoire de France* (1968/1969), 27–38.

Godwin, Joscelyn. "'Main divers acors': Some Instrument Collections of the Ars Nova Period." *Early Music* 5.2 (1977), 148–59.

Göllner, Marie Louise. "Un res d'Alemaigne." In *Festschrift für Horst Leuchtmann zum 65. Geburtstag*. Ed. Stephan Hörner and Bernhold Schmid. Tutzing: Schneider, 1993. Pp. 147–60.

———. "Interrelationships Between Text and Music in the Refrain Forms of Guillaume de Machaut." In *Songs of the Dove and the Nightingale: Sacred and Secular Music c.900–c.1600*. Ed. Greta Mary Hair and Robyn E. Smith. Basel: Gorden and Breach Publishers, 1995. Pp. 105–23.

———. *Essays on Music and Poetry in the Late Middle Ages*. Tutzing: Schneider, 2003.

Goodich, Michael. *The Unmentionable Vice: Homosexuality in the Later Medieval Period*. Santa Barbara, CA: Ross-Erikson, 1979.

Gourmont, Remy de. "Le roman de Guillaume de Machaut et de Peronne d'Armentières." In *Promenades Littéraires, V*. Paris: Mercure de France, 1913. Pp. 7–37.

Gower, John. *Confessio Amantis*. Ed. Russell A. Peck, with Latin translations by Andrew Galloway. 3 vols. Kalamazoo, MI: Medieval Institute Publications, 2000–06.

———. *Vox Clamantis.* In *The Complete Works of John Gower.* Ed. G. C. Macaulay. Oxford: Clarendon Press, 1899–1902. Pp. 3–313.

Green, D. H. *Women Readers in the Middle Ages.* Cambridge: Cambridge University Press, 2007.

Green, Richard Firth. "*Le roi qui ne ment* and Aristocratic Courtship." In Busby and Kooper. Pp. 211–25.

Grentes, Georges, Geneviève Hasenohr-Esnos, and Michel Zink, eds. *Dictionnaire des lettres françaises, Le Moyen Age.* Paris: Fayard, 1992.

Gröbner, Gustav. *Grundriss der romanischen Philologie.* 2 vols. Strasbourg: Trübner, 1902.

Guido delle Colonne. *Historia Destructionis Troiae.* Ed. and trans. Mary Elizabeth Meek. Bloomington, IN: Indiana University Press, 1974.

Guillaume de Lorris and Jean de Meun. *Le Roman de la Rose.* Ed. Félix Lecoy. Paris: Honoré Champion, 1965.

———. *Roman de la Rose.* Ed. and trans. J. V. Fleming. Princeton, NJ: Princeton University Press, 1969.

———. *Roman de la Rose.* Ed. and trans. Charles Dahlberg. Hanover and London: University Press of New England, 1971.

———. *Roman de la Rose: Édition d'après les manucrits BN 12786 et BN 378.* Trans. Armand Strubel. Paris: Librairie Générale Française, 1982.

Gunn, Alan F. *The Mirror of Love: a Re-interpretation of "The Romance of the Rose."* Lubbock, TX: Texas Tech Press, 1952.

Günther, Ursula. *The Motets of the Manuscripts Chantilly, Musée Condé, 564 (olim 1047) and Modena, Biblioteca Estense a.M.5.24 (olim lat. 568).* Rome: American Institute of Musicology, 1965.

———. "Problems of Dating in Ars Nova and Ars Subtilior." In *L'Ars nova italiana del Trecento IV.* Ed. Agostino Ziino. Certaldo: Centro di Studi sull'Ars nova italiana del Trecento, 1978. Pp. 292–93.

Guthrie, Steven R. "Meter and Performance in Machaut and Chaucer." In *The Union of Words and Music in Medieval Poetry.* Ed. Rebecca A. Baltzer, Thomas Cable, and James I. Wimsatt. Austin, TX: University of Texas Press, 1991. Pp. 72–100.

———. "Machaut and the *Octosyllabe.*" In Palmer, *Chaucer's French Contemporaries.* Pp. 111–36.

Gybbon-Monnypenny, G. B. "Guillaume de Machaut's erotic 'autobiography': precedents for the form of the *Voir-Dit.*" In *Studies in Medieval Literature and Language, in Memory of Frederick Whitehead.* Ed. W. Rothwell, W. R. J. Barron, David Blamires, and Lewis Thorpe. Manchester: Manchester University Press, 1973. Pp. 133–52.

Haidu, Peter. "Making It (New) in the Middle Ages: Towards a Problematics of Alterity." *Diacritics* 4.2 (1974), 2–11.

———. *The Subject Medieval/Modern: Text and Governance in the Middle Ages.* Stanford, CA: Stanford University Press, 2004.

Hamburger, Jeffrey F. *St. John the Divine: The Deified Evangelist in Medieval Art and Theology.* Berkeley, CA: University of California Press, 2002.

Hanf, Georg. "Über Guillaume de Machauts *Voir Dit.*" *Zeitschrift für romanische Philologie* 22 (1898), 145–96.

Harrison, Frank. *Motets of French Provenance.* Monaco: L'Oiseau-Lyre, 1968.

Hassell, James Woodrow, Jr. *Middle French Proverbs, Sentences, and Proverbial Phrases.* Toronto: Pontifical Institute of Mediaeval Studies, 1982.

Hasselman, Margaret P. "Teaching Machaut's *Remede de Fortune* in an Undergraduate Humanities Course." *Studies in Medieval and Renaissance Teaching* 8.2 (2000), 27–36.

Heinrichs, Katherine. "'Lovers' Consolations of Philosophy' in Boccaccio, Machaut, and Chaucer." *Studies in the Age of Chaucer* 11 (1989), 93–115.

———. *The Myths of Love: Classical Lovers in Medieval Literature.* University Park, PA: Pennsylvania State University Press, 1990.

———. "The Language of Love: Overstatement and Ironic Humor in Machaut's *Voir Dit.*" *Philological Quarterly* 73.1–2 (1994), 1–9.

———. "Troilus' 'Predestination Soliloquy' and Machaut's *Jugement du Roy de Behaigne.*" *Le Moyen Français* 35–36 (1996), 7–15.

Herlihy, David. *The Black Death and the Transformation of the West*. Cambridge, MA: Harvard University Press, 1997.

Herold, Christine. "Boethius's *Consolatio Philosophiae* as a Bridge between Classical and Christian Concepts of Tragedy." *Carmina Philosophiae: Journal of the International Boethius Society* 3 (1994), 37–52.

Hieatt, Constance B. "*Un Autre Fourme*: Guillaume de Machaut and the Dream Vision Form." Chaucer Review 14.2 (1979), 97–115.

———. "Falconry and Fantasy in Guillaume de Machaut's *Dit de l'alerion*." In Palmer, *Chaucer's French Contemporaries*. Pp. 163–86.

Higgins, Paula. "Parisian Nobles, a Scottish Princess and the Woman's Voice in Late Medieval Song." *Early Music History* 10 (1991), 145–200.

———. "The 'Other Minervas': Creative Women at the Court of Margaret of Scotland." In *Rediscovering the Muses: Women's Musical Traditions*. Ed. Kimberly Marshall. Boston: Northeastern University Press, 1993. Pp. 169–85.

Hippocrates. *Aphorisms*. In Vol. 4 of *Hippocrates: Heracleitus on the Universe*. Trans. W. H. S. Jones. Cambridge, MA: Harvard University Press, 1967. Pp. 97–221.

Hœpffner, Ernest. "Anagramme und Rätselgedichte bei Guillaume de Machaut." *Zeitschrift für Romanische Philologie* 30 (1906), 401–13.

Holsinger, Bruce W. *Music, Body and Desire in Medieval Culture: Hildegard of Bingen to Chaucer*. Stanford, CA: Stanford University Press, 2011.

The Holy Bible, Translated from the Latin Vulgate; Diligently Compared with the Hebrew, Greek and Other Editions in Divers Languages. The Old Testament First Published by the English College at Douay, A. D. 1609, and the New Testament First Published by the English College at Rheims, A. D. 1582; with Annotations, References and an Historical and Chronological Table. Baltimore, MD: John Murphy Company, 1914.

Homer. *Iliad*. Trans. Richmond Lattimore. Chicago: University of Chicago Press, 1951.

Hüe, Denis, ed. *"Comme mon coeur désire": Le Livre du Voir Dit*. Orléans: Paradigme, 2001.

Hülk, Walburga. "Geraubte Kinder: Die Genealogie und der Löwe in den altfranzösischen *Octavian*-Fassungen. Mit einem kleinen Anhang zum *Dit dou Lyon* des Guillaume de Machaut." In *Die Romane von dem Ritter mit dem Löwen*. Ed. Xenja von Ertzdorff and Rudolf Schulz. Trans. Winfried Baumann. Amsterdam: Rodopi, 1994. Pp. 451–71.

Huot, Sylvia. *From Song to Book: The Poetics of Writing in Old French Lyric and Lyrical Narrative Poetry*. Ithaca, NY: Cornell University Press, 1987.

———. *The Romance of the Rose and Its Medieval Readers*. Cambridge: Cambridge University Press, 1993.

———. "Patience in Adversity: the Courtly Lover and Job in Machaut's Motets 2 and 3." *Medium Ævum* 63.2 (1994), 222–38.

———. *Allegorical Play in the Old French Motet: The Sacred and the Profane in Thirteenth-Century Polyphony*. Stanford, CA: Stanford University Press, 1997.

———. "Reliving the *Roman de la Rose*: Allegory and Irony in Machaut's *Voir-Dit*." In Palmer, *Chaucer's French Contemporaries*. Pp. 47–69.

———. "Guillaume de Machaut and the Consolation of Poetry." *Modern Philology* 100.2 (2002), 169–95.

———. *Madness in Medieval French Literature: Identities Found and Lost*. Cambridge: Cambridge University Press, 2003.

———. "Reading across Genres: Froissart's *Joli Buisson de Jonece* and Machaut's Motets." *French Studies* 57.1 (2003), 1–10.

———. "Reading the Lies of Poets: The Literal and the Allegorical in Machaut's *Fonteinne amoureuse*." *Philological Quarterly* 85.1–2 (2006), 25–48.

Hutcheon, Linda. *Narcissistic Narrative: The Metafictional Paradox*. New York: Routledge, 1984.

Imbs, Paul. Le Voir-Dit *de Guillaume de Machaut: étude littéraire*. Paris: Klincksieck, 1991.

Jeay, Madeleine. "*Le commerce des mots: l'usage des listes dans la littérature médiévale (XIIe–XVe siècles)*.

Geneva: Droz, 2006.

———. "Les Saisons du récit et les vicissitudes de l'amour dans le livre du *Voir Dit* de Guillaume de Machaut." In *Tempus in fabula: Topoï de la temporalité narrative dans la fiction d'Ancien Régime*. Ed. Daniel Maher. Saint-Nicholas: Presses de l'université Laval, 2006. Pp. 213–27.

Jewers, Catherine A. "'*L'Art de la musique et le gai sentement*': Guillaume de Machaut, Eustache Deschamps and the Medieval Poetic Tradition." In Sinnreich-Levi. Pp. 163–79.

Johnson, Leonard W. "'Nouviaus dis amoureux plaisans': Variation as Innovation in Guillaume de Machaut." *Le Moyen Français* 5 (1979), 11–28.

———. *Poets as Players: Theme and Variation in Late Medieval Poetry*. Stanford, CA: Stanford University Press, 1990.

Kay, Sarah. "Touching Singularity: Consolation, Philosophy, and Poetry in the French *Dit*." In Léglu and Milner. Pp. 21–38.

Keitel, Elizabeth. "The Musical Manuscripts of Guillaume de Machaut." *Early Music* 5 (1977), 469–72.

———. "La tradition manuscrite de Guillaume de Machaut." In Chailley, ed. *Poète et compositeur*. Pp. 75–94.

Kelly, Douglas. "Courtly Love in Perspective: The Hierarchy of Love in Andreas Capellanus." *Traditio* 24 (1968), 119–47.

———. *Medieval Imagination: Rhetoric and the Poetry of Courtly Love*. Madison, WI: University of Wisconsin Press, 1978.

———. "*Translatio Studii*: Translation, Adaptation, and Allegory in Medieval French Literature." *Philological Quarterly* 57.3 (1978), 287–310.

———. *The Conspiracy of Allusion: Description, Rewriting, and Authorship from Macrobius to Medieval Romance*. Leiden: Brill, 1999.

———. "The Genius of the Patron: The Prince, the Poet, and Fourteenth-Century Invention." In Palmer, *Chaucer's French Contemporaries*. Pp. 1–27.

———. *Machaut and the Medieval Apprenticeship Tradition: Truth, Fiction and Poetic Craft*. Cambridge: D. S. Brewer, 2014.

Kendrick, Laura. "The Art of Mastering Servitude: Eustache Deschamps's Deployment of Courtly Love." *Romanistische Zeitschrift für Literaturgeschichte* 16 (1992), 30–40.

Kenny, Anthony, and Jan Pinborg. "Medieval Philosophical Literature." In *The Cambridge History of Later Medieval Philosophy: From the Rediscovery of Aristotle to the Disintegration of Scholasticism 1100–1600*. Ed. Norman Kretzmann, Anthony Kenny, and Jan Pinbiorg. Cambridge: Cambridge University Press, 1982. Pp. 11–42.

Kibler, William W. "Poet and Patron: Froissart's *Prison amoureuse*." *Esprit Créateur* 18.1 (1978), 32–46.

Kibler, William W., and James I. Wimsatt. "Machaut's Text and the Question of His Personal Supervision." In Palmer, *Chaucer's French Contemporaries*. Pp. 93–110.

Kraft, Christine. *Die Liebesgarten-Allegorie der "Echecs Amoureux."* Frankfurt: Lang, 1977.

Kügel, Karl. "Frankreich und sein direkter Einflussbereich." In *Die Musik des Mittelaters*. Ed. Hartmut Möller and Rudolph Stephan. Laaber: Laaber-Verlag, 1991. Pp. 352–84.

Lacassagne, Miren. "'*L'Art de dictier*': Poetics of a 'New' Time." In *Eustache Deschamps, French Courtier-Poet: His Work and His World*. Ed. Deborah M. Sinnreich-Levi. New York: AMS, 1998. Pp. 181–93.

Ladner, Gerhart B. *Images and Ideas in the Middle Ages: Selected Studies of History and Art*. 2 vols. Rome: Edizioni di Storia e Letteratura, 1983.

Laidlaw, James. "L'Innovation métrique chez Deschamps." In *Autour d'Eustache Deschamps: actes du colloque du Centre d'études médiévales de l'Université de Picardie-Jules Verne, Amiens, 5-8 novembre 1998*. Ed. Danielle Buschinger. Amiens: Presses du Centre d'études médiévales, Université de Picardie-Jules Verne, 1999.

Lanoue, David G. "History as Apocalypse: The 'Prologue' of Machaut's *Jugement dou roy de Navarre*." *Philological Quarterly* 60.1 (1981), 1–12.

———. "*La Prise d'Alexandrie*: Guillaume de Machaut's Epic." *Nottingham Medieval Studies* 29 (1985), 99–108.

Lassahn, Nicole. "The Patron in the Poem: Machaut's *Dit de la fonteinne amoureuse* in its Historical

Context." *RLA: Romance Languages Annual* 11 (1999), 48–55.

———. "Signatures from the *Roman de la Rose* to Guillaume de Machaut: the Beginnings of the Dream-Poem Genre in France." *RLA: Romance Languages Annual* 10 (1999), 75–81.

Leach, Elizabeth Eva. "Love, Hope, and the Nature of *Merci* in Machaut's Musical Balades *Esperance* (B13) and *Je ne cuit pas* (B14)." *French Forum* 28 (2003), 1–17.

———, ed. *Machaut's Music: New Interpretations*. Woodbridge: Boydell and Brewer, 2003.

———. *Sung Birds: Music, Nature and Poetry in the Later Middle Ages*. Ithaca, NY: Cornell University Press, 2007.

———. *Guillaume de Machaut: Secretary, Poet, Musician*. London and Ithaca, NY: Cornell University Press, 2011.

———. "Poet as Musician." In McGrady and Bain. Pp. 49–68.

———. "Machaut's First Single-Author Compilation." In *Manuscripts and Medieval Song: Inscription, Performance, Context*. Ed. Helen Deeming and Elizabeth Eva Leach. Cambridge: Cambridge University Press, 2015. Pp. 247–70.

Lechat, Didier. *"Dire par fiction": métamorphoses du je chez Guillaume de Machaut, Jean Froissart et Christine de Pizan*. Paris: Honoré Champion, 2005.

Leech-Wilkinson, Daniel. *Machaut's Mass: An Introduction*. Oxford: Clarendon Press, 1992.

———. *"Le Voir Dit* and *La Messe de Nostre Dame*: aspects of genre and style in late works of Machaut." *Plainsong & Medieval Music* 2 (1993), 43–73.

———. *"Le Voir Dit*: A Reconstruction and Guide for Musicians." *Plainsong & Medieval Music* 2 (1993), 103–40.

Lefèvre, Sylvie. "Longue demouree fait changier ami: De la lettre close à la lyrique dans le *Voir Dit* de Guillaume de Machaut." *Romania* 120 (2002), 226–34.

Lefferts, Peter, and Sylvia Huot. *Five Ballades for the House of Foix*. Newton Abbot: Antico Editions, 1989.

Léglu, Catherine E. and Stephen J. Milner, eds. *The Erotics of Consolation: Desire and Distance in the Late Middle Ages*. New York: Palgrave Macmillan, 2008. Pp. 141–64.

Leo, Domenic. "The Program of the Miniatures in Manuscript A." In *Machaut's Mass: An Introduction*. Ed. Daniel Leech-Wilkinson. Oxford: Clarendon Press, 1992. Pp. xci–xciii.

———. "Authorial Presence in the Illuminated Machaut Manuscripts." Ph.D. Dissertation: New York University, Institute of Fine Arts, 2005.

———. "The Beginning is the End: Guillaume de Machaut's Illuminated *Prologue*." In Plumley, Di Bacco, and Jossa. Pp. 96–112.

———. "The Pucellian School and the Rise of Naturalism: Style as Royal Signifier?" In *Jean Pucelle, A Medieval Artist: Innovation and Collaboration in Manuscript Painting*. Ed. Kyunghee Choi and Anna Russakoff. Turnhout: Brepols, 2013.

———. "Art-historical Commentary." In Earp, *Ferrell-Vogüé Machaut Manuscript*, vol. 1. Pp. 95–126.

———. "BnF, FR. 1584: An Art Historical Overview." In *The Works of Guillaume de Machaut*. Web. Accessed May 2016. Online at http://machaut. exeter.ac.uk/?q=node/2171.

Lermack, Annette. "Fit for a Queen: The Psalter of Bonne of Luxembourg at the Cloisters." Ph.D. Dissertation: University of Iowa, 1999.

Leupin, Alexandre. *Fiction and Incarnation: Rhetoric, Theology, and Literature in the Middle Ages*. Minneapolis, MN: University of Minnesota Press, 2003.

Leupin, Alexandre, and Peggy McCracken. "The Powerlessness of Writing: Guillaume de Machaut, the Gorgon, and *Ordenance*." *Yale French Studies* 70 (1986), 127–149.

Lewis, Flora. "The Wound in Christ's Side and the Instruments of the Passion: Gendered Experience and Response." In *Women and the Book: Assessing the Visual Evidence*. Ed. Lesley Smith and Jane H. M. Taylor. London: British Library, 1996. Pp. 204–29.

Little, Patrick. "Three Ballades in Machaut's *Livre du Voir-Dit*." *Studies in Music* 14 (1980), 45–60.

Lochrie, Karma. "Mystical Acts, Queer Tendencies." In *Constructing Medieval Sexuality*. Ed. Karma Lochrie, Peggy McCracken, and James A. Schultz. Minneapolis, MN: University of Minnesota Press, 1997. Pp. 180–200.

Löfstedt, Leena. Review of *"Un Engin si soutil": Guillaume de Machaut et l'écriture au XIVe siècle*, by

Jacqueline Cerquiglini. *Neuphilologische Mitteilungen* 88.2 (1987), 230–32.

Luce, Simeon. *Chroniques de J. Froissart: 1360–1366*. Vol. 6 of *Chroniques de J. Froissart*. Paris, Librairie de la Societé de l'Histoire de France, 1876.

———. *Chronique des Quatre Premiers Valois*. Paris: Librairie de la Société de l'Histoire de France, 1862.

———. *Histoire de Bertrand du Guesclin et de son Epoque, tome I: La Jeunesse de Bertrand (1320–1364)*. Paris: Hachette, 1876.

Lukitsch, Shirley. "The Poetics of the *Prologue*: Machaut's Conception of the Purpose of His Art." *Medium Ævum* 52.2 (1983), 258–71.

Machabey, Armand. *Guillaume de Machault, 130?-1377: La vie et l'œuvre musical*. 2 vols. Paris: Richard-Masse, 1955.

Magnan, Robert. "Eustache Deschamps and His Double: Musique naturele and Musique artificiele." *Ars Lyrica* 7 (1993), 47–64.

Margolis, Nadia. "Guillaume de Machaut." In *Literature of the French and Occitan Middle Ages: Eleventh to Fifteenth Centuries*. Eds. Deborah M. Sinnreich-Levi and Ian S. Laurie, eds. Vol. 208 of *The Dictionary of Literary Biography*. Detroit, MI: Gale, 1999. Pp. 181–98.

Martinez-Göllner, Marie Louise. *Essays on Music and Poetry in the Late Middle Ages*. Tutzing: H. Schneider, 2003.

Maw, David. "Machaut and the 'Critical' Phase of Medieval Polyphony." *Music & Letters* 87.2 (2006), 262–94.

Maxwell, Sheila Kate. "Guillaume de Machaut and the *Mise en Page* of Medieval French Sung Verse." Ph.D. Dissertation: University of Glasgow, 2009.

McGrady, Deborah L. "Le *Voir dit*: réponse à l'*Ovide moralisé*?" Ed. Emmanuèle Baumgartner. Special issue, *Cahiers de recherches médiévales* 9 (2002), 99–113.

———. *Controlling Readers: Guillaume de Machaut and His Late Medieval Audience*. Toronto: University of Toronto Press, 2006.

———. "'Tout son païs m'abandonna': Reinventing Patronage in Machaut's *Fonteinne amoureuse*." *Yale French Studies* 110 (2006), 19–31.

———. "Guillaume de Machaut." In *The Cambridge Companion to Medieval French Literature*. Ed. Simon Gaunt and Sarah Kay. Cambridge: Cambridge University Press, 2008. Pp. 109–22.

———. "A Master, a *Vilain*, a Lady and a Scribe: Competing for Authority in a Late Medieval Translation of the Ars amatoria." In *Poetry, Knowledge and Community in Late Medieval France*. Ed. Rebecca Dixon and Finn E. Sinclair. London: D. S. Brewer, 2008.

———. "Machaut and His Material Legacy." In McGrady and Bain. Pp. 361–86.

McGrady, Deborah, and Jennifer Bain, eds. *A Companion to Guillaume de Machaut*. Leiden and Boston: Brill, 2012.

Ménagier de Paris. Ed. Georgine E. Brereton and Janet M. Ferrier. Paris: Librairie Générale Française, 1994.

Miller, Anne-Hélène. "Guillaume de Machaut and the Forms of Pre-Humanism in Fourteenth-Century France." In McGrady and Bain. Pp. 33–48.

Morris, Rosemary. "Machaut, Froissart, and the Fictionalization of the Self." *The Modern Language Review* 83.3 (1988), 545–55.

Mühlethaler, Jean-Claude. "De Guillaume de Machaut aux rhétoriqueurs: A la recherche d'un Parnasse français." In *Histoire des Poétiques*. Ed. Jean Bessière, Eva Kushner, Roland Mortier and Jean Weisgerber. Paris: Presses Univérsitaires de France, 1997. Pp. 85–101.

———. "Un poète et son art face à la postérité: lecture des deux ballades de Deschamps pour la mort de Machaut." *Studi Francesi* 99 (1989), 387–409.

———. "Entre amour et politique: métamorphoses ovidiennes à la fin du Moyen Age, La fable de Céyx et Alcyoné, de *l'Ovide moralisé* à Christine de Pizan et Alain Chartier." *Cahiers de Recherches Médiévales et Humanistes* 9 (2002), 145–56.

Mullally, Robert. "Dance Terminology in the Works of Machaut and Froissart." *Medium Ævum* 59.2 (1990), 248–59.

Muscatine, Charles. *Chaucer and the French Tradition: A Study in Style and Meaning*. Berkeley, CA:

University of California Press, 1957.

Musso, Noël. "Comparaison statistique des lettres de Guillaume de Machaut et de Peronne d'Armentière dans *Le Voir Dit.*" In Chailley, ed. *Poète et compositeur.* Pp. 175–93.

Nádas, John L., and Michael Scott Cuthbert. *Ars nova: French and Italian Music in the Fourteenth Century.* Burlington, VT: Ashgate, 2009.

Nederman, Cary J., and Kate Langdon Forhan, eds. *Medieval Political Theory — A Reader: The Quest for the Body Politic, 1100–1400.* London and New York: Routledge, 1993.

Nelson, Jan A. "Guillaume de Machaut as Job: Access to the Poet as Individual Through his Source." *Romance Notes* 23.2 (1982), 185–90.

Newes, Virginia. "Turning Fortune's Wheel: Musical and Textual Design in Machaut's Canonic Lais." *Musica Disciplina* 45 (1991), 95–121.

———. "Symmetry and Dissymmetry in the Music of the *Lay de Bonne Esperance.*" In *Machaut's Music: New Interpretations.* Ed. Elizabeth Eva Leach. Woodbridge: Boydell and Brewer, 2003. Pp. 1–11.

———. "'Qui bien aimme a tart oublie': Guillaume de Machaut's *Lay de plour* in context." In Clark and Leach. Pp. 123–40.

Newton, Stella Mary. *Fashion in the Age of the Black Prince: A Study of the Years 1340–1365.* Woodbridge: Boydell Press, 1999.

Nichols, Stephen G. "Ekphrasis, Iconoclasm, and Desire." In Brownlee and Huot. Pp. 133–66.

———. "Textes mobiles, images motrices: L'Instabilité textuelle dans le manuscrit médiéval." *Littérature* 99 (1995), 19–32.

Nicholson, Peter. *Love & Ethics in Gower's* Confessio Amantis. Ann Arbor, MI: University of Michigan Press, 2005.

Nouvet, Claire. "Pour une économie de la dé-limitation: La *Prison amoureuse* de Jean Froissart." *Neophilologus* 70.3 (1986), 341–56.

———. "The 'Marquerite': A Distinctive Signature." In Palmer, *Chaucer's French Contemporaries.* Pp. 251–76.

O'Meara, Cara Ferguson. *Monarchy and Consent: The Coronation Book of Charles V, British Library Manuscript Cotton Tiberius B. VIII.* London: Harvey Miller Publishers, 2001.

Ordonnances des Roys de France de la Troisième Race. Vol. 3: 1355–64. Ed. Denis François Secousse. Paris: De l'Imprimerie Royale, 1732.

Oton de Granson. *Poems.* Ed. Peter Nicholson and Joan Grenier-Winther. Kalamazoo, MI: Medieval Institute Publications, 2015.

Oulmont, Charles. *Les débats du clerc et du chevalier dans la littérature poétique du moyen-âge.* Geneva: Slatkine, 1974. Originally published in Paris: Honoré Champion, 1911.

Ovid. *L'Ovide moralisé.* Ed. Cornelis De Boer. 4 vols. Amsterdam: Müller, 1915–38.

———. *The Metamorphoses.* Ed. and trans. Mary M. Innes. London: Penguin, 1955.

———. *Heroides.* In *Heroides and Amores.* Ed. and trans. Grant Showerman. Second edition. Rev. G. P. Goold. Cambridge, MA: Harvard University Press, 1977. Pp. 1–314.

———. *The Art of Love.* In *Ovid.* Vol. 2. Trans. J. H. Mozley. Second edition. Cambridge, MA: Harvard University Press, 1979. Pp. 11–175.

Page, Christopher. *Discarding Images: Reflections on Music and Culture in Medieval France.* Oxford: Oxford University Press, 1993.

Palmer, R. Barton. "Vision and Experience in Machaut's *Fonteinne Amoureuse.*" *Journal of the Rocky Mountain Medieval and Renaissance Association* 2 (1981), 79–86.

———. "Transtextuality and the Producing-I in Guillaume de Machaut's Judgment Series." *Exemplaria.* 5.2 (1993), 283–304.

———. "Rereading Guillaume de Machaut's Vision of Love: Chaucer's *Book of the Duchess* as Bricolage." In *Second Thoughts: A Focus on Rereading.* Ed. David Galef. Detroit, MI: Wayne State University Press, 1998. Pp. 169–95.

———. *Chaucer's French Contemporaries: The Poetry/Poetics of Self and Tradition.* New York: AMS Press, 1999.

———. "The Metafictional Machaut: Reflexivity in the Judgment Poems." In Palmer, *Chaucer's French Contemporaries*. Pp. 71–92.

———. "Guillaume de Machaut's La Prise de Alixandrie and the Late Medieval Chivalric Ideal." In *Chivalry, Knighthood, and War in the Middle Ages*. Ed. Susan J. Ridyard. Sewanee, TN: University of the South Press, 1999. Pp. 195–204.

———. "Chaucer's *Legend of Good Women*: The Narrator's Tale." In *New Readings of Chaucer's Poetry*. Ed. Robert G. Benson and Susan J. Ridyard. Cambridge: Brewer, 2003. Pp. 183–94.

———, ed. and trans. *Medieval English and French Legends: An Anthology of Religious and Secular Narrative*. Glen Allen, VA: College Publications, 2006.

———, ed. and trans. *Medieval Epic and Romance: An Anthology of English and French Narrative*. Glen Allen, VA: College Publications, 2006.

———. "Guillaume de Machaut and the Classical Tradition: Individual Talent and (Un)Communal Tradition." In McGrady and Bain. Pp. 241–60.

Patch, Howard Rollin. "Fortuna in Old French Literature." *Smith College Studies in Modern Languages* 4.4 (1923), 1–45.

———. *The Goddess Fortuna in Mediaeval Literature*. Cambridge, MA: Harvard University Press, 1927.

———. *The Tradition of Boethius: a Study of his Importance in Medieval Culture*. New York: Oxford University Press, 1935.

Patterson, Lee. "Court Politics and the Invention of Literature: The Case of Sir John Clanvowe." In *Culture and History, 1350–1600: Essays on English Communication, Identities and Writing*. Ed. David Aers. New York: Harvester Wheatsheaf, 1992. Pp. 7–42.

Peck, Russell A., ed. *Heroic Women from the Old Testament in Middle English Verse*. Kalamazoo, MI: Medieval Institute Publications, 1991.

Perkinson, Stephen. *The Likeness of the King: A Prehistory of Portraiture in Late Medieval France*. Chicago: University of Chicago Press, 2009.

Petit de Julleville, Louis. "La poésie française au XIVe siècle — Guillaume de Machaut." *Revue des cours et conférences* 1 (1892–93), 330–37.

———. "Les derniers poètes du moyen âge." In *Moyen Age*. Vol 2 of *Histoire de la langue et de la littérature française des origines à 1900*. Paris: Armand Colin, 1896. Pp. 336–98.

Phillips, Helen. "Fortune and the Lady: Machaut, Chaucer and the Intertextual 'Dit'." *Nottingham French Studies* 38.2 (1999), 120–36.

Picherit, Jean-Louis. "Les *Exemples* dans le *Jugement dou roy de Navarre* de Guillaume de Machaut." *Lettres Romanes* 36.2 (1982), 103–116.

Pietri, François. *Chronique de Charles le mauvais*. Paris: Éditions Berger-Levrault, 1963.

Pizan, Christine de. *The Book of the Duke of True Lovers*. Trans. Thelma S. Fenster and Nadia Margolis. New York: Persea, 1991.

———. *Le livre de la mutacion de fortune par Christine de Pisan*. Ed. Suzanne Solente. 4 vols. Paris: Picard, 1959–1966.

———. *Le livre du duc des vrais amans*. Ed. and Trans. Thelma S. Fenster. Binghamton, NY: Medieval and Renaissance Texts and Studies, 1995.

Plaisse, André. *Charles, dit le mauvais: comte d'Evreux, roi de Navarre, capitaine de Paris*. Evreux: Société Libre de l'Eure, 1972.

Planche, Alice. "*Une approche de l'infini*: Sur un passage du *Voir Dit* de Guillaume de Machaut." In *Écrire pour dire: Études sur le Dit médiéval*. Ed. Bernard Ribémont. Paris: Klincksieck, 1990. Pp. 93–108.

Plumley, Yolanda. *The Grammar of 14th Century Melody: Tonal Organization and Compositional Process in the Chansons of Guillaume de Machaut and the Ars Subtilior*. New York: Garland, 1996.

———. "Citation and Allusion in the Late *Ars Nova*: The Case of *Esperance* and the *En Attendant* Songs." *Early Music History* 18 (1999), 287–363.

———. "An 'Episode in the South'? Ars Subtilior and the Patronage of French Princes." *Early Music History* 22 (2003), 103–68.

———. "Intertextuality in the Fourteenth-Century Chanson." *Music & Letters* 84.3 (2003), 355–77.

————. "Playing the Citation Game in the Late 14th Century Chanson." *Early Music* 31.1 (2003), 20–38.

————. "Self-Citation and Compositional Process in Guillaume de Machaut's Lyrics with and without Music: The Case of 'Dame, se vous n'avez aperceü' (Rondeau 13)." In McGrady and Bain. Pp. 159–184.

————. *The Art of Grafted Song: Citation and Allusion in the Age of Machaut*. New York and Oxford: Oxford University Press, 2013.

Plumley, Yolanda, and Uri Smilansky. *A Courtier's Quest for Cultural Capital: New Light on the Original Owner of Machaut MS F-G*. Forthcoming.

Plumley, Yolanda, Giuliano Di Bacco and Stefano Jossa, eds. *Citation, Intertextuality and Memory in the Middle Ages and Renaissance*. 2 vols. Exeter: University of Exeter Press, 2011–13.

Poirion, Daniel. *Le poète et le prince: l'évolution du lyrisme courtois de Guillaume de Machaut à Charles d'Orléans*. Paris: Presses Universitaires de France, 1965.

————. *Le Moyen Age*. 2 vols. Paris: Arthaud, 1971.

————. "The Imaginary Universe of Guillaume de Machaut." In Cosman and Chandler. Pp. 199–206.

————. "Écriture et ré-écriture au moyen âge." *Littérature* 41 (1981), 109–18.

————, ed. *La littérature française aux XIVe et XVe siècles*. Heidelberg: Carl Winter, 1988.

Possamaï-Pérez, Marylène. *L'Ovide Moralisé: Essai d'interprétation*. Paris: Honoré Champion, 2006.

Prioult, A. "Un poète voyageur: Guillaume de Machaut et la "Reise" de Jean l'Aveugle, roi de Bohême, en 1328–1329." *Lettres Romanes* 4.1 (1950), 3–29.

Pucci, Joseph. *The Full-Knowing Reader: Allusion and the Power of the Reader in the Western Literary Tradition*. New Haven, CT: Yale University Press, 1998.

Quillet, Jeannine. *Charles V: Le roi lettré*. Paris: Librairie Académique Perrin, 1984.

Quittard, Henri. "Notes sur Guillaume de Machaut et son œuvre." *Revue de Musicologie* 1 (1917–19), 91–105, 123–38.

Rabel, Claudia. "L'Illustration de *L'ovide moralisé* dans les manuscrits français du XIVe siècle: essai pour une étude iconographique." M.A. Thesis: University of Paris, Sorbonne, 1981.

Reaney, Gilbert. "Voices and Instruments in the Music of Guillaume de Machaut." *Revue Belge de Musicologie / Belgisch Tijdschrift voor Muziekwetenschap* 10.1/2 (1956), 3–17.

————. "Voices and Instruments in the Music of Guillaume de Machaut (Continuation)." *Revue Belge de Musicologie / Belgisch Tijdschrift voor Muziekwetenschap* 10.3/4 (1956), 93–104.

Regalado, Nancy Freeman. "Le Porcher au palais: *Kalila et Dimma*, Le Roman de Fauvel, Machaut et Boccace." *Études Littéraires* 31.2 (1999), 119–32.

————. "Swineherds at Court: *Kalila et Dimna*, *Le Roman de Fauvel*, Machaut's *Confort d'ami* and *Complainte*, and Boccaccio's *Decameron*." In *"Chançon legiere a chanter": Essays on Old French Literature in honor of Samuel N. Rosenberg*. Ed. Karen Fresco and Wendy Pfeffer. Birmingham, AL: Summa, 2007. Pp. 235–54.

Rehyansky, Katherine Heinrichs. "Wise Birds: Chaucer's Crow and Machaut's." *Tennessee Philological Bulletin* 29 (1992), 23–33.

Ringbom, Sixton. "Some pictorial conventions for the recounting of thoughts and experiences in late medieval art." In *Medieval Iconography and Narrative: A Symposium*. Ed. Flemming G. Andersen, Esther Nyholm, Marianne Powell, and Flemming Talbo Stubkjær. Odense: Odense University Press, 1980. Pp. 38–69.

Robertson, Anne Walters. *Guillaume de Machaut and Reims: Context and Meaning in his Musical Works*. Cambridge: Cambridge University Press, 2002.

Roccati, G. Matteo. "Guillaume de Machaut, 'Prologue' aux oeuvres: la disposition du texte dans le ms. A (Paris, B. N. F., fr. 1584)." *Studi Francesi* 44.3 (2000), 535–40.

The Romance of Flamenca: A Provençal Poem of the Thirteenth Century. Ed. and Trans. Merton J. Hubert and Marion E. Porter. Princeton, NJ: Princeton University Press, 1962.

Roncaglia, Aurelio. "La statua d'Isotta." *Cultura Neolatina* 31 (1971), 41–67.

Root, Jerry. "'Space to Speke': Confessional Practice and the Construction of Character in the Works of Geoffrey Chaucer, Guillaume de Machaut, and Juan Ruiz." Ph.D. Dissertation: University of Michigan, 1990.

———. *'Space to Speke': The Confessional Subject in Medieval Literature*. New York: Peter Lang, 1997.

Rouse, Richard H., and Mary A. Rouse. *Manuscripts and Their Makers: Commercial Book Producers in Medieval Paris 1200–1500*. 2 vols. Turnhout: Harvey Miller Publishers, 2000.

Ruhe, Ernstpeter. *De Amasio ad Amasiam: Zur Gattungsgeschichte des mittelalterlichen Liebesbriefes*. Munich: Fink, 1975.

Rychner, Jean. "La flèche et l'anneau." *Revue des Sciences Humaines* 183 (1981–83), 55–69.

Sanders, Julie. *Adaptation and Appropriation*. Oxford: Routledge, 2006.

Sandler, Lucy Freeman. "Jean Pucelle and the Lost Miniatures of the Belleville Breviary." *Art Bulletin* 66.1 (1984), 73–96.

Saslow, James M. *Ganymede in the Renaissance: Homosexuality in Art and Society*. New Haven, CT: Yale University Press, 1986.

Schibanoff, Susan, "Sodomy's Mark: Alan of Lille, Jean de Meun, and the Medieval Theory of Authorship." In Burger and Kruger. Pp. 28–56.

Schilperoort, Johanna Catharina. *Guillaume de Machaut et Christine de Pisan (étude comparative)*. The Hague: de Swart, 1936.

Schmidt, Gerhard. Review of *The Portraits of Charles V of France (1338–80)*, by Claire Richter Sherman. *Zeitschrift für Kunstgeschichte* 34.1 (1971), 72–88.

Sherman, Claire Richter. *Imaging Aristotle: Verbal and Visual Representation in Fourteenth-Century France*. Berkeley, CA: University of California Press, 1995.

Singer, Julie. "Instrumental Comparisons: Machaut's Shorter *Dits*." In McGrady and Bain. Pp. 293–310.

Sinnreich-Levi, Deborah M., ed. *Eustache Deschamps, French Courtier-Poet: His Work and His World*. New York: AMS, 1998.

Sinnreich-Levi, Deborah M., and Ian S. Laurie, eds. *Literature of the French and Occitan Middle Ages: Eleventh to Fifteenth Centuries*. Detroit, MI: Gale, 1999.

Slerca, Anna. "L'*Advision Cristine*, Guillaume de Machaut, Boccace et le thème de la rétractation." In *Desireuse de plus avant enquerre . . . Actes du VIème Colloque internationale sur Christine de Pizan (Paris, 20–24 juillet 2006). Volume en hommage à James Laidlaw*. Ed. Liliane Dulac, Anne Paupert, Christine Reno, and Bernard Ribémont. Paris: Honoré Champion, 2008. Pp. 315–26.

Smilansky, Uri. "A Labyrinth of Spaces: Page, Performance, and Music in Late Medieval French Culture." In *Ritual and Space in the Middle Ages: Proceedings of the 2009 Harlaxton Symposium*. Ed. Frances Andrews. Donington: Shaun Tyas, 2011. Pp. 130–47.

Smith, Geri L. "Models of Authority in the *Rose*, Machaut, and Christine de Pizan: A Feminine Recasting of 'songe/mensonge' in *Le Dit de la Pastoure*." *Women in French Studies* 14 (2006), 11–26.

Smith, Nicole D. *Sartorial Strategies: Outfitting Aristocrats and Fashioning Conduct in Late Medieval Literature*. Notre Dame, IN: University of Notre Dame Press, 2012.

Solterer, Helen. *The Master and Minerva: Disputing Women in French Medieval Culture*. Berkeley and Los Angeles, CA: University of California Press, 1995.

Sonnemann, Günter. "Die Ditdichtung des Guillaume de Machaut." Ph.D. Dissertation: University of Göttingen, 1969.

Spearing, A. C. *Textual Subjectivity: The Encoding of Subjectivity in Medieval Narratives*. Oxford: Oxford University Press, 2005.

———. *Medieval Autographies: the "I" of the Text*. South Bend, IN: University of Notre Dame Press, 2012.

Spenser, Edmund. *The Faerie Queene*. Ed. A. C. Hamilton. Text edited by Hiroshi Yamashita and Toshiyuki Suzuki. Harlow, NY: Pearson Education, 2001.

Stäblein-Harder, Hanna. *Fourteenth-Century Mass Music in France*. Rome: American Institute of Musicology, 1962.

Stahuljak, Zrinka. "History's Fixers: Informants, Mediators, and Writers in the *Prise d'Alexandre*." In McGrady and Bain. Pp. 277–92.

Stehling, Thomas, trans. *Medieval Latin Poems of Male Love and Friendship*. New York: Garland Publishing, 1984.

Steiger, Veronica. "Hören und Staunen — Islamische Musikinstrumente an den europäischen

Herrscherhöfen." In *Dichtung und Musik der Stauferzeit.* Ed. Volker Gallé. Worms: Worms Verlag, 2011. Pp. 175–89.

Steinle, Eric M. "The Medieval Lyric Romance." Ph.D. Dissertation: University of California at Berkeley, 1984.

Sterling, Charles. *La Peinture Medievale a Paris 1300–1500.* Vol. 1. Paris: La Bibliothèque des Arts, 1987.

Stevenson, Kay Gilliland. "Readers, Poets, and Poems Within the Poem." *Chaucer Review* 24 (1989), 1–19.

Stewert, H. F., E. K. Rand, and S. J. Tester. *Boethius: The Theological Tractates [and] The Consolation of Philosophy.* Cambridge, MA: Harvard University Press, 1973.

Stone, Anne. "A Singer at the Fountain: Homage and Irony in Ciconia's 'Sus une fontayne'." *Music & Letters* 82.3 (2001), 361–90.

Sturges, Robert S. "Speculation and Interpretation in Machaut's *Voir-Dit.*" *Romance Quarterly* 33.1 (1986), 23–33.

———. *Medieval Interpretation: Models of Reading in Literary Narrative, 1100–1500.* Carbondale, IL: Southern Illinois University Press, 1991.

———. "Textual Scholarship: Ideologies of Literary Production." *Exemplaria* 3.1 (1991), 109–31.

———. "The Critical Reception of Machaut's *Voir-Dit* and the History of Literary History." *French Forum* 17.2 (1992), 133–51.

———. "Medieval Authorship and the Polyphonic Text: From Manuscript Commentary to the Modern Novel." In *Bakhtin and Medieval Voices.* Ed. Thomas J. Farrell. Gainesville, FL: University of Florida Press, 1995. Pp. 122–37.

Suchier, Hermann. "Das Anagramm in Machauts *Voir Dit.*" *Zeitschrift für Romanische Philologie* 21 (1897), 541–45.

Swift, Helen J. "(Un)covering Truth: Speaking 'proprement' in late medieval French Poetry." *Nottingham Medieval Studies* 48 (2004), 60–79.

———. *Gender, Writing, and Performance: Men Defending Women in Late Medieval French Poetry (1440–1538).* Oxford: Oxford University Press, 2008.

———. "*Tamainte consolation / Me fist lymagination*: A Poetics of Mourning and Imagination in Late Medieval *dits.*" In Léglu and Milner. Pp. 141–64.

———. "The Poetic I." In McGrady and Bain. Pp. 15–32.

Switten, Margaret. "Guillaume de Machaut: Le *Remède de Fortune* au carrefour d'un art nouveau." *Cahiers de l'Association internationale des études françaises* 41 (1989), 101–16.

Tarbé, Prosper. *Poésies d'Agnès de Navarre-Champagne, dame de Foix.* Paris: Aubry, 1856.

Taruskin, Richard. *Music From the Earliest Notations to the Sixteenth Century.* New York: Oxford University Press, 2010.

Taylor, Jane H. M. "Machaut's Livre du Voir-dit and the Poetics of the Title." In Aubailly et al. Pp. 1351–62.

Taylor, Karla. "Chaucer and the French Tradition." In *Approaches to Teaching Chaucer's* Troilus and Criseyde *and the Shorter Poems.* Ed. Tison Pugh and Angela Jane Weisl. New York: Modern Language Association of America, 2007. Pp. 33–37.

Taylor, Steven M. "Portraits of Pestilence: The Plague in the Work of Machaut and Boccaccio." *Allegorica* 5 (1980), 105–18.

Thomas, Antoine. "Guillaume de Machaut et l'*Ovide Moralisé.*" *Romania* 41 (1912), 382–400.

Thompson, Wendy. *Classical Composers: A Guide to the Lives and Works of the Great Composers from the Medieval, Baroque, and Classical Eras.* London: Southwater, 2002.

Trachsler, Richard. "Cent sénateurs, neuf soleils et un songe: Encore sur Machaut, la sibylle et le chaînon manquant." *Romania* 116 (1998), 188–214.

Tucoo-Chala, Pierre. *Gaston Fébus et la Vicomté de Béarn (1343–1391).* Bordeaux: Bière, 1960.

Turel, Noa. "Living Pictures: Rereading 'au vif,' 1350–1550." *Gesta* 50.2 (2011), 163–82.

Tuve, Rosemond. "Notes on the Virtues and Vices." *Journal of the Warburg and Courtauld Institutes* 27 (1964), 42–72.

Tyson, Diana B. "Authors, Patrons and Soldiers — Some Thoughts on Four Old French Soldiers'

Lives." *Nottingham Medieval Studies* 42 (1998), 105–20.

Uitti, Karl D. "From *Clerc* to *Poète*: The Relevance of the *Roman de 1a Rose* to Machaut's World." In Cosman and Chandler. Pp. 209–16.

Urbain V. *Lettres Communes des Papes du XIVe siècle: Urbain V (1362–1370), Lettres communes*. Ed. Michel Hayez. Rome: Ecole Française de Rome, 1974.

Van Buren, Ann Hagopian. "Thoughts, Old and New, on the Sources of Early Netherlandish Painting." *Simiolus: Netherlands Quarterly for the History of Art* 16.213 (1986), 93–112.

Venette, Jean de. *The Chronicle of Jean de Venette*. Ed. Richard A. Newhall. Trans. Jean Birdsall. New York: Columbia University Press, 1953.

Virgil. *The Aeneid*. Ed. and Trans. Robert Fitzgerald. New York: Random House, 1990.

Vitz, Evelyn Birge. *Orality and Performance in Early French Romance*. Woodbridge: D. S. Brewer, 1999.

———. "Minstrel Meets Clerk in Early French Literature: Medieval Romance as the Meeting-Place Between Two Traditions of Verbal Eloquence and Performance Practice." In *Medieval Cultures in Contact*. Ed. Richard F. Gyug. New York: Fordham University Press, 2003. Pp. 189–209.

———. "La lecture érotique au Moyen Age et la performance du roman." *Poétique* 137 (2004), 35–51.

Wallen, Martha. "Biblical and Mythological Typology in Machaut's *Confort d'ami*." *Res Publica Litterarum* 3 (1980), 191–206.

Walters, Lori. "Illuminating the *Rose*: Gui de Mori and the Illustrations of MS 101 of the Municipal Library, Tournai." In Brownlee and Huot. Pp. 167–200.

Weimann, Robert. "Text, Author-Function, and Appropriation in Modern Narrative: Toward a Sociology of Representation." *Critical Inquiry* 14.3 (1988), 431–47.

Westervelt, L. A. "The Medieval Notion of Janglery and Chaucer's *Manicple's Tale*." *Southern Review* 14 (1981), 107–15.

Whiting, Bartlett Jere, and Helen Wescott Whiting. *Proverbs, Sentences, and Proverbial Phrases*. Cambridge, MA: Belknap Press of Harvard University Press, 1968.

Wilkins, Nigel E. "A Pattern of Patronage: Machaut, Froissart and the Houses of Luxembourg and Bohemia in the Fourteenth Century." *French Studies* 37.2 (1983), 257–84.

———. *Music in the Age of Chaucer*. Second edition. Woodbridge: Boydell and Brewer, 1995.

Willard, Charity Cannon. "Concepts of Love According to Guillaume de Machaut, Christine de Pizan, and Pietro Bembo." In *The Spirit of the Court: Selected Proceedings of the Fourth Congress of the International Courtly Literature Society (Toronto 1983)*. Ed. Glyn S. Burgess and Robert A. Taylor. Cambridge and Dover, NH: Brewer, 1985. Pp. 386–92.

Williams, Sarah Jane Manley. "An Author's Role in Fourteenth Century Book Production: Guillaume de Machaut's 'Livre où je met toutes mes choses.'" *Romania* 90 (1969), 433–54.

———. "The Lady, the Lyrics and the Letters." *Early Music* 5.4 (1977), 462–68.

———. "Machaut's Self-Awareness as Author and Producer." In Cosman and Chandler. Pp. 189–97.

———. "The Lyrics of Machaut's *Voir Dit*: 'Voir' and 'Veoir.'" *Ars Lyrica* 7 (1993), 5–15.

Wimsatt, James I. *Chaucer and the Poems of 'Ch' in University of Pennsylvania MS French 15*. Cambridge: Boydell and Brewer, 1982.

———. *Chaucer and His French Contemporaries: Natural Music in the Fourteenth Century*. Toronto: University of Toronto Press, 1991.

———. "Reason, Machaut, and the Franklin." In *The Olde Daunce: Love, Friendship, Sex, and Marriage in the Medieval World*. Ed. Robert R. Edwards and Stephen Spector. Albany, NY: State University of New York Press, 1991. Pp. 201–10.

———. "Machaut's *Voit dit* as Game." *Ars Lyrica* 7 (1993), 17–24.

Wolfzettel, Friedrich. "Guillaume de Machaut: Dichter und Welt im Zeichen der Dame Rhétorique." In *Literatur im Umkreis des Prager Hofs der Luxemburger: Schweinfurter Kolloquium 1992*. Ed. Joachim Heinzle, Peter L. Johnson, and Gisela Vollmann-Profe. Berlin: Schmidt, 1994. Pp. 42–57.

Work, James A. "The Manciple's Tale." In *Sources and Analogues of Chaucer's Canterbury Tales*. Ed. W.F. Bryan and Germaine Dempster. Chicago: University of Chicago Press, 1941. Pp. 699–722.

Yri, Kristen. "Performing Machaut's Messe de Notre Dame: From Modernist Allegiances to the Postmodern Hinterland." In McGrady and Bain. Pp. 333–60.

Zeeman, Nicolette. "The Lover-Poet and Love as the Most Pleasing 'Matere' in Medieval French Love
     Poetry." *Modern Language Review* 83.4 (1988), 820–42.
Zink, Michel. "Les toiles d'Agamanor et les fresques de Lancelot." *Littérature* 38 (1980), 43–61.
———."The Time of the Plague and the Order of Writing: Jean le Bel, Froissart, Machaut." In
     "Contexts: Styles and Values in Medieval Art and Literature." Ed. Daniel Poirion and Nancy
     Freeman Regalado. Special issue, *Yale French Studies* (1991), Pp. 269–80.
———. *Froissart et le temps*. Paris: Presses Universitaires de France, 1998.
———. *Nature et poésie au Moyen Age*. Paris: Fayard, 2006.
Zumthor, Paul. "Intertextualité et mouvance." *Littérature* 41 (1981), 8–16.
———. "Le texte médiéval entre oralité et écriture." In *Exigences et perspectives de la sémiotique: recueil
     d'hommages pour Algirdas Julien Greimas*. Ed. Herman Parret and Hans-George Ruprecht. Vol. 2.
     Amsterdam: John Benjamins Publishing, 1985. Pp. 827–43.

✒ MIDDLE ENGLISH TEXTS SERIES

The Floure and the Leafe, The Assembly of Ladies, The Isle of Ladies, edited by Derek Pearsall (1990)

Three Middle English Charlemagne Romances, edited by Alan Lupack (1990)

Six Ecclesiastical Satires, edited by James M. Dean (1991)

Heroic Women from the Old Testament in Middle English Verse, edited by Russell A. Peck (1991)

The Canterbury Tales: Fifteenth-Century Continuations and Additions, edited by John M. Bowers (1992)

Gavin Douglas, *The Palis of Honoure*, edited by David Parkinson (1992)

Wynnere and Wastoure and The Parlement of the Thre Ages, edited by Warren Ginsberg (1992)

The Shewings of Julian of Norwich, edited by Georgia Ronan Crampton (1994)

King Arthur's Death: The Middle English Stanzaic Morte Arthur and Alliterative Morte Arthure, edited by Larry D. Benson, revised by Edward E. Foster (1994)

Lancelot of the Laik and Sir Tristrem, edited by Alan Lupack (1994)

Sir Gawain: Eleven Romances and Tales, edited by Thomas Hahn (1995)

The Middle English Breton Lays, edited by Anne Laskaya and Eve Salisbury (1995)

Sir Perceval of Galles and Ywain and Gawain, edited by Mary Flowers Braswell (1995)

Four Middle English Romances: Sir Isumbras, Octavian, Sir Eglamour of Artois, Sir Tryamour, edited by Harriet Hudson (1996; second edition 2006)

The Poems of Laurence Minot, 1333–1352, edited by Richard H. Osberg (1996)

Medieval English Political Writings, edited by James M. Dean (1996)

The Book of Margery Kempe, edited by Lynn Staley (1996)

Amis and Amiloun, Robert of Cisyle, and Sir Amadace, edited by Edward E. Foster (1997; second edition 2007)

The Cloud of Unknowing, edited by Patrick J. Gallacher (1997)

Robin Hood and Other Outlaw Tales, edited by Stephen Knight and Thomas Ohlgren (1997; second edition 2000)

The Poems of Robert Henryson, edited by Robert L. Kindrick with the assistance of Kristie A. Bixby (1997)

Moral Love Songs and Laments, edited by Susanna Greer Fein (1998)

John Lydgate, *Troy Book Selections*, edited by Robert R. Edwards (1998)

Thomas Usk, *The Testament of Love*, edited by R. Allen Shoaf (1998)

Prose Merlin, edited by John Conlee (1998)

Middle English Marian Lyrics, edited by Karen Saupe (1998)

John Metham, *Amoryus and Cleopes*, edited by Stephen F. Page (1999)

Four Romances of England: King Horn, Havelok the Dane, Bevis of Hampton, Athelston, edited by Ronald B. Herzman, Graham Drake, and Eve Salisbury (1999)

The Assembly of Gods: Le Assemble de Dyeus, or Banquet of Gods and Goddesses, with the Discourse of Reason and Sensuality, edited by Jane Chance (1999)

Thomas Hoccleve, *The Regiment of Princes*, edited by Charles R. Blyth (1999)

John Capgrave, *The Life of Saint Katherine*, edited by Karen A. Winstead (1999)

John Gower, *Confessio Amantis*, Vol. 1, edited by Russell A. Peck; with Latin translations by Andrew Galloway (2000; second edition 2006); Vol. 2 (2003; second edition 2013); Vol. 3 (2004)

Richard the Redeless and Mum and the Sothsegger, edited by James M. Dean (2000)

Ancrene Wisse, edited by Robert Hasenfratz (2000)

Walter Hilton, *The Scale of Perfection*, edited by Thomas H. Bestul (2000)

John Lydgate, *The Siege of Thebes*, edited by Robert R. Edwards (2001)

Pearl, edited by Sarah Stanbury (2001)

The Trials and Joys of Marriage, edited by Eve Salisbury (2002)

Middle English Legends of Women Saints, edited by Sherry L. Reames, with the assistance of Martha G. Blalock and Wendy R. Larson (2003)

The Wallace: Selections, edited by Anne McKim (2003)

Richard Maidstone, *Concordia (The Reconciliation of Richard II with London)*, edited by David R. Carlson, with a verse translation by A. G. Rigg (2003)

Three Purgatory Poems: The Gast of Gy, Sir Owain, The Vision of Tundale, edited by Edward E. Foster (2004)

William Dunbar, *The Complete Works*, edited by John Conlee (2004)

Chaucerian Dream Visions and Complaints, edited by Dana M. Symons (2004)

Stanzaic Guy of Warwick, edited by Alison Wiggins (2004)

Saints' Lives in Middle English Collections, edited by E. Gordon Whatley, with Anne B. Thompson and Robert K. Upchurch (2004)

Siege of Jerusalem, edited by Michael Livingston (2004)

The Kingis Quair and Other Prison Poems, edited by Linne R. Mooney and Mary-Jo Arn (2005)

The Chaucerian Apocrypha: A Selection, edited by Kathleen Forni (2005)

John Gower, *The Minor Latin Works*, edited and translated by R. F. Yeager, with *In Praise of Peace*, edited by Michael Livingston (2005)

Sentimental and Humorous Romances: Floris and Blanchefiour, Sir Degrevant, The Squire of Low Degree, The Tournament of Tottenham, and The Feast of Tottenham, edited by Erik Kooper (2006)

The Dicts and Sayings of the Philosophers, edited by John William Sutton (2006)

Everyman and Its Dutch Original, Elckerlijc, edited by Clifford Davidson, Martin W. Walsh, and Ton J. Broos (2007)

The N-Town Plays, edited by Douglas Sugano, with assistance by Victor I. Scherb (2007)

The Book of John Mandeville, edited by Tamarah Kohanski and C. David Benson (2007)

John Lydgate, *The Temple of Glas*, edited by J. Allan Mitchell (2007)

The Northern Homily Cycle, edited by Anne B. Thompson (2008)

Codex Ashmole 61: A Compilation of Popular Middle English Verse, edited by George Shuffelton (2008)

Chaucer and the Poems of "Ch," edited by James I. Wimsatt (revised edition 2009)

William Caxton, *The Game and Playe of the Chesse*, edited by Jenny Adams (2009)

John the Blind Audelay, *Poems and Carols*, edited by Susanna Fein (2009)

Two Moral Interludes: The Pride of Life and Wisdom, edited by David Klausner (2009)

John Lydgate, *Mummings and Entertainments*, edited by Claire Sponsler (2010)

Mankind, edited by Kathleen M. Ashley and Gerard NeCastro (2010)

The Castle of Perseverance, edited by David N. Klausner (2010)

Robert Henryson, *The Complete Works*, edited by David J. Parkinson (2010)

John Gower, *The French Balades*, edited and translated by R. F. Yeager (2011)

The Middle English Metrical Paraphrase of the Old Testament, edited by Michael Livingston (2011)

The York Corpus Christi Plays, edited by Clifford Davidson (2011)

Prik of Conscience, edited by James H. Morey (2012)

The Dialogue of Solomon and Marcolf: A Dual-Language Edition from Latin and Middle English Printed Editions, edited by Nancy Mason Bradbury and Scott Bradbury (2012)

Croxton Play of the Sacrament, edited by John T. Sebastian (2012)

Ten Bourdes, edited by Melissa M. Furrow (2013)

Lybeaus Desconus, edited by Eve Salisbury and James Weldon (2013)

The Complete Harley 2253 Manuscript, Vol. 2, edited and translated by Susanna Fein with David Raybin and Jan Ziolkowski (2014); Vol. 3 (2015); Vol. 1 (2015)

Oton de Granson Poems, edited and translated by Peter Nicholson and Joan Grenier-Winther (2015)

The King of Tars, edited by John H. Chandler (2015)

John Hardyng Chronicle, edited by James Simpson and Sarah Peverley (2015)

Richard Coer de Lyon, edited by Peter Larkin (2015)

✒ COMMENTARY SERIES

Haimo of Auxerre, *Commentary on the Book of Jonah*, translated with an introduction and notes by Deborah Everhart (1993)

Medieval Exegesis in Translation: Commentaries on the Book of Ruth, translated with an introduction and notes by Lesley Smith (1996)

Nicholas of Lyra's Apocalypse Commentary, translated with an introduction and notes by Philip D. W. Krey (1997)

Rabbi Ezra Ben Solomon of Gerona, *Commentary on the Song of Songs and Other Kabbalistic Commentaries*, selected, translated, and annotated by Seth Brody (1999)

John Wyclif, *On the Truth of Holy Scripture*, translated with an introduction and notes by Ian Christopher Levy (2001)

Second Thessalonians: Two Early Medieval Apocalyptic Commentaries, introduced and translated by Steven R. Cartwright and Kevin L. Hughes (2001)

The "Glossa Ordinaria" on the Song of Songs, translated with an introduction and notes by Mary Dove (2004)

The Seven Seals of the Apocalypse: Medieval Texts in Translation, translated with an introduction and notes by Francis X. Gumerlock (2009)

The "Glossa Ordinaria" on Romans, translated with an introduction and notes by Michael Scott Woodward (2011)

Nicholas of Lyra, Literal Commentary on Galatians, translated with an introduction and notes by Edward Arthur Naumann (2015)

Early Latin Commentaries on the Apocalypse, edited by Francis X. Gumerlock (2016)

🖉 SECULAR COMMENTARY SERIES

Accessus ad auctores: Medieval Introduction to the Authors, edited and translated by Stephen M. Wheeler (2015)

The Vulgate Commentary on Ovid's Metamorphoses, *Book 1*, edited and translated by Frank Coulson (2015)

Brunetto Latini, La rettorica, edited and translated by Stefania D'Agata D'Ottavi (2016)

🖉 DOCUMENTS OF PRACTICE SERIES

Love and Marriage in Late Medieval London, selected, translated, and introduced by Shannon McSheffrey (1995)

Sources for the History of Medicine in Late Medieval England, selected, introduced, and translated by Carole Rawcliffe (1995)

A Slice of Life: Selected Documents of Medieval English Peasant Experience, edited, translated, and with an introduction by Edwin Brezette DeWindt (1996)

Regular Life: Monastic, Canonical, and Mendicant "Rules," selected and introduced by Douglas J. McMillan and Kathryn Smith Fladenmuller (1997); second edition, selected and introduced by Daniel Marcel La Corte and Douglas J. McMillan (2004)

Women and Monasticism in Medieval Europe: Sisters and Patrons of the Cistercian Reform, selected, translated, and with an introduction by Constance H. Berman (2002)

Medieval Notaries and Their Acts: The 1327–1328 Register of Jean Holanie, introduced, edited, and translated by Kathryn L. Reyerson and Debra A. Salata (2004)

John Stone's Chronicle: Christ Church Priory, Canterbury, 1417–1472, selected, translated, and introduced by Meriel Connor (2010)

🖉 MEDIEVAL GERMAN TEXTS IN BILINGUAL EDITIONS SERIES

Sovereignty and Salvation in the Vernacular, 1050–1150, introduction, translations, and notes by James A. Schultz (2000)

Ava's New Testament Narratives: "When the Old Law Passed Away," introduction, translation, and notes by James A. Rushing, Jr. (2003)

History as Literature: German World Chronicles of the Thirteenth Century in Verse, introduction, translation, and notes by R. Graeme Dunphy (2003)

Thomasin von Zirclaria, Der Welsche Gast (The Italian Guest), translated by Marion Gibbs and Winder McConnell (2009)

Ladies, Whores, and Holy Women: A Sourcebook in Courtly, Religious, and Urban Cultures of Late Medieval Germany, introductions, translations, and notes by Ann Marie Rasmussen and Sarah Westphal-Wihl (2010)

🖉 VARIA

The Study of Chivalry: Resources and Approaches, edited by Howell Chickering and Thomas H. Seiler (1988)

Studies in the Harley Manuscript: The Scribes, Contents, and Social Contexts of British Library MS Harley 2253, edited by Susanna Fein (2000)

The Liturgy of the Medieval Church, edited by Thomas J. Heffernan and E. Ann Matter (2001; second edition 2005)

Johannes de Grocheio, *Ars musice*, edited and translated by Constant J. Mews, John N. Crossley, Catherine Jeffreys, Leigh McKinnon, and Carol J. Williams (2011)

Aribo, De musica *and* Sententiae, edited and translated by T.J.H. McCarthy (2015)

🖉 TO ORDER PLEASE CONTACT:
Medieval Institute Publications
Western Michigan University • Kalamazoo, MI 49008-5432
Phone (269) 387-8755 • FAX (269) 387-8750
http://www.wmich.edu/medieval/mip/index.html

Typeset in 10/13 New Baskerville
and Golden Cockerel Ornaments display

Medieval Institute Publications
College of Arts and Sciences
Western Michigan University
1903 W. Michigan Avenue
Kalamazoo, MI 49008-5432
http://www.wmich.edu/medievalpublications

 WESTERN MICHIGAN UNIVERSITY